A Commentary On the New Code of the Canon Law

A COMMENTARY ON
THE NEW
CODE OF CANON LAW

By **THE REV. P. CHAS. AUGUSTINE, O.S.B., D.D.**
Professor of Canon Law

VOLUME VIII

BOOK V

Penal Code (Can. 2195-2414)
with complete index

B. HERDER BOOK CO.
17 South Broadway, St. Louis, Mo.
AND
68 Great Russell St., London, W. C.
1922

CUM PERMISSU SUPERIORUM

NIHIL OBSTAT

Sti. Ludovici, die 25. Aug., 1922.

F. G. Holweck,
Censor Librorum

IMPRIMATUR

Sti. Ludovici, die 25. Aug., 1922.

✠*Joannes J. Glennon,*
Archiepiscopus
Sti. Ludovici

CONTENTS

iii

CONTENTS

v

CONTENTS

CONTENTS

THE PENAL CODE

BOOK V

INTRODUCTION

"Brutal laws brutalize a people," is a well known dictum of Montesquieu. If this is true of all laws, it is even more so of penal laws. For penalty means pain or suffering, and if this is out of proportion with the crime, it becomes an incentive to rebellion against law, and finally against authority itself. Moderation in the penal code, therefore, should be the keynote of wise legislation.[1] We say this, not as if we had expected that the Code of Canon Law would fail in moderation, but for the reasons which follow. Modern criminology is too moderate; it even eliminates the very notion of penalty. This is due to an inevitable reaction. Legislators had not always followed wise moderation or sufficiently considered the physical and psychological condition of the delinquent. With regard to this point, and more especially the treatment of youthful delinquents, the modern theories of criminology deserve some consideration. On the other hand these theories cannot claim universal, either scientific or dogmatic, acceptance. For they are based on mere assumptions and neglect sound philosophical principles,

[1] This is true of all, including the purely technical decision of the prohibition laws, notwithstanding U. S. Supreme Court.

tween guilt and penalty and the various purposes of the
latter illustrated in the course of our Commentary. We
pay no special attention here to the right of the Church
to employ coercion, for this shall be set forth under can.
2214. But one thing needs stressing, namely, that the
sentimentality of modern criminologists is not conducive
to public welfare. It would be much better for our
legislators to borrow correct ideas from the penal code of
the Church, which is at the same time a specimen of
true moderation and of the spirit in which penal laws
ought to be made and executed.

Concerning the *sources* (*fontes*) of the penal code, it
must be understood above all that the *ancient sources
now have only an interpretative value* (see can. 6). For
the Code is *the sole authentic* source of ecclesiastical law,
to the exclusion of all others, whether found singly or in
collections. *Single* penal laws were enacted at particular
as well as general councils, and some of them found their
way into collections.[10] Gratian's Decree contains penal
laws dispersed throughout, and an attempt at systematic treatment is made in Causae I–III. The fifth book
of the *Decretals* is more compactly, though not exclusively, penal, as may be seen from title 33 on privileges.
After the "classical" period of Canon Law no systematic digest of the penal law was attempted,—if
we except the so-called "*Reserved Cases*" in the Bull
"*In Coena Domini*," — until the time of Pius IX. This
Pontiff revised the penal law, as far as *censures* are concerned, in his well-known Constitution "*Apostolicae
Sedis*," of Oct. 12, 1869.

Other penal laws were scattered in the papal constitu-

---

10 Here the Penitential Books
may be cited, *e.g.*, Wasserschleben,
Die Bussbücher der abendländ.
Kirche, 1851; Schmitz, *Die Bussbücher und Bussdisciplin der Kirche*,
1883.

tions that emanated from time to time after the Clementine Collection, *i. e.*, after 1317. Among these the one called "*Ad vitanda scandala*," of Martin V (1418) is of special importance because of the distinction it makes between *excommunicati vitandi* and *tolerati*. Otherwise, as stated above, no exhaustive and complete redaction was attempted until the promulgation of the new Code.

The Code has taken cognizance of the postulates of the French and German Bishops at the Vatican Council, who wished to see the number of censures and reserved papal cases diminished. [11] A comparison with the "*Apostolicae Sedis*" shows this. Besides, the formulation of the present penal laws has been modified to such an extent that only a few former texts have been inserted entirely (*ex integro*) in the new Code. This should serve as a caution to the reader who is tempted to follow the old interpreters.

The *literature* on the penal laws of the Church is considerable, though now-a-days antiquated for more than one reason. Besides the commentaries on Book V of the Decretals, there are some specific treatises which deserve mention. They are:

C. A. THESAURUS, S. J., *De Poenis Ecclesiasticis*, 1640, re-published with notes and additional laws up to the year 1760, by Ubaldus Giraldi, whose edition of 1831 we use;

F. SUAREZ, *Disputationes de Censuris*, etc., Paris edition of 1861, t. xxiii;

F. KOBER, *Der Kirchenbann nach den Grundsätzen des*

---

11 Cfr. Granderath-Kirch, *Geschichte des Vatik. Konsils*, 1903, Vol. I, p. 441, p. 444; U. Stutz, *Der Geist des Codex Iuris Canonici*, 1918, p. 153 f.

Kanonischen Rechtes, 1863; ID., *Die Suspension der Kirchendiener,* 1862; ID., *Das Interdict,* in the *Archiv für kath. K-R.,* 1869.

Since the promulgation of the "*Apostolicae Sedis,*" 1869, the following commentaries have been published:

D'ANNIBALE, *Commentarius in Const. Apostolicae Sedis,* Prati, 1894.

AVANZINI, *De Constitutione Ap. Sedis,* Romae 1883.

HILARIUS a SEXTEN, *Tractatus de Censuris Ecclesiasticis cum Appendice de Irregularitate,* Moguntiae 1898.

PENNACHI, *Commentaria in Const. Ap. Sedis,* 1883.

Of a more general character are the following works:

P. HINSCHIUS, *Das Kirchenrecht der Katholiken und Protestanten in Deutschland,* Vol. IV, 1888; V, 1895; VI, 1897. The author, being a non-Catholic, could not always free himself from prejudice, but none the less his work is a fountainhead of historical and practical knowledge.

SMITH, *Elements of Eccl. Law,* Vol. III, ed. 3, N. Y. (*s. a.*)

Useful for the student of secular criminal law is:

KENNY-WEBB, *Outlines of Criminal Law,* New York, 1907.

Worthy of especial mention are:

J. HOLLWECK, *Die kirchlichen Strafgesetze,* 1899. He formulates the whole penal law into 301 paragraphs and then offers a commentary on the same.[12]

F. WERNZ, S. J., who entitles Vol. VI of his *Ius*

---

12 Msgr. Hollweck was an active member of the Commission on the Penal Code. We remember his telling us how difficult it was to arrange these canons. "It is," he said, "like taking a stone out of a building if you remove one censure or the other." We notice that Hollweck's arrangement has been adopted by the Code.

Decretalium, Ius Poenale Ecclesiae Catholicae, Rome 1913.

M. LEGA, *De Iudiciis Eccl.*, Vols. III et IV, 1906 ff.

Since the promulgation of the Code there have been issued:

H. A. AYRINHAC, *Penal Legislation*, N. Y. 1920.

F. M. CAPPELLO, S. J., *De Censuris iuxta Cod. I. C.*, 1919.

E. EICHMANN, *Das Strafrecht des Codex I. C.*, 1920.

A. PERATHONER, Auditor S. R. R., *Kirchliches Gerichtswesen und kirchl. Strafrecht*, 1919 (for the most part only a translation of the respective canons of the Code).

J. SOLE, *De Delictis et Poenis*, Rome 1920.

Our Code divides the whole fifth book into three parts, as follows:

Part I:
De Delictis
{ 1. Nature of crime and its division.
2. Imputability and circumstances.
3. Attempted crimes.

Part II:
De Poenis
{ 1. Nature, kinds, interpretation, application.
2. Power of inflicting penalties.
3. Subjects of penalties.
4. Pardoning power.
5. Censures in general and particular: excommunication, interdict, suspension.
6. Vindictive penalties for clergymen in general and in particular.
7. Penal remedies and penances.

aut post confessionem delinquentis in iudicio factam
ad normam can. 1750;

3.° *Notorium notorietate facti,* si publice notum sit
et in talibus adiunctis commissum, ut nulla tergiversatione celari nulloque iuris suffragio excusari possit;

4.° *Occultum,* quod non est publicum; *occultum
materialiter,* si lateat delictum ipsum; *occultum formaliter,* si eiusdem imputabilitas.

Can. 2198

Delictum quod unice laedit Ecclesiae legem, natura
sua, sola ecclesiastica auctoritas persequitur, requisito
interdum, ubi eadem auctoritas necessarium vel opportunum iudicaverit, auxilio brachii saecularis; delictum quod unice laedit legem societatis civilis, iure
proprio, salvo praescripto can. 120, punit civilis auctoritas, licet etiam Ecclesia sit in illud competens ratione peccati; delictum quod laedit utriusque societatis legem, ab utraque potestate puniri potest.

The Code first defines crime, then describes its qualities and guilt, and then enumerates the various kinds of
crimes, so far as the *forum internum* and *externum,* the
ecclesiastical and civil court, are concerned.

A crime, in ecclesiastical law, is an external and morally
imputable transgression of a law to which is attached a
canonical sanction, at least in general.

1. *Delictum* is taken from the word *delinquere* (*de* and
linquere, to forsake, to leave, to omit) and means an
offence in the general sense. However, by common usage
the term is restricted to a public offence or crime against
the juridical order or law. Therefore it is called a *transgression of the law,* whether divine or human, *i. e.,* merely
ecclesiastical. It is the law, either eternal or positive,

that governs order, the relation of man to God and of man to man, and any defection from that order constitutes a frustration of the designs of Providence.

2. But the transgression which the ecclesiastical law considers is not merely the guilty mind (*mens rea*), but the *act*,—i. e., an outward manifestation of a vicious intention, or a breach of the law as externally apprehensible. This may be positive or negative, or, in other words, it may consist in an act or in an omission. Thus a sacrilege is a positive act, but neglect of pastoral duties is an omission. It is essential to the notion of *delictum* that it be an *external act*, either of speech or deed, although it need not necessarily be provable.

3. Externality, however, does not exclude imputability, and hence the definition contains the addition, *morally imputable*. The vicious act, therefore, presupposes a guilty mind (*mens rea*).[1] Why? A transgression of the law is an act, and the transgressor, therefore, is an agent, and when that agent is intelligent and free, and acts as such, we say that the effects caused by such an agent are to be imputed or credited to him. Because an intelligent being has dominion over its actions, it is capable of moral proprietorship in the praise or blame justly due to its deliberate acts, according as they are seen to be good or bad.[2] In this feature crime shares the notion of sin, for every crime is a sin, though not conversely. For a sin (*e. g.*, mental apostasy or heresy) may be committed by the mind only, whereas a crime supposes an external act.

---

1 English lawyers for nearly 800 years have been familiar with the maxim: "*Actus non facit reum nisi mens sit rea*," the origin of which is attributed to St. Augustine; see

Kenny-Webb, *Outlines of Criminal Law*, 1907, p. 33.

2 W. Hill, S. J., *Ethics*, 8th ed., p. 47.

It may be asked whether *imputability* is required under all conditions. In general there is no doubt that every crime supposes personal imputability. An apparent exception seems to be the local interdict, which may affect guilty as well as innocent persons. But provision for these is made by can. 2276.

A more serious objection might arise from the existence of *pure penal laws,* which many moralists assert. However, in the first place, it would have to be proved that these laws really are laws. We cannot regard the prohibition of wine and beer, for instance, as a true law, because it neither pertains to reason nor is it intended for the public good, unless we identify the latter with the aims of fanatics. Secondly, it would have to be proved that the conscience does not feel guilty at all in transgressing such penal laws, *e. g.,* the constitutions of religious communities. No matter what the constitutions may say, it is a solemn and certain fact that religious do feel the sting of conscience when they transgress the rules laid down.[3] Be that as it may, the Code does not contain a single purely penal law.

4. But what does the addition *" cui addita sit sanctio canonica saltem indeterminata"* mean? The transgression is accompanied by penal sanction, at least in general terms. This means that there is neither crime nor punishment without a penal law.[4] It is, therefore, as stated above, the law which is infringed and which punishes. Superficially considered, this appears quite plausible and perhaps sufficient. Yet there are some philosophico-

---

[3] On this question see *Tübinger Quartalschrift,* 1900, pp. 204–281; 1902, pp. 574–620. Layman, S. J., appears to hit the nail on the head when he says: *" Si recte attendimus, eiusmodi constitutiones aut or-* *dinationes non sunt proprie leges."* (*Theol. Moral.,* l. I, tr. 4, c. 15, n. 1.)

[4] *" Nullum crimen, nulla poena sine lege poenali,"* was the adage of the School; Eichmann, *l. c.,* p. 27.

juridical questions involved in this simple answer. Thus it may be asked, why the law punishes certain transgressions, while it leaves others unpunished? Take, for instance, the reading of forbidden books, which is not punished generally (can. 1395), but only in particular cases (can. 2318); hunting by clergymen (can. 138), etc. Yet these forbidden actions cannot be called crimes in the sense of the ecclesiastical law.

There is another element implied in the word crime: it means a serious violation of the *public or social order,* which, when disturbed, requires reparation. We may indeed say that punitiveness or non-punitiveness forms a test between civil and criminal procedure, or between crimes proper and civil offences, and may even add, as a further distinction the legal power of remitting the sanction, yet the intrinsic and doubtless first intended demarcation is the amount or degree of social disturbance.[5] Sin may be a merely ethical transgression, but crime will ever be an ethico-juridical offence against the order established by law, and declared punishable at least in general terms.

The *sanctio canonica indeterminata* signifies a penalty to be meted out according to the good pleasure of the judge or superior (can. 2217, § I, n. I). It follows that, although no special penalty is provided for the transgression of a law, yet if that law embodies the provision that the punishment of the transgressor is left to the prudent judgment of the Ordinary, this is sufficient to mark the transgression as a crime, provided the other neces-

---

5 Kenny-Webb, *l. c.,* p. 3, enters upon this question thoroughly, yet when he says that the final distinction between civil and criminal lies "in the legal power of remitting the sanction" (*l. c.,* p. 15 f.) he seems to beg the question; for unless we assume that legal power to be absolute, it cannot remit penal sanction *ad libitum* or without the supposition of justice or some kind of law.

sary marks are not wanting. Instances of this kind are enumerated in can. 2170, 2183, and 2391. There is one exception to this general rule, however, *viz.*, can. 2222, § 1, which, as shall be seen, is nothing but an external corroboration of the idea of reparation and the supreme law of the Church, *viz.*, the welfare of souls.

§ 2 of can. 2195 ascribes the criminal character also to the violation or the *non-observance of a precept given under a penal sanction*. A specimen of such a precept is that mentioned in can. 2173 and 2176. But the precept must have been duly given and intimated according to can. 2310. Besides, the essential features of a crime must not be sacrificed in these violations, which consequently must be external and imputable.

Can. 2196 establishes the quality and determines the grievousness of crimes (*qualitas et quantitas*). Moralists, when speaking of the different species of sin, are wont to lay down a threefold rule for determining them. Two of these rules coincide with the quality of crime stated in the first clause of our canon. Crimes differ from one another in quality by reason of the different objects of the law. However, since every law has in view special acts, it is evident that crimes differ specifically according to their formal objects. Thus the crimes against faith and unity of the Church differ from those against religion, even though faith belongs to religion,[6] the sins against property and life differ from one another, although all are directed against the virtue of justice, because they are morally specified by their formal objects.

The *gravity of a crime* depends on the conditions mentioned, *viz.*, the objective gravity or importance of the law violated, the greater or less imputability, and the

6 See can. 2314, 2319, and can. 2320–2329.

damage done. The *objective* gravity of a law can easily be gauged by the gravity of the penalty attached to it. A law provided with a penal sanction (*lex perfecta*) is manifestly more important than a law destitute of such a sanction. Besides, the *subjective condition of the transgressor* must be considered, of which more under Title II. Lastly, an action which might be considered less weighty in its nature and on account of diminished imputability, might still entail very serious consequences[7] and thus enhance responsibility. English and American criminal law distinguishes between indictable and petty offences, and the former are classified as treasons, felonies, and misdemeanors.[8] There can be no doubt that this law is bottomed on the natural distinction of heinousness. Consequently, also, the procedure is different.

PUBLICITY OF CRIMES

Can. 2197 distinguishes three kinds of crimes,— public, notorious, and occult.

1. A crime is *public* if committed under, or accompanied by, circumstances which point to a possible and likely divulgation thereof. Canonists[9] enumerate different degrees of publicity: *almost occult* (*pene occultum*), which is known to at least two witnesses; *famosum* or *manifestum*, which not only can be proved, but is known to many; and, finally, *notorium*. From this it will be seen that a real intrinsic distinction be-

---

[7] Take, for instance, an operation performed by an unskilled surgeon or midwife, or an innocent hunting trip by a clergyman.

[8] Cfr. Kenny-Webb, *l. c.*, p. 84 ff. The French law distinguishes *crimes, délits, contraventions;* the German: *Verbrechen, Vergehen, Uebertretun-*

gen; the Roman: *facta, dicta, scripta, consilia;* l. 16, Dig. 48, 16; see c. 19, Dist. 1, *de Poenit.*

[9] Reiffenstuel, V, 1, 241 ff.; Schmalzgrueber, V, 1, n. 1 ff.; Hollweck, *l. c.*, p. 67 f.; Wernz, *l. c.*, VI, n. 17, p. 21.

tween a *public crime* and a *crime notorious in fact* can
hardly be established.[10]   (We shall point out one distinctive trait below.)   To fix the number of persons required for making a crime a public one [11] is rather
hazardous, though it may furnish a certain rule which will
enable the judge to decide as to the secrecy or public
character of a crime.   Many canonists hold that *at least
six persons* in a community, even the smallest (for instance, a religious house of 10 or 12 inmates), must know
of a crime, to render it public.[12]   Nor should there be
any doubt about the character of the persons who are
witnesses to the crime.   Furthermore, the interest they
may have in the crime should be weighed.[13]

2. A crime is *notorious* by notoriety of law (*notorietate
iuris*) if it has become an adjudged matter, according to
can. 1902–1904, or judicially confessed, according to can.
1750.   Extrajudicial confessions do not render a crime
notorious by notoriety of law.   Here we must take issue
with the assertion that the Code acknowledges such confessions.   Thus it has been stated [14] that it would be a
notorium juris if the bishop or vicar-general would catch
a clergyman *in flagranti!*   The Code contains nothing to
that effect, but requires (*can. cit.*) a confession before
the judge sitting in court.

A crime is notorious *notorietate facti* when it is pub-

10 The sources are not consistent;
see c. 17, C. 2, q. 1; c. 8, X, III, 2,
where the *notorium* is called *publicum* and *manifestum*.

11 Wernz, *l. c.*, VI, p. 22, note 35.

12 Reiffenstuel, V, 1, n. 252; unless, he says, it has been committed
in the presence of the competent authority who enjoys power *in foro
externo*.

13 Eichmann, *l. c.*, p. 32; for instance, in adultery.

14 Hollweck, *l. c.*, p. 67, note 4,
quotes Reiffenstuel, V, 1, 267; but
Reiffenstuel is cautious enough not
to make such a general statement,
for he demands that the judge sur-
prise the delinquent before witnesses. This is evident, otherwise
the judge would at the same time
be the accuser. That the pastor
does not constitute a public person
in judiciary matters is clear.

licly known and has been committed under such circumstances that it cannot be concealed by any artifice or be excused by any legal assumption or circumstantial evidence. The term *nulla tergiversatione celari* is equivalent to the other used in the Decretals.[15] The second clause refers to imputability, which may be lessened by extenuating circumstances, according to can. 2201–2206. Hence not only the fact itself must be notorious, but also its criminal character.[16] Thus, for instance, the fact of alienation may easily be proved by a legal deed, but whether it was criminal must be ascertained by other means; because it may be that the administrator or procurator had due permission and therefore acted lawfully. It is this element of inexcusability or of knowledge of the criminal character of the deed that appears to distinguish a public from a notorious crime. For the text manifestly lays stress on divulgation with regard to public crimes and emphasizes the criminal character as known and inexcusable.

3. Every *crime* which is not public, says our text, is occult or *secret*. The Code distinguishes a twofold secrecy, *viz.:* merely material *(materialiter occultum)*, which exists when the fact is unknown, or known only to the perpetrator and a few reticent persons; and formal *(formaliter occultum)*, when the moral and juridical guilt is unknown. An example may illustrate the distinction. If a *percussor clericorum* beats a pastor at night, his identity may remain unknown, though the effects point to a crime; if the priest was beaten in a public row, there may be a reasonable doubt as to the real perpetrator. The authors,[17] therefore, assumed that a crime committed at night could not be notorious or public. However,

15 C, 10, X, III, 2.
16 Reiffenstuel, V, 1, n. 265; Hollweck, *l. c.*, p. 68.
17 Schmalzgrueber, V, 1, n. 5.

this theory cannot be accepted in this general sense. Take, for instance, a sacrilegious burglary.[18] If a sufficient number of persons witnessed such a crime and recognized the perpetrator, the crime could not be styled occult. Neither does it seem true that a duel is always a secret crime, as some maintain.[19] For although duels are generally held in a secret place, yet there are, as a rule, witnesses and signs which admit of a perfectly safe judgment that a duel has taken place. [20]

ECCLESIASTICAL, CIVIL, AND MIXED CRIMES

The Code does not distinguish between private and public crimes, as far as prosecution is concerned, but it draws a line of demarkation between ecclesiastical, civil, and mixed crimes.

As *ecclesiastical crimes* were acknowledged manifest and serious transgressions of the law of the Church,[21] and as typically canonical crimes were considered: homicide, *moechia*, and apostasy. However it would be vain to look for a fixed list of so-called ecclesiastical crimes. The fact is that, since the fourth and fifth centuries, besides the three above named crimes, usury, simony, *crimen falsi*, and intercourse with excommunicated persons were also adjudged by the ecclesiastical courts.[22] The Decretals enumerate quite a list of crimes subject to ecclesiastical judicature: apostasy, heresy, usury, simony, sacrilege, incest, adultery, bigamy, usurpation of ecclesiastical power, and so forth, so that the whole Decalogue was more or

---

18 Kenny-Webb, *l. c.*, p. 171.

19 Hollweck, *l. c.*, p. 68, note 3.

20 When students enter the schoolroom with seared and bandaged faces and smelling from carbolic acid, there seem to be "loud" signs, nor do they, as a rule, make any secret of the duel.

21 Cfr. cc. 21, 22, C. 11, q. 3.

22 Cfr. Hinschius, *l. c.*, IV, p. 746.

less included.[23]   This is not surprising, since, with the exception of purely political crimes, the others were all taken to imply the *ratio peccati,* which the Church is certainly competent to judge.[24]   Our Code greatly reduces this list, as may be seen from the bare enumeration of the titles, *viz.,* Title XI, Title XIII, and Titles XVI-XIX.

Crimes that violate an ecclesiastical law are prosecuted by ecclesiastical authority, as the nature of the crime, and, we may add, the nature of the Church as an autonomous society, require.   If the Church should deem it necessary, or opportune, she may ask for the assistance of the secular power.   This aid, of course, will be offered by the State only in countries where the separation of the two societies has not yet become an accomplished fact, and where the mutual relations of both are regulated by concordats.

The text: "*requisito interdum auxilio brachii saecularis,*" has a diplomatic tinge.   Formerly, *e. g.,* in the time of Innocent III or Boniface VIII, it went without saying that the State was obliged to lend a helping hand to the Church.   The secular sword was supposed to be at the disposal of the Church (*ad nutum ecclesiae*) and the Roman Pontiffs did not hesitate to remind rulers of their duty.   Thus heretical disturbances, which usually caused also civic disorders, were frequently quelled by the civil authority at the request of the Church.[25]   The same course was taken in prosecuting those who attacked ecclesiastical personages of higher rank.[26]

The separation of State and Church, brought about by

---

[23] See lib. V, *Decretal.;* Eichmann, *l. c.,* p. 13.

[24] C. 13, Novit., X, II, 13.   Even political crimes were looked upon as heinous and had to be considered as such because of the intimate relation between Church and State.

[25] Cfr. cc. 9, 13, x, V, 7; c. 11, 6°, V, 2; see Scholz, *Publisistik zur Zeit Philipps des Schönen und Bonifaz VIII.* (Stutz, *K.-R. Abhandl.*)

[26] See c. 5, 6°, V, 9.

the religious breach of the XVIth century, lessened the
influence of the spiritual upon the temporal society.
Royal absolutism grew jealous of the power of the
Church and fomented aversion towards her in quarters
which had every reason to sustain her authority.   Thus
it came about that the rights of the Church were often
trampled under foot and she had no longer the means to
enforce them.   This is an actual condition, but it is not
the proper relation intended by the Governor of the Universe, who desires peaceful and harmonious coöperation
between the two societies, sovereign in their respective
spheres.[27] Hence it is that the Church still claims the
right of being helped and supported in the attainment of
her ends.   Evil-doers in the bosom of the Church can
hardly be desirable citizens, and permanent tranquillity
can be established only by the elimination of disorderly
elements.   This requires a firm and effective means of
righting wrong whenever it makes itself felt, even in the
ecclesiastical order, and the civil power should be aware
that the civil order must necessarily suffer if and whenever the ecclesiastical order is seriously disturbed.

Whilst the Church claims the right of punishing crimes
of a merely ecclesiastical character and of invoking the
civil power in the exercise of this right, she avoids interference in the prosecution of *merely civil crimes,* such as
treason, revolution, counterfeiting, evading the payment
of duties and taxes, etc.   These crimes fall within the
exclusive purview of the State, provided the clerical privilege is safeguarded according to can. 120, where it has
not been abolished by concordats or lawful custom.   But
the text adds: " although the Church, too, would be competent concerning such crimes, in as far as moral guilt

27 See Leo XIII, " *Immortale Dei,*" Nov. 1, 1885.

is concerned" For moral guilt touches the soul and consequently the salvation of men, which belongs to the spiritual power. Just here it may be perceived how well the State would fare if it coöperated with the Church. The authority of the State would be greatly strengthened, men would realize that a crime against the civil authority is abhorred also by the representative of Him from whom all power is derived,[28] and thus be made to understand that they are not mere cogs in a machine, but responsible members of an organism which has the spiritual power behind it.

A third class of crimes is called *mixed*. It comprises such crimes as offend against the moral-juridical order of both societies. Both Church and State are interested in the prosecution of crimes which include offences against religion in general, as mentioned in Title XII, crimes committed against life, liberty, property, good name and morals, as stated in Title XIV, forgers of official documents, as mentioned in can. 2362, because ecclesiastical documents may also serve state purposes.[29] These mixed crimes may be prosecuted by both the civil and the ecclesiastical power, with due regard to prevention [30] and to the ruling of can. 1933, § 3, concerning laymen, who, after being duly punished by the civil authority, should not be prosecuted by the Church.

---

28 Rom. 13, 1.
29 Cfr. Kenny-Webb, *l. c.*, p. 241; most of the so-called mixed crimes are also mentioned in the civil code (*ibid.*).
30 See can. 1553, § 2; can. 1568.

TITLE II

IMPUTABILITY, AGGRAVATING OR EXTENUATING CIRCUMSTANCES, AND JURIDICAL EFFECTS OF CRIME

Imputability was explained above as moral proprietorship in the praise or blame justly due to deliberate acts performed by a free agent. Hence a crime, to be imputable, must proceed from a deliberate intention, which presupposes knowledge and free will. The Code first explains imputability in general and the excusing, extenuating or aggravating influences bearing upon it, then sets forth some circumstances or conditions of this influence, in particular, the aggravating circumstances, then concurrence in crime, and, lastly, its juridical effects.

IMPUTABILITY IN GENERAL

Can. 2199

Imputabilitas delicti pendet ex dolo delinquentis vel ex eiusdem culpa in ignorantia legis violatae aut in omissione debitae diligentiae; quare omnes causae quae augent, minuunt, tollunt dolum aut culpam, eo ipso augent, minuunt, tollunt delicti imputabilitatem.

Can. 2200

§ 1. **Dolus heic est deliberata voluntas violandi legem, eique opponitur ex parte intellectus defectus cognitionis et ex parte voluntatis defectus libertatis.**

22

§ 2. Posita externa legis violatione, dolus in foro externo praesumitur, donec contrarium probetur.

The imputability of a crime depends on two essential conditions of the perpetrator, *viz.*, (1) deliberation (*dolus*), and (2) speculative or practical guilt (*culpa*). *Dolus* or malice is here taken as the deliberate will of transgressing the law, as opposed to lack of knowledge on the part of the intellect, and to deficiency on the part of the will. This follows from the complex nature of human acts which require knowledge as well as will (" *nihil volitum nisi cognitum* ") [1] and hence, where the voluntary element is entirely wanting, there can be neither *dolus* nor *culpa*, and where volition is impeded, this defect diminishes the guilt.

But the text adds (can. 2200, § 2), that if the fact of the violation of a law is certain, the intention or *dolus* is presumed until the contrary is proved. Hence the proof of ignorance rests on the perpetrator. This is also recognized by civil law. For criminal liability may exist even though the offender had no intention to commit the particular crime which he did in fact commit, and consequently it suffices to commit any crime, whatever it may have been. [2] This is the meaning of the legal maxim: *"Ignorance of fact, not of the law, excuses."* [3] How far deliberation and knowledge may affect culpability or immunity from criminal punishment depends on the mental condition of the perpetrator, but also on the wording of the law, as is evident from can. 2228 f. This supposes that for any punishable act there are required:

---

[1] Cfr. S. Thomas, *Summa Theol.*, I–II, q. 6; W. Hill, *Ethics*, 8th ed., p. 46; according to general usage in English. the term *voluntary* means free.

[2] Kenny-Webb, *l. c.*, p. 36.

[3] *Reg. Iuris 18 in 6°*; cfr. *Reg. Iuris 23 in 6°*: "*Sine culpa, nisi subsit causa, non est aliquis puniendus.*"

Knowledge that what the offender is doing is criminal, and *will* or power of volition, *i. e.*, the offender must be able to abstain from doing what he does: if either condition fails, immunity from criminal punishment will arise. This is sound theological as well as juridical doctrine, provided always that the law may add a specific clause as to the degree of knowledge or malice, as can. 2229 plainly indicates.[4]

The *culpa*, as distinguished from the *dolus*, may arise from ignorance and carelessness. Concerning ignorance, see can. 2202. The *omissio debitae diligentiae* may be the result of carelessness, or of negligence, or of thoughtlessness. Different occupations and conditions require more or less diligence.

Thoughtlessness must, however, be in one or the other way connected with volition or the exercise of the will, or what the theologians call *voluntarium in causa*. For in order to render an act imputable it is required that the evil effect be foreseen, at least in a general or confused way, that the agent had it in his power or was free to posit the cause, and, lastly, that there was an obligation to avoid the evil effect that followed the cause.

Any act, therefore, which is not a human act, *viz.*, one that does not proceed from reason and free will, cannot be imputed to a human agent. But since either reason or free will may be affected, not entirely, but partially, the degree of imputability or guilt is proportionate to the mental state in which the agent was at the time he committed the criminal act. Hence, § 2 of can. 2199 very appropriately states that every cause that increases, diminishes, or takes away the *dolus* or *culpa*, also

[4] Kenny-Webb, *l. c.*, p. 35. If the law determines no further degree of *dolus* or *culpa*, it is understood that the degree required for constituting a mortal sin is sufficient. Hollweck, *l. c.*, p. 75, note 6.

increases, diminishes, or takes away responsibility for the *delictum*. This, of course, presupposes the existence and exercise of freewill, but it does not exclude the possibility of so-called biological or physiological influences on the morality of human acts.   No psychologist denies the possible alteration of the ethical element by reason of the composite nature of man.   An eminent philosopher has stated it as follows: " That there are certain unfortunate individuals who, owing to mental derangement, are irresponsible, is beyond doubt and has never been disputed. That there are others who, while able to form correct judgments on speculative matters, are incapable of resisting solicitations to evil, does not contradict any point of our doctrine but seems rather to be established by experience.   It may not be even impossible that there exists, as Lombroso professed, ' a criminal type,' that is to say, monsters irresistibly given over to crime who can be recognized by certain anatomical, physiological, and pathological characteristics.   Such characteristics are to be found more or less numerous among most criminals. Further, we may also admit, though the experiments on which this assertion rests must be viewed with caution, that a person may under the influence of hypnotic suggestion lose the use of his liberty.   All these facts are not incompatible with the theory of free-will, as the exception does not disprove the rule." [5]

DEFECTUS COGNITIONIS

Can. 2201

§ 1. **Delicti sunt incapaces qui actu carent usu rationis.**

[5] D. Mercier, *A Manual of Modern Scholastic Philosophy*, Engl.   Transl., 1917, Vol. II, p. 225 f.

§ 2. Habitualiter amentes, licet quandoque lucida intervalla habeant, vel in certis quibusdam ratiocinationibus vel actibus sani videantur, delicti tamen incapaces praesumuntur.

§ 3. Delictum in ebrietate voluntaria commissum aliqua imputabilitate non vacat, sed ea minor est quam cum idem delictum committitur ab eo qui sui plene compos sit, nisi tamen ebrietas apposite ad delictum patrandum vel excusandum quaesita sit; violata autem lege in ebrietate involuntaria, imputabilitas exsulat omnino, si ebrietas usum rationis adimat ex toto; minuitur, si ex parte tantum. Idem dicatur de aliis similibus mentis perturbationibus.

§ 4. Debilitas mentis delicti imputabilitatem minuit, sed non tollit omnino.

Can. 2202

§ 1. Violatio legis ignoratae nullatenus imputatur, si ignorantia fuerit inculpabilis; secus imputabilitas minuitur plus minusve pro ignorantiae ipsius culpabilitate.

§ 2. Ignorantia solius poenae imputabilitatem delicti non tollit, sed aliquantum minuit.

§ 3. Quae de ignorantia statuuntur, valent quoque de inadvertentia et errore.

The degree of imputability is in proportion to the degree of *dolus* and *culpa*. *Dolus* or intention supposes a normal condition of the reasoning faculties, which in turn depends on organic conditions, which may be either actual or habitual, *i. e.*, more or less permanent. Besides, even in a normal condition ignorance may play a part in forming an imputable judgment. Can. 2201 treats of abnormal organic conditions, whilst can. 2202 has ignorance in view.

1. *Incapable of committing a crime are those who are actually deprived or destitute of the use of reason.* Hence acts committed in sleep or in a frenzied or furious state of mind cannot be imputed.[6] The text also includes insanity.

2. Those *habitually insane*[7] are *presumed* to be incapable of committing a crime, even though they may have lucid moments or may appear sane as to certain processes of reasoning or certain acts. Insanity is a disturbance of the mental faculties and, as such, influences the legal aspect of crime. Modern criminologists attribute insanity to pathological conditions and speak of the epileptic, the neurasthenic, and the psychopathic states.[8] *Moral insanity*, so-called, " in which all the upright sentiments are eliminated, while the intelligence presents' no disorders, "[9] is inadmissible and *de facto* rejected in American and English law. There are, on the other hand, different degrees of mental unsoundness, but " the very difficult practical question as to where the line of demarcation should be drawn " is yet unsolved.[10] Two classes of mentally unsound persons are: (a) lunatics over whom the threats and prohibitions of the criminal law exercise no control; and (b) those whose insanity is so slight that they would not yield to it if a policeman were at their elbow.[11] This rather technical distinction has been accepted by jurists ever since the case of Daniel McNaughten, A. D. 1843. We quote the replies given by the

6 Cfr. cc. 1, 3, Dist. 6.

7 C. 12, C. 15, q. 1, would inflict a milder penance after the return of normal conditions, which is inconsistent with our Code.

8 De Quirós, *l. c.*, p. 52 ff.

9 *Ibid.*, p. 9.

10 Kenny-Webb, *l. c.*, p. 48.

11 *Ibid.*

judges, because they not only are the norm of modern criminal law, but are also, to some extent, in accord with our Code.

(I) Every man is presumed to be sane, and to possess a sufficient use of reason to be responsible for his crime, until the contrary has been proved to the satisfaction of a jury.

(II) To establish a defence on the ground of insanity, it must be clearly shown that, at the time of committing the act, the party accused was laboring under such defect of reason, from disease of the mind, as not to know the nature and quality of the act he was performing, or if he did know, not to know that what he was doing was wrong.

(III) As to his knowledge of the wrongfulness of the act, the judges say: " If the accused was conscious that the act was one which he ought not to do, and if the act was at the same time contrary to the law of the land, he is punishable." Thus the test is the power of distinguishing between right and wrong, not, as was once supposed, in the abstract, but in regard to the particular act committed.

(IV) When a criminal act is committed by a man under some insane delusion as to the surrounding facts, which conceals from him the true nature of the act he is doing, he will be under the same degree of responsibility as if the facts with respect to which the delusion exists, had been as he imagined them to be.

We say, these principles agree with the new Code *to some extent*, because on account of the rules governing imputability these rules may be accepted *in globo*. However, the Code is very liberal in presuming immunity from criminal intent or responsibility, even for lesser or intermittent insanity. But this is only a *praesumptio iuris* and not a *praesumptio iuris et de iure*.[12] Hence the burden of proof is thrown upon the defendant, *i. e.*, the one accused of crime. The proof of insanity is furnished by the preponderance of evidence. Experts are to be called in and the rules laid down under can. 1762–1805 applied.

All the persons mentioned in can. 2201, § 2, are to be treated as habitually insane, which, of course, presupposes a morbid disease and not merely an *irrational impulse*. However, such an impulse, which sometimes takes on the nature of an irresistible force, may only be the symptom of a latent though not violent habitual madness, and in that case it must be treated like habitual insanity, although courts of some states of our country and England exclude it as a plea of defence. [13]

One form of insane impulse is *kleptomania*, because the impulse to steal really seems to arise from actual insanity. [14]

With regard to *hypnotism* note that it has not yet become a subject of sufficient judicial consideration to justify the attempt to formulate any rules [15] for it, and hence it must be treated like intoxication and passion, which are to be considered as to their antecedent causes and the intent.

3. *Intoxication* or drunkenness, if deliberate, *does not entirely take away responsibility* for a crime committed in that state, although it diminishes imputability, thus rendering the crime less offensive than when committed in the state of complete responsibility, unless indeed the state of intoxication was brought about purposely in order to commit or excuse the crime. Responsibility is to be fixed

12 See can. 1825–1828.   14 *Ibid.*
13 Kenny-Webb, *l. c.*, p. 52.   15 *Ibid.*, p. 55.

according to the degree of drunkenness, because it is this
that determines the measure of voluntariness. But to excuse entirely a deed done in the state of voluntary intoxication would be to excuse one wrongful act by another,
which neither the ecclesiastical nor the civil law [16] can
permit. For no one is allowed to put himself into a state
of irresponsibility or to deprive himself of the use of
reason without adequate cause. There is no difference between intoxication produced by alcoholic liquor and the
state superinduced by certain drugs, such as opium, mor-
phine, and cocaine. Even blameable drunkenness may
sometimes have the effect of diminishing criminal responsibility. Thus it may easily cause a mistake in regard to
facts which in itself excuse an otherwise unlawful act.
Take, for instance, a *percussor clericorum,* who in a
drunken condition is not aware of the clerical character of his victim. Besides, intoxication may also lessen
the guilty intent necessary for a particular crime. Thus
murder in the first degree may be reduced to homicide.
An exception is *intentional drunkenness brought about for
the purpose of committing a crime.* But this supposes
that the criminal had the wicked act in mind before getting drunk. Thus a pregnant woman who drank im-
moderately to brace herself for committing abortion
would have no defence or excuse; on the contrary she
would commit two distinct crimes.

The next clause of § 3, can. 2201, mentions *involuntary intoxication.* This, if it takes away the use of
reason, also takes away responsibility, and diminishes imputability in proportion to the diminished use of reason.
Biblical examples are well known.[17] Such a state may be
caused by malicious companions or by the administration

---

16 *Ibid.*

17 Noah, Gen. 9, 20 f.; Lot, Gen.
19, 32 ff.; see c. 9, C. 15, q. 1.

of alcohol for medical purposes, or by exceptional susceptibility to stimulants. It will be no defence, however, for a person to say that he did not intend to get drunk,[18] although the fact may lessen his imputability in the court of conscience. The degree of responsibility is gauged by the control one has over his reasoning faculties.

The text adds: "*Idem dicatur de aliis similibus mentis perturbationibus.*" These "other similar disturbances of the mind" may be caused by extraordinarily strong emotions of the irascible power. Thus the loss of dear ones may cause a sudden excitement, external natural causes such as fires, earthquakes, shipwrecks, etc., are apt to create a panic, and so forth. Hither also belong spiritistic and hypnotic suggestions and evocations which tend to upset the nerves.

4. Finally the Code says that *imbecility of mind lessens*, though it does not take away, responsibility. Among imbeciles are reckoned the *minus habentes*, the half-stupid and, we believe, also such as are physically very weak, because there can be no doubt that great feebleness of the body also affects the mind, no matter of what age the person may be. Concerning age consult can. 2204.

Canon 2202 has in view *ignorance*, which is not nescience, or absence of all knowledge, but properly means an absence of knowledge that is morally imputable to the free agent.[19] Such ignorance may be culpable or inculpable, and hence our text says

1. That *inculpable ignorance* of the law renders one immune from responsibility for transgressing it, while culpable ignorance diminishes the degree of imputability

18 Kenny-Webb, *l. c.*, p. 55 f.

19 Arregui, *Summarium Theol. Moral.*, 1919, ed. 4, n. 11: "*Caren-* *tia scientiae moraliter debitae*"; cfr. c. 9, X, V, 36: "*si scire debuisti.*"

only in proportion to the obligation one is under of acquiring the necessary knowledge. Here the distinction between vincible and invincible ignorance is properly employed, whereas the distinction between antecedent and consequent ignorance has little or nothing to do with our text, as all agree that antecedent ignorance is not imputable. Thus if a clergyman goes hunting, he may be reasonably ignorant that hunting is forbidden, because really only the *chase* in the proper sense is forbidden, not simple hunting. He may also be ignorant about the game laws, and become aware of the unlawfulness of hunting only after a fine has been imposed.

Ignorance is *vincible* if it can be removed by the use of ordinary means proportionate to the matter and the person who has to employ these means. If it cannot be remedied except by extraordinary means which are required neither by the thing itself nor by the state or vocation of the person who is supposed to be obliged to use such means, ignorance is called *invincible*.

There are different degrees of vincible ignorance: *affected*, when one purposely avoids knowing the laws, so as to escape the burden of observing them; *supine* or *crass*, when one is ignorant of the law through indolence or carelessness. Both affected and supine ignorance, being consequent, render a crime simply involuntary.[20]

2. *Ignorance of the penalty does not take away imputability*, but to some extent diminishes it. The reason is that penalty indeed deters from committing a crime too readily, but the *mens rea*, the remorse of conscience, is

---

[20] Ignorance, if purely affected, approaches *dolus*, and is still further distant from *culpa*, as far as this signifies carelessness; but it is related to *culpa*, inasmuch as it bears upon the necessary or required knowledge of the law; ignorance enters *dolus* as well as *culpa*; see c. 102, C. 11, q. 3; concerning penalties see can. 2229.

there and convicts the perpetrator of sin. However, since the penalty is, as a rule, proportionate to the gravity of the crime, it is but natural that ignorance of the penalty should diminish responsibility. What kind of ignorance is here intended is not explicitly stated. But since the term is used generally, it appears to include both vincible and invincible ignorance, as far as responsibility is concerned, though not as far as incurring the penalty is implied.

3. What has been stated with regard to ignorance, must also be applied to *inadvertence* and *error*. Hence if one is not sure that a certain occupation or action may cause harm, he is supposed to be innocent of guilt.[21] The same is true concerning error, for instance, if one is mistaken about the law prohibiting intercourse with *excommunicati vitandi,* he does not incur the penalty of excommunication.[22] Note, however, that error and inadvertence as well as ignorance excuse from criminal responsibility in a higher or lesser degree according to the wording of the law.[23] For laws which have the clause: *scienter praesumpserit, ausus fuerit,* require a higher degree of knowledge and attention, and on the other hand excuse more easily from criminal intent. This is a decidedly superior concept of law and responsibility than we find in secular codes. For, according to civil criminologists, a mistake in regard to the law, even though it be inevitable, does not afford an excuse for crime.[24] This is quite intelligible, for the State has in view chiefly the public order.

21 C. 23, C. 22, q. 4: "*Hoc est innocentem esse, ignorare quod noceat.*"

22 C. 102, C. 11, q. 3.
23 Compare can. 2365, 2369, 2371.
24 Kenny-Webb, *l. c.,* p. 62.

Can. 2203

§ 1. Si quis legem violaverit ex omissione debitae diligentiae, imputabilitas minuitur pro modo a prudenti iudice ex adiunctis determinando; quod si rem praeviderit, et nihilominus cautiones ad eam evitandam omiserit, quas diligens quivis adhibuisset, culpa est proxima dolo.

§ 2. Casus fortuitus qui praevideri vel cui praeviso occurri nequit, a qualibet imputabilitate eximit.

Carelessness, although it may approach *dolus*, is, according to Can. 2199, rather to be referred to *culpa* or lack of attention. But since many circumstances which puzzle the judge may surround the agent as well as the criminal act, he is to decide according to the common or ordinary circumstances. But if carelessness amounts, as it were, to forethought, it is more culpable. The text therefore says, *a breach of law committed by omitting the required diligence is less imputable*, but the degree of imputability is left to be fixed by the judge, who must weigh all the circumstances. The judge, therefore, is not to set up the law, but to consider whether the act is punishable by law, *i. e.*, whether a law exists that would punish such an act, at least in general.

Diligence is taken here as the contrary of negligence; and therefore omission of it spells negligence, or carelessness, or thoughtlessness, etc. All these terms clearly refer to the intellectual (either speculative or practical) attitude of man with regard to a determined law, *e. g.*, the prohibition of homicide. If the term " *debita*," is added to diligence, this cannot mean all possible diligence or attention, for to use such is not in the power of man; nor is it the intention of the lawgiver, else we should have to recur to the Sovereign Pontiff in each individual case.[25] Diligence therefore must be gauged by the object itself, *ex rei gravitate*. For greater diligence is required in important cases than in cases of a less serious nature. Besides, diligence must be applied in proportion to the position or condition of the agent or person, *ex qualitate personae*. For persons in a responsible position, like prelates, physicians, and lawyers, are justly supposed to employ more attention, and to consider more carefully than ordinary human beings the circumstances and consequences of an action they are about to perform. The general rule is that a man shall omit nothing of his own accord that he can and must do in order to dispel ignorance. Hence it must be in his power and he must be under obligation to dispel noxious ignorance. For instance, can. 1269 states the rules for preserving the Holy Eucharist. Now if a priest to whose care the Blessed Sacrament is committed, would leave the place without taking proper precautions, he would be responsible if a sacrilege were committed through his negligence, and his responsibility would be as great as his thoughtlessness had been.[26]

But, continues can. 2203, *if a person has been able to foresee the event* (or effect of an action) *and has nevertheless omitted to take the precautions which ordinary diligence would have dictated, carelessness approaches vicious intent or dolus.* Thus a clergyman may not be guilty of voluntary homicide if he throws a stone and

25 Ballerini-Palmieri, *Opus Theol. Morale*, 1892, ed. 2, Vol. I, p. 35, n. 64 ff.

26 See c. 1, X, III, 44; on negligence in civil courts one may find interesting matter in Kenny, *A Selection of Cases Illustrative of English Law of Tort*, 1904, p. 531 ff.

kills some one, [27] but if he goes hunting and omits the necessary precautions, he cannot be declared free of guilt in case a stray bullet from his gun kills or injures some one. Similarly, a clergyman exercising surgery (which he should not do) and omitting the necessary precautions or neglecting to acquire the necessary skill, cannot be declared guiltless. [28]

The next case considered by the Code is a *casual one*, or, as we call it, an accident, something that is not *foreseen or, if foreseen, could not be avoided*. Such an accident cannot be imputed. For instance, if a woman who has made her escape from her abductor jumps into a river and drowns, she is not considered a suicide who must be deprived of ecclesiastical burial. [29] Thus also a homicide committed in self-defence against an unjust aggressor who could not otherwise be repelled, would not render one liable to excommunication; nor would a woman who suffered abortion by an unlucky fall be subject to the penalty established for that crime. [30] How far carelessness may enter here must be judged according to what was said above on diligence. But the power and obligation there mentioned are a sure indication of the measure of diligence to be used. A fortuitous case, however, presupposes that it could not be foreseen or, at least, that it was unlikely to happen. [31]

27 C. 37, Dist. 50.

28 Cfr. can. 139, § 2; c. 19, X, V, 12.

29 C. 11, X, III, 28; see can. 1240, § 1, n. 3.

30 See c. 3, X, V, 39; can. 2350.

31 C. 25, X, V, 12: a priest intended to build a new church and in tearing down the old one, the roof fell and killed a workingman, who had been warned by the priest.

AGE

CAN. 2204

Minor aetas, nisi aliud constet, minuit delicti imputabilitatem eoque magis quo ad infantiam propius accedit.

Here only imputability is considered, for the diverse penalties are stated in can. 2230. Unless the contrary is evident, youth diminishes responsibility in proportion to its closeness to infancy. The Roman law regarded *impuberes* as entirely incapable of *dolus*.[32] Canon Law, and the Decretals particularly,[33] do not exclude responsibility, but admit that it may be lessened, more especially with regard to the sixth commandment. The Church is also very indulgent to minors (*i. e.*, those who have not yet completed the twentieth year of age) when the right of immunity, or rather the *ius asyli* is concerned. Thus Clement XIII vindicated this right to minors even in case of homicide; because, he said, full malice cannot be attributed to youths and atrocious crimes are committed by them but rarely.[34] This may have been true at that time, but newspaper reports now-a-days tell a sad story of youthful depravity. Therefore our Code adds: *nisi aliud constet, i. e.*, if malice does not supply the lack of age. Juvenile courts have been established of late years for youthful offenders and they deal with them more leniently than the lay courts were wont to do, not only at the time of Clement XIII, but also up to a comparatively recent date.[35]

32 L. 3, Dig. 47, 10=c. 2, C. 15, q. 1.

33 Cc. 1, 2, X, V, 23.

34 " *Quemadmodum*," May 25, 1763, § 5 f. (*Bull. Rom. Continuatio*, ed. Prati, 1862, Vol. IV, p. 754).

35 Kenny-Webb, *l. c.*, p. 45 f.

Can. 2205

§ 1. Vis physica quae omnem adimit agendi facultatem, delictum prorsus excludit.

§ 2. Metus quoque gravis, etiam relative tantum, necessitas, imo et grave incommodum, plerumque delictum, si agatur de legibus mere ecclesiasticis, penitus tollunt.

§ 3. Si vero actus sit intrinsece malus aut vergat in contemptum fidei vel ecclesiasticae auctoritatis vel in animarum damnum, causae, de quibus in § 2, delicti imputabilitatem minuunt quidem, sed non auferunt.

§ 4. Causa legitimae tutelae contra iniustum aggressorem, si debitum servetur moderamen, delictum omnino aufert; secus imputabilitatem tantummodo minuit, sicùt etiam causa provocationis.

§ 1. *Violence, which takes away all freedom of action, excludes responsibility and consequently the guilt of crime.*

Violence means external physical compulsion applied to force one to act against one's own will, as when a young man is haled before the ordaining bishop by his foolish parents. The doctrine of St. Thomas [36] is very clear on this subject. The act of the will is twofold: one is its immediate act, as it were, elicited by it, namely *to wish;* the other is an act of the will commanded by it, and put into execution by means of some other power, such as *to walk* and *to speak,* which are commanded by the will to be executed by means of the motive power. As regards the commanded acts of the will, the *actus imperati,*

[36] *Summa Theol.,* I–II, q. 6, art. 4 et 5; translated by the Fathers of   the English Dominican Province, 1914.

the will can suffer violence, in so far as violence can
prevent the exterior members from executing the will's
command. But as to the will's own proper act, the *actus
elicitus*, violence cannot be done to the will. The reason
is that the act of the will is nothing else than an inclination proceeding from the interior principle of knowledge.
On the other hand violence or compulsion proceeds from
an exterior principle or agent. It is contrary to the
nature of the will that it should be subject to compulsion
or violence, just as it is contrary to the nature of a natural inclination or movement to be bent in a contrary direction. Violence, therefore, is directly opposed to the voluntary as well as to the natural. For the voluntary and
the natural have this in common, that both are from an
intrinsic principle; whereas violence is from an extrinsic
principle. And for this reason, just as in things of
knowledge violence effects something against nature (*e. g.*,
a stone thrown upwards); so in things endowed with
knowledge it effects something against the will. Now
that which is against nature is said to be *unnatural;* and
in like manner that which is against the will is said to be
involuntary. Therefore violence causes involuntariness,
and consequently an act done under such external influence
is no human act, because a human act is always a
voluntary act. Violence, in other words, renders an act
irresponsible. However, note well, violence must be
complete and adequate and referable to the act in question; in other words, there must be a causal connection
between the violent act and the act commanded or intended by violence, as stated expressly in can. 1087. See
also can. 214 concerning ordination under compulsion, the
impediment of abduction (can. 1074), and acts against
faith commanded by idolatrous or heretical parents who
may be wicked and powerful enough to compel their

children to come with them into non-Catholic temples, etc.

§ 2. Fear, *even though relatively grave, necessity,* and *even a serious* loss or *detriment,* if merely ecclesiastical laws are violated, often *take away responsibility* and therefore the guilt of crime.

(a) Fear, or *trepidatio mentis ob malum imminens,* has been sufficiently explained elsewhere.[37] Since fear does not render a human act purely involuntary, but leaves it substantially free, it is evident that an act done from fear is imputable. Wherefore we need not be surprised that *" duress per minas "* forms a very rare defence in English-American law. [38]

(b) The same is true of *necessity,* which is a moral-physical state of man that prompts him to violate the law. Necessity has its degrees which depend on the helplessness of the person that is in need, and on the necessity of having or obtaining what is needed. Therefore extreme, grave, and light necessity are distinguished. *Extreme* [39] would be the necessity which would concern life or death, material or spiritual. *Grave* is the necessity which would cause a serious spiritual or material loss of property, name, honor, social condition. *Light* is the necessity if the loss threatened is of little importance, or if the damage, though great, can easily be warded off or repaired. The Code is very generous, as far as the external forum is concerned, in admitting any kind of necessity, which, as Gratian says, [40] knows no law.

---

[37] See this Commentary, Vol. II, p. 30; Vol. V, p. 245 f.

[38] Kenny-Webb, *l. c.,* p. 69.

[39] Theologians distinguish *extrema et quasi-extrema.*

[40] Dictum ad c. 39, C. 1, q. 1; cfr. c. 5, X, I, 40; c. 2, X, III, 46.

Whether *gravis,* in our text, is also to be referred to *necessitas* may reasonably be doubted; for the adjective grave is repeated before *incommodum,* but not before *necessitas.*

(c) *Incommodum* means inconvenience, trouble, bother, loss, detriment, and is related to necessity, with this difference, that necessity signifies rather a negative condition, or want, whereas *incommodum* may involve the positive deprivation of something that is convenient, or becoming, to one's state of life. However, the inconvenience must be *great*. *Incommodum* is a very elastic term, and may be referred to the person affected as well as to the object that causes convenience or inconvenience.

(d) Grave fear, necessity, and grave inconvenience excuse from crime only if the violation concerns an *ecclesiastical law*. For it is generally understood that merely positive laws do not oblige under great inconvenience, inasmuch as the human legislator is supposed not to wish to lay a too heavy burden upon man under such conditions. Thus the law of alienation without papal indult (can. 1532, 2347, n. 3) may really prove too burdensome, nay even detrimental, and therefore does not oblige under certain conditions.

§ 3. On the other hand, § 3 of can. 2205 states that *an intrinsically evil act or an act which implies contempt of faith or ecclesiastical authority or injury to souls may be excused* on the grounds of grave fear, necessity, and grave inconvenience, but can never be declared entirely immune from criminal imputability.

(a) Ethics teaches that the morality of an act arises from the object, the circumstances, and the end intended by the agent. These determinants make an act either good or bad; and since the moral quality is something objective, the act itself is objectively tainted by the defect of the intrinsic quality of the object, the circumstances or the end. Of course, the intention can be rectified, provided the object and circumstances are either good or indifferent. However, this rather belongs to the internal forum.

(b) To the external forum may be referred three kinds of acts here specified, namely, contempt of faith, contempt of ecclesiastical authority, and spiritual damage. Contempt of faith spells apostasy or heresy, contempt of authority implies schism, if not also heresy, and spiritual damage may be summed up under the heading of co-operation, scandal, and hatred. The synod of Ancyra (314 A. D.) issued three canons concerning the reception of the *lapsi, i. e.,* those fallen in the persecution, to whom clemency is shown, but who are nevertheless censured for the crime they had committed against the faith. Of course, the compulsory offering of incense to pagan idols was free of guilt, but whether the act was done under compulsion could be proved only by the fact that the priests and deacons suffered torments or confiscation and protested their faith.[41]

Spiritual damage would be perjury, which is not allowed under any circumstances.[42]

§ 4. *The motive of legitimate self-defence against an unjust aggressor, provided the measure of necessity is not exceeded, takes away the criminal offence,* and, like provocation, diminishes imputability. The reason for the clause is that a man may rightfully prefer his own life to that of an unjust assailant, who certainly and actually intends his death, when one or the other must die or will surely be killed. For the unjust assailant forfeits the right of his own life by intending to kill another.

The so-called *moderamen inculpatae tutelae* requires: (a) that no more force is used than necessary to ward off the attack; (b) that the assailant is *hic et nunc* in the act

---

41 See c. 32, Dist. 50. 42 C. 1–3, C. 22, q. 5.

of aggression; (c) that no other means of escape are at
hand, and (d) that the intention is (at least implicitly)
directed not to the killing, but to the defence.[43]

Whether this plea of self-defence may also be made in
cases where one's honor, liberty, or fortune are at stake, is
not explicitly stated in our text. However, it is certain
that no one would be allowed to kill a calumniator even
though the calumny or detraction could not be warded off
by any other means. Nor is it allowed to kill a thief for
a small amount of money, say one gold ducat, or to kill a
man for the sake of a property right to be possessed only
in future or by way of inheritance; or to kill one who
retains an inheritance, etc. [44]

Provocation and actual aggression not infrequently
overlap, and it is difficult to distinguish one from the
other.[45] A real challenge often amounts to great danger.

THE PASSIONS

CAN. 2206

**Passio, si fuerit voluntarie et deliberate excitata vel
nutrita, imputabilitatem potius auget; secus eam
minuit plus minusve pro diverso passionis aestu; et
omnino tollit, si omnem mentis deliberationem et
voluntatis consensum praecedat et impediat.**

A passion is a movement or disturbance of the sensible
appetite which follows the imagination of good or evil,
and has various degrees, from vehemence to mere appre-

[43] Hill, *l. c.*, p. 209.

[44] Cfr. prop. damn. by the H. O.,
March 4, 1679, nn. 30–33 (Denzinger, nn. 1047–1055).

[45] This certainly was the case in

Papiensi, S. C. C., May 18, 1726
(Richter, *Trid.*, p. 93, n. 9), yet a
dispensatio ad cautelam was imparted.

hension. The composite nature of man, *i. e.*, his rational and appetitive constituents, influence morality, the latter not directly, because, being seated in the appetite, they are "blind," but indirectly, inasfar as they are subject to the will. It is evident that passions here are understood, not as consequent, but as *antecedent, i. e.*, as preceding the will and the deliberate action of the will. *Consequent* passions, *i. e.*, such as follow the free act, cannot affect its free nature, although they may influence other subsequent acts. Antecedent passions sometimes pull in the same direction as the will, sometimes in opposition to it. But no matter in what direction they may pull, freedom of will does not cease entirely, except in rare cases. Yet it is also true that self-control, the characteristic feature of freedom, is lost in proportion as sensible emotion increases. How far it may affect the moral imputability of an act is very difficult to determine, because each individual differs in sensitive or appetitive constitution and the organic or material conditions of temperament and heredity, habits of life, climate and temperature also differ greatly and influence different individuals in greater or less degree.[46] Thus also one individual may have the irascible passions more developed whilst another may be more under the influence of the concupiscible.

This premised, the text says that the passions, when willfully and deliberately excited and fostered, increase imputability; otherwise, *i. e.*, if neither nurtured nor stirred up by wilful coöperation, but simply taken as they objectively affect human nature as a whole and individually, they diminish responsibility in proportion to the degree of strength with which they work on the imagina-

---

[46] Cfr. S. Thom., I–II, q. 24; *De Veritate*, q. 22, art. 9; Hill, *l. c.*, p. 73; Mercier, *l. c.*, II, p. 226.

tion. Should they precede and impede the deliberation of the mind and the consent of the will, the act following could not be imputed.

AGGRAVATING CIRCUMSTANCES

CAN. 2207

Praeter alia adiuncta aggravantia, delictum augetur:
1.° Pro maiore dignitate personae quae delictum committit, aut quae delicto offenditur;
2.° Ex abusu auctoritatis vel officii ad delictum patrandum.

CAN. 2208

§ 1. Recidivus sensu iuris est qui post condemnationem rursus committit delictum eiusdem generis et in talibus rerum ac praesertim temporis adiunctis ut eiusdem pertinacia in mala voluntate prudenter coniici possit.

§ 2. Qui pluries deliquerit etiam diverso in genere, suam auget culpabilitatem.

Circumstances which enhance a man's responsibility may arise from the quality of the person and his office as well as from a repetition of crimes.

Can. 2207 considers the *personal and official circumstances.* The higher the *dignitary* who commits a crime or against whom a crime is committed, the greater the crime itself. For not only is the scandal greater,[47] but the law itself surrounds these persons with greater protection and inflicts severer penalties for crimes commit-

47 Cfr. c. 4, C. 25, q. 1; c. 12, X,II, 24.

ted against them.[48] Consequently clergymen are more severely punished than laymen.[49] A heavier penalty must be meted out to calumniators of the clerical state than to detractors of the lay state.[50] Heresy is more severely punishable in clerics than in laymen.[51]

But *authority and office* may be *abused,* and such abuse is the more detestable, the higher the office, and being an abuse of a public trust, also enhances imputability. Hither belongs the acceptance of gifts by ecclesiastical judges;[52] also the *crimen falsi,* wherefore ecclesiastics who falsify papal or episcopal documents are more guilty than laymen;[53] here also belong the abuse of the confessional[54] and all the crimes mentioned in Title XIX of this book.

Relapse into the same crime also increases culpability. The text first defines a *recidivus* in the juridical sense. He is one who, after a judicial sentence of condemnation, again commits the same crime under such conditions and circumstances, especially of time (for instance, soon after the sentence) that stubbornness in the practice of evil may be prudently presumed. This may be the case concerning those faults enumerated in can. 2168 ff. (non-residing clergymen) and can. 2176 f. (concerning concubinage with the same or another person). But it must be noted that *pertinacia* presupposes ill will, *i. e.,* resistance to either paternal or canonical warnings after formal condemnation.

Responsibility or culpability is increased also if one relapses into *crimes of a diverse kind.* The reason for

---

48 Can. 2343 f.
49 Can. 2323, 2336, 2340, § 2, 2345 etc.
50 C. 1, X, V, 1.
51 C. 13, X, V, 7.

52 Cfr. can. 1624, 1941, § 2; 2037, § 1.
53 Cfr. can. 2360, 2363; c. 4, C. 25, q. 1.
54 Can. 2367 f.; also can. 1665, § 2; can. 2408.

this law must be sought in the increased *mens rea*, just as the virtues united in the one virtue of prudence enhance the good habit.[55] The civil law also takes into consideration whether or not a criminal has been sentenced before.

PARTIES TO A CRIME

CAN. 2209

§ 1. Qui communi delinquendi consilio simul physice concurrunt in delictum, omnes eodem modo rei habentur, nisi adiuncta alicuius culpabilitatem augeant vel minuant.

§ 2. In delicto quod sua natura complicem postulat, unaquaeque pars est eodem modo' culpabilis, nisi ex adiunctis aliud appareat.

§ 3. Non solum mandans qui est principalis delicti auctor, sed etiam qui ad delicti consummationem inducunt vel in hanc quoquo modo concurrunt, non minorem, ceteris paribus, imputabilitatem contrahunt, quam ipse delicti exsecutor, si delictum sine eorum opera commissum non fuisset.

§ 4. Si vero eorum concursus facilius tantum reddidit delictum, quod etiam sine eorundem concursu commissum fuisset, minorem imputabilitatem secumfert.

§ 5. Qui suum influxum in delictum patrandum opportuna retractatione abduxerit plene, ab omni imputabilitate liberatur, etiamsi exsecutor delictum ob alias causas sibi proprias nihilominus patraverit; si non abduxerit plene, retractatio minuit, sed non aufert culpabilitatem.

[55] Cfr. can. 2234.

§ 6. Qui in delictum concurrit suum dumtaxat officium negligendo, imputabilitate tenetur proportionata obligationi qua adigebatur ad delictum suo officio impediendum.

§ 7. Delicti patrati laudatio, fructuum participatio, delinquentis occultatio et receptatio aliive actus delictum iam plene absolutum subsequentes, nova delicta constituere possunt, si nempe poena in lege plectantur; sed, nisi cum delinquente de illis actibus ante delictum conventum fuerit, non secumferunt delicti patrati imputabilitatem.

The present canon enumerates various kinds and degrees of participation in criminal acts. The first two sections (§ 1 and § 2) have in view conspirators and accomplices,[56] the following four deal with principals, as they are called in criminal law, who influence others more or less efficaciously, while the last section treats of cooperation after the act. But all kinds fall under the generic name of coöperation, which may be defined as physical concurrence in the evil act of another. However, since the act is supposed to be a criminal one, the distinction between material and formal coöperation is of little value here, because material coöperation presumes the act not to be evil or at least to be indifferent, if such acts exist.

1. *Conspirators* are those who, by mutual counsel to commit a crime, concur physically or actually in its perpetration. They are equally responsible with the criminal unless *de facto* circumstances increase or diminish their culpability. Thus in rape or sacrilegious burglary the

---

[56] The difference between conspirators and accomplices may be thus stated: Agreement makes conspirators, crime, accomplices.

robbers are held equally responsible.[57] *Percussores clericorum,* if they concur in the same criminal act, are all guilty, even though only one may strike the blow.[58] Conspiracy, of course, being supposed to be entered into by agreement, must be manifested in some way. But if the participants actually share in the criminal act, conspiracy is presumed, and it is incumbent on the participator to prove that he was no partner to the conspiracy. Thus Alexander III decided in the case of Thomas à Becket that all those who had come with the intention of killing or wounding the archbishop, even though they did not lay hands on him, were equally or almost equally guilty with the actual murderers.[59] Hence it is not too much to say that the mere fact of the parties having entered into such an agreement suffices to constitute a conspiracy.[60]

2. *Accomplices* are partners in a crime which, by its very nature, requires a helper. They are equally responsible with the criminal, unless circumstances lessen, increase or remove imputability. An accomplice is required in simony, which is equally punished in those who give, receive, and consent; religious superiors who simoniacally receive members, and bishops who bless abbots for the same motive are equally guilty.[61] Accomplices are also essential to adultery. However, here the culpability is diminished if one party does not know that the other is married.[62] Another crime which necessarily requires accomplices is duelling.[63] Those who claim ignorance or plead " not guilty " must prove their ignorance or innocence.

[57] See cc. 1, 4, C. 36, q. 2: the *reptantes, cooperantes, conniventes* are subject to the same penalty.

[58] C. 34, C. 23, q. 8.

[59] C. 6, X, V, 12.

[60] Kenny-Webb, *l. c.*, p. 272.

[61] Cfr. c. 21, C. 12, q. 2; cc. 8, 30, 39, V, 3; can. 2371, 2392.

[62] Cfr. c. 5, X, V, 16; can. 2388.

[63] Can. 2351.

3. *Principals or participators in a crime* may take part therein by a more or less efficacious influence, or they may withdraw their coöperation, or they may concur only in a negative way in the perpetration of the crime.

(a) Principals in the first degree are, as per § 3, the (1) *mandans* or principal author of a crime; (2) the instigators and (3) the aiders and abettors in whatsoever form. All these are no less guilty than the criminal himself, provided the crime would not have been perpetrated without their coöperation and provided all other things are equal. For instance, a prelate ordering celebration of divine office in an interdicted church would be a *mandans* and both the prelate and the celebrant would incur the same penalty.[64] An instigator *(ad delictum inducens)* would be a religious inviting outsiders to violate the papal enclosure.[65] The same crime may have abettors or aiders *(concurrentes)*, for instance, in the usurpation or alienation of ecclesiastical property,[66] in procuring abortion and duelling,[67] in forging papal documents, and in the election,[68] presentation or nomination of candidates to ecclesiastical offices.[69] *Ceteris paribus* means that the guilt may be less in the one or other of the coöperators, because of ignorance of the law, or the greater dignity and official character of the author, instigator or aider.

(b) *Principals in a less degree*, according to § 4 of can. 2209, are those who aid in the perpetration of a crime, but not so that the crime would not have been committed if they had not concurred, in other words, they are, as it were, merely concomitant perpetrators. These are less responsible, provided, however, they were not acting as

---

64 Can. 2338, § 3.
65 Can. 2342, n. 1.
66 Can. 2347 f.

67 Can. 2350, § 1; 2351, § 1.
68 Can. 2360.
69 Can. 2394.

conspirators. Thus, for instance, in the usurpation of ecclesiastical property the main robber may be a high personage and his tools incur less responsibility because the former was bent on carrying out his plans, even though the others would have resisted.

(c) Those who *withdraw their coöperation* in a crime in a proper and efficacious way are freed from every responsibility, even though the perpetrator commits the crime for reasons of his own; if the withdrawal is only half-hearted, the responsibility is lessened, but not taken away entirely. For instance, in a simoniacal election the money must be entirely refunded and every promise cancelled before election. A druggist who offered medicine for abortion must take it back; if he only dilutes or mixes it with other counteracting ingredients, he is guilty to some extent should abortion result; but he is not guilty at all if the medicine is taken back, and abortion results nevertheless.[70]

(d) *Official* aiders or abettors in crime are those who neglect their duty and thereby aid in the commission of crimes. Their responsibility is proportionate to the obligation by which they are bound, in virtue of their office, to prevent the crime. For instance, a pastor deserving removal for the reasons mentioned in can. 2182 or in can. 2176, should be removed by the bishop, and if the latter fails to remove him, he himself becomes responsible for the ensuing damage (decrease of Christian training, detriment to divine worship, scandal, etc.). There is now little excuse for not proceeding in such cases, because the law has rendered procedure less diffi-

---

[70] But even in this case a druggist or a physician may be somewhat guilty, if the bottle or box had the formula written on it, because it could be copied before it was returned.

cult and the obligation is incumbent on the Ordinary.[71]

4. *Principals or accessories "after the fact"* are such as laud and approve a crime, or share in the booty or fruits of the same, or hide and shelter criminals, or abet the crime after it has been perpetrated. Each of these acts constitutes a crime in itself if forbidden under penal sanction; otherwise they exclude imputability, unless conspiracy has preceded.

Can. 2338, § 2, which prohibits intercourse with *excommunicati vitandi,* affords an example of *patrati delicti laudatio* or *receptatio delinquentis;* can. 2338, § 3, would punish the *admittentes;* can. 2339 concerning ecclesiastical burial affords a similar case, though it appears as an independent crime.

The *fructum participantes* or *detinentes* of can. 2345 are here included, because they participate in the theft, provided they are aware of the injustice of the act.[72]

CONSEQUENCES OF CRIMES

CAN. 2210

§ 1. Ex delicto oritur:

1.° Actio poenalis ad poenam declarandam vel infligendam et ad satisfactionem petendam;

2.° Actio civilis ad reparanda damna, si cui delictum damnum intulerit;

§ 2. Utraque actio explicatur ad normam can. 1552–1959; et idem iudex in criminali iudicio potest ad instantiam partis laesae civilem actionem ad examen revocare et definire.

---

71 There may indeed be some impediments which prompt the Ordinary not to proceed; but there also are purely imaginary obstacles, such as fear of trouble and sheer indolence or ignorance.

72 Cfr. c. 4, X, V, 18.

Can. 2211

Omnes qui in delictum concurrunt ad normam can. 2209, §§ 1-3 obligatione tenentur in solidum expensas et damna resarciendi quae ex delicto quibuslibet personis obvenerint, licet a iudice pro rata damnati.

The Code calls these things *efféctus*, we prefer to speak of *consequences*, since effect means the immediate and direct result of an act. These consequences are two: criminal and civil action (can. 2210), which must be proportionately applied to the principals in crime.

From crimes may arise:

1.° *A penal or criminal action* looking either to a declaration or condemnation to penalty and satisfaction or to retribution;

2.° *A civil action* looking to a repair of the damage done if any was done.

Both actions have been set forth in can. 1552–1959; but 'the present text adds that the judge in a criminal trial may, if the injured party demands it, also examine and settle the civil action or damage suit. Thus if damage was done by beating a cleric or by sacrilegious theft, the criminal court may decide the amount of reparation.

Can. 2211 states the *obligation of repairing the damage to be imposed on the conspirators, accomplices and instigators,* as mentioned under can. 2209, §§ 1–3. This threefold class of participants in a crime are held *in solidum* to repair the expenses and damage caused by the crime to any and every person who suffered by it. For instance, if two or three persons committed a theft, or three elected a fourth illegally, *i. e.*, simoniacally, to an office, each is held responsible for the whole amount of expenses and damages, just as if he were the only perpetrator, even, says the text, if he were condemned by the judge only to a *pro rata* payment. Therefore if A was condemned to pay $100, B $150, and C $200, A is liable for $450 in case the other two prove insolvent. Of course A may fall back on B and C by instituting a suit in the civil court, which would certainly recognize the claim of A independently of any criminal action.

TITLE III

CONATUS DELICTI OR INCHOATE CRIMES

CAN. 2212

§ 1. Quicunque actus posuerit vel praetermiserit qui ad exsecutionem delicti natura sua conducunt, sed delictum non consummaverit, sive quia consilium suum deseruit, sive quia delictum propter insufficientiam vel ineptitudinem mediorum perficere non potuit, *delicti conatum* committit.

§ 2. Cum omnes actus positi vel omissi sunt qui ad exsecutionem delicti natura sua conducunt et ad delictum perficiendum sufficiunt, si ex alia causa, praeter voluntatem agentis, effectum sortiti non sint, delicti conatus dicitur proprio nomine delictum *frustratum.*

§ 3. Conatui delicti accedit actio illius qui alium ad delictum committendum inducere studuerit, sed inefficaciter.

§ 4. Si conatus delicti peculiari poena in lege mulctetur, verum constituit delictum.

CAN. 2213

§ 1. Delicti conatus suam habet imputabilitatem, eo maiorem, quo magis ad consummationem accedit, quanquam minorem prae delicto consummato, salvo praescripto § 3.

§ 2. Delictum frustratum magis culpabile est, quam simplex delicti conatus.

§ 3. Ab omni imputabilitate liberatur qui sponte

55

PART II
PENALTIES

PENALTIES IN GENERAL

CAN. 2214

§ 1. Nativum et proprium Ecclesiae ius est, independens a qualibet humana auctoritate, coercendi delinquentes sibi subditos poenis tum spiritualibus tum etiam temporalibus.

§ 2. Prae oculis autem habeatur monitum Conc. Trid., sess. XIII, *de ref.*, cap 1: "Meminerint Episcopi aliique Ordinarii se pastores non percussores esse, atque ita praeesse sibi subditis oportere, ut non in eis dominentur, sed illos tanquam filios et fratres diligant elaborentque ut hortando et monendo ab illicitis deterreant, ne, ubi deliquerint, debitis eos poenis coercere cogantur; quos tamen si quid per humanam fragilitatem peccare contigerit, illa Apostoli est ab eis servanda praeceptio ut illos arguant, obsecrent, increpent in omni bonitate et patientia, cum saepe plus erga corrigendos agat benevolentia quam austeritas, plus exhortatio quam comminatio, plus caritas quam potestas; sin autem ob delicti gravitatem virga opus erit, tunc cum mansuetudine rigor, cum misericordia iudicium, cum lenitate severitas adhibenda est, ut sine asperitate disciplina, populis salutaris ac necessaria, conservetur et qui correcti fuerint, emendentur aut, si resipiscere noluerint, ceteri, salubri in eos animadversionis exemplo, a vitiis deterreantur."

This canon vindicates to the Church a right which flows from her very constitution, namely, *the right to punish subjects who transgress her laws with spiritual as well as temporal penalties.* This right is natural and inherent in the Church, and therefore independent of human authority. It is what we call the coercive or restrictive power, sometimes also styled *potestas executiva,* although the English term executive does not accurately convey the idea embodied in the Latin word.

The Code uses three adjectives to determine the character of this coercive power:

1. It is called *nativum, i. e.,* an inherent or natural right. The proof for this dogmatic thesis [1] lies in the fact that Christ founded a visible autonomous society endowed with the means to achieve its appointed end.[2] The Church, indeed, is not merely a teaching institution, but a juridical society, the object of which is the common and individual spiritual welfare of men. It is therefore an *a priori* wrong conception of the Church, if only teaching and preaching penance is emphasized, whilst the binding character of the obligations imposed by membership is neglected. Christ granted power to rule His Church to Peter and the other Apostles, and this power is as wide and deep as the creative word that produced it.[3] There is no limitation or restriction or exception made of the power of binding and loosing. It embraces all things,

---

[1] *Trid.,* sess. 7, can. 14, *de baptismo;* Martin V, *"Inter cunctas,"* Feb. 22, 1418, art. 31, 33 (Denzinger, n. 575, 577); Pius VI, *"Auctorem fidei,"* Aug. 28, 1794 propp. 4,

[5] (Denzinger, n. 1367 f.); Pius IX, *Syllabus,* prop. 24 (Denzinger, n. 1572).

[2] See Hollweck, *l. c.,* p. IX ff.

[3] Cfr. Matth. 16, 19; 28, 18 ff.

all men who, by the regeneration of Baptism, are incorporated with the visible body of Christ. Neither is this power a merely internal persuasion produced by external exhortation. It means a reality that is sensibly manifested. For those who reject the authority of the Church and refuse to listen to her, are segregated from the body of Christ and must be treated as separated, *i. e.*, as heathen and publicans. [4]

The Apostles commanded as well as preached and were endowed with the power of punishing the disobedient.[5] We cannot imagine that the words addressed to them by Christ are merely strong metaphors inculcating obedience or penance. They rather communicate a power given by One who is the Governor of the universe.

This power of enforcing authority was understood and used by the Church throughout the course of her history. We will only point here to the fact of public penance and the ecclesiastical penalties inflicted on delinquent clerics. All this goes to show that the Church possessed and was conscious of possessing a vindictive power, and consequently it must be admitted that Christ laid down that authority in the constitution of the Church.

2. It is, however, a *ius proprium*, not merely in the sense of possession, but of a *characteristic power*. For the coercive power granted to the Church must not be considered as *an end,* but as a means to an end. Since the purpose of the Church is spiritual, the means, too, must partake of the same nature and therefore be spiritual. We clearly perceive from our Code that the spiritual element prevails. For most of the penalties are censures which directly reflect the spiritual element of the coercive power. In this respect the Church is superior to

4 Matth. 18, 17 f.   5, 4 ff.; II Cor. 8, 8; 10, 5 f.
  5 Cfr. Acts 15, 28; I Cor. 4, 21;

the State, which reaches only the external order of human society. However, this too must be understood in the right way. For we do not say that the Church is limited to merely spiritual means. This would be contrary to the nature of man, who is compounded of body and soul. Besides our text would give us the lie if we were to assume in the Church a merely spiritual (often confounded with internal) power.

3. The legislator further circumscribes this coercive power by the phrase: *independens a qualibet humana auctoritate,* a power that is independent of every human authority. This is merely a corollary of the *nativum ius,* for if this power is a constitutional, and therefore divine right of the Church, no human power can destroy or attack it with impunity. We do not read that St. Paul consulted the Proconsul of Achaia before he inflicted on the incestuous a severe punishment which had visible and external consequences. Neither did the Church borrow her power from the emperors. Quite a different thing is the personal immunity of Church dignitaries from the jurisdiction of lay courts. For this privilege may have been brought about and enlarged with the coöperation of the civil power. But the coercive power is not identical or coextensive with personal immunity. The abettors of Louis the Bavarian were dazzled by the imperial power, which they traced to imperial Rome, and therefore asserted that the Church, even as a whole, could not inflict coercive punishment on any man unless the emperor granted her this power. This error was promptly rejected by John XXII, who in this regard acted as the champion of an innate power, not of the papacy alone, but of the Church at large.[6]

_____
[6] " *Licet,*" Oct. 23, 1327, art. 5 (Denzinger, n. 427).

That the Church has been hampered and often unjustly handicapped in exercising this power is apparent
from the so-called "appeal from abuses" which the Gallican Liberties asserted as a privilege of the Frankish
Church. The Church could not accept such a curtailment
of her God-given power. She may tolerate abuses, as she
has tolerated persecution, but she can never allow the
substantial and necessary powers she has received from
her Founder to slip from her.

4. The *extent* of this coercive power is either formal or
material. Formal are the various kinds of punishment,
and *material* are the subjects over whom this power may
be wielded (see Title VI).

Here a word may be added concerning the various
canonical penalties in general. The text says that these
may be either *spiritual* or *temporal*. It may be said that
this contradicts our statement, made above, that the
means of exercising the coercive power must be com-
mensurate with the spiritual purpose of the Church, and
therefore spiritual. But we did not forget to say, at the
same time, that man is a being who must be treated with
human measure in meting out punishments. Now it is
a fact, always supposing that the Church is a visible,
autonomous society, that men, even clerics, are sometimes
more afraid of temporal, sensible punishments than of
the spiritual weapon of censures. This all the more where
faith has suffered shipwreck or at least has been weak-
ened. Consequently we find even in our Code some fines
and detention in houses of correction for clerical offenders. Yet even these penalties clearly have a spiritual aspect: they are inflicted for the purpose of amendment.

The *development* in the practice of imposing penalties
has kept pace with the outward growth and development

of the Church and her relation to the State. Excommunication or exclusion from the ecclesiastical body is the oldest penalty; its civil effects are noticeable already in the Apostolic writings.[7] Very severe was the punishment for the relapsed, as the history of the penitential discipline abundantly shows. Reconciliation took place gradually and by way of stations, the gradation of which is a matter of dispute. Clergymen were removed from their office and functions.

After Catholicism had become the religion of the State, the number of delinquents increased and a varied system of penalties became imperative. Excommunication became twofold, major and minor, to which was later added the personal interdict. Clergymen, too, experienced a variety of penalties, the severity of which varied in different countries. Characteristic of all these penalties was their vindictive nature, as well as the element of atonement or expiation contained in them.[8]

The relation of the Church to the State after the thirteenth century naturally widened the field of penal laws, inasmuch as many crimes which were at first purely ecclesiastical, were now considered civil, and *vice versa*. Not only ecclesiastical penalties, such as censures, but also temporal penalties were meted out by the ecclesiastical authorities: prison, exile, branding, slavery, loss of civil honor and civil rights, and so forth. The Decretals contribute the last stone to the building of the Church's Penal Code. After this classical period there was a demand — and a most legitimate one — for mitigation.

The inquiring reader may expect an answer to the question whether the *ius gladii* or right of inflicting capital punishment belongs to the Church as an inherent right.

---

7 Cfr. I Cor. 5; III Joh. 10; II Thess. III, 14.

8 See Hinschius, *l. c.*, IV, 747 ff.; Eichmann, *l. c.*, p. 7.

We think not. For to vindicate this right to the Church would entail danger of interference in the right of the State, and besides, the maxim: " *Ecclesia non sitit sanguinem* " is incompatible with the right of shedding blood. The spirit of the Church is, or at least should be, the spirit of Christ, which spells meekness and mercy. Moreover, one of the purposes of punishment is the correction or amendment of the delinquent. But this purpose is simply frustrated if the criminal is killed.[9] Furthermore, persuasion rather than force is to be used even with regard to the most serious ecclesiastical crimes, heresy and schism, which may be compared to treason in civil law. Yet the Code itself forbids compulsion in matters of faith (can. 1351), according to St. Augustine, who thought it expedient to call for armed resistance only after bloody crimes had been committed by the Donatists. We are aware of the objections that are drawn from the history of the Inquisition,[10] and do not wish to extenuate the stain it has left upon the annals of the Church; but it must be said to the honor of the latter that she always recommended clemency, even when she delivered stubborn recusants up to the secular arm. Besides it must not be forgotten that in the ages of faith heresy was punishable also as treason by the civil government. And finally we must not apply our kidglove notions of criminology and penal law to the ruder Middle Ages.

After this somewhat lengthy digression it remains to explain the term *delinquentes*. However, this has already been the subject of the first part, for delinquency is related to *delictum,* and consequently a delinquent means

---

9 Thus Hollweck, *l. c.,* p. XXVII.

10 The literature on this subject is immense; but we would recommend particularly the popular pamphlet by Eliza Atkins Stone, *A Brief for the Spanish Inquisition,* reprinted from *The Ave Maria.*

one who has committed a crime in the ecclesiastical sense of the word.

§ 2 of can. 2214 recalls the wise admonition of the Council of Trent to the bishops when compelled to use the punitive power. It is essentially the same doctrine as that inculcated by the Apostles [11] and may be divided into three parts:

1. Being pastors, not tyrants, they should first use persuasion and paternal admonition in order to deter men from evil-doing;

2. If some through human frailty have been delinquent, they should be reproved, entreated, and rebuked, but benevolently rather than austerely, by exhortation rather than threats;

3. If, however, the seriousness of the crime requires the rod, gentleness should be combined with firmness, judgment with mercy, and leniency with severity. Thus the faithful shall not be exasperated and wholesome discipline shall be maintained, correction shall lead to amendment, or where malice is combined with stubbornness, the deterring example shall at least be a warning to others.

11 I Tim. IV, 2; I Pet. V, 2.

TITLE IV

DEFINITION, KINDS, INTERPRETATION AND APPLICATION OF PENALTIES

DEFINITION

CAN. 2215

Poena ecclesiastica est privatio alicuius boni ad delinquentis correctionem et delicti punitionem a legitima auctoritate inflicta.

This text is quoted from the Council of Trent. It contains all the elements of penalty as now defined. For an ecclesiastical penalty means the privation of some good, inflicted by the lawful authority for the correction of the delinquent and the punishment of his crime.

Three elements are clearly discernible in this definition: the effect of penalty, its object and source.

1. The effect is privation of some good (*privatio alicuius boni*). This is the generic feature common to all penalties or pains, for *poena* means pain or suffering. St. Thomas says that it is essential to pain or penalty that it be an affliction against one's own will for some guilt or crime.[1] Hence man must be made aware of it either in body or mind. Every privation, however, be it in the natural or the supernatural order, causes pain because it is a want of perfection or lack of something that perfects and completes the well-being of man. If the Code

[1] *Summa Theol.*, I–II, q. 46, art 6, ad. 2.

66

insists on privation or denial of some good, it is in accordance with modern ideas of criminal law, which emphasize privation rather than positive infliction of pain, thereby excluding the notion of torment or torture. It must be added that even privation should be based on ethical principles. It would be against these rules if those who are entitled to inflict penalties would not observe the limits of justice and morality nor take into consideration the grievousness of the crime committed. An immoral penalty or brutal treatment of criminals [2] is against human nature and invariably misses its purpose.

The *bonum* of which one may be deprived is determined according to the kind of punishment. If it is a spiritual punishment, supernatural or spiritual goods, such as sacraments and divine worship, are withdrawn; if it is a temporal penalty, natural goods, such as liberty and fortune, are taken away, in whole or in part.

2. The *purpose of punishment* is twofold, reformatory and punitive. It is notable that the Code emphasizes the *reformatory* feature first. There is little difficulty among modern criminologists in admitting the reformatory or corrective character of punishment. In fact, there is quite a tendency to proclaim this the sole legitimate object of punishment.[3] But this contention goes too far. There is a wide gulf between Church and State, the latter looking solely to the temporal order of things, whereas the Church considers the whole man, soul and body.

The Code mentions " *delicti punitionem.*" What does that mean? Penalty supposes guilt, and guilt is caused by the breach of an obligation set up either by natural or positive law. Law means order, coördination or sub-

---

[2] The old maxim " *reus res sacra,*" even a criminal is a sacred thing, should guide also the judge and the criminologist.

[3] Kenny-Webb, *l. c.,* p. 28.

ordination. It is evident that a crime is a breach of law and order, more specifically, a crime against public law, and a discord in human society. And since crime is a defection from public law and order, it naturally follows that human society requires atonement and expiation, not necessarily in the sense of revenge, but as a restoration of the public order by public punishment.[4]

This doctrine may or may not be distasteful to the great majority of modern writers.[5] At the bottom of all criminal law is the sense of public justice outraged by crimes, and the sense of ethical retribution demanding expiation.[6]

Furthermore it cannot be denied that public authority, being the guardian of law and order, must be entitled and obliged to *prevent* crime. This is the *preventive* element to be noticed in penalties. Certain reformers would deny that right to the State, but it is obviously implied by the right of self-preservation. " The right to punish must ever remain founded, in part at least, upon the idea of retributive justice. Pain must ever follow wrong-doing. While vengeance is a divine prerogative, human governments are the means and agencies through which divine Providence controls human affairs, and it is, therefore, not only the right but the duty of the State to punish those acts which are deemed subversive of society, quite apart from motives merely prudential or reformatory." [7]

We may, therefore, sum up the purpose of ecclesiastical law as follows: it is reformatory in its main tendency, owing to the nature of the Church as an institution for

---

[4] Lynching, though it cannot be defended, may be understood as growing out of the deep-rooted sentiment of public indignation and as a demand for justice.

[5] Kenny-Webb, *l. c.*, p. 28, rather incline to the conservative view.

[6] Foerster, *Schuld und Sühne*, 1911, p. 72 f.

[7] Kenny-Webb, *l. c.*, p. 29.

saving souls, but it is also expiatory, preventive or deterring, in order to preserve divine and human laws, to keep the public order intact and to show forth the true nature of crime to the guilty as well as to the innocent. A society founded by God cannot dispense with these elements of genuine criminal law.

3. The penalty must be inflicted by *lawful authority*. For law is not a mere contractual order of things, but a participation in the will of God or divine Providence, and a breach of it therefore requires the intervention of the lawful custodian and guardian of the law. Penalty is neither revenge nor self-affliction, because, as stated above on the authority of St. Thomas, it means affliction against one's own will. Revenge is a private or first right, which, far from restoring the disturbed public order, disturbs it still more. Only the legitimate authority, as the founder of law and the representative of the supreme Ruler, is entitled to demand justice and inflict the necessary penalties on transgressors. Besides, in meting out the penalty, there must be an objective standard for measuring the crime as well as the punishment. The criminal himself or other interested individuals might be either too lenient or too cruel. The golden mean to be observed even in meting out punishment, demands an even balance, which can best be held by the administrators and executors of justice.

DIFFERENT KINDS OF PENALTIES

Can. 2216

In Ecclesia delinquentes plectuntur:
1.° Poenis medicinalibus seu censuris;
2.° Poenis vindicativis;
3.° Remediis poenalibus et poenitentiis.

Can. 2217

§ 1. Poena dicitur:

1.° *Determinata*, si in ipsa lege vel praecepto taxative statuta sit; *indeterminata*, si prudenti arbitrio iudicis vel Superioris relicta sit sive praeceptivis sive facultativis verbis;

2.° *Latae sententiae*, si poena determinata ita sit addita legi vel praecepto ut incurratur ipso facto commissi delicti; *ferendae sententiae*, si a iudice vel Superiore infligi debeat;

3.° *A iure*, si poena determinata in ipsa lege statuatur, sive latae sententiae sit sive ferendae; *ab homine*, si feratur per modum praecepti peculiaris vel per sententiam iudicialem condemnatoriam, etsi in iure statuta; quare poena ferendae sententiae, legi addita, ante sententiam condemnatoriam est *a iure tantum*, postea *a iure* simul et *ab homine*, sed consideratur tanquam *ab homine*.

§ 2. Poena intelligitur semper ferendae sententiae, nisi expresse dicatur eam esse *latae sententiae* vel *ipso facto* seu *ipso iure* contrahi, vel nisi alia similia verba adhibeantur.

The Code deals with *three* kinds of penalties: censures or corrective (medicinal) penalties, vindictive penalties, and penal remedies and penances.[8]

1. *Censures* are called corrective or medicinal penalties because they principally, though not exclusively, aim at amending the delinquent. Consequently, if this purpose is achieved, the penalty is to be removed and the criminal may claim absolution from censure.[9] For, the chief purpose being reformatory, the contumacy or stubbornness is

---

8 See can. 6, n. 5.　　　　　　　9 Can. 2241, § 1; can. 2248, § 2.

broken. It also follows that censures are not inflicted for crimes which are mere *facta* without reference to the future, or, once committed, have no further consequences.[10] But it must also be understood that, although the main object of censures is reformation or correction, yet the purpose of penalty in general, *vis.:* ethical retribution or reparation, is not excluded. For it is of public interest that each and every crime be duly punished, in order to deter others and thus prevent criminality.[11] The penal character of censures lies in this, that they deprive the delinquent of certain spiritual goods, which may entail temporal consequences, as in the case of an *excommunicatus vitandus.*

2. *Vindictive* penalties are intended directly to avenge crimes. Their primary purpose, therefore, is not reformation, but reparation of the violated public order.[12] They may be temporal or spiritual. As far as inflicted on the clergy, they are exhaustively enumerated in can. 2298, whilst vindictive penalties threatened against clergy and laity are mentioned in can. 2291. We need not refer to the former practice which abounded in temporal penalties, as mutilation, *decalvatio* or scalping, scourging, exile, deportation, galleys, fines, etc.[13] The Code has modified the use of such penalties and limited them to fines and detention in houses of correction.

3. *Penal remedies and penances* are purely preventive means, though they partake of the penal character, otherwise they would not be enumerated under the heading of penalties. They may indeed also have the purpose of

---

10 Wernz, *l. c.,* Vol. VI, n. 145, p. 150.

11 C. 35, X, V, 39; c. 1, Clem. I, &

12 These penalties may be dispensed, not absolved from, and call for judiciary procedure; can. 1933, § 4; can. 1889, § 2; can. 2207; Eichmann, *l. c.,* p. 54 f.

13 Cfr. Wernz, *l. c.,* n. 99, p. 100 f.

mere prevention. For an enumeration see can. 2306 ff.

Penances, even when inflicted in the external forum, differ in character from vindictive penalties, as they generally depend upon acceptance and execution on the part of the penitent and chiefly aim at atonement made to God.[14]

A *subdivision of penalties* is that based upon the measure and mode of infliction, as per can. 2217.

1. A *fixed* penalty is one so clearly determined by law or precept, that no room is left for doubting what is meant. Thus, if the law says: "they incur excommunication," "are deprived of office," etc., this and no other penalty must be understood.

Another element must be considered in order to understand the term *taxative*, which means an accurately defined measure of punishment. An example is that of suspension *ex informata conscientia*, which must be clearly determined as to effect and time (can. 2188). The term *taxative* also implies that the circumstances of imputability have been duly weighed, else the judge would have a wide margin left for determining the penalty. This becomes more evident in penalties which are inflicted by a precept, (*praecepto*). For precept means an order of the judge or superior directly affecting the delinquent and indirectly the crime.[15]

An *undetermined* or arbitrary[16] penalty is one, the infliction of which is left to the prudent discretion of the judge or superior. The discretion may, however, concern the question whether any penalty is to be meted out at all,

14 *Ibid.*, n. 96, p. 98.

15 Precept differs from *verba praeceptiva*, because precept means a single order or injunction given under threat of incurring penalty, either *ferendae* or *latae sententiae*, whereas *verba praeceptiva* include the penalties stated in law, and merely state that these penalties must, as a rule, be inflicted, according to can. 2223.

16 See Wernz, VI, n. 61, p. 70.

or what kind of a penalty, and in what measure. For the law may determine that a penalty must be inflicted, but leave the kind and measure to the judge; *e. g.*, where the phrase is used: "*pro gravitate delicti.*" Take, for instance, can. 2170. It says that the Ordinary *must* decree privation of income, but *may* inflict other penalties in addition thereto. Hence the law sometimes prescribes one penalty and intimates others. The law may also establish the minimum of penalties, and leave it to the judge to inflict a severer punishment.[17] Preceptive or obligatory terms in general are: *debet puniri, puniendus est, privandus, declarandus* or *declaretur infamis;* facultative or arbitrary terms: *pro gravitate culpae, ad arbitrium superioris,* etc.

2. A distinction of the ecclesiastical law which has been made a target of attacks against the Church is that between penalties *latae* and *ferendae sententiae.* A fixed penalty is *latae sententiae* if it is attached either by law or precept to the commission of the crime. The law uses, for instance, the terms *ipso facto, ipso iure incurrit excommunicationem*[18] (can. 2343, *privilegium canonis*); the superior decrees (*per modum praecepti*) suspension to be *ipso facto* incurred for a certain kind of crime: these are penalties *latae sententiae. Ferendae sententiae* are those which are to be inflicted by the judge or superior, although perhaps appointed by law.[19]

3. A fixed penalty *latae sententiae* as well as *ferendae sententiae* may be established by law (*a iure*). For instance, clerics who violate the *privilegium canonis* against cardinals and papal legates incur two penalties *ipso iure latae sententiae* and, besides, are to be deprived of their

17 Cfr. c. 2, X, V, 21; c. 3, X, IV, 3.

18 The Const. "*Vacante Sede*,"

for instance, uses the term: *innodamus.*

19 Cfr. can. 2324, 2328 etc.

benefices, offices, dignities, which is a penalty *ferendae sententiae,* although both kinds of penalties are laid down in law (can. 2343).

Ab homine is a penalty which, though established by law, is inflicted by way of a special order *per modum praecepti peculiaris,* or by a condemnatory judiciary sentence. For instance, the Ordinary may compel recusants to fulfill the terms of a last will, even by censures, because the law (can. 2348) gives him that right. In this case the Ordinary may simply issue a particular order, or, if the case has been brought before the ecclesiastical court, he may issue a sentence of excommunication, or, in the case of a clerical recusant, of suspension. Hence, continues our text, a penalty *ferendae sententiae* established by law, as in the case of can. 2343, § 2, n. 3, is one *a iure tantum* as long as no condemnatory sentence has been issued; but after such a sentence has been rendered, it becomes a penalty *a iure et ab homine,* although considered a penalty inflicted *ab homine.* The difference is very palpable in can. 2244, § 2 f., and can. 2247, § 2. A condemnatory sentence differs from a declaratory sentence in so far as the latter affects the execution or observance of the penalty as stated under can. 2232.

§ 2 of can. 2217 rules that the penalty must always be understood to be *ferendae sententiae,* unless *ipso iure,* or *ipso facto,* or similar terms are used.[20]

Why can the Church, unlike the State, inflict a penalty *latae sententiae?* It appears unjust and unworthy of a perfect society to condemn one before he is heard. But we must not forget that the Church is a peculiar society, with a religious character that does not remain on the surface, but penetrates and encompasses the whole man.

---

[20] For instance, can. 2315: *habeatur tanquam haereticus, haereticorum poenis obnoxious.*

She reaches into the court of conscience. Besides, the most sacred offices might be neglected and abused without punishment because of lack of witnesses and plaintiffs, and the fear of penalty and final exposure may check malice and carelessness.[21] Therefore the first traces of censures *latae sententiae* coincide with the spread of evil influences in the sixth and seventh century. In order to protect ecclesiastical discipline more efficaciously, this quasi self-executory remedy was found most efficient and secure.[22] Although the Church has now formally mitigated the practice of inflicting *ipso facto* penalties by demanding a declaratory sentence in most cases (see can. 2232), it would be against the mind of the legislator to maintain that sentences called *ipso facto* have no other significance or effect than that of a serious threat.[28]

THE APPLICATION OF PENALTIES

Can. 2218

§ 1. In poenis decernendis servetur aequa proportio cum delicto, habita ratione imputabilitatis, scandali et damni; quare attendi debent non modo obiectum et gravitas legis, sed etiam aetas, scientia, institutio, sexus, conditio, status mentis delinquentis, dignitas personae quae delicto offenditur, aut quae delictum committit, finis intentus, locus et tempus quo delictum commissum est, num ex passionis impetu vel ob gravem metum delinquens egerit, num eum delicti poenituerit eiusdemque malos effectus evitare ipse studuerit, aliaque similia.

---

21 See Hollweck, *l. c.*, p. xx f.
22 See Hinschius, *l. c.*, IV, 841; V, 85 ff.

28 Prop. 47 damn. by "*Auctorem fidei*," Aug. 28, 1794 (Denzinger, *l. c.*, n. 1410).

§ 2. Non solum quae ab omni imputabilitate excusant, sed etiam quae a gravi, excusant pariter a
qualibet poena tum latae tum ferendae sententiae
etiam in foro externo, si pro foro externo excusatio
evincatur.

§ 3. Mutua iniuria compensatur, nisi una pars
propter maiorem iniuriae ab eadem illatae gravitatem
damnari debet, deminuta, si casus ferat, poena.

1. Penalties must be proportionate to the crime, which
is to be judged according to its imputability and the scandal and damage caused. This is the *objective* standard
for the meting out of penalties. It may be noted by the
way that the legislator here again takes the public order
and public safety as the basis for criminal law.

There is also a *subjective* proportion, to be taken, not
mathematically, as they say, but geometrically, that is to
say, not only the objective importance of the law and the
objective grievousness of the transgression must be considered in weighing the penalty, but also the circumstances
under which, and the end for which the crime was perpetrated. All this has been sufficiently discussed under
the title of imputability. Age, knowledge, education, sex,
profession (*conditio*), the mental status of the delinquent,
the dignity of the offender as well as of the person offended,[24] the purpose for which the crime was committed
must be duly considered as well as the time (*e. g.*, during
divine service) and the place (sacred or profane).

Imputability may be lessened or increased according to
the degree and cause of passion or fear. The promptness
of repentance, efforts made in curbing the evil effects,
and similar individual circumstances should also be taken
into account.

24 See, for instance, the gradation in can. 2343.

2. Those *circumstances* which relieve one from all guilt, as well as those which excuse the perpetrator from grievous sin, also render him immune from every penalty, *latae* as well as *ferendae sententiae*, even in the external forum, if he has sufficiently proved his defence in the external forum. The reason for this rule lies in the fact that penalties, especially censures, are grievous and therefore presuppose a grievous fault or crime.[25] The law, being intended chiefly for the upkeep of the external order, supposes such guilt and therefore requires proof of " not guilty," which must be furnished by the accused. Note the term " *in foro externo.*" If the defence is considered valid *in foro externo*, it is also valid *pro foro interno;* but not conversely. Compare canon 2251 on censures. Hence the *regula juris* 23 in 6° : " *sine culpa, nisi subsit causa, non est aliquis puniendus,*" that is, no one should be punished who is without *dolus* or *culpa,* unless for a special reason which involves the public welfare.[26]

3. *Mutual injury* is levelled or compensated, and therefore quashed, provided there is some proportion between the injury done on both sides. There may be an injury of the same nature complained of by two priests. This is looked upon as condoned by mutual calumny. But between a bishop and a priest there is no strict proportion and mutual condonation cannot be supposed *ex aequo.* It may, however, lessen the penalty, and thus become an extenuating circumstance, when punishment must be dealt out.

---

[25] See c. 41, C. 11, q. 3.

[26] Cfr. can. 723; Reiffenstuel, *Comment in Reg. Iuris 23.*

INTERPRETATION OF PENALTIES

Can. 2219

§ 1. In poenis benignior est interpretatio facienda.

§ 2. At si dubitetur utrum poena, a Superiore competente inflicta, sit iusta, necne, poena servanda est in utroque foro, excepto casu appellationis in suspensivo.

§ 3. Non licet poenam de persona ad personam vel de casu ad casum producere, quamvis par adsit ratio, imo gravior, salvo tamen praescripto can. 2231.

The general rules of interpretation must also be applied to penal laws. For although the judge may use discretion and "fill up the gaps of the law"— *lacunae legis* — or mitigate the rigor of the penalty, yet an ecclesiastical judge, being inferior to the Pope, is only a minister and executor of the law, and hence, if the penalty is clearly expressed, and the fact is established, he must apply the penalty according to can. 2223.[27]

1. Rule 49 in Sexto: "In penalties the more favorable interpretation should be adopted," must be understood according to the general rules of interpretation, as stated above. If the penalty is clearly stated in law, it must be applied to the criminal, provided the crime and responsibility for it are ascertained. Therefore the *benignior interpretatio* concerns only dubious or disjunctive penalties, for instance, if the law uses *either — or,* and especially if it leaves the measure of punishment to the discretion of the judge.

---

[27] Cfr. C. 11, Dig. 48, 19; Reiffenstuel in Reg. Iuris 49 in 6°; somewhat ambiguous, Wernz, *l. c.,* VI, p. 76, n. 67.

There is also another rule in 6° (15) which may find a place here: "*Odia restringi et favores convenit ampliari.*" Its interpretation causes difficulty, for a law generally is a restriction and therefore disagreeable, although it may be favorable to another. Thus criminal laws are very hateful to careless citizens and criminally inclined individuals, yet at the same time very beneficial to the commonwealth.[28] It would not do to favor a criminal and provoke a peaceful community. This rule, therefore, must be understood in the light of imputability, damage and scandal. An example may illustrate this. Compare can. 1063, § 2, with can. 2319, § 1, n. 1, where the excommunication *latae sententiae,* reserved to the Ordinary, is inflicted on those who celebrate a marriage before a non-Catholic minister because scandal is given to the congregation.

2. If there is *doubt* whether a penalty inflicted by the competent superior is *just or unjust,* the penalty must be borne in both the internal and external forum, unless an appeal was lodged which has a suspensory effect. The reason for this rule lies in the character of the penal law as a safeguard of the public welfare as well as in the necessity of upholding lawful authority. Therefore an excommunicated person, even though innocent in conscience and justified by public opinion, must conduct himself as guilty.[29]

The meaning of the clause, "*excepto casu appellationis in suspensivo*" is evident from can. 2243, where censures

[28] The laws in favor of religion must, although restrictive of human liberty, be widely interpreted; S. C. P. F., July 2, 1827 (*Coll.*, n. 796). If the law is divisible, *i.e.*, partly favorable and partly unfavorable, the favorable part may be amplified, but the unfavorable must be restricted.

[29] Cfr. cc. 1, 31, C. 11, q. 3; see can. 1904. The example of Savonarola is a case in point.

are declared to have only devolutive recourse attached. Consequently, one who is censured must bear the censure until it is reversed.

3. *Analogy is not admitted* in interpreting penal laws. Hence there is no stretching from one person to another, no extending from one case to another, even if the reasons or circumstances of persons and cases are quite alike, nay the reasons for extending the penalty seem even stronger. This, of course, depends on the terms which the law uses for persons; for instance, the pronoun *qui* is of a general tenor, and comprises females as well as males.[30] The term " religious " also comprehends both sexes, unless the context forbids this interpretation.[31] But if the term *parochus* is used, the penalty threatened must not be extended to other persons, even though they may have some qualities in common with pastors. If the pastor is mentioned, the assistant or curate is not included; if a priest is named, deacons and inferior clerics are excluded.[32] One case is not stretched to cover another because, although circumstances apparently seem to point to sameness, yet each single case has its own peculiar character and circumstances. Thus two pastors may be absent from their homes for the same length of time without the bishop's permission, yet on account of particular circumstances the one may be excused but not the other. Thus also in cases of *sollicitatio,* where the words used may be understood by one person but not by another. For the interpretation of the penal laws now in force for the whole Church can. 6, n. 5 is to be consulted. In other words, no penalties, temporal or spiritual, corrective or vindictive, are in force at present, except those mentioned in the Code. If these agree

30 Cfr. can. 2350, § 2; can. 2353.
31 Can. 490.

32 Can. 2387; concerning a distinction of persons, see can. 2358.

verbally and substantially with penalties formerly in vogue, they may be interpreted according to the old forensic practice and theory of authors. If they agree with the old law only in part, the interpretation must be made according to the old practice as far as they agree, but according to the general laws from the wording and context, as far as they disagree.[88]

---

[88] See can. 6, n. 2 and 3; can. 2351 on duelling. Analogy, although forbidden when application is concerned, may be admitted even in penal laws when competency as to application is in question, or if formalities only are concerned; cfr. can. 2296, § 1; 2310; Eichmann, l. c., p. 116, note 2; 124, note 1.

TITLE V

SUPERIORS WHO WIELD COERCIVE POWER

Can. 2220

§ 1. Qui pollent potestate leges ferendi vel praecepta imponendi, possunt quoque legi vel praecepto poenas adnectere; qui iudiciali tantum, possunt solummodo poenas, legitime statutas, ad normam iuris applicare.

§ 2. Vicarius Generalis sine mandato speciali non habet potestatem infligendi poenas.

The rule is that coercive power follows legislative power; for even though we may distinguish sovereignty into the three well-known departments, legislative, judiciary, and coercive, radically and virtually they must be held by one and the same sovereign power, otherwise authority would be divisible, which is absurd.[1] Therefore the Code says that *those who enjoy legislative power are authorized to attach a penal sanction to their laws.* This is done in order to render laws effective.

But the Code adds to these legislators another class, *viz.:* those who are entitled to *impose precepts.* These, too, it says, may attach penalties to their precepts or orders.

There is a notable distinction between precept and law. For a precept may be imposed also in virtue of

---

[1] Montesquieu in his *L'Esprit des Lois* advocated a complete division, in order to counteract State omnipotence.

merely domestic power, *e. g.*, a community of religious
women may have a precept, which is not law, imposed
on them. Furthermore a precept concerns the individual, not territory, and follows the subject everywhere,
but ceases to oblige when the authority who has given
the precept ceases to exist in whatever manner, unless
it was given in writing or in the presence of two witnesses.[2] Taking precept as distinct from law, therefore,
it follows that the power of attaching a penal sanction to
a precept must be understood of penalties in general, not
of censures. Were it otherwise, superioresses of religious
congregations would be entitled to inflict censures, which
is contrary to ecclesiastical law. On the other hand it
would not be exceeding one's power if one endowed with
jurisdiction in the external forum would attach a censure to the enforcement of a precept. The general rule,
however, is that legislative and coercive power are correlated.

Different from the power of the legislator is that of
the *judge,* as such; he can only administer justice or
apply the penal laws already established according to the
rules laid down in the Code. We say the judge, *as such;*
for when the Ordinary acts as judge, he may apply the
laws, as far as permissible, in proportion to his ordinary
power.

The Code first sets forth the coercive power, explaining how far those endowed with this power may extend
it; then it lays down rules for judges.

COERCIVE POWERS

Can. 2221

Legislativam habentes potestatem, possunt intra

2 See can. 24; can. 2143.

limites suae iurisdictionis, non solum legem a se vel
a decessoribus latam, sed etiam, ob peculiaria rerum
adiuncta, legem tam divinam, quam ecclesiasticam a
superiore potestate latam, in territorio vigentem, congrua poena munire aut poenam lege statutam aggra-
vare.

Can. 2222

§ 1. Licet lex nullam sanctionem appositam habeat,
legitimus tamen Superior potest illius transgressionem, etiam sine praevia poenae comminatione,
aliqua iusta poena punire, si scandalum forte datum
aut specialis transgressionis gravitas id ferat; secus
reus puniri nequit, nisi prius monitus fuerit cum comminatione poenae latae vel ferendae sententiae in casu
transgressionis, et nihilominus legem violaverit.

§ 2. Pariter idem legitimus Superior, licet probabile
tantum sit delictum fuisse commissum aut delicti certe
commissi poenalis actio praescripta sit, non solum ius,
sed etiam officium habet non promovendi clericum de
cuius idoneitate non constat, et, ad scandalum evitan-
dum, prohibendi clerico exercitium sacri ministerii aut
etiam eundem ab officio, ad normam iuris, amovendi;
quae omnia in casu non habent rationem poenae.

1. Those who have legislative power may attach penal
sanctions to their laws within the limits of their jurisdiction. Hence

a) The *Pope* has coercive power over and in the whole
Church, and may abrogate, modify, and circumscribe
penal laws.

b) *Ordinaries* and those who go by that name may do
the same as far as their territory or subjects or powers

reach. But their power is limited by the common law and must be interpreted acording to the rules laid down in the following canons.

c) *Metropolitans* enjoy coercive power in the dioceses of their suffragans only as far as can. 274, n. 5 admits.

d) The *Vicar-General*, according to can. 2220, § 2, requires a *special commission* from his Ordinary to inflict penalties.

e) *Religious superiors* of exempt clerical communities enjoy coercive power within the limits of the common law and their own constitutions. But their subjects, *i. e.*, regulars, are liable to be punished by the local Ordinaries in certain cases.[8]

f) Religious superiors who *enjoy only domestic power, i. e.*, no jurisdiction proper *in foro externo*, may indeed attach penalties to the enforcement of their precepts as far as the domestic power permits;[4] but they must abstain from inflicting censures or any other penalty that would savor of abuse of jurisdiction *in foro externo*. Neither can *pastors* or simple priests as such inflict censures.[5]

2. Those who have real legislative (not preceptive) power, that is, all except those mentioned above under f, are permitted by can. 2221:

a) To add a penal sanction to their own law or to any law issued by their predecessor which was a *lex minus quam perfecta, i. e.*, lacking a penal sanction;

b) To add to or to increase a penal sanction already attached by law to a divine or an ecclesiastical law issued by a superior lawgiver for that respective territory, if special circumstances demand such an addition or increase

---

8 Cfr. can. 616, § 2;; 619; 631; 1435, § 2; 2269, § 2.
4 Cfr. can. 501, § 1.

5 S. C. P. F., May 5, 1654 (*Coll.,* n. 120); some missionaries seem to have claimed this power.

of penalty. Thus a general prohibition had been issued
for the Christians of the Malabaric Rite not to play any
kind of musical instruments for the purpose of idol worship. This was placed under excommunication and enforced with great rigor.[6]

Ordinaries may also use rigor in order to eradicate
certain local or provincial vices, as stated under can. 897.

However, it should be noted that the canon just quoted,
which treats of reservation, supposes that the crimes are
atrocious, not merely conventional. An atrocious crime
would be robbery, incendiarism, or keeping children away
from religious instruction or sending them without necessity to non-Catholic schools, where Catholic schools are
available.[7]

3. Can. 2222 instructs *superiors how to proceed* when
inflicting a penalty for the transgression of laws which
have no penal sanction attached (*leges minus quam per-
fectae*). Thus canon 140 forbids a cleric to attend
theatres or balls. There is no penalty provided against
the transgressors of this canon. Yet the Ordinary could
mete out a just punishment. Therefore § 1 of can. 2222
distinguishes thus:

a) The general rule is that *no penalty is to be inflicted
without a threat or canonical warning*. This warning
must contain a penalty of either *ferendae* or *latae sententiae* before the transgression happens. Only in case the
transgression is proved does the penal sanction go into
effect. Thus, in the case mentioned, the Ordinary would
have to forbid theatre-going under penalty of either
ferendae or *latae sententiae,* otherwise the delinquent
could not be punished.

---

6 Benedict XIV, " *Omnium solli-*   7 See can. 1372–1374; can. 2319, §
citudinum, Sept. 12, 1744, § 14,   1, n. 4.
dub. XIII (*Coll. P. F.,* n. 347).

b) The first clause states an exception to this general rule: the lawful superior may inflict a just penalty even without previous canonical warning or threat of punishment, if *scandal has been given or the transgression is of a particularly serious character*. This may happen if the theatre is one of the lower type and perhaps offensive also to religion. For the rest, we refer to what was said on suspension *ex informata conscientia,* which the lawgiver undoubtedly had in mind.[8]

§ 2 of can. 2222 grants the lawful superior *preventive power* and also obliges him to make use of this power in case of a *probable* crime and of a crime against which criminal action cannot be brought on account of *prescription*.[9] But this canon concerns only *clergymen*. Therefore in either of these two cases, *viz.,* of a probable[10] crime or a crime for which a penalty is prescribed, the lawful superior (also of exempt religious),

1.° May and should not promote to either minor or major orders a cleric of whose unfitness he is certain;

2.° He may and should prohibit such a cleric from exercising the sacred ministry, in order to avoid scandal;

3.° He may and should, to avoid scandal, remove such a cleric from office according to the rules laid down in can. 2147–2161.

But this preventive suspension *has not the character of an ecclesiastical penalty,* and consequently its transgression does not induce irregularity (cfr. can. 985, n. 7).

---

8 See can. 2186–2194; Vol. VII, p. 471 ff.

9 See can. 1704, § 2; Vol. VII, 147 f.

10 A probable crime may be called one which cannot be fully proved, yet is testified to by at least one trustworthy witness or known to the superior *extra-sacramentaliter.*

THE JUDGE

Can. 2223

§ 1. In poenis applicandis iudex nequit poenam determinatam augere, nisi extraordinaria adiuncta aggravantia id exigant.

§ 2. Si lex in statuenda poena ferendae sententiae facultativis verbis utatur, committitur prudentiae et conscientiae iudicis eam infligere, vel, si poena fuerit determinata, temperare.

§ 3. Si vero lex utatur verbis praeceptivis, ordinarie poena infligenda est; sed conscientiae et prudentiae iudicis vel Superioris committitur:

1.° Poenae applicationem ad tempus magis opportunum differre, si ex praepropera rei punitione maiora mala eventura praevideantur;

2.° A poena infligenda abstinere, si reus perfecte fuerit emendatus, et scandalum reparaverit, aut sufficienter punitus sit vel puniendus praevideatur poenis auctoritate civili sancitis;

3.° Poenam determinatam temperare vel loco ipsius aliquod remedium poenale adhibere aut aliquam poenitentiam iniungere, si detur circumstantia imputabilitatem notabiliter minuens, vel habeatur quidem rei emendatio aut inflicta a civili auctoritate castigatio, sed iudex vel Superior opportunam praeterea ducat mitiorem aliquam punitionem.

§ 4.° Poenam latae sententiae declarare generatim committitur prudentiae Superioris; sed sive ad instantiam partis cuius interest, sive bono communi ita exigente, sententia declaratoria dari debet.

Can. 2224

§ 1. Ordinarie tot poenae quot delicta.

§ 2. Si tamen propter numerum delictorum nimius esset poenarum infligendarum cumulus, prudenti iudicis arbitrio relinquitur aut poenam omnium graviorem infligere, addita, si res ferat, aliqua poenitentia vel remedio poenali, aut poenas intra aequos terminos moderari, habita ratione numeri et gravitatis delictorum.

§ 3. Si poena constituta sit tum in conatum delicti tum in delictum consummatum, hoc admisso, infligi tantum debet poena in consummatum delictum statuta.

Can. 2225

Si poena declaretur vel infligatur per sententiam iudicialem, serventur canonum praescripta circa sententiae iudicialis pronuntiationem; si vero poena latae vel ferendae sententiae inflicta sit ad modum praecepti particularis, scripto aut coram duobus testibus ordinarie declaretur vel irrogetur, indicatis poenae causis, salvo praescripto can. 2193.

The judge, as such, is the minister of justice and executor of the coercive power. He is bound by, and not above, the law,[11] and consequently must be guided by the text of the law, carefully weigh the number and nature of the crime, whether fully perpetrated or only attempted, and, finally, observe the rules of procedure.

1. He must consider the *law*, and, therefore:

a) Is not *allowed to increase* a fixed penalty, unless extraordinary circumstances demand a severer punishment,

11 C. 2, X, I, 2.

e. g., the atrocity of a crime, the scandal given, etc. The increase may consist of multiplication or added intensity, for instance, suspension and detention in a house of correction, or suspension from office and benefice, etc.[12]

b) If the penal law *ferendae sententiae* is couched in arbitrary terms (*verbis facultativis*), it is left to the conscience and prudence of the judge to mete out the penalty or dictate the minimum penalty if this is fixed.[13]

c) If the wording of the penal law is compulsory (*verbis praeceptis*), the *penalty* must, as a rule, be *inflicted*. There is a precept in terms used in the subjunctive or gerundive forms: *privetur, privandi sunt, debet puniri, suspendi, removeri, etc.* Yet even in this case the legislator leaves it to the conscience and prudence of the judge, both of which qualities suppose that he decides objectively, not subjectively or under the influence of passion.

a) He may *delay* the application of the penalty to a more opportune time if he foresees greater evils from premature or hurried punishment. This depends on circumstances of time and person.[14]

β) He may abstain from inflicting the penalty if the delinquent shows that he has thoroughly reformed and repaired the scandal given, or has undergone or will probably undergo a proportionate punishment at the hands of the civil authority. This, of course, supposes a so-called mixed crime, which the civil as well as the ecclesiastical authorities provide for in their penal codes.

γ) He may *mitigate a fixed penalty* or substitute for it either a penal remedy or some penance.[15] Thus he may inflict partial instead of total suspension, instead of a fine

---

12 Cfr. can. 2324, 2337 etc.
13 Cfr. can. 2405, 2406, § 2.
14 In countries where Church and State are separate, interference from the latter should not easily occur; still popular commotion may bring it about; see can. 2337.
15 Of these see can. 2306 ff.

he may decree alms, etc. But this mitigation *supposes* that a notably alleviating circumstance speaks in favor of lesser imputability on the part of the delinquent, or that he has given proof of amendment, or that a civil punishment has already been inflicted, and the ecclesiastical judge nevertheless deems it opportune to mete out a mitigated punishment. This action is justified because the ecclesiastical judge thereby emphasizes the fact that the Church has the right to exercise coercive power and to show her abhorrence of public crimes.

d) As a rule it is left to the *discretion of the superior* to *declare* that a penance has been incurred, *i.e.*, to issue a declaratory sentence. However, this sentence *must* be issued if the interested party insists, for instance, on getting satisfaction or removing suspicion, or if the public welfare demands it, for instance, in the case of a corruptor, or briber, or dangerous heretic.

2. The judge must furthermore, under can. 2224, consider the *number* of crimes committed. As a rule each crime demands its separate penalty. However, if the numer of crimes would call for too great a number of penalties, the judge should use prudent judgment. He may, therefore, inflict the heaviest penalty and, if circumstances demand it, add some penances or penitential remedies. He may, also, after having weighed the number and gravity of the crimes committed, mitigate the penalties according to the rules of equity. If an inchoate and a consummated crime have distinct penalties in law, the judge shall inflict only the penalty established for the consummated crime if this had been committed.

3. Finally, the judge *must observe the rules of procedure* according to can. 2225, as follows:

a) If a penalty is declared or inflicted by way of a

judiciary sentence which presupposes at least a summary trial, he must observe the rules laid down in can. 1968 ff.

b) If a penalty, more especially a censure, either *latae* or *ferendae sententiae,* is to be inflicted by way of a *particular order* or precept, it must be declared to have been incurred (*latae sententiae*), or actually inflicted, *in writing* or before two witnesses, and the reasons for it given. The text says *ordinarie,* as a rule, because the *suspensio ex informata conscientia* (see can. 2193) does not require that the reasons be indicated.

TITLE VI

WHO ARE LIABLE TO THE COERCIVE POWER OF THE CHURCH

The Code first determines the obligatory force of penal laws, as such (and the exceptions, can. 2227) ; then it fixes responsibility for the crime, psychologic conditions and partnership, the moment for incurring the penalty and its actual infliction, and, finally, it deals with plural and inchoate crimes.

GENERAL RULES AND EXCEPTIONS

CAN. 2226

§ 1. Poenae adnexae legi aut praecepto obnoxius est qui lege aut praecepto tenetur, nisi expresse eximatur.

§ 2. Licet lex poenalis posterior abroget anteriori, si tamen delictum, quando lex posterior lata est, iam commissum erat, applicanda est lex reo favorabilior.

§ 3. Quod si lex posterior tollat legem vel poenam tantum, haec statim cessat, nisi agatur de censuris iam contractis.

§ 4. Poena reum ubique terrarum tenet, etiam resoluto iure Superioris, nisi aliud expresse caveatur.

CAN. 2227

§ 1. Poena nonnisi a Romano Pontifice infligi aut declarari potest in eos de quibus in can 1557, § 1.

§ 2. **Nisi expresse nominentur, S. R. E. Cardinales sub lege poenali non comprehenduntur, nec Episcopi sub poenis latae sententiae suspensionis et interdicti.**

1. The general rule is that those who are subject to laws or precepts are also subject to the penal sanctions attached thereto, unless they are expressly exempted. Hence

a) The *lawgiver* himself is not subject to purely ecclesiastical penalties by compulsion (*vi coactiva*), though morally speaking, or from a sense of propriety (*vi directiva*), he may be said to be subject to them. Practically it is better to say that he is not subject to his own penal laws.

b) *Rulers* of nations and their offspring and successors are immediately subject to the Roman Pontiff, who alone can issue a condemnatory or declaratory sentence against them (can. 2227, § 1).

c) *Cardinals* are immune from penal laws, unless they are expressly mentioned as subject to them. Thus in the Constitution of Pius X, "*Vacante Sede*," (*e. g.*, n. 51) they are threatened with excommunication *latae sententiae* if they reveal the proceedings of a papal conclave. They are also mentioned in can. 2397, concerning the oath they have to take.

d) *Bishops,* also titulars, are not subject to the penalties *latae sententiae* of suspension and interdict, unless they are expressly mentioned, as in can. 2370 and also in can. 2373. Although the name "bishop" does not occur in the latter canon, it certainly applies to Ordinaries. Other penalties, like excommunication and privation of income (can. 2398) they may also incur.

e) Exempt *religious* are subject to the penalties established by common law, and as far as the common law subjects them to the coercive power of the local Ordinary.[1] *Religious who do not enjoy the privilege of exemption,* are subject to the penal laws of the Code and also to those established by the particular laws of their territory, unless their approved Constitutions modify, restrict, or enlarge the power of the local Ordinary over them.

f) As to *peregrini* and *vagi,* see can. 14.

2. Sections 2 and 3 of can. 2226 establish the *relation of a later to a former penal law and to the consequence.* A later law abrogates a former one, but a crime committed before the later law was passed is punishable according to that one which is more favorable to the delinquent. Thus, for instance, can. 2319, § 1, n. 1, is more favorable than the old law to those who have contracted mixed marriages before a non-Catholic minister; for the Ordinary may absolve them, even though they have contracted the marriage before the Code went into effect (May 18, 1918).[2]

If the later law abolishes the former entirely, or only as to its penal sanction, the penalty ceases immediately and the delinquent is therefore immune from punishment, no matter whether he has not yet been punished or has undergone part of the punishment. On the privation of active and passive vote or of office, *e. g.,* in alienation, see can. 2347. An *exception* to this last named rule (§ 3) are *censures,* which remain if contracted by reason of a former law now abolished (can. 2248, § 1).

3. An ecclesiastical penalty *binds* the delinquent *everywhere,* even after the superior who inflicted it has gone out of office. This applies to penal laws in general, for

---

1 See can. 616 f.; 1425, § 2. Concerning the interdict, a probable opinion formerly exempted regulars from incurring the same, if *clerus* only is mentioned; Hollweck, *l. c.,* p. 132; however, see 2269, § 2.

2 Formerly they were suspected of heresy, according to " *Apostolicae Sedis,*" n. 1.

there are, *e. g.,* local interdicts which are merely territorial (see can. 2247, § 2). A priest suspended by
his bishop from saying Mass cannot say Mass in another diocese, *"unless the penalty contains a clause to
the contrary."* Thus it may be that the bishop suspends one from saying Mass in his diocese [3] only because
of scandal given there. The reason for this law lies
in the fact that the coercive power emanates from the
supreme lawgiver, who holds the keys of the whole
Church and watches over the unity and uniformity of
ecclesiastical discipline. The *Orientals,* however, are not
subject to the ecclesiastical penalties established in the
Code (Can. 1.).

THE CRIMINAL ACT

CAN. 2228

**Poena lege statuta non incurritur, nisi delictum
fuerit in suo genere perfectum secundum proprietatem
verborum legis.**

Since every penalty supposes a crime, it is evident that
no penalty established by law can be incurred, unless the
crime defined in the law has been fully committed. Hence
a diagnosis must precede. For instance, if one is accused
of simony in conferring or obtaining an ecclesiastical office, it must be proved that a bribe or price was offered
and accepted, or that an unlawful contract was made.[4]
If women violate the enclosure of men's convents, the
fact of violation must be established; if the limits of

---

[3] Whether the suspension *ex informata conscientia* ceases with the
bishop's departure from office is not
expressly stated in the Code (can.

2188; thus Eichmann, *l. c.,* p. 67),
but implied by the warning that the
penalty should be temporary only.

[4] Cfr. c. 4, X, V, 3; can. 2392.

enclosure are not clearly indicated, there can be no breach of enclosure. [5]

The means for proving criminal acts are pointed out in can. 1747–1836. Experts and ocular inspection have a place here.

PSYCHOLOGICAL AND PHYSIOLOGICAL REQUISITES OF CRIME AND CRIMINAL COÖPERATION

CAN. 2229

§ 1. A nullis latae sententiae poenis ignorantia affectata sive legis sive solius poenae excusat, licet lex verba de quibus in § 2 contineat.

§ 2. Si lex habeat verba: *praesumpserit, ausus fuerit, scienter, studiose, temerarie, consulto egerit* aliave similia quae plenam cognitionem ac deliberationem exigunt, quaelibet imputabilitatis imminutio sive ex parte intellectus sive ex parte voluntatis eximit a poenis latae sententiae.

§ 3. Si lex verba illa non habeat:

1.° Ignorantia legis aut etiam solius poenae, si fuerit crassa vel supina, a nulla poena latae sententiae eximit: si non fuerit crassa vel supina, excusat a medicinalibus, non autem a vindicativis latae sententiae poenis;

2.° Ebrietas, omissio debitae diligentiae, mentis debilitas, impetus passionis, si, non obstante imputabilitatis deminutione, actio sit adhuc graviter culpabilis, a poenis latae sententiae non excusant;

3.° Metus gravis, si delictum vergat in contemptum fidei aut ecclesiasticae auctoritatis vel in publicum animarum damnum, a poenis latae sententiae nullatenus eximit.

5 See can. 2342, n. 2.

§ 4. Licet reus censuris latae sententiae ad normam § 3, n. 1 non teneatur, id tamen non impedit quominus, si res ferat, congrua alia poena vel poenitentia affici queat.

CAN. 2230

Impuberes excusantur a poenis latae sententiae, et potius punitionibus educativis, quam censuris aliisve poenis gravioribus vindicativis corrigantur; puberes vero qui eos ad legem violandam induxerint vel cum eis in delictum concurrerint ad normam can. 2209, §§ 1-3, ipsi quidem poenam lege statutam incurrunt.

CAN. 2231

Si plures ad delictum perpetrandum concurrerint, licet unus tantum in lege nominetur, ii quoque de quibus in can. 2209, §§ 1-3, tenentur, nisi lex aliud expresse caverit, eadem poena; ceteri vero non item, sed alia iusta poena pro prudenti Superioris arbitrio puniendi sunt, nisi lex peculiarem poenam in ipsos constituat.

In can. 2202 the Code referred to ignorance as taking away or diminishing imputability. This is the mental or psychologic element which must be considered also in meting out penalties. Besides ignorance, there are other mental conditions, either transient or habitual, which may influence the superior or judge in inflicting penalties. These are mentioned in can. 2229 sqq. The general rule is that the penalty must be proportioned to the responsibility of the criminal.

1. Affected ignorance (*ignorantia affectata*), *i.e.*, the

kind that is purposely fostered in order to avoid the trouble of finding out the law and to have a pretext for transgressing it, does not render one immune from incurring the penalties *latae sententiae,* no matter whether this ignorance concerns the law itself or its penal sanction,— not even if the law contains words like these: *praesumpserit, ausus fuerit, scienter, studiose, temerarie, consulto egerit, i. e.,* even though the law expressly demands a *dolus.* The reason is evident. For such ignorance is culpable and arises from a *dolus,* the degree of which is therefore not only diminished but increased. A cleric, therefore, who would *purposely* abstain from reading the penal Code or from informing himself of its provisions, could hardly be excused from *dolus,* and the penalties *latae sententiae* could be declared against him.

2. If the law contains the terms quoted above: *praesumpserit,* etc., or similar ones which require full knowledge and deliberation, every degree of diminished imputability, either of the intellect or the will, renders the offender with such lessened responsibility immune from penalties *latae sententiae;* not so much because of the objective verification of the criminal act, as on account of his subjective state of mind. For instance, one who knowingly reads a book forbidden in virtue of can. 2318, § 1, incurs excommunication especially reserved to the Apostolic See, but if he did not know that it was a heretical book, or one forbidden by Apostolic letter, he does not incur excommunication.

3. If the law *does not contain the terms praesumpserit, ausus fuerit,* etc.:

a) Crass or supine ignorance (*crassa vel supina ignorantia*) *exempts* from *no* penalty *latae sententiae.* This ignorance supposes, not so much a positive as a negative attitude towards the law; hence *crassa vel supina igno-rantia* is imputed to one who takes little or no trouble to find out the truth. Such ignorance, of course, is imput-able in proportion to the obligation one is under to acquire the knowledge in question. Less imputable is the ignor-ance called purely vincible, for it supposes that one has at least made an effort, even though insufficient, to over-come one's ignorance. Such ignorance (here called " *non crassa vel supina* ") excuses from censures (*a medicinali-bus*), but not from vindictive penalties *latae sententiae*. The reason for this difference must be sought in the in-tensiveness of the corrective penalties and their more individual character, whereas the vindictive penalties are intended more or less for the public weal and order, just as irregularities, the ignorance of which does not excuse from incurring them, concern the clerical decorum *in directo* and the person *in obliquo*.

b) *Drunkenness, carelessness, mental weakness, im-petuous passions do not exempt* from penalties *latae sen-tentiae*, provided the responsibility, though somewhat diminished, is still grievously culpable; thus *procuratio abortus* (can. 2350), though committed in the heat of passion, would still be subject to excommunication.

c) Grave fear by no means excuses from penalties *latae sententiae*, if the crime involves contempt of faith or of ecclesiastical authority, or public damage to souls. Hence no one is excused from the penalty laid down in can. 2314, § 1 (apostasy from faith), nor from that estab-lished in can. 2335, which forbids membership in Masonic societies which conspire against ecclesiastical and civil authority. The public welfare is jeopardized by the vio-lation of the seal of confession (can. 2369).

§ 4, lastly, rules that a delinquent who, on account of purely vincible ignorance, does not incur censures, may nevertheless be punished, if expedient, by some penalty or penance. This, of course, should be guaged according to the publicity, scandal, and damage incurred.

Can. 2230 considers, first, *impuberes* as such, and then as instruments of *puberes,* whilst can. 2331 properly defines partnership in crime.

1. *Impuberes, i. e.,* boys before the fourteenth and girls before the twelfth year of age, completed, are excused from penalties *latae sententiae,* and should be punished rather by reformatory educational means than by censures and severe vindictive penalties. To the point is can. 2342, n. 2, concerning the breach of enclosure in men's convents. There women are named, but girls (*impuberes*) do not incur the excommunication, whereas religious superiors and others who admit a girl under age incur it.[6] The difference is palpable.

2. Therefore *puberes* who induce *impuberes* to violate a law or who are partners to a crime, according to can. 2209, §§ 1–2, incur the legal penalty, though the *impuberes* who are coaxed into, or coöperate in, the crime are free from any penalty *latae sententiae.* This difference is based upon responsibility, and the age limit must here be taken mathematically; because this is the more benign interpretation and more secure in the application. The maxim *" malitia supplet aetatem "* should not be applied here.

3. In cases of *partnership in crime* can. 2209, §§ 1–3 must be consulted as to the responsibility of the parties. Those who concur in a crime by conspiracy, or as accomplices or effective counsellors and coöperators, are subject to the same penalty, though only one (in the singular) is mentioned in the penal law; unless the text has a con-

6 Yet there is a controversy concerning the point, as shall be seen under said canon.

trary provision.[7] Others mentioned under can. 2209 are
to be punished proportionately, according to the prudent
discretion of the superior, unless the law provides a special penalty.

WHEN PENALTIES TAKE EFFECT

CAN. 2232

§ 1. Poena latae sententiae, sive medicinalis sive
vindicativa, delinquentem, qui delicti sibi sit conscius,
ipso facto in utroque foro tenet; ante sententiam tamen
declaratoriam a poena observanda delinquens excusatur quoties eam servare sine infamia nequit, et in
foro externo ab eo eiusdem poenae observantiam ex-
igere nemo potest, nisi delictum sit notorium, firmo
praescripto can. 2223, § 4.

§ 2. Sententia declaratoria poenam ad momentum
commissi delicti retrotrahit.

CAN. 2233

§ 1. Nulla poena infligi potest, nisi certo constet
delictum commissum fuisse et non esse legitime praescriptum.

§ 2. Licet id legitime constet, si agatur de infligenda
censura, reus reprehendatur ac moneatur ut a contumacia recedat ad normam can. 2242, § 3, dato, si
prudenti eiusdem iudicis vel Superioris arbitrio casus
id ferat, congruo ad resipiscentiam tempore; contumacia persistente, censura infligi potest.

1. A penalty *latae sententiae,* whether corrective or
vindictive, binds the delinquent *ipso facto* both in the ex-

---

[7] Conspirators, can. 2331, § 2; can.   2342, nn. 1, 2; 2351; cooperators,
2347; accomplices, can. 2338, § 2;   can. 2362, 2371, etc.

ternal and in the internal forum, provided he is conscious of the crime. For instance, a bishop-elect who neglects to receive episcopal consecration within the time prescribed, is bound in conscience and publicly to apply to himself the penalty stated in can. 2398.

However, says the text, if defamation should actually follow the application of this penalty, the delinquent is excused from executing the penalty as long as no declaratory sentence has been issued. This clause does not state in what forum, whether the external or the internal, the delinquent is excused. The word *infamia* seems to point to the external forum, because the penitential forum appears, to us at least, not to entail defamation. Therefore we should say that in the internal forum the penalty must be observed if it can be done without the loss of good name and if the penalty is divisible.[8] Thus in the example taken from can. 2398, the bishop-elect might apply the forfeited income to charitable purposes without great risk of defamation. The second clause of can. 2398 could hardly be observed without defamation.

The text continues: and *in the external forum no one is allowed to demand this self-execution of the penalty on the part of the delinquent, unless the crime is notorious,* with due regard, however, to can. 2223, §4, which leaves the issuance of a declaratory sentence to the discretion of the superior and demands it only when the parties insist or when public welfare is at stake. Thus a priest may be interested in the declaration of a sentence against another because of the title he has to a parish.

A declaratory sentence does not constitute a penalty, but simply affirms that a penalty has been incurred, and hence throws the penalty back to the moment when the

8 Wernz, *l. c.,* VI, n. 63, p. 74.

crime was committed. The consequence is plain, especially with regard to fines, which run from the moment when the crime was committed. [9]

2. *No penalty can be inflicted unless it is certain that the crime has been perpetrated* and legitimate prescription has not set in, according to can. 1703–1705. Besides, although these conditions may be verified, no *censure* should be inflicted (*censura ferendae sententiae*) except after rebuke and warning have been administered to the delinquent. To that purpose also a certain term should be granted, according to the prudent discretion of the judge or superior, and only if contumacy is persisted in, should the censure be inflicted.

It may be well to add that theory at least permits one who is accused and condemned to a manifestly unjust sentence, not to heed the sentence, at least in the internal forum.[10]

MULTIPLIED AND ATTEMPTED CRIMES

Can. 2234

Qui plura delicta commisit, non modo gravius puniri, sed si, prudenti iudicis arbitrio, res id ferat, subiici etiam vigilantiae vel alii remedio poenali.

Can. 2235

Delictum frustratum aut conatus delicti, nisi tanquam distincta delicta lege plectantur, possunt con-

---

9 As to the effects of excommunication and suspension, see can. 2261, 2264, 2284.

10 As to the *external forum*, see can. 2219; many authors permit the manifestly innocent to shirk the penal consequences if no scandal or contempt of authority is to be feared; Eichmann, *l. c.*, p. 68.

grua poena pro gravitate puniri, salvo praescripto can. 2213, §3.

Those who have committed *several crimes,* either of the same kind, or of different kinds, should not only be *more severely punished,* but also subjected to vigilance and other penal remedies. A *frustrated* or attempted *crime* may be punished proportionately to the actual crime, unless the attempt itself is punishable in law as a distinct crime (see can. 2213, §3.)

TITLE VII

REMISSION OF PENALTIES

The Code certainly takes *poenarum remissio* for the authoritative removal of penalties. For by committing a crime one has incurred the bond of guilt (*vinculum culpae*), which in turn introduces another bond, *viz.*, that of penalty (*vinculum poenae.*) This juridical bond, established by the coercive power, can be solved only by the same authority. The Code does not take into consideration the cessation of penalties by the death of the delinquent and by atonement. Death dissolves everything, but not the effect of censures. Atonement extinguishes penalties, inasmuch as it has the character of a temporarily fixed penalty.[1] Thus the fasts and pilgrimages of the penitential discipline may be looked upon as temporary punishments, which cease after the lapse of time for which they were decreed. But the Code does consider prescription, by which the criminal action may be quashed (can. 2240; see can. 1703).

WHO MAY GRANT PARDON

Can. 2236

§ 1. Remissio poenae sive per absolutiouem, si agatur de censuris, sive per dispensationem, si de poenis vindicativis, concedi tantum potest ab eo qui poenam tulit, vel ab eius competente Superiore aut successore, vel ab eo cui haec potestas commissa est.

[1] Wernz, *l. c.*, VI, n. 82 f., p. 90 f.

§ 2. Qui potest a lege eximere, potest quoque poenam legi adnexam remittere.

§ 3. Iudex qui ex officio applicat poenam a Superiore constitutam, eam semel applicatam remittere nequit.

§ 1. Penalties may be removed by way of *absolution* or *dispensation*. The former is applied to *censure*, the latter to *vindictive penalties*. But both presupposes jurisdiction over the person as well as over the matter at issue, because of the juridical tie contracted by penalty.

Therefore *only he can absolve or dispense* who has established or inflicted the penal law or penalty. Only, the *Pope* can absolve or dispense from all penalties, even without the valid reason [2] otherwise required for dispensations and absolutions imparted by prelates inferior to the Sovereign Pontiff. A sufficient reason is the amendment and the reparation of damage or scandal.

Ordinaries may dispense or absolve from penalties which they themselves, not the common law, have established or inflicted.[3]

The successors of these ecclesiastical authorities are endowed with the same powers as their predecessors. The *superior* ecclesiastical authority can dispense or absolve from penalties inflicted by the inferior; hence the Roman Pontiff may dispense or absolve from penalties inflicted by the Ordinaries in virtue of their ordinary power, even if the case was reserved, not by common, but by diocesan law.

Finally, those who are *commissioned* by superiors may

[2] He needs no reason because of his plenitude of power *in foro externo*, but if the contrition or attrition required for absolution in the sacramental forum should be wanting, the absolution may be valid *in foro externo*, but without effect *in foro interno*.

[3] *Ratione delicti* (can. 1566, § 1) the ordinary in whose diocese the crime has been committed, is competent to absolve.

dispense or absolve in virtue of that commission within the limits of their mandate. The *Vicar-General*, as he needs a special commission to inflict penalties,[4] also needs a special commission to dispense or absolve from them.

§ 2. Those who *may exempt* from the observance of a law, may also remit the penal sanction attached to the same, and consequently render the delinquent immune from punishment. Note that the inferior, say the Ordinary, cannot exempt from common law, because *eximere a lege* supposes a legislative power not granted to the Ordinaries with regard to the common law. For this the Ordinaries, *i. e.*, all prelates inferior to the Pope, need special faculties. However, can. 81 would also seem to apply here;[5] also can. 66, § 3, which requires a faculty in order to be capable of receiving a favor or privilege. The faculty to dispense from certain laws, *e. g.*, impediments, does not include the faculty to absolve from the penalties, *e. g.*, of excommunication, but only the power to absolve from the penalty *ad hoc, i. e.*, to obtain the favor.[6]

§ 3. The *judge* who *ex officio* applies a penalty established by a superior, cannot remit the penalty once inflicted. Having rendered the sentence, his office is completed.

The judge is not above the law, but subject to it.

THE ORDINARY'S POWER WITH REGARD TO COMMON LAW

Can. 2237

§1. In casibus publicis potest Ordinarius poenas latae sententiae iure communi statutas remittere, exceptis:

---

4 See can. 2220, § 2.
5 Concerning censures, special provisions are made in can. 2254.

6 See can. 2265, § 2; Eichmann, *l. c.*, p. 72.

1.° Casibus ad forum contentiosum deductis;

2.° Censuris Sedi Apostolicae reservatis;

3.° Poenis inhabilitatis ad beneficia, officia, dignitates, munera in Ecclesia, vocem activam et passivam eorumve privationis, suspensionis perpetuae, infamiae iuris, privationis iuris patronatus et privilegii seu gratiae a Sede Apostolica concessae.

§ 2. In casibus vero occultis, firmo praescripto can. 2254 et 2290 potest Ordinarius poenas latae sententiae iure communi statutas per se vel per alium remittere, exceptis censuris specialissimo vel speciali modo Sedi Apostolicae reservatis.

§ 1. The Ordinary may remit all penalties *latae sententiae*, either corrective or vindictive, established by common law, except the following:

a) *Cases brought before the civil ecclesiastical court,* as when civil action is instituted in order to obtain damages for a crime.[7]

b) *Cases reserved to the Apostolic See*, either simply, or especially, or most especially.[8]

c) *Penalties entailing inability to hold benefices, offices,*[9] *dignities* in the Church, penalties referring to the active and passive vote and privation thereof, perpetual suspension, infamy by law, privation of advowson, and privileges or favors granted by the Apostolic See.

As to the public character of crimes, see can. 2197.

The power of Ordinaries is here restricted perhaps more than some authors were inclined to admit.[10] But the underlying reason is that given by these authors, *viz.,*

---

7 See can. 2210, § 1, n 2.
8 See can. 2245, § 3.
9 *Munera*, i. e., charges of any kind, for instance, rector, lector, sexton.
10 Thesaurus-Giraldi, *l. c.*, P. I, c. 23, *ed. cit.*, p. 30.

that too frequent recourse to the Apostolic See be not required. Besides, there is no doubt that minor crimes also are here supposed, because all the reserved censures are excluded. But the text also excludes from the power of the Ordinary a category which was formerly considered as included therein, at least if the penalty had no special clause attached.[11] The reason for this restriction is palpable: all the cases enumerated under n. 3 concern the public welfare of the Church, not merely that of the delinquent.

The term "*Ordinary*" is limited here, as the Ordinary cannot delegate another (can. 2237, § 2). But all the Ordinaries mentioned in can. 198 are included. And since the text simply says "Ordinary," the *superiors of exempt clerical orders* enjoy this power over their subjects.

§ 2 of can. 2237 refers to *occult cases* with due regard to censures (can. 2254) and occult vindictive penalties (can. 2290). Now in such cases *latae sententiae*, established by common law, the Ordinary as well as any one delegated by him may remit the penalties. An *exception* to this general rule are the censures which are reserved either *specialissimo* or *speciali modo* to the Holy See. In occult cases, the Ordinary may delegate another, as per can. 199, § 2, either for each separate case or habitually.

CONDITIONS AND MODE OF PARDON

Can. 2238

Poenae remissio, vi aut metu gravi extorta, ipso iure irrita est.

---

11 Thesaurus-Giraldi, *l. c.*

Can. 2239

§1. Poena valide remitti potest praesenti vel absenti, absolute vel sub conditione, in foro externo vel interno tantum.

§2. Licet poena etiam oretenus remitti possit, si tamen scripto inflicta fuerit, expedit ut etiam eius remissio scriptis concedatur.

Can. 2240.

Ad praescriptionem actionis poenalis quod attinet, servetur dispositio can. 1703.

The remission of any penalty, whether by absolution or dispensation, if extorted by physical compulsion or grave fear, is *ipso iure* invalid. Hence serious threats to use the civil power, which the abominable *appellatio ab abusu* [12] sometimes resorted to, are without avail either in the internal or the external forum.

A penalty may be remitted not only *when the person is present,* but also when he *is absent,*[13] either unconditionally or with a condition attached, for instance, to present himself to the superior, or provided the amendment has lasted for a certain length of time. A remission may be valid either in the court of conscience only or in the external forum only.

Although a penalty may be remitted by word of mouth it is more expedient that it be done in writing, if the penalty was inflicted in writing. But writing is not required for the validity of a dispensation or absolution. As to prescription of penal actions see can. 1703 (Vol. VII of this commentary, pp. 148 sqq.).

---

12 Cfr. can. 2334, n. 4.
13 Of course, in *foro interno* or, rather, in the sacramental forum, personal presence is required.

SECTION II
PENALTIES IN PARTICULAR

TITLE VIII
CORRECTIVE PENALTIES OR CENSURES

CHAPTER I

CENSURES IN GENERAL

Can. 2241

§1. Censura est poena qua homo baptizatus, delinquens et contumax, quibusdam bonis spiritualibus vel spiritualibus adnexis privatur, donec, a contumacia recedens, absolvatur.

§2. Censurae, praesertim latae sententiae, maxime excommunicatio, ne infligantur, nisi sobrie et magna cum circumspectione.

Can. 2242

§1. Censura punitur tantummodo delictum externum, grave, consummatum, cum contumacia coniunctum; potest autem ferri censura etiam in delinquentes ignotos.

§2. Si agatur de censuris ferendae sententiae, contumax est qui, non obstantibus monitionibus de quibus in can. 2233, §2, a delicto non desistit vel patrati delicti poenitentiam cum debita damnorum et scandali reparatione agere detrectat; ad incurrendam vero censuram latae sententiae sufficit transgressio legis vel praecepti cui sit adnexa latae sententiae poena, nisi reus legitima causa ab hac excusetur.

§ 3. Contumaciam desiisse dicendum est, cum reum vere delicti commissi poenituerit et simul ipse congruam satisfactionem pro damnis et scandalo dederit aut saltem serio promiserit; iudicare autem utrum poenitentia vera sit, satisfactio congrua aut eiusdem promissio seria, necne, illius est, a quo censurae absolutio petitur.

The term censure is derived from the Latin *censura*, which originally signified registration, much in the same sense as our modern census. The office of *censores* was created in 443 B. C. and gradually extended to the *regimen morum*, or supervision of public morals, later to the arrangements for the collection of the public revenue and the execution of public works. As censors or inspectors of public morals the *censores* were empowered to brand with disgrace (*ignominia*) those guilty of acts which, although not forbidden by any penal statute, were denounced by public opinion. The branding with disgrace was termed *notio*, or *notatio*, or *animadversio censoria*, and the disgrace inflicted by it, *nota censoria*. To inflict this note no previous judicial investigation or examination of witnesses was required, and the only effect of the *nota censoria*, in itself, was to affix a stigma to the individual. But, in addition to the mere disgrace thus inflicted, the censors could, to a certain extent, deprive the object of their displeasure of public honors and privileges, but neither the dishonor nor the degradation were necessarily permanent.[1]

1 Ramsay-Lanciani, *Roman Antiquities*, 1901, p. 198 ff.

Ecclesiastical terminology was uncertain up to the time of Innocent III (1198–1216), inasmuch as all kinds of ecclesiastical penalties were understood by censures. But a decretal of the above-named Pontiff restricted the term *censura* to interdict, suspension, and excommunication,[2] and this meaning was thenceforth permanently established.[3] A censure then is *defined* by the Code as *a penalty by which a baptized person, delinquent and contumacious, is deprived of certain spiritual goods or goods connected with spiritual ones, until he has given up his contumacy, and obtained absolution.*

1) Censures generically belong to the class of penalties, because they contain all the marks of a *penalty*.[4] Hence, although the corrective element is foremost in censures, the character of penalty as retribution and reparation is not entirely wanting.

2) The *subject* of censures must be baptized, delinquent, and stubborn.

a) *Homo baptizatus* alone is the subject of censures; no brute[5] is capable of punishment in the proper sense. Baptism is necessary because the Church does not exercise her judiciary power except over those who belong to her fold.[6] Consequently not even catechumens are subject to ecclesiastical censures. On the other hand, any one who is validly baptized, no matter what religion or creed or sect he may profess, is *de iure* subject to ecclesiastical censures.[7] Baptized *non-Catholics*, because of the

---

2 C. 20, X, V, 40.

3 Hinschius, *l. c.*, V, 125, note 4; Hollweck, *l. c.*, p. 84, note 1.

4 See can. 2215.

5 The *anathema* sometimes hurled at irrational creatures—as we read in ancient documents—must be understood of execration and de-

testation, not of punishment involving guilt; Ballerini-Palmieri, *Opus Theol. Morale*, 1894, ed. 2, Vol. VII, p. 20, n. 49.

6 *Trid.*, Sess. XIV, c. 2. *de ref.*

7 *Trid.*, Sess. VII, can. 7; can. 12; Suarez, *De Censuris*, disp. V, sect. 1, n. 25 (XXIII, 156).

indelible character of Baptism, are also theoretically subject to censures, but these are not enforced against them by reason either of opportunity, or lack of the necessary assistance, or infeasibility. Besides, there is no doubt that the legislator has only Catholics in view, at least directly.

It is hardly necessary to state that only a *living* man can be properly censured. If excommunication was at one time inflicted on the dead, it was only as a warning to the living not to give them ecclesiastical burial or offer ecclesiastical suffrages for their repose. Consequently also the absolution given to such as died with signs of penance, refers to the living and not to the dead.[8]

b) A censure can be inflicted only for a *delictum* (crime). This is described in can. 2195, and further explained in can. 2242, § 1. Only an external, grievous, consummated and stubborn crime is censurable.

External is here used in opposition, not to occult, but merely to internal sinful acts, as, for instance, an internal heresy which remains entirely within the mind and is never manifested.[9] A crime on the other hand (for instance, homicide), may be wholly occult, and yet external.

The crime must be grievous or *grave*, because the external act itself must be grievously culpable. The reason lies in the gravity of the penalty, which, ultimately meaning exclusion from the kingdom of heaven, should

8 Ballerini-Palmieri, *l. c.*, n. 48.
9 *Ibid.*, p. 64, n. 133: *"neque sufficit, quod quis, v.g., intendens haeresim confirmare, mensam percutiat aut dicat: ita est, quia per hoc non significatur haeresis exterius."* But if one would say to himself: "I don't believe," or purposely and with heretical intent refuse to genuflect or bow (like the Greeks) to the Blessed Sacrament, he would manifest his heretical belief externally.

not be inflicted except for such crimes as render one unworthy to enter that kingdom.[10]   But it must be observed that, according to the common teaching of the schools, a censure may be threatened even for a less serious transgression, which in itself would not amount to a grievous or mortal sin, provided the matter may become serious by reason of scandal, or danger, or the purpose for which the censure is threatened. Thus a theft, the matter of which would constitute only a light fault, might cause serious loss to a church.[11] Thus, also, a *percussio levis clericorum* (see can. 2343, §4) may be placed under excommunication in order to prevent greater evil and to enforce respect for the clerical state.

The proportion between the penalty and the reason for which it is threatened must be reasonable.

The next characteristic of a crime is that it be consummated (*comsummatum sive completum in genere suo*). This is verified when the effect of the forbidden act has followed. Beyond the intention of the legislator the penal law cannot bind. For instance, the violation of enclosure is complete if the whole body has moved within the forbidden precinct (can. 2343). However, the legislator may also punish an inchoate or attempted crime. For instance, can. 2333 lays under excommunication the *prohibentes promulgationem vel executionem litteras vel acta Apostolicae Sedis*. This class of persons incur excommunication, but the Apostolic letters may be promulgated or executed notwithstanding this unjust prohibition, which is against ecclesiastical liberty. Therefore the wording and context of the law must be weighed.[12]

---

10 S. Thomas, *Summa Theol.*, III, Suppl., qu. 21, art. 3.

11 Suarez, *l. c.*, disp. IV, sect. 6, n. 12 f.; see can. 2326.

12 Ballerini-Palmieri, *l. c.*, VII, p. 65, n. 135 f. and n. 139.

c) The person to be censured must be *contumacious*, in other words, crime must be connected with contumacy. Although contumacy in legal parlance is defined as contempt of court, the term has also a wider meaning, *viz.*, persistent disobedience, which is more explicitly described in can. 2242, § 2.

Persistent disobedience presupposes knowledge of the law which forbids acts under censure (can. 2209). It also supposes that the act perpetrated against the law is not only a past act, but endures as to its vicious character; because censures are corrective penalties.[13] Hence if penance is done and reparation is made, no censures can be inflicted.

When does contumacy exist? The Code, can. 2242, §2, distinguishes between a censure *ferendae* and a censure *latae sententiae*. The former requires a canonical admonition. Hence the ecclesiastical superior must, according to can. 2143, issue a formal warning, in the presence either of the chancellor or of another official of the episcopal court, or before two witnesses, or by registered letter, bidding the culprit to cease his criminal conduct or to do penance for the crime committed and to repair the damage and scandal done. Time must be given in order to await the result of the warning, and only after the term granted has expired without the desired result, may contumacy be assumed.[14] If no criminal warning was issued, the sentence, even though valid,[15] is unjust, and recourse or appeal is open to the censured. This warning may, but need not, be repeated.

The judgment as to the existence of contumacy lies with the superior. In order to incur a censure *latae sententiae*,

---

13 Wernz, *l. c.*, VI, n. 155, p. 164.
14 See can. 2283, § 2.
15 It would be invalid in the cases

mentioned in can. 1892 and 1894; Eichmann, *l. c.*, p. 77.

all that is required is to transgress the law or precept to which the penalty *latae sententiae* is attached, unless the culprit has a lawful reason or excuse. Consequently, there is no need of canonical admonition, since the penal law itself, threatening the penalty to be incurred *ipso facto*, contains this admonition.[16] The clause: *" nisi reus legitima causa ab hac excusetur"* must be referred to the reasons for or against imputability, as explained in can. 2199–2206 and 2229.

Contumacy may be said to *cease* (can. 2242, §3) when the delinquent repents of the crime he has committed, makes proportionate satisfaction for the damage he has caused and repairs the scandal given, or at least seriously promises to do so. Whether the repentence is sincere, the satisfaction sufficient, or the promise serious, must be judged by the one who is asked to give absolution.

Here it may be added that a promise under oath is not demanded by our text, although the Roman Ritual [17] appears to require it.

It should be clearly understood that *these marks of crime must all concur simultaneously;* if but one of them is lacking no censure is incurred.

3. The effect of a censure is *privation of certain spiritual goods* or things connected therewith. This is the proximate purpose or effect of censures, which are spiritual penalties and therefore deprive the delinquent of *spiritual benefits.* When *temporal goods* are mentioned, they must be related to spiritual goods. Thus, *e. g.,* a suspension (*qua* censure) may deprive a cleric of bene-

16 Cfr. c. 26, X, II, 28. Concerning a declaratory sentence required for a censure *latae sententiae*, see can. 2223, § 4. A censure *latae sententiae* which requires a declaratory sentence only, need not be preceded by a canonical admonition; see Suarez, *l. c.,* disp. III, sect. 10, n. 19 ff.; Ballerini-Palmieri, *l. c.,* VII, p. 82, n. 165 f.

17 Tit. III, c. 3, n. 2; see c. 15, X, V, 39.

ficiary emoluments, but only in relation to his office, which is something spiritual. Excommunication may deprive one of exercising legitimate functions, but only in order to ecclesiastical office; it may also render one *vitandus,* but only with regard to the faithful as such. The specific benefits of which the censured are deprived are enumerated under the single headings. Although privation is the main and primary effect of censure enforcement, yet obedience and submission, repair of damage and scandal are also intended as subordinate ends.[18]

4. Censures do not cease automatically with contumacy and subsequent amendment, but *require formal absolution.* It would be scandalous, to say the least, to teach that censures cease in the court of conscience after the culprit has amended his conduct and is no longer contumacious;[19] see can. 2248 ff.

Can. 2241, §2 admonishes all concerned to make a *sober and careful use of censures,* especially of censures *latae sententiae,* and more particularly of excommunication. This warning of the Council of Trent[20] has repeatedly been emphasized. Thus missionaries were told not to be misled by civil governors into pronouncing censures in order to ascertain the temporal estates of deceased persons.[21] The S. Congregation also refused to permit Vicars Apostolic to censure those who trafficked in or used opium or arach. The reason given was that censures constitute the very nerve of ecclesiastical discipline and should therefore be used sparingly and for grave, canonical, and approved reasons only.[22]

---

18 Suarez, *l. c.,* disp. VI, sect. 1, nn. 1–3 (XXIII, 175).
19 Prop. 44. damn. a S. O., March 18, 1666 (Denzinger, n. 1015).
20 Sess. XXIV, c. 3, *de ref.*

21 S. C. P. F., Aug. 18, 1760 (*Coll.,* n. 434).
22 S. C. P. F., June 23, 1830; Sept. 30, 1848 (*Coll.,* nn. 815, 1085).

Excommunications may also be inflicted on unknown delinquents, says can. 2242, §1. For although the intention must be directed to a certain subject, yet if that person is determined in one way or another, it is sufficient for the censure to bind him, even though he may be unknown as such or such, but merely as the perpetrator. [28] There is no difficulty as to a censure *latae sententiae,* because this censure is incurred by the very perpetration of the deed, but it may need a declaratory sentence. Censures *ferendae sententiae* require canonical admonition. A public edict issued either in the church or in some official publication would be sufficient.[24]

APPEAL OR RECOURSE FROM CENSURES

Can. 2243

§1. Censurae inflictae per sententiam iudicialem, statim ac latae fuerint, exsecutionem secumferunt, nec ab eis datur appellatio, nisi in devolutivo; item a censuris ad modum praecepti inflictis datur recursus, sed in devolutivo tantum.

§2. Appellatio vero vel recursus a sententia iudiciali vel praecepto comminante censuras etiam latae sententiae nondum contractas, nec sententiam aut praeceptum nec censuras suspendunt, si agatur de re in qua ius non admittit appellationem vel recursum etiam cum effectu suspensivo; secus censuras suspendunt, firma tamen obligatione servandi id quod sententia aut praecepto mandatur, nisi reus appellationem vel recursum interposuerit non a sola poena, sed ab ipsa quoque sententia vel praecepto.

---

23 Suarez, *De Censuris,* disp. V. sect. 2, n. 2 f. (Vol. XXIII, 158 f.)

24 *Ibid.,* disp. III, sect. 11, n. 5 (XXIII, 65).

Ecclesiastical discipline requires that prelates in inflicting penalties for the correction and reformation of morals should not be handicapped by dilatory appeals.[25] Therefore, the Code safeguards the authority of the ecclesiastical judge by clearly eliminating censures *latae sententiae,* which require no execution of the sentence, but go into effect automatically. But a censure inflicted *a iure tantum* may here be understood because, according to can. 2217, §1, n. 3, it may require a condemnatory sentence, which would certainly mean a judicial sentence. But a censure inflicted *ab homine,* by way of a special precept, like that of the *suspensio ex informata conscientia,* is here expressly mentioned.

Note the difference between appeal and recourse; an appeal supposes a judiciary sentence, a recourse, either a decree or a decision; an appeal is permitted to a tribunal only, recourses are disposed of administratively by the Roman Congregations.[26]

§1 of can. 2243 rules:

1. That *censures inflicted* by judiciary sentence take *effect* immediately and must, as a rule, be carried out. An *appeal,* if properly lodged, has a *devolutive* effect, *i. e.,* the whole case is thrown upon the court of appeal, but the one thus censured must conduct himself as if he were censured, *i. e.,* abstain from every act of order, jurisdiction, or administration forbidden by the censure. However, this text evidently presupposes that the sentence was valid; and since the text speaks of a judiciary sentence, its validity may be impaired for three reasons; (a) if the judge had no jurisdiction at all, as, for instance, a superior who has resigned or otherwise gone out of office; (b) if an essential form was neglected, for

25 C. 13, X, I, 31.   26 Can. 1601.

instance, the summons; (c) if the reason was unjust or insufficient, because the penalty, being a grave one, requires a just and reasonable cause for being inflicted. Whenever one of these reasons occurs, the censure does not bind. What is to be done? The whole judgment must be reversed, for an appeal proper is impossible, as can. 1880, 3° clearly states. But here it must also be noted that, although the exception of nullity may be lodged after a definite sentence (Benedict XIV, " *Ad militantis*," n. 36), yet the exception of nullity does not, *as a rule*, impede the execution of the sentence. We said " *as a rule*," for if the nullity is evident or notorious, or can be immediately proved, the exception quashes the effect of the sentence or execution.[27]

2. The text states that from *censures inflicted by way of precept* only *recourse*, and that *in devolutivo*, is permitted. Thus a *suspensio ex informata conscientia* admits *only* recourse to the S. C. Concilii, *in devolutivo*. But note well that only censures, not vindictive penalties, have this devolutive effect.

§2 of can. 2243 regards censures not yet inflicted or incurred, but merely *threatened*. The threat may be pronounced by a judge in the form of a judiciary sentence, although the law itself may have determined the penalty (*i. e.*, censure), or it may be pronounced by a superior in the form of a special precept, as is prescribed for non-residing pastors. A superior of exempt clerical religious may issue such a precept in an important matter of discipline. Again notice the difference between appeal and recourse with suspensive or devolutive effect:

1. *If the matter is such as to admit of no appeal or recourse with suspensive effect*, such an appeal or recourse

27 Can. 1892.

suspends neither the judiciary sentence (or precept) nor the censure threatened but not yet incurred, even though it be a censure *latae sententiae*. No appeal is allowed in the cases mentioned in can. 1880. Recourse *in devolutivo* only is provided in can. 345, 513, §2, 1340, §3, 1395 and 1428, §3.

2. If the *matter in question admits of an appeal or a recourse with suspensive effect*, then a twofold hypothesis is possible.

a) The appellant may lodge his appeal *against the censure* only, without dodging or shirking the obligation of fulfilling the command stated in the sentence or precept. In that case the *censure is suspended,* but the obligation of complying with the substance of the sentence or precept remains. For instance, the sentence may demand restitution of stolen church property or reparation of damage caused by homicide, robbery, incendiarism,[28] or by giving up a supposed marriage or concubinage.[29]

b) If the appeal or recourse is lodged not only against the penalty (*i. e., the censure*), but also against the sentence or precept which supposedly contains both penalty and obligation, *both* are suspended. Hence the appellant is neither censured nor obliged to repair eventual damages or perform the act prescribed by the sentence or precept.

MULTIPLICATION OF CENSURES

Can. 2244

§1. Non solum diversae, sed etiam eiusdem speciei censura potest in eodem subiecto multiplicari.

§2. Censura latae sententiae multiplicatur:

---

[28] See can. 2346; 2348; 2354; 2401. [29] See can. 2356; 2357, § 2.

1.° Si diversa delicta, quorum singula censuram se..
cumferunt, eadem vel distincta actione committantur;

2.° Si idem delictum, censura punitum, pluries re-
petatur ita ut plura sint delicta distincta;

3.° Si delictum, diversis censuris a distinctis
Superioribus punitum, semel aut pluries com-
mittatur.

§3. Censura ab homine multiplicatur, si plura praecepta vel plures sententiae vel plures distinctae partes
eiusdem praecepti aut sententiae suam quaeque censuram infligant.

The whole or at least the main difficulty concerning the
multiplication of censures seems to arise from their effect,
i. e., the privation of spiritual benefits. Suarez refutes it
effectively.[30] Privation is indeed the primary object or
end of censures, not, indeed, mere privation, but its positive cause, and this may be multifarious. Mortal sin,
for instance, deprives the soul of sanctifying grace, and,
when multiplied, produces a multitude of stains.

Besides, one censure does not exhaust the power of the
ecclesiastical judge, which, on the contrary, remains intact,
and may, therefore, again be used against the same
delinquent.

Finally, multiplied censures are intended to terrify and
deter, and to lend additional weight to the authority of
the law.

The multiplication of censures is necessarily bound up
with the specific and numerical distinction of sins; and
therefore the difficulties besetting this subject also adhere
in the one here under discussion.

The Code begins by stating that censures may be multiplied, *not only specifically, but also numerically in one*

30 *De Censuris,* disp. V, sect. 2, n. 6.

and the same subject. Thus a man may be excommunicated, suspended, and interdicted all at the same time, as we know from the common formula of absolution. Neither is there any difficulty in that, because these privations differ. The objection mentioned above is directed only against the same kind of censure. May one be twice excommunicated? The Code says, yes, and then distinguishes between censures *latae sententiae* and censures *ab homine.*

1. Censures *latae sententiae* are multiplied:

a) When *several crimes,* each of which has a censure attached, are committed by the same act or by different acts.

This is a specific distinction of crimes, although the act may be one and the same, or the acts may be morally and physically distinct. If the acts differ, the case is evident. But if the act is, at least physically, one and the same, it seems strange that two or more censures should follow. Yet if we distinguish the reasons for the sources from which the censures are established, it is but logical to assume diversity, as of causes, so of effects. Take the example of one dragging a bishop by force before a lay tribunal. There would be a violation of can. 2341 and of can. 2343, §3 (*privilegium fori* and *canonis*). A nun with solemn vows and papal enclosure, who would leave the enclosure to contract civil marriage before a non-Catholic minister, would incur four censures, *viz., under* can. 2319, §1, n. 1, can. 2341, 3, can. 2385 (as apostate), and can. 2388,—all these being specified censures inflicted for specific reasons.

b) There is also multiplication if *the same crime is repeated so that the repeated acts constitute distinct crimes.* Two characteristics distinguish acts from one another:

interruption and diversity of object. If an act is morally and physically *interrupted,* so that the posterior act is not coherent with the anterior, these acts are distinct. On the other hand, if an act lasts for some time, but is inspired by the same motive and continued under the same impetus, the act is one, for instance, a protracted beating of a clergyman.[31] When the *object* or *matter* of one criminal act is diverse, authors differ as to the multiplication of censures. For instance, if one would bring two clergymen before a lay tribunal or converse with two *vitandi* at the same time, or would kill two clerics by the same stroke, Suarez and others believe it probable that only one censure would be incurred, because the action is essentially one and constitutes but one sin.[32] The Code is not against this assumption.

c) *If a crime laid under diverse censures by various superiors* is perpetrated once or oftener, a multiplication of censures may be incurred. The reason is that the two superiors may have different reasons for decreeing the censure. However, it must be clearly understood that there is question here not only of a double or emphatic prohibition, but of a double or multiplied censure. Now can. 2247, §1 forbids Ordinaries to put under censure crimes which are already forbidden under the same penalty by the Apostolic See. Consequently the censures mentioned in the Code as reserved to the Apostolic See cannot again be inflicted by inferior prelates. Note that we here treat of censures *latae sententiae,* which need no admonition.[33] Hence the case can concern only a lay-

---

[31] C. 27, X, V, 39.
[32] *De Censuris,* disp. V, sect, 3, n. 3 ff.
[33] What Suarez (*l. c.,* disp. V, sect. 3, n. 13) and Ballerini-

Palmieri (*l. c.,* Vol. VII, n. 113, p. 55 ff.) say, is not to the point; and what Ayrinhac (*l. c.,* p. 93) says, appears like an evasion of the difficulty.

man or a clergyman or religious who has different superiors. Thus if a layman has several bishops, because he has more than one domicile, the different bishops may censure him; a religious, too, may have different superiors, —the provincial or general of his institute, and the local Ordinary as far as pastoral duties are concerned.

One difficulty remains: What is meant by "*diversis censuris*"? Does it mean specifically or numerically different censures? If specifically different, it would mean excommunication or suspension or interdict. This seems to be the meaning of our text, although the Decretals,[34] from which it is apparently taken, only mention excommunication, which is said to have been incurred severally, because inflicted by several prelates.

2. The next class of multiplied censures is that of *censurae ab homine*. There is no difficulty as to the multiplication of these, because the various reasons constitute as many titles, and each sentence presupposes a clear title for a distinct pronunciamento on diverse matters judged or commanded. Therefore, if several ordinances or several sentences (which of course suppose diverse objects) have been issued under censure, censures are multiplied in proportion to the number of precepts and sentences transgressed. Besides, if the sentence or precept is divisible, and hence composed of several parts, each of which is emphasized by a special censure, the censures are also multiplied. Here the intention of the superior or judge must be clearly manifested, and besides, the admonition must be made for each and every sentence or precept and for every specific part thereof.[35]

---

[34] C. 42, X. V, 39; but c. 27 *ibid.* refers to diverse crimes; thus one may be interdicted by the Pope and excommunicated or suspended by the ordinary; Eichmann, p. 80.

[35] Suarez, *l. c.*, disp. V, sect. 2, n. 13.

In asserting a multiplication of censures, either *latae sententiae* or *ab homine,* it must be remembered that all the conditions enumerated above must concur, not only in one, but in each and every censure; else one censure may be incurred, but not the other. The consequence of such verified or not-verified multiplication is important in reference to absolution.

RESERVATION OF CENSURES

Can. 2245

§1. Censurae aliae sunt reservatae, aliae non reservatae.

§2. Censura *ab homine* est reservata ei qui censuram inflixit aut sententiam tulit, eiusve Superiori competenti, vel successori aut delegato; ex censuris vero *a iure* reservatis aliae sunt reservatae *Ordinario,* aliae *Apostolicae Sedi.*

§3. E reservatis Apostolicae Sedi aliae sunt *reservatae simpliciter,* aliae *speciali modo,* aliae *specialissimo modo.*

§4. Censura latae sententiae non est reservata, nisi in lege vel praecepto id expresse dicatur; et in dubio sive iuris sive facti reservatio non urget.

Can. 2246

§ 1. Ne reservetur censura, nisi attenta peculiari gravitate delictorum et necessitate aptius providendi disciplinae ecclesiasticae et medendi conscientiis fidelium.

§2. Reservatio strictam recipit interpretationem.

§3. Reservatio censurae impedientis receptionem

Sacramentorum importat reservationem peccati cui censura adnexa est; verum si quis a censura excusatur vel ab eadem fuit absolutus, reservatio peccati penitus cessat.

Can. 2247

§1. Si censura Sedi Apostolicae reservata sit, Ordinarius nequit aliam censuram sibi reservatam in idem delictum ferre.

§2. Reservatio censurae in particulari territorio vim suam extra illius territorii fines non exserit, etiamsi censuratus ad absolutionem obtinendam e territorio egrediatur; censura vero ab homine est ubique locorum reservata ita ut censuratus nullibi absolvi sine debitis facultatibus possit.

§3. Si confessarius, ignorans reservationem, poenitentem a censura ac peccato absolvat, absolutio censurae valet, dummodo ne sit censura ab homine aut censura specialissimo modo Sedi Apostolicae reservata.

Elsewhere,[86] in sketching the historical development of reservation, we said that reservation to the " Apostolic Lord " of the more atrocious crimes was a well-known practice, especially since the twelfth century, and was connected with pilgrimages to Rome as well as with the decline of public penance. Can. 893, §2 calls the restriction of the absolving power an *avocatio, i. e.,* a calling of certain cases before a higher tribunal. By earlier authors reservation was defined as " *restrictio iurisdictionis in odium delinquentis.* " This definition gave way to another, called the most common one by St. Alphonsus: " *restrictio iurisdictionis, ut delinquentes judicium prudentiorum*

---

[86] See Vol. IV, of our *Commentary*, pp. 311 ff.

subeant." [87]   This latter definition may appeal to tender
souls, but historically and theologically speaking it has not
much foundation, if exclusively understood of the higher
and more prudent judgment to which the penitent has to
submit.   For there is no doubt that the grievousness or
atrocity of the crime was the decisive element in reserving cases.   To bring home to the delinquent the fact of
the heinousness of his crime was another object of
reservation.   That by undertaking a pilgrimage to Rome
in those days this thought was vividly presented to the culprit, goes without saying.   Thus the Church did a truly
social work.   It appears to us that the idea of the mere
prudent judgment of a case overlooks the penal character
of censures and their corrective or reformatory purpose.[88]
No doubt some prelates may have had misgivings or suffered from lack of necessary knowledge in treating very
serious cases.   But this was not true of all, nor could there
have been wanting suitable clergymen to advise the bishops.   The Code, in the definition quoted above, treats
reservation as restrictive of jurisdiction, which is quite
intelligible from a juridical point of view.   However, our
view of reservation seems to receive weight from can.
2246, §1.

The common-law (*a iure*) censures reserved to the *Ordinary* are the following mentioned in can. 2319; 2326;
2339; 2341 (third clause) ; 2342, § 4; 2350; 2375; 2388,
§2. Can 2385 reserves the case of apostasy to the exempt
religious superior.

Censures reserved *simpliciter* to the *Holy See* are those
named in can. 2327, 2335; 2338, §1 ; 2338, §2; 2341 (sec-

---

[87] *Theol. Moralis*, VI, n. 581.   107; Ballerini in the notes to Gury's
[88] Thus also Hollweck, *l. c.*, p.   *Theol. Moral.*, II, n. 571.

ond clause); 2342; 2346; 2351, §1; 2370; 2371; 2372; 2373; 2387; 2388, § 1; 2392, n. 1; 2405.

Can. 2245 distinguishes

1° between *reserved* and *non-reserved censures*

2°	Reserved 1° *ab homine*	a) to the one who inflicted the censure or sentence b) to the former's superior, successor or delegate.		
	or Reserved 2° *a jure*	a) to the Ordinary (81 cases or canons) b) to the *Apostolic See* reserved	a) *simpliciter* (16) b) *speciali modo* (13) c) *specialissimo modo* (4)	

Speciali modo reserved to the *Apostolic See* are those mentioned in can. 2341; 2318, § 1; 2322, n. 1; 2330 (and "*Vacante Sede*," n. 81); 2332; 2333; 2334; 2341 (first clause); 2343, §2, n. 1; 2343, §3; 2345; 2360, §1; 2363.

Specialissimo modo reserved to the Apostolic See are those mentioned in can. 2320; 2343, §1; 2367; 2369, §1.

§4 of can. 2245 states that censures *latae sententiae* are reserved only if the *reservation is expressly stated* in the law or precept which contains or threatens the reservation. *If there be a doubt concerning reservation, the latter need not be observed, i. e.,* any confessor may absolve therefrom.[39]

The doubt may concern either the law (*dubium iuris*) or

---

[39] Neither is an absolution *ad cautelam* there and then required, nor is recourse necessary, or a renewed absolution, if the doubt has afterwards been cleared away; · Cappello, *l. c.*, p. 24.

a fact (*dubium facti*). A solid doubt in regard to law is, for instance, in a case of abortion, whether the law comprises the *mandatarius* as well as the *mandans* (see can. 2350). A *dubium facti* would be whether the non-Catholic minister before whom the parties contracted a marriage, acted as minister of his denomination or merely as justice of the peace, *i. e.*, as civil magistrate. Note, however, that the doubt here mentioned does not concern the censured person as much as the one who is to absolve him from censure. Of course, if the parties did not know of the censure, there can be no contumacy, and consequently no censure. [40]

Can. 2246, §1 enjoins *moderation* in the reservation of censures, and mentions three reasons for which a censure may be reserved: (1) the specially serious or *grievous character* of the *crime*, as stated in can. 897, and inculcated by the Council of Trent; [41] (2) the necessity of properly *guarding ecclesiastical discipline*, because it may be that at sundry times and in diverse places reservation may do more harm than good, as, for instance, in times of persecution, in provinces far distant with but few ministers, [42] whilst certain tendencies and public manifestations of specified vicious inclinations may demand more radical means; (3) the necessity of offering *a remedy to the conscience of the faithful*, whose character and conduct also differ in different places, at various times, and under various conditions. [43]

§2 of can. 2246 sets forth the well-known rule that the *reservation of censures must be strictly interpreted*, be-

---

[40] Hence it would be well to ask the parties whether they knew that such a marriage was forbidden under censure.

[41] Sess. 14, c. 7, *de poenit.*

[42] S. C. P. F., June 6, 1817, n. 14 (*Coll.*, n. 723).

[43] Benedict XIV, "*A quo primum*," June 14, 1757, § 8; *De Syn. Dioec.*, V, 5; see this Commentary, Vol. IV, p. 323 t.

cause restrictions are not favors which may be stretched, and because penalties should be interpreted in the milder sense.[44] However, it is evident that when the wording of a reserved censure is plain, it must be taken in its obvious sense. Besides, a reserved censure may have a twofold aspect: It may be favorable to a certain class of persons and unfavorable to another class. Thus the *privilegium canonis* (2343) is favorable to the clerical state and may therefore be widely interpreted; but as far as it concerns those who attack clerics, it is unfavorable, and must therefore be restricted to " *percussores* " in the strict sense.[45] Hence no extension from person to person, from case to case, in other words, no analogous interpretation is permissible.

If the wording is ambiguous the interpretation of the school, and consequently any probable opinion, may be followed.[46]

§3 of can. 2246 settles a controversy concerning episcopal reserved censures. The text has two clauses, and the first contains a condition not specially expressed.

1. Reservation of a censure may (a) *prevent one from receiving the sacraments,* and such a reservation involves reservation of the sin to which the censure is attached. This is the case in excommunication; *e.g.*, can. 2319, §1, n. 1, says that parties contracting marriage before a non-Catholic minister cannot licitly receive the sacraments until the censure is removed by the Ordinary. This reservation, therefore, concerns the sin itself.

(b) Reservation may *not prevent* one from receiving the sacraments, and then the sin is not reserved, even though the censure is. Consequently, a suspended cleric

---

44 Reg. *Iuris* 15 and 49 in 6°.   46 Ballerini-Palmieri, *Opus Theol.*
45 Reiffenstuel, in Reg. Iuris 15,   *Morals,* V, n. 725, p. 397, ed. 2.
n. 9.

rule." This can mean nothing else than that the bishops should not make it a rule to reserve to themselves cases already reserved to them by law, or reserved to no one by law.

This is the grammatical-verbal interpretation of can. 898. Is there any solid reason to depart from it? We cannot see any such reason. For if it is stated that it is naturally repugnant that bishops should reserve to themselves cases from which they can absolve only by delegated power, the answer is: Concerning the cases reserved to the Apostolic See *specialissimo* or *speciali modo,* there might be some shadow of a reason. But as to cases simply reserved to the Apostolic See, or reserved to the bishops by law, or reserved to no one, there cannot be any reason. For in these cases they absolve *propriâ auctoritate,* granted by law or general faculties. Besides, if the Bishop wishes to impress the faithful with the seriousness of a crime, he may bind himself, or rather shift the odium of the reservation to the Apostolic See. Lastly, it matters little whether he absolves *potestate propriâ* or *delegatâ.* It must, however, be observed that the Code strictly enjoins Ordinaries not to make cases reserved to the Apostolic See episcopal cases. This is deducible from the first proposition. But it must be added that invalidity of such reservations cannot be read into the text. The term *" abstineant "* cannot be stretched that far, nor can the *" nequit ferre "* of can. 2247, §1 be simply taken as involving invalidity. For the *" nequit "* alone does not warrant such interpretation. If the legislator had intended invalidity, he would have expressed it, as, for instance, in can. 782, § 3: *" valide uti nequeunt."*

Legislator quod voluit, expressit; quod noluit, tacuit.

§2 of can. 2247 determines the *territorial extent and*

force of reservation and distinguishes between a reserved censure *a iure* and one *ab homine*. Of course it is understood that this law *(a iure)* affects a diocese or province only, not the Church at large, because the common law binds everywhere. Thus diocesan statutes formerly forbade entering a saloon under suspension, to be incurred *ipso facto*. This was a censure *a iure particulari*.

a) The reservation of censures made for a particular territory—by way of a territorial law—is restricted to the limits of the respective territory, diocese or province and has no binding force outside these boundaries, even though the person censured would leave this territory in order to be absolved, in other words, if he would leave his home *in fraudem legis*.

b) If, however, an Ordinary or judge would inflict a censure and reserve it to himself by virtue of a special ordinance or condemnatory sentence (can. 2217, §1, n. 3), such a reserved censure would bind the person thus censured everywhere, so that he could not be absolved by any confessor unless the latter had obtained special faculties for the purpose. This also concerns *religious of exempt institutes*. A censure issued in virtue of the law for a whole order or exempt congregation binds in the whole of that order or congregation. If a religious superior issues a special precept or a condemnatory sentence *(ab homine)*, the person thus censured cannot be absolved by another superior, unless the latter has obtained special faculties from the respective superior or the constitutions permit.

However, can. 519 must be considered here. Hence a religious who has incurred a censure decreed as *a iure* by his institute may be absolved by any approved confessor; but if the censure is *ab homine, i. e.,* incurred by a special precept or condemnatory sentence, he cannot be absolved by any confessor, because can. 519 reads: "*a censuris in religione reservatis.*"

Neither can ignorance of the confessor be a pretext, for §3 of can. 2247 precludes this assumption. It says indeed that if a confessor, *unaware of the reservation,* absolves a penitent from censure and guilt, the absolution from censure would be valid, but adds: the absolution, even in case of ignorance, would be invalid if given for a censure *ab homine* or for a censure reserved *specialissimo modo* to the Apostolic See. What kind of ignorance, whether culpable or inculpable, is required, is not stated nor does the Code distinguish. Similar to ignorance is inadvertence, and therefore inadvertence also must be admitted as an excuse and the absolution be regarded as valid. [53]

The phrase "*a censura ac peccato*" should be compared with can. 2246, § 3, where it is stated that absolution from censure implies cessation of reservation of sin, provided the censure is not one which prevents the reception of the Sacraments.

Take can. 894, the false accusation of an innocent priest. This is a case reserved as a sin, or by the very nature of the offence, and, besides, it is reserved to the Apostolic See *speciali modo,* under censure, in virtue of can. 2363. The question arises whether the confessor, not knowing of, or not adverting to, the reservation when he absolves the penitent from "censure," also absolves him from the sin, so that the penitent can receive the Sacraments. A different answer is given by different authors. Under can. 894 we maintained that "neither ignorance nor doubt as to

[53] Cfr. Cappello, *l. c.,* p. 25. See, for instance, can. 2338, § 1, which supposes a *dolus,* according to can. 2229, § 2, *i. e.,* full knowledge and deliberation.

the law of reservation excuses from this reservation." This view is shared by others, *e. g.*, Ayrinhac (*Penal Legislation*, p. 310 ff.), but it is contradicted by Arregui (*Summarium Theol. Moralis*, 4th ed., no. 607), although his argumentation did not convince us. However, since can. 209 admits a probable and positive doubt as to the "*supplet ecclesia*," it is but meet that we should here supplement what we said under can. 894 (Vol. IV, p. 318), to the effect that the absolution from sin in this case (Can. 894) should be considered valid and licit.

The censure reserved *modo speciali* to the Apostolic See may be validly removed if the confessor does not know or is not aware of it. If the sin is not reserved *ratione sui*, for its own sake, but only as far as a censure is attached to it, absolution from censure also involves absolution from sin. For instance, if an apostate religious who has incurred excommunication reserved to the Ordinary (or religious superior, can. 2385), goes to a confessor who does not know of that reservation and absolves from both censure and sin, the penitent is absolved from both. For the text simply says: "*ignorans reservationem*" without qualification, and thus appears to admit ignorance of reservation of both censure and sin, and therefore no distinction need be made as to censures preventing and censures not preventing the reception of the Sacraments. This should also be applied to episcopal cases.

ABSOLUTION FROM CENSURES

It was said elsewhere that the bishops were formerly wont to send penitents guilty of enormous crimes to Rome, to present themselves to the Sovereign Pontiff in order to receive a penance or to ask for the benefit of a change or absolution. Personal appearance before the higher court was then required, as also absolution, *i. e.*, a formal decision. For although the purpose of a censure is to amend the delinquent, yet, since the infliction of such a penalty implies an act of jurisdiction, more generally in the external forum, it is a logical consequence that the removal of such a juridical-moral tie requires an act of jurisdiction. Hence no one, even though perfectly contrite and willing to reform, can promise himself freedom from censures incurred, unless he has a warrant from the ecclesiastical court. But since the salvation of souls is the supreme law of the Church, it follows that the external régime may be relaxed or modified in cases of imperative need or greater spiritual progress for the benefit of the *cura animarum*. Such, in brief, is the development of the penitential discipline as related to censures. Personal appearance is no longer required and the burden of being subject to censures for a space of time that would prove intolerable or dangerous to the spiritual welfare of man has been relieved. At the same time the seriousness of censures has been preserved and the heinousness of the more atrocious crimes is still brought home to recusants.

NECESSITY OF AND CLAIM TO ABSOLUTION—REVIVAL OF CENSURES

Can. 2248

§1. Quaelibet censura, semel contracta, tollitur tantum legitima absolutione.

§2. Absolutio denegari nequit cum primum delinquens a contumacia recesserit ad normam can. 2242, §3; a censura autem absolvens, potest, si res ferat, pro patrato delicto congruam vindicativam poenam vel poenitentiam infligere.

§3. Censura, per absolutionem sublata, non reviviscit, nisi in casu quo onus impositum sub poena reincidentiae impletum non fuerit.

1. *Necessity.* That *a censure once contracted can be removed only by a lawful absolution,* follows from the definition given in can. 2236, §1. There is, then, no other way of obtaining relief except by absolution, leaving the rest to God and the disposition of the individual.[54] Absolution is *legitima* if imparted by competent authority. Competent is the one who has inflicted the censure, or his superior, delegate, or successor (can. 2245, §2).

The text furthermore says: "*semel contracta.*" A censure may be threatened by a special ordinance of the superior, as it were conditionally: "If you violate this ordinance, then etc." Such precepts cease for particular individuals with the cessation of the authority who issued them, unless indeed they were formulated in a legitimate document or given in the presence of two witnesses.[55] If the censure was not yet incurred when the superior who issued the precept goes out of office, it ceases and therefore no special authority is needed for absolution.

2. *Claim to Absolution.* As stated, the purpose of censures is the amendment of the delinquent. Consequently, *if he recedes from contumacy* or persistent disobedience, *he is entitled to absolution and it cannot be licitly withheld from him.*

Repentance alone, however, is not sufficient for purging oneself of contumacy, but satisfaction and reparation of scandal are required, according to can. 2242, §3. Hence

---

[54] Cfr. c. 1, X, V, 41.   [55] See can. 24.

the one who absolves from censure must judge whether the acts performed by the penitent are sufficient. Besides, *he may also impose a vindictive penalty, or penance, proportionate to the crime committed, should the case require this.*

But what if the party who was offended by the criminal act would refuse to make peace or consider the satisfaction insufficient? This would not interfere with the absolution, and the latter should not, therefore, be withheld, if the delinquent has performed the works prescribed.[56]

The imposition of such a vindictive penance is left to the one who absolves from censures, and he should judge the case or situation objectively. If the one absolved should fail to comply with his obligation of assuming a vindictive penance, the absolution would nevertheless be valid.

3. *Revival* of censures. *A censure duly removed never revives.* This is the rule. However, the *absolvens* may impose a work, vindictive penalty or penance, retraction, restitution, petition for absolution or any kind of work under penalty of relapse into the censure if the imposed penance is not complied with. This is called *absolutio sub poena reincidentiae.* It is a conditional absolution, which, while it *hic et nunc* completely removes the censure and its effects, eventually depends on the fulfillment of the condition by the person who was thus absolved.

Hence, if the condition is complied with, the censure

---

[56] S. C. EE. et RR., Aug. 4, 1579 (Bizzarri, *l. c.,* p. 225). One had committed a violent act against a priest, who was not satisfied with the reparation made. But the delinquent had done everything prescribed in the rescript of absolution and therefore the bishop was told to absolve him. See also *Reg. Iuris* 4. et 5. in 6°.

remains removed; but if it is not fulfilled, the censure returns (*reviviscit*). Whether a new guilt is incurred, is a controverted question. However, there can be no doubt that a new and culpable contumacy is required, since the censure has been taken away completely, and every censure requires contumacy. It may be said, therefore, that the old sentence revives with the same censure if the contumacy is verified in the second instance.[57] The reason why the censure revives is the protection of authority.[58]

The clause of reincidence must, of course, be expressly stated in law, as is the case in can. 2252, 2254, §§1, 3, or by the one who inflicts or absolves from censure.

ABSOLUTION FROM SEVERAL CENSURES

Can. 2249

§1. Si quis pluribus censuris detineatur, potest ab una absolvi, ceteris minime absolutis.

§2. Petens absolutionem, debet casus omnes indicare, secus absolutio valet tantum pro casu expresso; quod si absolutio, quamvis particularis petitio facta sit, fuerit generalis, valet quoque pro reticitis bona fide, excepta censura specialissimo modo Sedi Apostolicae reservata, non autem pro reticitis mala fide.

A censure may be incurred for various reasons and crimes, and it may be inflicted by different superiors. Although one mortal sin cannot be remitted without the

57 Cfr. Ballerini-Palmieri., *Opus Theol. Morale*, VII, n. 289; ed. 2, p. 146 ff. Different from this conditional absolution is the provisional (*absolutio ad cautelam*) which is sometimes given to receive a favor or for a certain time, and produces a limited effect; *ib.*, n. 291.

58 See c. 22, 6° V, 11: "*nec sic illudant censurae ecclesiasticae.*"

other mortal sins weighing upon the soul, yet *one censure may be removed without the others being taken away.* This is to be explained according to can. 2244, being evident from the diverse effects which diverse censures may produce, especially since censures are intended more for the public welfare of Christian society than for the court of conscience.

Hence it is, as §2 of can. 2249 rules, that one who has incurred several *censures, when asking for absolution, must mention all the censures he has incurred; otherwise the absolution will be good only for the censure expressed in the petition.* The reason for this rule lies in the above-mentioned fact of the possibility of several censures being inflicted for various crimes and reasons by various superiors. Therefore even the power, not only the will, may be wanting in the one who absolves.

The second clause of this section reads: *If, however, absolution was imparted in general terms, even though the censured person had asked to be absolved from one particular censure, the absolution holds good for all censures which were concealed in good faith.* But this general absolution is not valid in case of censures reserved *specialissimo modo* to the Apostolic See, *nor is it valid* for censures *concealed in bad faith.*

This law contains both a positive and a negative assertion. It admits absolution for censures *bona fide reticitis,* or as they are sometimes called, *oblitis, i. e.,* censures which the penitent forgot to mention either in confession or in his petition.

The first supposition, of course, is that the one who is asked for absolution has the power, either ordinary or delegated, of absolving from the censures in question.

The second supposition is that the penitent has *bona fide*

omitted to mention some censures incurred by him, whether reserved or not. Here the whole question turns about the will of the superior to absolve from censures which were not mentioned. The Code says implicitly that this will must be presumed if he uses a formula indicating general absolution, as is the case in the formula "*in quantum possum et tu indiges.*" Hence, if the tenor or wording of the absolution was general, the absolution frees the penitent from all censures, including those he omitted to mention.[59]

The negative clause is restrictive and, first, excludes from the absolution in general terms the *four censures most specially reserved to the Pope.* Secondly, it denies the benefit of absolution from censures that have been concealed purposely or *mala fide.* One reason for this is that it depends on the will of the superior, who is not supposed to coöperate with sinful and deliberate deception, as his power is not for destruction, but for edification. Another reason is to safeguard the dignity of censures.

Quite different from this question is that of an invalid confession, in which the censures were either mentioned or *bona fide* omitted. This question is not solved by our text.[60]

ABSOLUTION FROM SIN AND CENSURE

Can. 2250

§1. Si agatur de censura quae non impedit Sacramentorum receptionem, censuratus, rite dispositus et

59 Ballerini-Palmieri, *l. c.,* Vol. V, n. 753, p. 414 ff.

60 The more probable opinion admits the validity of the absolution from censures confessed in an invalid confession; Ballerini-Palmieri, *l. c.,* Vol. V, n. 760, p. 417.

a contumacia recedens, potest absolvi a peccatis, firma censura.

§2. Si vero agatur de censura quae impedit Sacramentorum receptionem, censuratus nequit absolvi a peccatis, nisi prius a censura absolutus fuerit.

§3. Absolutio censurae in foro sacramentali continetur in consueta forma absolutionis peccatorum in libris ritualibus praescripta; in foro non sacramentali quolibet modo dari potest, sed ad excommunicationis absolutionem regulariter formam adhiberi convenit in eisdem libris traditam.

Since the administration of the Sacraments and their efficacy depend solely on the will and institution of Christ, whereas absolution from censures depends on the will of man, *i. e.,* the superior or positive law, it follows that absolution from sin and absolution from censures are two different acts, even though they may be performed by means of the same formula.

1. Hence *one may be absolved from sin,* and therefore be in the state of grace, yet remain under censure. This is admitted by the text in case of a censure which *does not prevent the censured from receiving the Sacraments,* provided the penitent is properly disposed for receiving the Sacrament of Penance and gives up his contumacy, according to can. 2242, §3. Thus one placed under suspension, local interdict or interdict *ab ingressu ecclesiae* (can. 2276) may validly and licitly be absolved from sin, and yet remain suspended or interdicted. Of course, if the censure entailed a prohibition of saying Mass, he could not licitly perform this function.

2. If, on the other hand, there is question of a censure which *prevents the reception of the Sacraments, absolution*

from censure must be imparted before absolution from sin can licitly [61] *be granted.* This is the case with excommunication. The reason for this distinction lies in the separable effects of the respective censures as well as in the will of the lawgiver; see also can. 2247, §3.

3. *Formula of Absolution.* The text distinguishes *two fora,* the sacramental and the non-sacramental. The latter is again distinguished according to the kind of censures involved. Hence:

a) If absolution is given in the tribunal of penance *(in foro sacramentali),* the usual form contained in the Roman Ritual [62] should be employed.

b) In the non-sacramental forum *(in foro non-sacramentali),* either for the court of conscience or for the external forum, any formula may be used if no excommunication is implied; hence also the short formula for the confessional is permitted.

c) If, however, absolution is to be given *from excommunication,* the formula prescribed in the Roman Ritual (or Pontifical) should, as a rule, be employed.[63] *Regulariter,* therefore, admits a departure from the general rule, and in urgent cases the confessional or even the abbreviated formula may be used.

There is also in the Ritual [64] a formula for absolving a person who has been under excommunication, but has given signs of repentance before dying. The purpose of this absolution, as is evident from the same Ritual, con-

---

61 The text does not call for invalidity; Cappello, *l. c.,* p. 28.

62 Tit. III, c. 2 (ed. Pustet, 1913, p. 66 f.). " *Misereatur tui. . . . Indulgentiam. . . . Dominus noster. . . . Passio. . . .*" In urgent cases: "*Ego te absolvo ab omnibus censuris et peccatis in nomine Patris et Filii et Spiritus Sancti.*"

63 *Ibid.,* tit. III, c. 3 (ed. cit., p. 68 ff.).

64 Tit. III, c. 4, where *verberare corpus* means to touch the body or coffin with the (penitential) rod, which is a reminder of the *virga* of I Cor. IV, 21.

sists in permitting ecclesiastical burial. Absolution from censures may be imparted validly in any form, written or oral, nor is it required that the party be personally present; even absent and unwilling persons may be absolved.[65]

ABSOLUTION IN THE EXTERNAL AND INTERNAL FORUM

Can. 2251

Si absolutio censurae detur in foro externo, utrumque forum afficit: si in interno, absolutus, remoto scandalo, potest uti talem se habere etiam in actibus fori externi; sed, nisi concessio absolutionis probetur aut saltem legitime praesumatur in foro externo, censura potest a Superioribus fori externi, quibus reus parere debet, urgeri, donec absolutio in eodem foro habita fuerit.

The formula of absolution, although distinct as to the two fora (sacramental and non-sacramental), does not touch the effects of absolution in either. But the case is different when we say that absolution was given in *the external forum,* and when we say it was imparted in *the internal forum,* either in the Sacrament of Penance or outside this Sacrament, but for the court of conscience. The reason for this distinction lies in the effects and the purpose of censures, which concern the public welfare of the Church, the avenging of crime, and the reparation of scandal or damage. This can more efficaciously be obtained and urged if the absolution given *in foro interno* is not admitted as sufficient in the external forum.[65] But

65 Capello, p. 29. Laymann, P. 6 (*ed Venet.*, 1690, Vol. I, *Theol. Moral.*, I, tract, 5, P. I, c. 7. p. 91).

our text is very cautiously worded and avoids any insinuation as to the validity of an absolution given in the internal forum which would properly require an absolution for the external forum. Take, for instance, can. 2319, §1, n. 1. A marriage contracted before a non-Catholic minister is no doubt a notorious or public crime, entailing excommunication reserved to the Ordinary. Therefore the pastor or curate who has received from the Ordinary the faculty to absolve the guilty party, should give the absolution *in foro externo* in order to make sure of its validity.[66]

The text says:

1.° Absolution given *in foro externo* affects both fora, the internal as well as the external; concerning this there never was a doubt.[67]

2.° If the absolution was given *in foro interno,* the person thus absolved may conduct himself as one absolved or freed from censure also concerning acts of the external forum, provided *the scandal has been removed.*

Returning to our case (can. 2319), a priest endowed with the proper faculties may impart absolution *in foro interno, i. e.,* either in the Sacrament of Penance or outside of it. If the couple is unknown in the place of absolution, there will be no scandal; but there might be if they were well known and would stay away from the Sacraments. Consequently, the parties may go to the Sacraments and perform other legal ecclesiastical acts, even if they were absolved only *in foro interno,* or, as we say, privately.

3.° However, continues the text, *if absolution was given*

---

[66] And since it is an excommunication, the *formula propria* should be used according to *Rit. Rom.,* tit. III, c. 3.

[67] S. Poenit., April 27, 1886, ad 4 (*Coll. P. F.,* n. 1655).

privately only, the superiors of the external forum, before whom the censured person is bound to appear, may insist upon the censure until absolution is given in the external forum, unless evidence is furnished that absolution was granted, or may be lawfully presumed, for the external forum.

Notice (a) that the text does not imply invalidity [68] of the absolution given privately, provided of course the power or faculty was not wanting; (b) that the superior enjoying jurisdiction *in foro externo* is not obliged to urge the censure unconditionally, but only under the condition (c) that evidence is wanting or presumption. Evidence may be had from the certificate of absolution or through an official document issued by the one who absolved *in foro interno*. Presumption or circumstantial evidence would be the giving of satisfaction, also witnesses who had seen the party go to confession or heard of it.[69]

Urgere censuram means to demand that the parties conduct themselves as censured, and therefore abstain from performing any and all acts forbidden by the censure. The Ordinary is entitled to urge the censure in the case of can. 2319 and of can. 2314, §2. In cases of *occult censures,* if neither scandal nor promulgation or denunciation are involved, absolution given in the internal forum would certainly be sufficient.[70]

Regulars cannot absolve penitents from censures for the external forum, and those whom they do absolve, if denounced by the Ordinaries, must conduct themselves

---

[68] Missionaries could absolve apostates and heretics only *in foro conscientiae,* and those thus absolved had to present themselves before the Holy Office or the Ordinary, "*si velint esse tuti in foro ex-* *teriori*"; S. O., Jan. 3, 1640; Sept. 28, 1672 (*Coll. P. F.,* nn. 98, 204).

[69] Ballerini-Palmieri, *l. c.,* VII, n. 320, p. 162.

[70] Laymann, *l. c.;* see can. 2237, § 2.

as censured.[71] The reason is substantially the same: the bishop is entitled to have a guarantee of absolution and satisfaction, especially if the censure was publicly declared or is likely to cause a juridical investigation;[72]— in other words, if it should become notorious.

THOSE EMPOWERED TO ABSOLVE FROM CENSURES

The following three canons point out three distinct classes of cases. The first treats of the danger in which any priest may absolve; the second outlines the regular administration under normal conditions, and the last provides for urgent and special situations. They show how the Church adapts her laws to the exigencies of the times.

I. ABSOLUTION IN DANGER OF DEATH

Can. 2252

Qui in periculo mortis constituti, a sacerdote, specialis facultatis experte, receperunt absolutionem ab aliqua censura ab homine vel a censura specialissimo modo Sedi Apostolicae reservata, tenentur, postquam convaluerint, obligatione recurrendi, sub poena re-incidentiae, ad illum qui censuram tulit, si agatur de censura ab homine; ad S. Poenitentiariam vel ad Episcopum aliumve facultate praeditum, ad normam can. 2254, §1, si de censura a iure; eorumque mandatis parendi.

The Decretals [73] demanded, as a rule, personal

---

71 Clement X, "Superna," June 21, 1670, § 7.

72 S. C. P. F., Jan. 14, 1726 (Coll., n. 305).

73 Cfr. cc. 3, 26, 58, X, V, 39. C. 22, 6°, V, 11.

appearance before the " Apostolic Lord " to receive his order in case of a reserved censure. At the same time they admitted exceptions in the cases of women, old or sickly persons, and especially in cases where there was danger of death. But in this latter instance the obligation of a personal visit to Rome remained, as soon as the patient recovered sufficiently, under pain of falling back into censure. [74] The Friars Preachers and Friars Minor had obtained the faculty to absolve from censures in case of impending death, but under the same conditions. Every reservation ceased after the Council of Trent, whose ruling has passed into the Code.[74a] Hence any validly ordained priest, no matter what his juridical or moral standing, may absolve in danger of death from any sin or censure.

Our text also supposes that a *special faculty* required for absolving from reserved censures is *wanting in the priest* who otherwise may enjoy ordinary jurisdiction *in foro poenitentiae,* and says:

1°. When in *danger of death* [75] one may be absolved by any priest, even though the priest has no jurisdiction or faculties to absolve from the censure in question; but

2°. *After recovery, i. e.,* after being fully restored to health, the penitent is bound to have recourse to the proper authority, under penalty of falling back into the censure

3°. If absolution has been given from a censure reserved *ab homine,* or *modo specialissimo* reserved to the Apostolic

---

[74] C. I, *Extrav. Comm.,* V, 7 (Bened. XI, A. D. 1304). [74a] Sess. 4, c. 7, *de Poenit.,* can. 882.

[75] When the Archbishop of Cincinnati asked when the penitents could be said to be in danger or *in articulo* (at the point) of death the Holy Office referred him to approved authors; S. O., Sept. 13, 1859, ad 1 (*Coll. P. F.,* n. 1181). As a rule, the danger of death may be supposed when the penitent is in such a state that he has an equal chance for life or death, be the danger internal, (sickness, wounds, birth, old age) or external (war, perilous journey); Cappello, *l. c.,* p. 33.

See, *recourse* must be had to the one who inflicted the censure, if it was a censure *ab homine*. The recourse must be had to the S. *Poenitentiaria*, or to the bishop, or to another endowed with the faculty of absolving, if the censure was one *a iure, i. e., specialissimo modo* reserved to the Holy See.

4°. This recourse implies that the penitent *abide by the order* of the respective superiors. The term "*mandatis parendi*" implies willingness and promptness to carry out the injunctions given, either orally or in writing. Generally there is attached to the rescript of absolution the clause: "*iniunctis de iure iniungendis.*" This signifies:

(a) that the censured party must give satisfaction to those who were hurt or damaged by the criminal act for which he or she was censured;

(b) that scandal be repaired if any was given;

(c) that other imposed works, such as sacramental confession or penance, be accepted.[76]

Note that only the four cases reserved *specialissimo modo (i. e., a iure)* require recourse under penalty of reincidence. All other censures reserved *a iure* to the Apostolic See, either *simplici* or *speciali modo,* as well as the cases reserved by law to the Ordinary, do not call for such recourse.

The text alludes to the bishop or other priest, *aliumve facultate praeditum*. Ordinaries, therefore, also need faculties to receive such a recourse and to impart absolution in the four cases mentioned.[77]

---

[76] Cappello, *l. c.*, p. 80. The term "*standi mandatis ecclesiae*" has been explained as the obligation of having recourse, either personally or through the confessor, to the Roman Pontiff; S. O., Aug. 19, 1891; March 30, 1892 (*Coll. P. F.,* nn. 1764, 1788). This is expressed in the text.

[77] The faculties issued May 6, 1919, for the nuncios, internuncios, and Apostolic delegates do not

In can. 2254, §1, the rule is laid down that recourse should be made by letter or through the confessor. It also indicates the time within which recourse must be made, *i. e.*, a month from recovery.

2. ABSOLUTION WHEN THERE IS NO DANGER OF DEATH

Can. 2253

Extra mortis periculum possunt absolvere:

1.° **A censura non reservata, in foro sacramentali quilibet confessarius; extra forum sacramentale quicunque iurisdictionem in foro externo habeat in reum;**

2.° **A censura *ab homine*, ille, cui censura reservata est ad norman can. 2245, §2; ipse autem potest absolutionem concedere, etiamsi reus alio domicilium vel quasi-domicilium transtulerit;**

3.° **A censura *a iure reservata*, ille qui censuram constituit vel cui reservata est, eorumque successores aut competentes Superiores aut delegati. Quare a censura reservata *Episcopo* vel *Ordinario*, quilibet Ordinarius absolvere potest suos subditos, loci vero Ordinarius etiam peregrinos; a reservata *Sedi Apostolicae*, haec aliive qui absolvendi potestatem ab ea impetraverint sive generalem, si censura *simpliciter reservata* sit, sive specialem, si *reservata speciali modo*, sive denique specialissimam, si *reservata specialissimo modo*, salvo praescripto can. 2254.**

This canon regulates the ordinary administration, under normal conditions, of the penitential jurisdiction in the internal and external forum with regard to censures. It

contain this power; nor do those issued in 1920 to the Vicar-Apostolic of North Carolina.

is *the rule,* whenever danger of death or urgent cases do not justify a departure.

1. As to *non-reserved censures.* From these *every duly approved confessor* may validly and licitly absolve in the tribunal of penance for the internal as well as the external forum; but for the latter, absolution holds good only under the condition laid down in can. 2251. If absolution is to be given outside the confessional, it must be imparted by the one who has jurisdiction over the delinquent *in foro externo.* Therefore, a pastor or curate cannot absolve from non-reserved censures outside the confessional, unless he has received delegated power to do so from his bishop.

This absolution given in *foro externo* also affects the court of conscience (can. 2251).

2. As to *reserved censures ab homine.* From these only he who has inflicted the censure, or his competent superior, or his successor or delegate, can absolve, as stated under can. 2245, §5. However, he who is entitled to impart absolution may grant it also in a strange territory, *i. e.,* even though the delinquent has set up his domicile or quasi-domicile elsewhere. This is according to the *forum delicti,* as stated in can. 1566.

3. To absolve from censures reserved *a iure* the competency is first determined according to the general principle: " he can loose who can bind, " *i. e.,* he who set up the law enacting the censures can absolve from it.[78] But the supreme lawgiver reserves certain censures to the Ordinaries and to exempt religious superiors.

Therefore two points are to be observed: the *lawgiver* as far as he has enacted the censure as law, and the *reservation.* The general principle is that the *successors* of the lawgiver or those to whom the censures are re-

78 See cc. 29, 39, X, V, 39.

served, the competent superiors of these, and, finally, the *delegates* of either, may absolve.[79] These authorities are specially mentioned.

a) An *Ordinary* may absolve his subjects everywhere from censures reserved *Episcopo* or *Ordinario;* the *local* Ordinary may absolve also *peregrini.*

By Ordinaries must be understood

1.° All *bishops,* also titular bishops, who enjoy the privilege of choosing for themselves any confessor, and also their dependents, who by this very choice obtain jurisdiction to absolve from censures reserved to the Ordinary.[80]

2.° *Abbots or prelates nullius* who enjoy the same power, with the exception of the privilege just mentioned (can. 349), unless they are bishops.

3.° *Vicars-general, vicars-capitular* (administrators), *vicars* and *prefects Apostolic.*

4.° *The major superiors* of exempt clerical religious orders may either personally or through a delegate absolve their own subjects [81] from every censure *iure* reserved to the Ordinary.

The Ordinaries mentioned under n. 1 to 4, with the sole exception of titular bishops, may also absolve their subjects from *occult* censures reserved *simplici modo* to the Holy See.

Finally *Cardinals* enjoy the privilege of absolving from any censure, except the four *specialissimo modo* reserved to the Pope.[82]

---

79 *Delegatus* is referred to both superiors and successors and implicitly to the delegate of the lawgiver or *reservans* by law.

80 See can. 349, § 1, n. 1 as compared with can. 239, § 1, n. 2; but this is a personal privilege, not communicable to others, except as far as the canon permits.

81 A prelate cannot absolve one who is not his subject by reason of profession or obedience, unless the approved Constitutions give him that right.

82 Can. 239, § 1, n. 1 f.

It goes without saying that the *Sovereign Pontiff* may, either himself or through his delegates, absolve from any censure reserved either *a iure* or *ab homine*.

b) Only the Apostolic See itself can *de iure* absolve from censures *reserved to the Apostolic See;* every inferior needs faculties, which are of a threefold kind:

1.° A *special faculty* is required for absolving from censures which are reserved to the Apostolic See *simplici modo*.

2.° A *special faculty* is required to absolve from censures reserved to the Apostolic See *modo speciali*.[83]

3.° A *most special* faculty is needed to absolve from the four cases reserved to the Apostolic See *modo specialissimo*.

3. ABSOLUTION IN MORE URGENT CASES

Can. 2254

§1. In casibus urgentioribus, si nempe censurae latae sententiae exterius servari nequeant sine periculo gravis scandali vel infamiae, aut si durum sit poenitenti in statu gravis peccati permanere per tempus necessarium ut Superior competens provideat, tunc quilibet confessarius in foro sacramentali ab eisdem, quoquo modo reservatis, absolvere potest, iniuncto onere recurrendi, sub poena reincidentiae, intra mensem saltem per epistolam et per confessarium, si id fieri possit sine gravi incommodo, reticito nomine, ad S. Poenitentiariam vel ad Episcopum

---

83 An Apostolic Delegate has the general and special, but not the most special, faculty; see Faculties, May 19, 1919, n. 4; Prelates regular, after the Constitution "*Apostolicae Sedis*," 1869, could no longer—nor can they now—absolve from cases *simpliciter* reserved to the Apostolic See; *S. Poenit.*, Dec. 5, 1873 (*Coll. P. F.*, n. 1409).

aliumve Superiorem praeditum facultate et standi eius mandatis.

§2. Nihil impedit quominus poenitens, etiam post acceptam, ut supra, absolutionem, facto quoque recursu ad Superiorem, alium adeat confessarium facultate praeditum, ab eoque, repetita confessione saltem delicti cum censura, consequatur absolutionem; qua obtenta, mandata ab eodem accipiat, quin teneatur postea stare aliis mandatis ex parte Superioris supervenientibus.

§3. Quod si in casu aliquo extraordinario hic recursus sit moraliter impossibilis, tunc ipsemet confessarius, excepto casu quo agatur de absolutione censurae de qua in can. 2367, potest absolutionem concedere sine onere de quo supra, iniunctis tamen de iure iniungendis, et imposita congrua poenitentia et satisfactione pro censura, ita ut poenitens, nisi intra congruum tempus a confessario praefiniendum poenitentiam egerit ac satisfactionem dederit, recidat in censuram.

Although the Decretals allude to legitimate impediments preventing a personal appearance in Rome, the case, as it is now formulated, is rather modern.[84] Besides the aforesaid Decretals demanded a sworn guarantee (*debita cautio sub iuramento*) before one could be absolved by a bishop or a simple priest. This more especially when the *privilegium canonis* had been violated.

The first section of can. 2254 states and circumscribes the case, §2 modifies it, and §3 mitigates the requirement of recourse.

1. In more *urgent cases any duly approved confessor*

[84] See cc. 29, 58, X, V, 39; c. 22, 6°, V, 11; S. O., June 23, 1886, (*Coll.* P. F., n. 1658): *"In casibus vere urgentioribus, in quibus. . . ."*

may validly and licitly absolve from each and every cen-sure, no matter how and to whom it is reserved, provided it is a censure *latae sententiae.*

Which cases are *more urgent,* is then stated as follows:

a) When *these censures cannot be exteriorly observed without serious danger of scandal or loss of reputation,* which may be the case if a priest would be obliged to exercise the sacred ministry, or if a layman in good standing would have to omit his Easter Communion; to judge whether this case is verified belongs to the confessor.[85]

b) Or if it would be *difficult for the penitent to remain in the state of grievous sin for the length of time required to obtain the necessary faculty from the competent superior.*[86] Whether and under what circumstances it would be difficult for a penitent to remain in this state, must be left to the judgment of the confessor, who certainly may apply the rule: "*Poenitenti credendum est.*" Therefore, if the penitent should say, one day would be hard, we think our canon could be applied, though some authors hold that at least a week, or three or four days, are required.[87]

The *obligation of the confessor* under such circumstances is:

a) That he absolve[88] in the *tribunal of penance;* hence he cannot absolve outside the confessional, because the *forum sacramentale* is not identical with the internal forum;

85 S. O., June 23, 1886, ad 2° (*Coll.,* n. 1658).

86 This reason is an enlargement of the former; S. O., June 16, 1897 (*Coll.,* n. 1971).

87 See Cappello, *l. c.,* p. 34. Frequent Communion should now-a-days also be reckoned with.

88 The absolution is a direct one, *i. e.,* one which remits the sin by virtue of the judicial (penitential) sentence given for that sin (under censure); S. O., Aug. 19, 1891, ad 3; March 30, 1892, ad 6 (*Coll. P. F.,* nn. 1764, 1788); Arregui, *l. c.,* p. 394.

b) That he impose *on the penitent* the strict and grievous *obligation of having recourse to the S. Poenitentiaria,* or to a bishop or other superior endowed with the necessary faculties to absolve him, and to abide by their orders;

c) That this recourse be imposed under penalty of reincidence (*sub poena reincidentiae*),[89] *i. e.,* of falling back into specifically the same censure from which he is now absolved;

d) To remind the penitent that recourse must be had *within a month,* to be reckoned probably from the day of absolution, or at least from the day when he became conscious of the obligation;

e) To tell the penitent that the recourse may be made by *letter,* in which case the proper names are to be entirely suppressed and fictitious names used, or personally, because a personal visit to Rome is not excluded;

f) For the confessor to remember that he, too, is bound to have recourse to the competent authority, unless a serious obstacle prevents him.

Here we may add two decisions of the *S. Poenitentiaria.*[90]

1.° That the recourse cannot be spared the penitent, even if the post-office authorities or civil power should open the letter, because fictitious names are given.

2.° If the penitent is a transient, whom the confessor may not meet again, it suffices that a serious promise be demanded of him to have recourse to the competent

---

[89] This reincidence concerns censures reserved to the Apostolic See *modo simplici,* and consequently also those reserved *speciali* and *specialissimo modo;* S. O., June 17, 1891, ad 2 (*Coll.,* n. 1756).

[90] S. Poenit., Nov. 7, 1888 (*Coll. P. F.,* n. 1695, ad. 5 et 6). The month is, of course, to be understood as the minimum, or, as we say, *ad urgendam,* not *ad finiendam, obligationem.*

authorities. In this case, we incline to believe, the burden of writing should not be urged against the confessor.

§2 says the penitent is at liberty to *approach another confessor endowed with the necessary faculties* and to obtain absolution from him. This right is granted even in case the penitent has already been absolved (in urgent necessity) and has had recourse to the competent authority. But the penitent has *again* to *confess* the *censured sin* to this other confessor, in order that the latter may know the nature of the case and impose the necessary injunctions. After that absolution the penitent has merely to carry out the orders given by the second confessor and is not bound to abide by the injunctions of the superior to whom recourse was had, which may reach him later.

§3 modifies the requirement of recourse. If in some extraordinary case, it says, *recourse should be morally impossible,* the confessor may grant absolution without imposing the obligation of recourse. However, in that case another obligation must be imposed, *viz., iniunctis de iure iniungendis,* and a proportionate penance and satisfaction for the censure. This obligation is so grave that if the penitent would not comply with the penance imposed and with the demand of satisfaction *within the time fixed* by the confessor, he would fall back into the same censure.

Recourse would be morally impossible, as the Holy Office has declared, if neither the penitent nor the confessor could write, and it would be hard for the penitent to approach another confessor; or if the penitent himself was unable to write, though the confessor was, but the latter would not be likely to meet the penitent again, in order to give him the answer.[91]

From this favor of omitting the recourse is *excluded the case of absolutio complicis* (can. 2367); and poverty or inconvenience to seek another confessor are not admitted as an excuse.[92]

[91] S. O., Nov. 9, 1898; Sept. 5, 1900 (*Coll.*, nn. 2023, 2095).

[92] S. O., June 7, 1899 (*Coll.*, n. 2052).

CHAPTER II

Can. 2255

§1. Censurae sunt:

1.° Excommunicatio;

2.° Interdictum;

3.° Suspensio.

§2. Excommunicatio afficere potest tantum personas physicas, et ideo, si quando feratur in corpus morale, intelligitur singulos afficere qui in delictum concurrerint; interdictum et suspensio, etiam communitatem, ut personam moralem; excommunicatio et interdictum, etiam laicos; suspensio, clericos tantum; interdictum, etiam locum; excommunicatio est semper censura; interdictum et suspensio possunt esse vel censurae vel poenae vindicativae, sed in dubio praesumuntur censurae.

Can. 2256

In canonibus qui sequuntur:

1.° Nomine divinorum officiorum intelliguntur functiones potestatis ordinis, quae de instituto Christi vel Ecclesiae ad divinum cultum ordinantur et a solis clericis fieri queunt;

2.° Nomine autem actuum legitimorum ecclesiasticorum significantur: munus administratoris gerere bonorum ecclesiasticorum; partes agere iudicis, auditoris et relatoris, defensoris vinculi, promotoris iustitiae et fidei, notarii et cancellarii, cursoris et apparitoris, advocati et procuratoris in causis ecclesiasticis; munus patrini agere in sacramentis baptismi et confirmationis; suffragium ferre in electionibus ecclesiasticis; ius patronatus exercere.

These two canons enumerate the censures, then state on whom and how they may be inflicted, and, lastly, set forth the significance of certain terms connected with the effects of censures.

I. There are *three kinds of censures:*

1. Excommunication,
2. Interdict,
3. Suspension.

This enumeration is complete and has never varied since the time of the Decretals.[1] Consequently, irregularity arising from crime (*ex delicto*) is no censure, although some have asserted it, as Benedict XIV says.[2]

II. §2 of can. 2255 determines the *subject* on whom censures may be inflicted, distinguishing between physical and moral or artificial persons, laymen and clergymen, persons and places.

a) *Excommunication* can affect *only single individuals.* Therefore, if this censure is inflicted on a corporation, the meaning can only be that the members of that corporation, as far as they are guilty of, or partakers in, the censured crime, are intended.

b) The *interdict* and *suspension* may be inflicted also on a *community* as such, *i. e.*, a corporation. The difference between excommunication and the interdict,

---

[1] See c. 20, X, V, 40; c. 1, 6°, V, 11. [2] "*Inter Praeteritos,*" Dec. 3, 1749, § 48.

as affecting or not affecting a corporation, lies in the respective effects. The effects of excommunication concern personal spiritual benefits and favors, *i. e.*, such as touch the soul and salvation of the individual, whereas the privation entailed by suspension or interdict is not of an individual spiritual character.[3] Hence excommunication can be inflicted only on real delinquents, although they may otherwise be punished as members of the corporation; for it is not necessary that each and every person be nominally censured (can. 2242, §1). If some authors go further and say that a corporation is not capable of being excommunicated because it forms a fictitious, not a real body, and has no soul (or rather will) in common,[4] they shoot beyond the mark. For a corporation has a collective will, and is capable of rights and obligations quite different from the rights and obligations inherent in its members as private citizens or non-members.[5] We need not stretch the imagination to comprehend a corporate will. It is the will of the community as expressed by its statutes and asserted by its lawful representatives. The *fictio iuris* is therefore quite superfluous; for since corporations are endowed with rights and obligations of their own, it is but logical that they should also be liable to punishment. This idea is not precisely embodied in the Roman, English or American law of old, but it prevails in modern times.[6] On the other hand, if a collective will were denied

---

[3] Cfr. Suarez, *De Cens.*, disp. 18, sect. 2, n. 3; Laymann, *Theol. Moral.*, l. I, tr. V, p. II, c. 1, n. 6.

[4] Thus Suarez, *I. c.*, c. 5. 6°, V, 11 insinuates the real reason: *"volentes animarum periculum vitare, quod exinde sequi posset, cum nonnunquam contingeret innoxios huiusmodi sententia irretire."*

[5] Wernz, *Ius Decret.*, VI, p. 24, n. 18.

[6] Kenny-Webb, *Outlines of Criminal Law*, 1907, p. 57 ff.; of course, the criminal liability of a corporation has its limits; for a corporation cannot be hanged, though it can be fined.

to a corporation, it is hardly conceivable that it could be interdicted or suspended. Hence we said that those who use this argument " shoot beyond the mark. " Consequently, the real and practical difference between excommunication not affecting a community as such on the one side, and interdict and suspension as affecting a community as such on the other hand, must be sought in the effects, *i. e.*, in the personal privation of intrinsically spiritual goods which properly concern the salvation of the soul.

c) *Excommunication* and *interdict* may be inflicted also on the *laity,* whilst *suspension* is for the *clergy* only.

d) An *interdict* may be laid on a *place,* not, of course, by reason of guilt or punishment in the proper sense, but as the container of culpable subjects or connected with an indictable crime.

e) *Excommunication* is always a censure, whereas *interdict* and *suspension* may be *either censures or vindictive penalties;* if it is doubtful whether they were inflicted as a censure or as a vindictive penalty, they are presumed to be censures. Thus an interdict or suspension *in perpetuum* or *ad tempus praefinitum,* or *ad beneplacitum superioris* (can. 2291, n. 1 f.; 2298, n. 2) is a vindictive penalty.

In order to remove every doubt, the censures should be named as to persons and species, and hence terms should be used which clearly indicate the nature of the penalty according to the common usage of the Church and the schools. This is true chiefly of a censure *ferendae sententiae,* or rather, let us say, of a censure *ab homine.* For a penalty *a iure* or *latae sententiae* is already clearly marked out and only requires the verification of the criminal act. Thus a censure *latae sententiae* does not demand a canonical admonition, though a declaratory sentence may be necessary in certain circumstances (can. 2232). The reason for this wording lies in the necessity of an external and sufficient manifestation of the superior's will.[7]

From this it is also apparent why the legislator *presumes censures* rather than vindictive penalties. For although censures are grievous penalties, yet absolution must be granted as soon as contumacy ceases (can. 2248, §2), whereas vindictive penalties may, but must not, be removed by dispensation or relaxation. Besides, vindictive penalties may be meted out for past crimes, but censures are inflicted for delinquencies which are of a prospective and enduring nature.[8] The presumption here mentioned is that called *iuris*, but not *iuris et de iure*, and hence admits direct as well as indirect evidence (can. 1825 f.).

III. Can. 2256 *explains* the *terms* used to designate certain effects or consequences of penalties which occur in the following canons.

a) By *divine offices*[9] are to be understood those functions of power of order (*potestatis ordinis*) which have been established by divine or ecclesiastical authority and are performed only by the clergy. Such are the celebration of Holy Mass, the administration of the Sacraments and sacramentals (blessings, sepulture, public service, preaching, choir service, processions) etc.

b) *Legal ecclesiastical acts* are those of official administrators of ecclesiastical property; those of the following persons employed in the ecclesiastical court: judge, auditor, relator, *defensor vinculi* (for marriage and ordination), fiscal promotor and promotor of faith

---

[7] Wernz, *l. c.*, VI, n. 165 ff., p. 169 f.

[8] Laymann, *l. c.*, n. 3.

[9] Cfr. can. 2259, § 1; private

(for beatification and canonization), courier and beadle, lawyer and proxy; those of sponsois at Baptism and Confirmation; — the (active) voice [10] or right of voting at ecclesiastical elections, including those held by monastic chapters and chapters of religious communities and acts of actual (not habitual) exercise of the *ius-patronatus* or advowson.

ART. I

EXCOMMUNICATION

In general terms excommunication means the act of excluding or the state of being excluded from the communion of the faithful; practically speaking, the Church is the society of *the* faithful.

Being therefore, an autonomous society, the Church is logically entitled to set up conditions not only for admittance, but also for remaining in what is a juridically closed society. In other words, the Church, like any other organization, has the power to deprive unworthy members of the rights and privileges of membership. Of course, a complete or radical loss of membership is impossible, since the baptismal character is indelible. But the bonds of external communion can be severed. This punishment was hinted at very plainly when our Lord said: " If he will not hear the church, let him be to thee as the heathen and publican." [11] Excommunication was no doubt also understood when the Apostle said: "deliver such a one to Satan" and "put away the evil one from among yourselves." [12]

devotions are not included in this term; Eichmann, *l. c.*, p. 90.

10 Since the text reads *suffragium ferre*, it can only mean the active, not passive, voice (can. 19); cfr.

Wernz, *l. c.*, n. 114, p. 117; Eichmann, *l. c.*, p. 90.

11 Matth. 18, 17.

12 I Cor. 5, 5, 13; II Thess. 3, 14; Kober, *Der Kirchenbann*, 1863, p. 9 ff.

The technical name for excommunication is ἀορισμός, sometimes with the adjective " entire " or accompanied by the word *anathema*. The words " *excommunicati et ecclesia eiecti* " are used by ancient synods.[13] The effect of excommunication was separation from the community of the faithful, in order to bring the delinquent to his senses, but also to purify and protect the community itself.

Besides this entire or full separation, there came into existence, towards the beginning of the fifth century, a milder form of exclusion, which consisted in forbidding the culprit to participate in the Eucharistic supper in certain parts of the public service, and in prayer. This *minor excommunication* was often connected with public penance, but after the public penitential system in the IXth century was abated, it developed into a separate excommunication of a peculiar disciplinary character. In virtue of the Decree of Martin V, " *Ad evitanda,* " of 1418, this penalty was incurred by those who unlawfully conversed or communicated with excommunicated persons and by such as were guilty of transgressing the *privilegium canonis, i. e.,* the notorious beaters of clerics.[14]

Mention was made above of *anathema* [15] as distinct from excommunication. The term occurs in the Decree of Gratian,[16] which permits us to look upon anathema as major or full excommunication, whilst excommunication without any further addition and as distinguished from or opposed to, anathema would be identical with minor excom-

---

[13] Thus the Synod of Antioch, A. D. 341, c. 1 (Mansi, *Coll. Concil.,* II. 1307): ἀκοινωνήτους καὶ ἀποβλήτους; those who refused to conform to the celebration of Easter as prescribed by the Council of Nicaea.

[14] The text is preserved in two somewhat different wordings; see Hollweck, *l. c.,* Appendix I, p. 355; *infra,* can. 2258.

[15] See Numb. XXI, 3; I Cor. XVI, 22; "*anathema, maranatha.*"

[16] See c. 12, C. 3, q. 4; c. 41, C. II, q. 3; Kober, *l. c.,* p. 37.

munication,[17] although the distinction is not very clear. Therefore Gregory IX simplified the terminology by defining excommunication pure and simple as full or major excommunication [18] and leaving "minor excommunication" untouched. *Anathema* then appears as the more solemn form of pronouncing or declaring excommunication. *Maranatha* [19] merely enhanced the outward solemnity. The *excommunicatio minor* was officially abolished by the Constitution "*Apostolicae Sedis*," 1869, and the commentators who held that it had been abolished —at least as *censura latae sententiae et iuris*—were upheld by an authentic decision of the Holy Office.[20] The Code leaves no room for minor excommunication in whatever form.

Our text first defines the nature and species of excommunication and then determines its effects.

NATURE AND DIVISION

Can. 2257

§1. **Excommunicatio est censura qua quis excluditur a communione fidelium cum effectibus qui in canonibus, qui sequuntur, enumerantur, quique separari nequeunt.**

§2. **Dicitur quoque** *anathema,* **praesertim si cum sollemnitatibus infligatur quae in Pontificali Romano describuntur.**

17 C. 58, X, V, 39.
18 Kober, *l. c.*, p. 38.
19 I Cor. XVI, 22. It means: Until the Lord cometh or returneth; see Suarez, *De Cens.*, disp. IX, sect. 2, n. 4 f.

20 S. O., Dec. 5, 1883 (*Coll. P. F.*, n. 1608); Hollweck, *l. c.*, p. 114. It would be well if the old formula for "*General Absolution*" granted on some occasions would also be recast.

Can. 2258

§1. Excommunicati alii sunt *vitandi,* alii *tolerati.*

§2. Nemo est vitandus, nisi fuerit nominatim a Sede Apostolica excommunicatus, excommunicatio fuerit publice denuntiata et in decreto vel sententia expresse dicatur ipsum vitari debere, salvo praescripto can. 2343, §1, n. 1.

§1. Excommunication is a censure excluding a person from the communion of the faithful and accompanied by the inseparable effects mentioned in the following canons.

In order to understand this exclusion it must be remembered that the Church is a juridical as well as a spiritual society, consisting of a body and a soul, similar to an individual or physical person. To the soul (*anima*) of the Church are referred sanctifying grace, the theological virtues (faith, hope, and charity), the supernatural moral virtues, as well as the gifts of the Holy Ghost. To the body *(corpus)* of the Church belong the visible members, as organized and governed by the lawful authority, also the external means conducive to the purpose of the Church, such as Sacraments and sacramentals, worship, the word of God, offices and benefices.[21]

The relation of the individual Catholic to the body of the Church is sometimes styled external communion, whilst his connection with the soul of the Church is called internal communion.[22] This latter communion is not *per se* severed by excommunication, as grace and charity can-

[21] Mazzella, *De Religione et Ecclesia,* 1892, p. 344 f.

[22] Reiffenstuel, V, 39, n. 55 ff., who, however, distinguishes communio pure interna, externa et mixta,—the two latter making up the external.

not be taken away by the penal sword of the Church, but
are lost only through grievous personal guilt.   And as this
guilt can be repaired by perfect contrition, it may happen
that one is excommunicated and yet lives in the friendship
of God.   Besides, faith and hope may coëxist with mortal
sin.[23]   Therefore, the exclusion from the communion of
the faithful concerns the external union with the Church
(*corpus Ecclesiae*) only.   But even this severance, as was
stated at the beginning of this article, cannot be radical,
otherwise an excommunicated person would have to be
rebaptized, which would imply the fallacy that the character of Baptism is not indelible.   Therefore an
aptitudinal or habitual relation to, or bond with, the body
of the Church remains even after the sentence of excommunication has gone into effect.   Nevertheless it is quite
true that, as St. Chrysostom says,[24] excommunication is
the heaviest and severest of all penalties.   For it entails
spiritual poverty and helplessness and exposure to more
vehement attacks from the powers of darkness, which are
apt to lead to obstinacy and final despair.

This spiritual helplessness is apparent from the *effects*
or consequences of excommunication.   These are called
inseparable from excommunication (*qui separari nequeunt*) because they always follow in its trail.   They
are neither modified nor extended, unlike suspension,
which admits restriction.

The text is also directed against the assumption of a
major and minor excommunication; and, therefore, the
sentence of minor excommunication (*ab homine*) must
be considered as abolished.   The reason for this
inseparability is easy to perceive.   Actual membership in
the Church is totally lost by excommunication.   Nor is

---

[23] C. 28, X, V, 39.   [24] *Contra Gentiles;* see Hollweck,
l. c., p. 115.

there any essential or juridical difference between excommunication and *anathema*, for the latter, as §2 of can. 2257 states, mainly means added solemnity, especially the solemn pronouncement of the formula of excommunication contained in the *Pontificale Romanum*.[25]

§2. Two *classes of excommunicated* persons are mentioned in can. 2258, *viz.:* those who are to be avoided (*vitandi*) and those who are tolerated (*tolerati*). This distinction is substantially, although not technically, embodied in the well-known decree of Martin V (1418), "*Insuper ad evitanda.*" Note, however, that this decree has come down in two different readings, one of them being that of the Council of Constance, as reported by St. Antoninus of Florence, the other that preserved in the acts of the Vth Lateran Council. The difference is rather substantial. For the Constance text mentions two kinds of *vitandi:* those publicly denounced and the notorious beaters of clerics; whereas the Lateran text enumerates three: the two just named and those who have so notoriously fallen into a sentence of excommunication that "no artifice can conceal it and no pretext of law excuse it."[26]

The Code, in §2 of can. 2258, rather favors the Constance text, which it considerably modifies, eliminating the notorious beaters of clerics and restricting personal denunciation to that made by the Apostolic See. Hence it says that *only those are vitandi who:*

a) Have been excommunicated nominally by the Apostolic See,

b) Whose excommunication was publicly announced, and

---

25 Title: "*Ordo excommunicandi et absolvendi*"; see also c. 106, C. II, q. 3, concerning the form of excommunication and anathema.

26 Hollweck, *l. c.*, Appendix I, p. 355.

c) Who have been expressly declared to be *vitandi* in the decree or sentence.

All these marks must *concur* in order to constitute an excommunicated person a *vitandus*.

Ad a). The *Apostolic See* is here understood as defined in can. 7, *viz.*: the Roman Pontiff or the Congregations, Tribunals, and Offices of the Roman Court.

Nominatim or by name means mentioning the excommunicated person's name or describing him so that no doubt remains as to his identity.[27] If only one name is mentioned, the accomplices, followers, and protectors of the *excommunicatus* are not *vitandi*, even though they commit an act forbidden under threat of excommunication, for there is no excommunication *latae sententiae* which renders one a *vitandus*.[28]

Ad b). The excommunication must be publicly announced (*publice denuntiata*), which is achieved by an authentic edict or decree; thus publication in the "*Acta Apostolicae Sedis*" would certainly be sufficient; also publication in a diocesan newspaper, if this is the official mouthpiece of the episcopal court. Publication in ordinary newspapers cannot claim an official character, and therefore one would not have to heed such a notice.[29] Neither would a denunciation before two witnesses be a public one, so that one thus denounced would become a *vitandus*.[30]

Ad c). The sentence or decree must expressly mention the fact that the excommunicated person is to be avoided; for, as stated above, there is no excommunication *latae*

27 Thus, for instance, Napoleon was excommunicated without mentioning his name, but clearly designated; Kober, *Der Kirchenbann*, p. 259.

28 Bened. XIV, *De Syn. Dioec.*, VII, 68, 4; Hollweck, *l. c.*, p. 123.

29 This applies also to the *Osservatore Romano*, because it is not *the* official organ of the Vatican.

30 Hollweck, *l. c.*, p. 123.

sententiae or *a iure* which *ipso facto* produces that effect. A *decree* is issued if no formal procedure is followed, because the fact of the criminal act and the contumacy are established. A *sentence* is issued after a trial.

Now, from these three combined conditions only one *exception* is made, *viz.*, that mentioned under can. 2343, §1, n. 1: for those who lay violent hands on the person of the Roman Pontiff. This is a remnant of the legislation concerning notorious beaters of clerics, but restricted to the sacred person of the Pontiff.

We may add that the distinction between *vitandi* and *tolerati* is not to be taken as intrinsically affecting the nature and consequences of excommunication. Both classes of *excommunicati* are equally cut off from the communion of the faithful, both experience the same effects, as far as religious communion is concerned.[31] The only difference regards civil intercourse, as will be seen under can. 2267.

INSEPARABLE EFFECTS

Suarez[32] notes that, although the adequate effect of excommunication is but one, namely, total exclusion from the communion of the faithful, yet in that communion may be distinguished several rights and favors. Privation of these rights, therefore, constitutes as many effects of excommunication.

The Code enumerates these effects, first, as to the

---

31 Suarez thought that an *excommunicatus toleratus* was still a member of the Church (*De fide*, disp. IX, sect. 1, n. 4); but Bellarmine (*De Ecclesia Milit.*, l. III, c. 6) held the correct doctrine; cfr. Mazzella, *De Religione et* Ecclesia, 1892, p. 474; Hollweck, l. c., p. 115 f. A difference is noted in can. 2262, § 2, n. 2, which seems to partake of the spiritual nature.

32 *De Censuris*, disp. IX, procem. (Vol. XXIII, p. 260).

officia divina, then as to *actus legitimi,* and, finally, as to civil intercourse.

EXCLUSION FROM DIVINE OFFICES

Can. 2259

§1. Excommunicatus quilibet caret iure assistendi divinis officiis, non tamen praedicationi verbi Dei.

§2. Si passive assistat toleratus, non est necesse ut expellatur; si vitandus, expellendus est, aut, si expelli nequeat, ab officio cessandum, dummodo id fieri possit sine gravi incommodo; ab assistentia vero activa, quae aliquam secumferat participationem in celebrandis divinis officiis, repellatur non solum vitandus, sed etiam quilibet post sententiam declaratoriam vel condemnatoriam aut alioquin notorie excommunicatus.

No excommunicated person has the right to assist at divine services; the only exception is hearing the word of God, which, therefore, is not forbidden. In the olden time even gentiles and heretics were allowed in church until the Mass of the catechumens began.[33] The sermon, though an ecclesiastical or divine office, and therefore specially mentioned in the text, is intended for instruction and correction.[34]

What *divine offices* are has been stated under can. 2256, n. 1, *viz.:* the acts of public worship performed in the name of the Church by her clergy, *e. g.,* the Holy Sacrifice of the Mass, the canonical office publicly recited by those who are obliged to recite it in virtue of can. 135 or can. 610, public prayers, processions (see can. 1290), blessings and consecrations performed according to the

[33] C. 67, Dist. 1, *de consecr.*   [34] C. 43, X, V, 39.

liturgical books of the Church.[35] Many popular devotions, like the Rosary, the Stations of the Cross, etc., even if recited under the leadership of a priest, are not divine offices in the sense of our text, and therefore an excommunicated person is not debarred[36] from them.

1. Assistance at sermons or lectures (*praedicatio verbi Dei*) does not permit assistance at the divine service,[37] preceding or following, as stated in §2.

2. Since the right of assisting at *Mass* is taken away, no obligation remains to hear *Mass* on Sundays and holydays. The most that can be asserted is the imputation of *voluntarium in causa* if an *excommunicatus* should neglect to ask for absolution for a considerable time[38] (but see can. 2254).

3. Somewhat different is the obligation of reciting the *Breviary*, privately, not in choir; all authors say that this duty remains, since the clergyman is a public person, and is, as a rule, furthermore obliged by reason of a benefice.[39]

§2 *of can.* 2259 determines more precisely the extent of the exclusion from divine offices. A twofold distinction is made: between active and passive assistance, and between *tolerati* and *vitandi*. *Active assistance* entails a certain participation in the celebration of divine offices; such as acting as sacristan, or acolythe, or sacred minister or organist, or choir-singer, or as a witness at weddings.[40] (For the matrimonial ceremony is both a

---

35 Laymann, *l. c.*, I., I, tr. V, p. II, c. 1, n. 6.

36 See *Stimmen der Zeit*, July 1920, Vol. 50, p. 316.

37 Laymann, *l. c.*

38 This is what Lehmkuhl says, II, n. 892, and is *sententia communis;* see Schmalzgrueber, V, 39, n. 131; Hollweck, *l. c.*, p. 119.

39 Laymann, *l. c.*, Lehmkuhl, *l. c.* The reciting clergyman should say "*Exaudi*," etc., instead of "*Dominus vobiscum*," *sub veniali*. He may also, for reasons of necessity or utility, employ a companion; Hilarius a Sexten, *l. c.*, p. 57.

40 C. 7, C. 11, q. 3. Congregational singing of liturgical songs, or

Sacrament on the side of the contracting parties, and a sacramental because of the nuptial blessing). *Passive attendance* may be understood as inactive or inert participation, which, of course excludes the recitation of prayers in common with the other faithful.

The text then says:

a) That *passive assistance may be permitted* to a *toleratus,* and it is not necessary to expel him from the assembly, *e. g.,* from the church or chapel, although the priest who says Mass and others may know of the excommunication.

b) *Active assistance* must be denied not only to *vitandi,* but also to any one who is excommunicated, even though *toleratus, after a declaratory or condemnatory sentence* has been issued or the excommunication has become notorious. This is in keeping with can. 2232, which safeguards the good name of the delinquent as long as no sentence or notoriety renders him disreputable.

c) *Vitandi* are denied active as well as passive assistance and must be *expelled* from the place where divine services are held.[41] Should expulsion be impossible,[42] because of great inconvenience, the divine office must cease at once, unless the rubrics demand a continuance. Thus, for instance, if Mass has already proceeded to the beginning of the Canon, it must be continued until Communion, inclusively, after which the priest should admonish the culprit to depart and, in case of resistance, leave the altar immediately if this can be done without serious conse-

---

participation therein, would fall under active assistance.

41 The constant formula in the Decretals is: *"excommunicatis et interdictis penitus exclusis";* cc. 43, 57, X, V, 39; c. 17, X, V, 40 and *passim.*

42 Formerly those who incited to disobedience in this regard or proved stubborn incurred the excommunication reserved to the Holy See; c. 2, Clem. V, 10.

quences.[43] The same applies to the distribution of Communion outside of the Mass. If quarrels or other evil results must be feared in case of interruption, the divine office may be completed. On the other hand, even a priest or religious who is *vitandus* may be expelled by laymen or a policeman without fear of violating the privilege of clerical immunity.[44]

RECEPTION AND ADMINISTRATION OF SACRAMENTS AND SACRAMENTALS

Can. 2260

§1. Nec potest excommunicatus Sacramenta recipere; imo post sententiam declaratoriam aut condemnatoriam nec Sacramentalia.

§2. Quod attinet ad ecclesiasticam sepulturam, servetur praescriptum can. 1240, §1, n. 2.

Can. 2261

§1. Prohibetur excommunicatus licite Sacramenta et Sacramentalia conficere et ministrare, salvis exceptionibus quae sequuntur.

§2. Fideles, salvo praescripto §3, possunt ex qualibet iusta causa ab excommunicato Sacramenta et Sacramentalia petere, maxime si alii ministri desint, et tunc excommunicatus requisitus potest eadem ministrare neque ulla tenetur obligatione causam a requirente percontandi.

§3. Sed ab excommunicatis vitandis necnon ab aliis excommunicatis, postquam intercessit sententia con-

---

43 He may finish in the sacristy or simply close the Mass there and then; Laymann, *l. c.*

44 Cfr. c. 16, X, V, 39; Laymann, *l. c.*

demnatoria aut declaratoria, fideles in solo mortis periculo possunt petere tum absolutionem sacramentalem ad normam can. 882, 2252, tum etiam, si alii desint ministri, cetera Sacramenta et Sacramentalia.

These two canons are closely related to each other, because both treat of the same subject, *viz.*: the Sacraments and Sacramentals. Can. 2260 determines the reception or passive use of the Sacraments, whilst can. 2261 treats of the minister or active administration of these means of grace.

1. *No excommunicated person can (lawfully) receive the Sacraments, and after a declaratory or condemnatory sentence he cannot even receive the Sacramentals.*[45] Notice the word "lawfully"; we have added it, within brackets, because it conveys the true meaning of the text; for the reception of the Sacraments by an excommunicated person would be valid, though illicit, with the exception of Penance. The reason is that the efficacy of the Sacraments in general does not depend on human or ecclesiastical will and command, but on the institution of Christ, but the validity of the Sacrament of Penance depends on jurisdiction, which may be taken away by ecclesiastical authority.[46]

The use of the *sacramentals* (can. 1144) by an excommunicated person is forbidden only after a declaratory or condemnatory sentence of excommunication has been issued. Sacramentals may be considered under a twofold aspect:

a) As acts or things of a private person or for private devotion and pious use, or

b) As sacred things purposely used for the sake of the

---

[45] See cc. 32, 59, X, V, 39. [46] Laymann, *l. c.*, c. I, tr. V, p. 5, c. 4, n. 1.

spiritual benefit which accrues to them from the blessing or consecration of the Church. As public or ecclesiastical means of devotion they are forbidden to the excommunicated. But in their private devotion they may make use of them. Thus the use of sacred images, Holy Water, the sign of the Cross is permitted them.[47]

Excommunicated persons may even enter a church privately to pray there. On the other hand, priests are not allowed to impart blessings to them, e. g., bless candles, bread, etc., for them or give them the blessing *post partum;* for this would be not merely private but public worship. It may also be noted that, as excommunicated persons are obliged *sub gravi* to abstain from receiving the Sacraments (urgent cases — see can. 2252, 2254 — excepted) so ministers are bound to refrain from administering these to such persons.[48]

Concerning *ecclesiastical burial* consult can. 1240, §1, n. 2, which excludes from this sacramental all excommunicated persons against whom a declaratory or condemnatory sentence has been issued; a *fortiori,* of course, the *vitandi.*

Can. 2261, §1 *prohibits excommunicated persons from administering the Sacraments and sacramentals,* and priests from saying Mass.

Here the text expressly uses *licite* (lawfully), which undoubtedly refers to all the Sacraments, except Penance, under certain conditions explained in can. 2264. As the power of order, which is required for the administration of the Sacraments, cannot be lost, the validity is not

---

47 The use of the Sacramentals is permitted, not in order to obtain the fruits derived from the blessing of the Church, but to venerate them; Hilarius a Sexten, *l. c.,* p. 56. It may even be useful, *ex opere operantis,* inasmuch as this act may produce a proper disposition on the part of the excommunicated person.

48 Suarez, *De Censuris,* disp. X, sect. 1 and 2; cfr. can. 855; can. 2364.

endangered. Neither is the Sacrament of Matrimony invalid if contracted by excommunicated parties,[49] provided of course the form be duly observed. The penalties [50] inflicted on such as violate this canon are stated under can. 2333, §3. Besides, they become irregular according to can. 985, n. 7.

However, there are *exceptions* stated in our canon, and consequently the penalty and irregularity just mentioned do not affect those administering the Sacraments under such circumstances. The exceptions are:

1. *Provided the minister is not a vitandus or under a declaratory or condemnatory sentence, the faithful may, for any just reason, ask him to administer the Sacraments and sacramentals to them.* This is more especially true if no other minister is available, in which case the excommunicated minister thus asked may administer the Sacraments and sacramentals without as much as inquiring for the reason why the petitioner wishes to receive them. Hence the faithful are to judge in such cases whether the reason is just. Any reason may be called just which promotes devotion or wards off temptations or is prompted by real convenience, for instance, if one does not like to call another minister.

This mitigation—such it is even in comparison with Martin V's decree "*Ad evitanda*" — is accorded only in case the minister is not *vitandus* nor under a declaratory or condemnatory sentence, according to

2. The second exception. If the minister, *i. e.*, priest, is a *vitandus* or *excommunicated in virtue of a condem-*

---

[49] For the parties themselves are the ministers of this Sacrament, neither would they receive it invalidly (though unworthily), if under censure; what the assisting priest has to do in such cases is explained in can. 1066.

[50] Formerly deposition was decreed for the ministers; see cc. 6, 7, C. 11, q. 3; c. 109, C. 11, q. 3 somewhat mitigated; cc. 3-6, X, V, 27.

natory or declaratory sentence, the faithful may demand from him *absolution* in danger of death, even *though other priests be present who are not excommunicated*,[51] but *other Sacraments or sacramentals they may receive* from such a priest only *if no other ministers are available*.

"*Deesse*" is not precisely synonymous with "*non adesse*" (see can. 1098, n. 2), for the former term, in classical language, means "to fail, to be wanting"; yet in connection with an object in the dative case it may also signify, "to be absent, not to be there."[52] Hence by a benign, though legitimate, interpretation we dare say that if no other non-excommunicated priests are present, an excommunicated one may administer all the Sacraments and sacramentals when there is danger of death. This interpretation is justified by the psychological condition of the sick person and affords another proof of the kindness of the Church.

EXCLUSION FROM THE SUFFRAGIA

Can. 2262

§1. Excommunicatus non fit particeps indulgentiarum, suffragiorum, publicarum Ecclesiae precum.

§2. Non prohibentur tamen:

1.° Fideles privatim pro eo orare;

2.° Sacerdotes Missam privatim ac remoto scandalo pro eo applicare; sed, si sit vitandus, pro eius conversione tantum.

We have retained in the inscription the old term (*suffragia*) common to all the acts mentioned in the text:

---

51 See can. 882, 2252.

52 Thus Cicero; *convivio puer defuit; bello defuisti.*

indulgences, suffrages, public prayers. The technical term for this effect of excommunication is "*privatio communium ecclesiae euffragiorum*," *viz.*: privation of the spiritual aids by which members of the Church assist one another in order either to atone for temporal punishments (*per satisfactionem*) or to obtain, either directly or indirectly, spiritual benefits (*per impetrationem*). If these suffrages are offered privately, by private persons in their own name, they may be applied to excommunicated persons, and therefore the canon has nothing to do with these.[53] But if they are offered in the name and by authority of the Church, they fall under the present law, because the Church wills to exclude the excommunicated from these suffrages.[54]

The text (§1) says that the *excommunicated do not partake of the indulgences, suffrages, and public prayers of the Church*, either by way of satisfaction or impetration.

a) *Indulgences* cannot be gained by, nor applied to, excommunicated persons, and no private application is possible because all indulgences flow from the treasury of the Church, over which her public authority has absolute control.

b) *Suffrages* are especially the fruits of Holy Mass, and prayers or good works, such as alms and penances, offered by way of satisfaction.

c) The *public prayers of the Church* may be understood as prayers chiefly, though not exclusively, of impetratory intercession, offered in the name of the

---

[53] Cfr. Suarez, *l. c.*, disp. IX, sect. 1, n. 1 ff. (Vol. 23, p. 260 f.); Hilarius a Sexten, *l. c.*, p. 58; Hollweck, *l. c.*, p. 118; private *suffragia*, i. e., such as are offered in his own name by the priest, may be performed for excommunicated persons; thus he may pray, fast, give alms, and even offer the holy Sacrifice in his own name for them.

[54] Suarez, *l. o.*

Church, such as all the liturgical prayers are: the choir service or recitation of the holy office, processions, and blessings, as far as they are contained in the liturgical books. Excommunicated persons, whether *vitandi* or *tolerati*, are excluded from all these. Navarrus [55] held that these *suffragia* could be applied by any priest, provided he was convinced that the excommunicated person was in the state of grace. This view is no longer tenable. Our text is plainly against it, but it does admit, what was quite commonly held and partly modified by previous decisions, namely, that

a) The faithful may *pray privately* for excommunicated persons, by way of impetration and satisfaction,[56] which, of course, depends solely on the acceptance of God.

b) *Priests may privately offer the Mass for a toleratus, provided no scandal is given; but for a vitandus only for his conversion.* What *private application* means is not expressly stated in our Code and would be difficult to define briefly. Private application may mean the application of the most special fruits of holy Mass, which the priest gains for himself as a private person. There cannot be any doubt that he may apply this fruit to any kind of excommunicated person.[57] As to the *fructus ministerialis*, or special fruit to be applied to one who asks for it, there is doubt. If we identify *privatim applicare* with a private Mass, it would mean that only a solemn or conventual or parochial Mass is excluded.[58] On

[55] Navarrus held this view against the clear text of the *"Ad evitanda"*; Hollweck, *l. c.*, p. 119, but was opposed by Suarez (*De Cens.*, disp., IX, sect. 3, n. 2); at least Suarez excluded any direct intention.

[56] Suarez, *l. c.*, disp. IX, sect. 5, n. 3: *"Dicendum est, licitum esse privatim pro excommunicato orare, propriam et personalem satisfactionem offerendo,"* and this he extends (*ib.*, n. 5) to the Memento in holy Mass.

[57] See preceding note from Suarez; also Hollweck, *l. c.*, p. 118.

[58] Thus Eichmann, *l. c.*, p. 94; Ayrinhac, *l. c.*, p. 124 seems to imply the same.

the other hand, if we interpret private application as meaning the priest's own fruits, then we should have to exclude the ministerial fruit, and no stipend (in the proper sense) could be accepted for such application. The intention of the lawgiver here is uncertain. The text says that a Mass may be applied even for a *vitandus*, but only for his conversion. This was allowed for Greek schismatics by a decision of the Holy Office, which also admitted the acceptance of a stipend.[59] May we not draw the legitimate conclusion: If application of the ministerial fruit is allowed because a stipend is permitted, when the purpose is conversion, even for a *vitandus*, it is logical to say that private application implies application of the ministerial fruit and acceptance of a stipend, provided the Mass is no conventual or parochial or solemn one and scandal is avoided, for instance, by not publishing the Mass or not making it known to any one. *A fortiori* a private application, if no scandal is given, is permitted for an *excommunicatus toleratus*. The Holy Office also wishes all scandal removed in case Freemasons should order Masses and forbids the clergy to accede to the pressure and commands of such if they insist on having the Masses published in papers or invitations.[60] It goes without saying that the priest is not allowed to countenance any disobedience or disregard of censures by a too free acceptance of Mass stipends. Solemn conventual or parochial Masses cannot be lawfully offered for excommunicated persons, either living or dead. Besides, it is a rather venturesome interpretation to allow a Mass to be said for a *dead vitandus*, *i. e.*, one who died under such an excommunication, because the text allows it to be

59 S. O., April 19, 1837 (*Coll. P. F.*, n. 858); see our Comment., Vol. IV, p. 143 f.

60 S. O., July 5, 1878 (*Coll. P. F.*, n. 1495).

done only for his conversion,[61] which after death is impossible. But for a *dead excommunicatus toleratus* a private application, provided no scandal arises therefrom, may and is permitted.

EXCLUSION FROM LEGAL ACTS

Can. 2263

Removetur excommunicatus ab actibus legitimis ecclesiasticis intra fines suis in locis iure definitos; nequit in causis ecclesiasticis agere, nisi ad normam can. 1654; prohibetur ecclesiasticis officiis seu muneribus fungi, concessisque antea ab Ecclesia privilegiis frui.

Can. 2264

Actus iurisdictionis tam fori externi quam fori interni positus ab excommunicato est illicitus; et, si lata fuerit sententia condemnatoria vel declaratoria, etiam invalidus, salvo praescripto can. 2261, §3; secus est validus, imo etiam licitus, si a fidelibus petitus sit ad normam mem. can. 2261, §2.

Can. 2265

§1. Quilibet excommunicatus:

1.° Prohibetur iure eligendi, praesentandi, nominandi;

61 Thus Ayrinhac, *l. c.*, p. 124; the quotations from Wernz and Gasparri do not prove his assumption; our text is too clear: " *sed pro eius conversione tantum.*" Therefore, what we said in Vol. IV, p. 145 f. of this Commentary, though we made no incorrect statement, must be supplemented and completed by what we say above. We add: From this it is evident that, if absolution from censures is given, even after death, every restriction as to the application of Masses is removed.

2.° Nequit consequi dignitates, officia, beneficia, pensiones ecclesiasticas aliudve munus in Ecclesia;

3.° Promoveri nequit ad ordines.

§2. Actus tamen positus contra praescriptum §1, nn. 1, 2, non est nullus, nisi positus fuerit ab excommunicato vitando vel ab alio excommunicato post sententiam declaratoriam vel condemnatoriam; quod si haec sententia lata fuerit, excommunicatus nequit praeterea gratiam ullam pontificiam valide consequi, nisi in pontificio rescripto mentio de excommunicatione fiat.

These three canons logically comprise the effects of legal acts, including acts of jurisdiction.

1. *Forensic and honorary* acts are those which the canon law permits the members of the Church to perform, especially in the ecclesiastical court and on ecclesiastical occasions.

a) The right of acting as *plaintiff* is denied to excommunicated persons except in their own case of excommunication, and an *excommunicatus* as well as his report or finding may be rejected as suspect; he is allowed to be neither arbiter nor counsel (lawyer).[62]

b) Excommunicated persons are not allowed to act as *sponsors* at Baptism or Confirmation, as far as stated under can. 765 f. and can. 795 f.

c) They are not allowed to act as *administrators of ecclesiastical property* or to perform *any* ecclesiastical commission, for all these are comprised by the name of ecclesiastical offices and functions.

d) They may not enjoy any *privileges or favors*

---

62 See can. 1654; 1754, § 2; 1795, §2; 1931; 2256, n. 2; c. 17, C. 6, q. 1; c. 8, 6°, V, 11.

granted by the Church before they were excommunicated, no matter whether these were given by higher or inferior prelates.[63]   Therefore absolution from censures, at least provisional, is added in most rescripts.

Note, however, that the text says: *fungi* and *frui*, from which it must be concluded that the prohibition only lasts until absolution from excommunication is granted, and no formal rehabilitation is required.   Besides, it appears quite reasonable that forensic acts, *i. e.*, acts in the ecclesiastical court, or rather exclusion from the office of judge, lawyer, auditor, counsel, promotor, should take effect only after a declaratory or condemnatory sentence. This seems necessary for the safety and certainty of juridical procedure.[64]

2. *Acts of jurisdiction* of the external and internal forum are mentioned in can. 2264 as follows:

a) Simply excommunicated persons can perform acts of jurisdiction *validly* (not licitly); their acts are not only valid, *but even lawful*, if the faithful ask such excommunicated persons to perform them, according to can. 2261, §2.

b) Persons excommunicated by a condemnatory or declaratory sentence, and *a fortiori vitandi*, can *neither validly nor lawfully* perform acts of jurisdiction, except in danger of death, according to can. 2261, §3.   Acts of jurisdiction are here expressly declared to comprise both the internal and the external forum.   An act of jurisdiction is the so-called *missio canonica*, because the commission to teach or preach, according to the more common

---

[63] The text does not especially mention (can. 2256, n. 2) papal favors; therefore also episcopal grants or favors of Ordinaries are excluded; see c. 1, 6°, I,

3; Hollweck, *l. c.*, p. 120, note 10.
[64] See can. 2223, § 4, because the persons being public, the public welfare seems involved; Eichmann. *l. c.*, p. 94 f.

doctrine, is an act emanating from jurisdiction. Consequently this mission also is lost by excommunication.[65]

However, here, too, must be applied what our text allows for those simply excommunicated without a special sentence. Therefore, if an excommunicated priest would be asked to preach or teach, he could do it lawfully.

3. Can. 2265 concerns *ecclesiastical offices and orders*, either in the active or passive sense.

a) Excommunicated persons are *excluded from the right of electing* (voting), *presenting, nominating;* but the vote or presentation (iuspatronatus) or nomination is not invalid unless made by a *vitandus* or one excommunicated by a declaratory or condemnatory sentence. If a chapter or college has the right of electing, presenting, or nominating, the act is valid or invalid according to can. 167, §2. This privation lasts until the excommunication is removed.[66]

b) *No excommunicated person may obtain any dignity, office, benefice, ecclesiastical pension, or other commission in the Church.* Here again the invalidity of the act conferring these dignities, offices, etc., attaches only to a *vitandus* or one who is under a declaratory or condemnatory sentence, as §2 states. It may be added that no dignity is excepted. "*Munus,*" which broadly signifies any office, may be understood of commissions or functions; thus, for instance, a proxy is not allowed or valid under given circumstances.[67]

65 Suarez, *De Cens.*, disp. XII, sect. 2, n. 4; Hollweck, *l. c.*, p. 121. Assistance at marriage is no act of jurisdiction; however, can. 1095, § 1, n. 1 must be consulted.

66 See can. 1470, § 4. Excommunicated Cardinals, pending the conclave or election, are not deprived of either the active or the passive vote, but only for this one occasion; ("*Vacante Sede,*" n. 29). If a curious reader should ask; but what if, by a very improbable supposition, an excommunicated cardinal should be elected Pope? Answer: he would go to confession or ask any confessor to absolve him from the censure. That is all.

c) *No one may be licitly promoted to orders* as long as he is excommunicated. *Order* is here taken according to can. 950, *i. e.*, including all orders, even tonsure; for there is no reason why the term should be restricted to " holy " orders, nor does the context call for a milder interpretation.[68] A question might arise as to minor orders and tonsure, whether they would be invalidly conferred by a prelate who is under a declaratory or condemnatory sentence of excommunication, because these orders are not, properly speaking, Sacraments, but merely sacramentals. Comparing can. 2372 with our text, their validity can be solidly defended.

d) *No one excommunicated* by a declaratory or condemnatory sentence, including *vitandi, can obtain any papal favor, unless mention is made of the excommunication in the papal rescript.* Therefore, any favor, *e. g.*, a monsignorship, a dispensation, an indulgence, etc., granted to such a person would be invalid unless it contained the clause: *" non obstante excommunicatione of quacumque censura "* or a similar one.[69]

---

67 See c. 15, X, I, 38; c. 24, X, II, 27; Hollweck, *l. c.*, p. 121; Schmalzgrueber (V, 39, n. 154) excepted pensions, but our Code is plainly against any exception.

68 Ayrinhac, *l. c.*, p. 126, says: "No one under excommunication should be promoted to *holy* orders."

69 Cfr. the *Ordo Servandus in S.*

Cong. Trib. Off., Sept. 29, 1908, III, n. 6, where, however, only *"nominatim excommunicati"* are mentioned. The *clausulae "ex plenitudine potestatis," "ex certa scientia"* would not be sufficient; Suarez, *De Cens.*, disp. XIII, sect. 2, n. 14.

LOSS OF INCOME FROM DIGNITY, OFFICE, etc.

Can. 2266

Post sententiam condemnatoriam vel declaratoriam excommunicatus manet privatus fructibus dignitatis, officii, beneficii, pensionis, muneris, si quod habeat in Ecclesia; et vitandus ipsamet dignitate, officio, beneficio, pensione, munere.

As the income or revenue from ecclesiastical offices is justly denied to those who are cut off from the communion of the Church,[70] it follows that the material part or income cannot be claimed by an *excommunicatus*. However, self-execution is not required until a formal sentence has been issued, and hence

1. After a declaratory or condemnatory sentence the excommunicated clergyman — for these the text has chiefly in view — remains *deprived of the fruits, i. e.*, revenues, salary, income, accruing from the dignity, office, benefice, pension, charge, which he holds in the Church.

A doubt indeed arises concerning the obligation of beneficiaries or office holders. Are they obliged in conscience (*in foro interno*) to make restitution of the fruits received from the time or moment in which the excommunication was incurred until the declaratory sentence was issued? The majority of authors say, yes.[71] However, this must be understood with due regard to can.

---

[70] C. 53, X, II, 28.

[71] Cfr. Suarez, *De Cens.*, disp. XIII, sect. 2, n. 7 ff.—A question may arise concerning a charge (*munus*), for instance, organist, sexton, etc., when paid by the government or civil authority. Would the incumbent lose the income if he were excommunicated? By ecclesiastical law he undoubtedly would; but we hardly believe that the Church would urge the forfeiture.

2232, §1, which says that a penalty *latae sententiae* binds in both fora, but need not be observed if defamation should follow, nor can its observance be urged if the crime was not notorious. Consequently, the obligation of restitution runs from the moment the censure was incurred, but does not urge either in the internal or the external forum if loss of reputation would follow or if the crime was occult.

2. A *vitandus* loses not only the fruits, but also his dignity, office, benefice, pension, or charge, and consequently all these dignities and offices become vacant (can. 183, §1).

SOCIAL OR CIVIL INTERCOURSE

Can. 2267

Communionem in profanis cum excommunicato vitando fideles vitare debent, nisi agatur de coniuge, parentibus, liberis, famulis, subditis, et generatim nisi rationabilis causa excuset.

The faithful shall avoid social intercourse with *vitandi*. From this obligation are *exempted* those bound by matrimonial bonds, parents, children, servants, and subjects. Besides, any reasonable cause may excuse others.

The extent of this avoidance was expressed in the following verse: *" Os, orare, vale, communio, mensa negatur."* [72]

[72] Cfr. the Glossa *ad verbum aliis*, c. 3, 6°, V, II; Hilarius a Sexten, *l. c.*, p. 63; Hollweck, *l. c.*, p. 124. But they also offered reasons which excused from this observance and put them in this verse: *"Utile, lex, humile, res ignorata, necesse."* *Utile* signified any spiritual or corporal utility; *lex*, the married couple; *humile*, submission or obedience, children and parents, masters and servants; *res ignorata*, ignorance of fact or law; *necessitas*, any spiritual or temporal necessity or need.

The *os* was taken as oral and epistolary intercourse; the *orare* as communion in private prayer; the *vale* as signs of special friendship, but not of common or usual salutations; *communio* as living in the same house and having commercial intercourse; *mensa* as eating at the same table and accepting invitations to banquets. Our text, being very broad, should not cause any alarm or misgiving, as if business would come to a standstill and social ties be rent assunder.

Art. II

THE INTERDICT

It is a rather venturesome attempt to say anything definite on the origin of this so-called censure. Broadly speaking, the opinion that the personal interdict was developed from temporary suspension, and the local interdict from excommunication, seems quite tenable.[1] Like other ecclesiastical disciplines, the interdict must not be presumed to have been introduced "cut and dried," but had its normal evolution from the ninth to the twelfth centuries,[2] when it appears as an independent penalty side by side with excommunication and suspension. It cannot, however, be denied that abuses had been committed, which may perhaps be excused, but cannot be defended on a juridical basis.[3] Local interdicts presuppose unity of faith and also, we dare say, the idea that

---

[1] See Kober, *Das Interdikt* (*Arch. für kath. K.-R.*, 1869, p. 3 ff.); Krebihl, *The Interdict, its History and Operation*, Washington 1909; Boudinhon, in *Cath. Encycl.*, Vol. VIII, p. 73 f.; Hollweck, *l. c.*, p. 126 ff.; Eichmann, *l. c.*, p. 17 f.; Hinschius, *K.-R.*, IV, 804 ff.; V, 13 ff.; 516 ff.; and the commentators on X, V, 39.

[2] We find traces of a partial local interdict already in the VIth century, when certain churches of a city were closed for service: but such cases were extremely rare.

[3] Boudinhon, *l. c.*

ecclesiastical authority laid a certain claim to territorial rights. The close interpenetration of Church and State in the Middle Ages made it possible to get this penalty respected by rulers and subjects. But the disruption of religious unity led to a mitigation of that "dangerous weapon" in the sixteenth century. The last general local interdict was imposed by Paul V, in 1606, on the Republic of Venice, without results. The interdict put on several Sicilian dioceses by Clement XI, in 1713, was also without practical effect. Of modern date are the vindictive interdicts imposed on the city of Adria, in 1909, and Galatina, in 1913, which are recorded in the official bulletin of the Holy See.[4] We also know that a congregation in one of our American dioceses was laid under the interdict some years ago by the Ordinary. But the use of this ecclesiastical penalty has, in the last two centuries, been exceedingly moderate.

The Code first defines an interdict, then sets forth who may inflict it and how far it extends, describes its effects, and, finally, mentions *ingressus ecclesiae* as a kind of interdict.

DEFINITION AND DIVISION

Can. 2268

§1. Interdictum est censura qua fideles, in communione Ecclesiae permanentes, prohibentur sacris quae in canonibus, qui sequuntur, enumeratur.

§2. Prohibitio fit vel directe per interdictum personale, cum personis ipsis usus eorum bonorum interdicitur; vel indirecte per interdictum locale, cum

---

[4] *A. Ap. S.*, I, 765; V, 517.

certis in locis eorundem dispensatio vel perceptio vetatur.

1. The Roman Law [5] mentions various interdicts, which, however, only remotely resemble the one described here. Formerly an interdict meant an order forbidding something to be done; but at present the term designates not only a pretorian restraint, but a particular penalty, with effects attached by common law. Hence the Code defines it as a *censure by which the faithful, while remaining in communion with the Church, are forbidden certain* [*sacred things or benefits*] enumerated in the following canons.

a) The generic nomenclature "*censura*" is here retained, although the interdict may also be inflicted as a vindictive penalty.[5a] In case of doubt, therefore, it is to be regarded as a censure.[6]

b) In *communione Ecclesiae permanentes* indicates an essential difference from excommunication, which does not leave union with or membership in the Church intact, but abolishes it. The interdict merely limits the practical use of that communion. Besides in an interdict the prohibition of sacred things is limited; but, unless so expressed in the law, it is unlimited in excommunication.

c) The term *fideles*, faithful, clearly insinuates that the interdict is also distinguished from suspension because the latter is inflicted on clerics only (can. 2256, §2); besides, suspension can never be local, but is always personal.[6a] This, of course, is also true of excommunication.

---

5 See *Inst.*, IV, 15; *Dig.*, 43, 1; 48, 22; *Cod.*, VIII, 1., see our Commentary, Vol. VIII, p. 125.

5a See can. 2291, n. 1–2.

6 Can. 2256, § 2. A purely local interdict, if such a penalty were inflicted, would not be a censure, which strictly supposes a grievous, morally imputable transgression.

6a Hilarius a Sexten, *l. c.*, p. 82.

d) Concerning the *effects* of an interdict, the text simply says: *"sacris,"* and to determine the import of these sacred things refers to the canons which immediately follow; besides these no others are enumerated. Note that the text does not mention inseparable effects, *qui separari nequunt.* This is logical, for the interdict does not disrupt communion with the faithful, and consequently we find that the extent is not the same for each kind of interdict.

2. *Division.* An interdict is *personal* when the prohibition directly concerns the personal use of certain sacred things, *i. e.,* when persons are directly intended by the interdict;

b) It is *local* when *in recto* the place, and only indirectly the persons living in that place, are struck by this penalty. In interdicted places the administration or reception of sacred things or spiritual benefits is forbidden.

These are the two main divisions mentioned in can. 2269.

§ 2. However, the subdivisions, as they may be called and are expressly referred to in the following canons, may just as well be added here.

c) A *general personal* interdict is one laid upon a corporation as such, for instance, the entire (Catholic) population of a realm, province, diocese, parish,[7] chapter, or all the members of a religious community.

A *general local* interdict is one inflicted upon a place comprising several distinct places or juridical entities, for instance, a diocese, or province, or parish.

d) A *special personal* interdict is one imposed on

---

7 Can. 2269, § 1, calls an interdict laid upon a parish a general interdict; in the old ecclesiastical law a parish was never regarded as an autonomous entity.

specified persons, for instance, on the pastor of a parish, or the administrator of a diocese.

A *particular local* interdict is one inflicted on a specified place, taking place (*locus*) in the stricter sense of locality, for instance, a specially designated church chapel, altar, or cemetery.[8]

AUTHORITIES WHO CAN INFLICT THE INTERDICT

Can. 2269

§1. Generale interdictum tam locale in territorium dioecesis, reipublicae, quam personale in populum dioecesis, reipublicae, ferri tantum potest a Sede Apostolica vel de eius mandato; interdictum vero generale in paroeciam vel paroeciae populum, et particulare sive locale sive personale, etiam Episcopus ferre potest.

§2. Interdictum personale sequitur personas ubique; locale non urget extra locum interdictum, sed in loco interdicto omnes etiam exteri aut exempti, excluso speciali privilegio, illud servare debent.

1. A *general local* interdict which is imposed upon the territory of a diocese or realm, and a *general personal* interdict which affects the people of a diocese or realm, can only be inflicted by the *Apostolic See* or by the latter's commission.

2. A *general interdict* which is to affect either an *entire parish* as such, or an *entire congregation* as such, or a

---

8 See Wernz, *l. c.*, VI, p. 124, n. 218; Hilarius a Sexten, *l. c.*, p. 83; Hollweck (*l. c.*, p. 127, § 52, note 3) calls the interdict the most flexible of all censures; the Code does not entirely abolish this flexibility; but it does away with the so-called *interdictum deambulatorium* (c. 8, Clem. V, 8), which directly affected places, but virtually the persons.

particular local or special interdict, may also be inflicted
by the bishop.

Here the text appears to mention only an interdict *ab
homine.* But there are a few interdicts which are incurred
ipso iure [9] and therefore need only a declaratory sentence
(can. 2223, §4; can. 2232, §1).

The *bishop,* and not the Ordinary, is mentioned, because the vicar-general cannot inflict such a penalty without a special mandate (can. 2220, §2). The *vicar
capitular* or administrator, on the other hand, cannot be
denied the right to place a parish under the interdict.[10]

Concerning the *prelates regular* of exempt religious,
Suarez [11] justly observes that, although they may inflict a
personal interdict by right and custom, yet custom denies
them the right to impose a local interdict. For such a
penalty is neither an adequate means of good government
nor apt to edify the faithful.

The *bishop may inflict an interdict without the consent
of his chapter or consultors* [12] and is not bound to call in a
collegiate body of judges, if he proceeds in a judiciary
way.[13] He may also impose it as a special order; [14] always
provided that he does not overstep the power laid down
in can. 2269, §1.

The question may arise whether the bishop could lay

9 The Code contains: one general interdict *modo speciali* reserved to the Ap. See (can. 2332);
one personal interdict contracted
ipso iure, but not reserved (can.
2338, § 4); two personal interdicts
ferendae sententiae, can. 2328,
2356; one *ab ingressu ecclesiae
ipso iure,* reserved to the ordinary,
can. 2339; one incurred *ipso iure*
but not reserved, can. 2338, § 3;
one *ferendae sententiae,* can. 2329.

10 *Trid.,* Sess. 24, c. 16, *de
ref.;* Wernz, *l. c.,* p. 229, n. 220.

11 *De Cens.,* disp. XXXVI, sect.
I, n. 3 (*ed. cit.,* Vol. 23, II, p.
253).

12 C. I, X, V, 31, calls for such
a consent, but custom has done
away with this requirement (Suarez, *l. c.,* n. 6); nor does the
Code require it.

13 He may, but is not obliged to,
entrust the judges with this affair;
can. 1576.

14 Can. 1933, § 4.

§2. In die Nativitatis Domini, Paschatis, Pentecostes, sanctissimi Corporis Christi te Beatae Mariae Virginis in caelum assumptae interdictum locale suspenditur, et prohibetur tantum collatio ordinum et sollemnis nuptiarum benedictio.

Can. 2271

Si interdictum fuerit locale generale et interdicti decreto aliud non caveatur expresse:

1°. Permittitur clericis, dummodo non sint ipsi personaliter interdicti, omnia divina officia et sacros ritus in quacunque ecclesia aut oratorio privatim obire, ianuis clausis, voce submissa et campanis non pulsatis;

2°. In ecclesia vero cathedrali, ecclesiis paroecialibus vel in ecclesia quae unica sit in oppido, in iisque solis, permittuntur unius Missae celebratio, asservatio sanctissimi Sacramenti, administratio baptismatis, Eucharistiae, poenitentiae, assistentia matrimoniis, exclusa benedictione nuptiali, mortuorum exsequiae, vetita tamen quavis sollemnitate, benedictio aquae baptismalis et sacrorum oleorum, praedicatio verbi Dei. In his tamen sacris functionibus prohibetur cantus et pompa in sacra supellectili et sonitus campanarum, organorum, aliorumve instrumentorum musicalium; sacrum autem Viaticum ad infirmos privatim deferatur.

Can. 2272

§1. In interdicto locali particulari, si interdictum fuerit altare vel sacellum alicuius ecclesiae, nullum sacrum officium seu sacer ritus in eisdem celebretur.

§2. Si interdictum fuerit coemeterium, fidelium

quidem cadavera sepeliri ibidem possunt, sed sine ullo ecclesiastico ritu.

§3. Si latum fuerit in certam ecclesiam vel oratorium:

1°. Si ecclesia fuerit capitularis nec interdictum sit Capitulum, valet praescriptum can. 2271, n. 1, nisi interdicti decretum praecipiat Missam conventualem celebrari et horas canonicas recitari in alia ecclesia aut oratorio;

2°. Si fuerit paroecialis, servetur praescriptum cit. can. 2271, n. 2, nisi interdicti decretum aliam ecclesiam pro interdicti tempore eidem substituat.

Can. 2273

Interdicta civitate, interdicta quoque manent loca accessoria etiam exempta et ipsa ecclesia cathedralis; interdicta ecclesia, interdicta sunt sacella contigua, non vero coemeterium; interdicto sacello, non est interdicta integra ecclesia nec, interdicto coemeterio, interdicta est ecclesia ipsi contigua, sed interdicta sunt omnia oratoria in coemeterio erecta.

1. *General Prohibition.* In a place laid either under a *general or a particular local interdict, no divine offices or sacred rites may be performed.* This is the general rule, and the terms must be employed according to their obvious meaning. Hence the celebration of Mass, the reservation of the Blessed Sacrament, preaching, administration of Sacraments or sacramentals or any ritual or liturgical function such as burials, may not take place in such places.[20] This, we said, is the rule.

---

[20] Here again the strictly liturgical devotions are intended; con-   sequently private devotions, such as the Rosary or the Stations of the

2. Now follow the *modifications* which affect any local interdict, general or particular, and may therefore be called general modifications, such as were granted by the Decretals,[21] and are partly extended by the Code:

a) It is permitted to administer the Sacraments and sacramentals to the *dying*. This includes Extreme Unction [22] as well as the Viaticum and the Last Blessing. What *servatis servandis* means may be deduced from can. 2271, n. 2: the Viaticum must be privately carried to the sick according to can. 849. But the clause also hints at the rubrics as found in the Roman Missal and Ritual.[23]

b) On Christmas, Easter, Pentecost, Corpus Christi, and the Assumption (Aug. 15) the local interdict is suspended, and only the conferring of orders and the solemn nuptial blessing are forbidden. Hence solemn service with all pomp and liturgical display may be celebrated, but only on these days themselves, not during the octave.[24] When Corpus Christi is transferred to a Sunday, the Sunday is favored.

The *particular modifications* of a *general* local interdict are stated in can. 2271, provided the wording of the decree of interdict does not contain anything to the contrary, for the clergy in particular and for the faithful in general,

1. The *clergy may privately perform all the divine*

Cross, confraternities, processions led by laymen, are allowed; for the term *"divina officia"* (can. 2256, n. 2) does not include these.

21 Especially by the well-known *caput* "*Alma*," c. 24, 6°, V, 11; see c. 5, X, V, 38.

22 Reiffenstuel, V, 39, n. 203.

23 *Missale Rom.*, tit. *De Defectibus*, c. VIII, n. 5; *Rit. Rom.*, tit. IV, c. 4, n. 6 f.

24 Martin V, "*Ineffabile*," May 26, 1429, § 3, extended the privilege to Corpus Christi; this is upheld by the Code. But the extension to the Octave of Corpus Christi granted by Eugene IV ("*Excellentissimum*," May 26, 1433) is not according to the Code, which says "*in die*." Whether the Spaniards still enjoy this favor on the feast of the Immac. Conception seems doubtful.

offices and sacred rites in any church or chapel.[25] But this general permission is conditional, and also circumscribed as to the manner in which these functions may be held.

a) The *condition* in the strict sense is that the clerics themselves be *not personally interdicted*, for if they were, can. 2275 would take effect.

b) The *manner* in which this service may be performed is described as follows: It is a *private* celebration, from which the faithful must be excluded.[26] It must be held *januis clausis, i. e.,* behind closed doors, which indicates that the clergy only may be admitted. However, if the priest would have no cleric to serve his Mass, a layman could and should be admitted.

It must be held *voce submissa, i. e.,* in a low voice, so that it can not be heard outside the church.[27]

It must finally be held without the bells being rung (*campanis non pulsatis*). However, canonists except from this prohibition the ringing of the Angelus bell and the bell for sermons.[28]

It may be added that this prerogative is granted to the *clerical state, as such,* whence it logically follows that every clergyman may hold such services. But mere assistance without coöperation could hardly be admitted. For the text clearly states *obire*, which signifies active service.

2. For *the faithful in general* the text grants the following mitigation under certain conditions:

a) The privileged churches are the *cathedral* and *the parish churches,* even though there may be several in one

25 Cfr. c. 24, 6°, V, 11.

26 Whether or not excommunicated or interdicted; Suarez, disp. XXXIV, sect. 1, n. 21 f.

27 Suarez, *ib.*, n. 12 f.

28 C. 11, X, V, 38. Suarez, l. c., n. 16 f.

city or town, and the *church which is the only one in a town*. In this latter clause a public oratory, which enjoys all the rights of a church,[29] is included among the privileged churches. Town may be taken in the sense of civil division, nor is any certain distance from one to another here indicated. The same cannot be said of semi-public and private oratories, which are therefore excluded from this prerogative, especially since the text adds: "*in iisque solis*," and this favor is intended for all the faithful, not for a privileged class only.[30]

b) The *divine or sacred functions* permitted are: the celebration of one Mass daily, under the restrictions mentioned below; the reservation of the Blessed Sacrament; the administration of Baptism with all its ceremonies and with sponsors; the administration of the holy Eucharist and of Penance; assistance at marriage, but without the nuptial blessing (which prohibition seems to exclude both blessings, that of the Ritual as well as that of the Missal); burial of the faithful, but excluding every solemnity, *i. e.*, external pomp of any kind;[31] blessing of the baptismal water and the holy oils; preaching the word of God.

c) The *restrictions* governing all these sacred functions are: no chanting is allowed, no display of *sacra supellex* (although, of course, the liturgical colors must be used), no ringing of bells, no playing of organs or other musical instruments; and the holy *Viaticum* must be brought to the sick privately, as is customary in our country. Hence only a low Mass is permitted, without sacred ministers, and without benediction of the Blessed

29 See can. 1191, § 1.

30 This text corrects the old law of c. 24, 6°, V, 11; what Suarez, (*l. c.*, n. 5 f.) and others, *e. g.*, Hilarius a Sexten (*l. c.*, p. 88) say, therefore, that private (*sic!*) oratories are included in this prerogative, is no longer tenable.

31 See can. 1204.

Sacrament. The exequies are to be performed in church according to the rubrics, but without the "*Libera,*" and also without a funeral sermon.

The *effects of a particular local interdict* are enumerated as follows:

1. If an *altar or chapel* in a church has been interdicted, no sacred office or rite may be performed there; from this rule no exception is allowed, not even in favor of non-liturgical devotions, for the text is not restricted to divine offices.[32]

2. If a *cemetery* is interdicted, the bodies of the faithful may be buried there, but without any ecclesiastical rites; these rites may, however, be supplied after the interdict is raised.

3. If a *specified church or oratory* is interdicted, it makes a difference whether the sacred edifice is a conventual (capitular) or parochial one.

a) If the church belongs to a *chapter,* for instance, of canons or regulars who really form a chapter, ecclesiastical corporation, or convent,[33] the chapter may make use of the favor granted under can. 2271, n. 1, concerning the clergy, provided, however, (1.°) that the chapter is not under a personal interdict, and (2.°) that the text of the interdict does not order the conventual Mass to be celebrated and the canonical hours to be recited in another church or oratory.

b) If the church is a *parochial* one, canon 2271, n. 2,

---

32 A reasonable doubt as to our statement is likely to arise from the word *sacer* (*ritus*) which, if taken to mean liturgical, would not exclude private or non-liturgical devotions; yet we are inclined to take it in the wider sense of *any sacred function.*

33 The meaning is: those churches which form a chapter or convent with the obligation of a conventual Mass and choir service; see can. 610, § 1, 2, wherefore convents of Sisters who have no such obligation can not claim the privilege here granted.

with all its favors and restrictions must be applied, unless
the interdict expressly provides that another church is to
be substituted for the one interdicted.

The *material extent* of local interdicts is explained in
can. 2273 as follows:

1. If a city is laid under the interdict, the accessory or
contributory places also are interdicted, including exempt
places and the cathedral.   This appears to be a rather
wide interpretation and was expressly acknowledged as
such by the Decretals,[34] where the reason is stated; *viz.,*
that interdicts be not vilified or contemned.

However, it may be justly doubted (we at least cannot read into the Decretal as much as others do) [35]
whether this provision can be stretched to cover two
different territories with different prelates.   For instance,
take Kansas City, Mo., and Kansas City, Kansas, or
Brooklyn and New York, between which the river forms
a line of demarkation dividing the two dioceses.   Hence
we suppose that the accessory premises or suburbs must
belong to the same diocese.   Thereby we do not, of
course, mean to deny that the Apostolic See could formulate an interdict so as to include the accessories of a city
situated in another diocese.

Exempt religious are included and must observe the
interdict even if they live in the suburbs, unless they
enjoy a special privilege.   The *cathedral* is especially
mentioned, because some authors, by reason of a
Decretal,[36] exempt it from interdicts.

2. If a church is interdicted, the *adjoining chapels* also

---

34 C. 17, 6°, V, II.

35 Thus Suarez, *l. c.,* disp.
XXXII, sect. 2, n. 23 f.; but the cc.
17, 6°, V, II would not justify the
assumption of Suarez.

36 C. 4, 6°, III, 4, which, however, as Suarez justly observes
(*l. c.,* n. 22), only speaks of benefices, not of favors granted to
churches.

are interdicted, but not the cemetery, even though adjoining.[87] The term *contigua* must be taken in its obvious sense, *i. e.*, bordering on or touching the church with which they form one whole, even though perhaps a little space is left between them.

3. If a *chapel* is interdicted, the whole *church* is not interdicted, whether this chapel be in the church or adjoining it; for there may be a special reason for interdicting the chapel, and besides, no inference may be drawn from the minor to the major, from the accessory to the principal; *accessorium sequitur principale*, but not *vice versa*.

4. If a cemetery is interdicted, the *adjoining church* is *not* interdicted, even though it belongs to the cemetery; but all oratories erected on the cemetery are included.

We conclude with a remark concerning local interdicts. Canon 2271 mentions three conditions for the lawful use of the favors granted during the time of an interdict; but it omits to add another condition: "*excommunicatis et interdictis exclusis*," which occurs in the old law.[88] Hence it may safely be concluded that there is no obligation positively to exclude the excommunicated and interdicted, except in case of can. 2259, §2 and can. 2275, n. 1. However, the clergy should take care that the interdict is not violated through their coöperation.

EFFECTS OF A PERSONAL INTERDICT

Can. 2274

§1. Si communitas seu collegium delictum perpetraverit, interdictum ferri potest vel in singulas

87 Corrects c. 17, 6°, V, II. 88 See c. 25, X, V, 33; c. 24, 6°. V, II.

personas delinquentes, vel in communitatem, uti talem, vel in personas delinquentes et in communitatem.

§2. Si primum, servetur praescriptum can. 2275.

§3. Si alterum, communitas seu collegium nequit ius ullum spirituale exercere quod ei competat.

§4. Si tertium, effectus cumulantur.

Can. 2275

Personaliter interdicti:

1°. Nequeunt divina officia celebrare eisve, excepta praedicatione verbi Dei, assistere; passive assistentes non est necesse ut expellantur; sed ab assistentia activa, quae aliquam secumferat participationem in divinis officiis celebrandis, repellantur interdicti post latam sententiam condemnatoriam vel declaratoriam, aut alioquin notorie interdicti;

2°. Prohibentur Sacramenta et Sacramentalia ministrare, conficere et recipere, ad norman can. 2260, §1, 2261.

3°. Praescripto can. 2265 etiam ipsi adstringuntur;

4°. Carent sepultura ecclesiastica ad normam can. 1240, §1, n. 2.

1°. It is evident that these two canons are related to each other, as both are concerned with the personal interdict. Since a personal interdict may be either general or special, can. 2274 considers the possible distinction between them, which is based upon the assumption that a personal interdict may be placed upon a body as such, or upon single members of that body. In the first case a censure can hardly be assumed;[39] whilst a special per-

---

[39] Hilarius a Sexten, l. c., p. 83, according to D'Annibale, I, n. 370.

sonal interdict in case of doubt, must be presumed to be a censure as per can. 2255, §2.

Communitas is a society less compactly organized, for instance, a parish, diocese, province.

Collegium is a more closely organized society or a corporation in the ecclesiastical and civil sense, as we say: *tres faciunt collegium.* Such are the cathedral and collegiate and monastic chapters, provided they have their own constitutions and enjoy autonomy (*societas imperfecta*). As stated above, modern laws presume that such communities and corporations are capable of committing a crime collectively, because they have a collective will. Consequently, they can also be punished collectively, and this is the fundamental supposition of an interdict.

The text says: 1.° An interdict may be placed upon *single persons* or members of *a community or college which is found guilty of a punishable crime,* and in this case the effects enumerated in can. 2275 follow. This is a special personal interdict.

2.° An interdict may be inflicted on a *community or corporation as such, i. e.,* as a community or corporation, and in this case the community *cannot exercise any spiritual right* that belongs to it as a *corporation or community.* These rights are the capitular, collegiate, or corporate rights, in as far as they are spiritual, such as the right of election,[40] postulation, nomination, presentation, etc. Thus a chapter of canons who could otherwise elect the bishop or a vicar capitular,[41] is deprived of this right when under an interdict, provided a declaratory or condemnatory sentence has been issued.[42] The same is true

40 Cfr. c. 16, X, I, 6; can. 161; can. 167.
41 See can. 432.
42 See can. 167, § 1, n. 3.

Bishops are not included in an interdict, either local or personal; see can. 2227, § 2; c. 4, 6°, V, II.

of a monastic chapter and a religious community. Neither could a parish choose its pastor, if this right belonged to the congregation according to can. 465.

Concerning our *consultors,* who ought to form some species of collegiate body, they scarcely have any truly spiritual rights, except that of electing the administrator, which would here certainly be concerned.[43] A *collegiate body of judges* who actually form a college according to can. 1576, is also included here.

3.° If the interdict has been imposed on *individual delinquents and* at the same time *on the whole community, its effects are bulked, i. e.,* the interdict produces a double effect—one affecting the community as such, *vis.,* privation of all corporate spiritual rights; the other affecting those personally interdicted (can. 2275). All this, of course, must be plainly expressed in the interdict itself, otherwise it may be presumed that the interdict is laid only upon the community as such (n. 2).

Those *personally interdicted, i. e.,* individual members of a community or corporation, or others,[44] if interdicted, suffer the following penalties according to can. 2275:

1. *They are not allowed to celebrate or assist at divine offices. Exception is made in favor of preaching,* at which they may assist. It is not necessary to expel such personally interdicted persons from an assembly gathered for divine service, provided they merely assist and take no active part in the ceremony. On the other hand, such as have been interdicted by a declaratory or condemnatory sentence, or are otherwise notoriously interdicted, must be refused all active assistance, *i. e.,* participation or coöperation in the celebration of the divine offices. From

---

[43] See S. C. Cons., Feb. 22, 1919 (*Eccl. Rev.,* Vol. 60, p. 532 f.); for Canada and Nova Scotia, S. C. Cons., May 8, 1919 (*Eccl. Rev.,* Vol. 61, p. 165).

[44] Cfr. can. 2328, can. 2356.

this text we may conclude that personally interdicted individuals may be permitted, if necessary, to take some part in the divine service, for instance, by serving at Mass, as long as no declaratory sentence has been pronounced or the fact of their being interdicted is not notorious.[45]

2. They are *forbidden to celebrate, administer, or receive any Sacraments or sacramentals* according to can. 2260, §1, and can. 2261. Thus the faculties for hearing confessions are lost by an interdict after a declaratory or condemnatory sentence; [45a] also the right of assisting at marriages.[46]

Irregularity follows a violation of this law, according to can. 985, n. 7; the reception of orders at the hands of an interdicted bishop is punishable by suspension.[47]

3. *Rights* denied to excommunicated persons are also denied to interdicted persons to the extent stated in can. 2265.

4. Those under a personal interdict lose the right to a *Christian burial,* as explained in can. 1240, §1, n. 2.

No mention is made of *actus legitimi,* except as far as can. 2265 falls under that heading. Consequently other legal acts may be validly and licitly performed by one who is personally interdicted.

MITIGATION FOR THE PERSONALLY INNOCENT

Can. 2276

Qui interdicto locali vel interdicto in communitatem seu collegium subest, quin eidem causam dederit, nec

45 For instance, they are not known as the leaders of a faction against the Ordinary.

45a Can. 873, § 3; Can. 1095, § 1, n. 1.

46 Can. 1095, §1, n. 1.

47 Can. 2372; cfr. can. 2338, § 3; 2364.

alia censura prohibeatur, potest, si sit rite dispositus,
Sacramenta recipere, ad normam canonum praeceden-
tium, sine absolutione ab interdicto aliave satisfactione.

Those who are laid under a local or personal interdict
that concerns a community or corporation, but have not
been the cause of that interdict, and are not otherwise
censured, may receive the Sacraments according to the
rules laid down in the preceding canons, provided they
are properly disposed.

This favor is granted without any other satisfaction,
and no absolution is required.

The term "*causam dederit*" [48] may give rise to doubts.
Who causes an interdict, either local or personal?
Suarez [49] justly observes that the culprit or delinquent
must, in one way or another, be intimately connected with
the place or community, so as to possess, rule or influence
it. The pastor of a parish, or town, or city, is held responsible for the actions of his subjects; also kings and
magistrates, especially in former days, were looked upon
as responsible for the crimes committed in their respective
territories. Concerning a community or corporation, a
decision of a chapter would throw the burden on the
whole body, because apparently approved by all. Here,
then, the ringleaders would undoubtedly be those who
provoked the interdict. That innocent persons sometimes suffer cannot be avoided, since the interdict is
intended not so much as a punishment, but as a defence
of the authority of the Church.

[48] C. 24, 6°, V, 11.   [49] *De Cens.*, disp. XXXVI, sect.
3.

THE INTERDICT FORBIDDING ONE TO ENTER A CHURCH

Can. 2277

Interdictum ab ingressu ecclesiae secumfert prohibitionem ne quis in ecclesia divina officia celebret vel eisdem assistat aut ecclesiasticam sepulturam habeat; si autem assistat, non est necesse ut expellatur, nec, si sepeliatur, oportet ut cadaver amoveatur.

As a species of personal [50] interdict is here mentioned that "*ab ingressu ecclesiae*," which occurs in the Decretals.[51] It may be inflicted upon laymen as well as clerics. Its effects are stated as follows:

1. Those so interdicted are *forbidden to celebrate the divine offices* in any church, even though it be not an interdicted church;

2. They are forbidden *to assist* at such offices, either passively or actively.

3. *Ecclesiastical burial* is denied them, *i. e.*, they must be buried without solemnity and without the ecclesiastical rites which are performed in church. For no doubt the burial here intended is that in the church, according to can. 1205, §2, *i. e.*, of civil and ecclesiastical princes and dignitaries, among them abbots.

This interdict *does not*, however, require that the interdicted person be expelled from a church where divine offices are being celebrated, or that these functions be interrupted or suspended on account of his presence. Neither does this interdict call for an *exhumation* of the corpse if such a person should have been buried in the church, either by fraud, violence, or ignorance.

---

50 Thus Suarez, *l. c.*, disp. XXXV, sect. 4, n. 3.

51 See the "*multum allegabile*," c. 12, X, V, 38, concerning annual confession and Paschal Communion.

ART. III

SUSPENSION OR CLERICAL CENSURE

Suspension is a mitigation of the ancient penalty of deposition and degradation, which occurs as early as the third century.[1] Its fuller development, however, commenced in the fourth century, which witnessed quite a change in public discipline, including the application of penalties to clerical offenders; removal from office, but not from the clerical ranks; privation of certain spiritual [2] and material rights; ineligibility for higher offices, whilst the bishops were denied intercourse with their fellow bishops.[3] When, in the sixth and later centuries, benefices were introduced and multiplied, it was natural that the revenues should play a conspicuous part as means of reaching delinquent clerics. Hence towards the end of the XIIth century we find a suspension from benefices beside and distinct from suspension from the exercise of orders and offices.[4] This is the status of suspension in the Decretals, to which the Council of Trent only added the suspension *ex informata conscientia*.[5] The Code has not simplified suspension.

Yet some progress is noticeable, especially as far as precision of terms and definition of the effects of different kinds of suspension are concerned.

1 See Kober, *Die Suspension der Kirchendiener*, 1862, p. 19 ff.; Hinschius, *K.-R.*, IV, 747 ff.; " *ab ordine depositus*"; *Syn. Aurel. III*, c. 19.

2 For instance, prohibition to say Mass for a certain time, *v. g.*, six months; *Syn. Aurel. III*, c. 6, 18.

3 *Syn. Aurel. III*, c. 6 (*l. c.,*): "*ab omnium fratrum caritate.*"

4 See c. 2, X, II, 20; c. 7, X, V, 19; c. 7, X, I, 6.

5 Sess. 14, c. 1, *de ref.*; see can. 2186.

Can. 2278

§1. Suspensio est censura qua clericus officio vel beneficio vel utroque prohibetur.

§2. Etiam suspensionis effectus separari queunt; sed nisi aliud constet, in suspensione generaliter lata comprehenduntur omnes effectus qui in canonibus huius articuli enumerantur; contra, in suspensione ab officio vel a beneficio omnes tantum effectus alterutrius speciei.

1. *Suspension is a censure by which a cleric is forbidden to exercise the rights attached to his office or benefice, or both.*

In as far as it is a *censure,* suspension must bear the marks and conditions of censures in general.

Suspension differs from *excommunication* in this that it concerns clerics only, and its effects are separable in various degrees. Suspension differs from an *interdict* in that its effects are strictly limited to clerical rights, leaving the spiritual benefits common to all Christians, such as ecclesiastical burial, untouched.

2. Since the *effects of suspension are separable,* it is evident that they follow the various kinds of suspension in varying degrees.

a) A *general suspension* deprives a cleric of all the rights pertaining to *his office as well as his benefice;* and if the suspension is not further determined in the decree or precept of the superior or judge,[6] a general

---

6 As a censure it may be inflicted by a judiciary sentence or in virtue of a special precept; see 1933, § 4; on provisional suspension, see can. 2222, § 2.

suspension is to be understood, *i. e.*, one accompanied by all the effects stated in this article.

c) A *special suspension* is twofold: from office or from benefice. The special suspension from office may be either *total* or *partial*, according as all the rights attached to the office, or some only, are taken away. The special suspension from benefice, too, may be total or partial, since the administration of the benefice may be taken away or only its revenues.

The distinction of *latae* and *ferendae sententiae* also applies to suspension. But the distinction between a *suspensus vitandus* and *toleratus* has no foundation in the Code.

EFFECTS OF SUSPENSION

Can. 2279

§1. Suspensio *ab officio* simpliciter, nulla adiecta limitatione, vetat omnem actum tum potestatis ordinis et iurisdictionis, tum etiam merae administrationis ex officio competentis, excepta administratione bonorum proprii beneficii.

§2. Suspensio:

1.° *A iurisdictione* generatim, vetat omnem actum potestatis iurisdictionis pro utroque foro tam ordinariae quam delegatae;

2.° *A divinis,* omnem actum potestatis ordinis quam quis sive per sacram ordinationem sive per privilegium obtinet;

3.° *Ab ordinibus,* omnem actum potestatis ordinis receptae per ordinationem;

4.° *A sacris ordinibus,* omnem actum potestatis ordinis receptae per ordinationem in sacris;

5.° *A certo et definito ordine exercendo*, omnem actum ordinis designati; suspensus autem prohibetur insuper eundem ordinem conferre et superiorem recipere receptumque post suspensionem exercere;

6.° *A certo et definito ordine conferendo*, ipsum ordinem conferre, non vero inferiorem nec superiorem;

7.° *A certo et definito ministerio*, ex. gr., audiendi confessiones, vel *officio*, ex. gr., cum cura animarum, omnem actum eiusdem ministerii vel officii;

8.° *Ab ordine pontificali*, omnem actum potestatis ordinis episcopalis;

9.° *A pontificalibus*, exercitium actuum pontificalium, ad normam can. 337, §2.

Can. 2280

§1. Suspensio a *beneficio* privat fructibus beneficii, excepta habitatione in aedibus beneficialibus, non autem iure administrandi bona beneficialia, nisi decretum vel sententia suspensionis ipsam administrandi potestatem suspenso expresse adimat et alii tribuat.

§2. Si, quamvis censura obstet, beneficiarius fructus percipiat, fructus restituere debet et ad hanc restitutionem cogi potest canonicis quoque, si opus sit, sanctionibus.

A suspension may be inflicted on individual clerics or on a body of clerics as a corporation.

1. The *effects of special suspension from office* are mentioned in can. 2279, §1. It is evident from can. 145 that *office* is to be taken in the strict sense, *i. e.*, for a charge, either divinely or ecclesiastically established, conveying some of the power of order or jurisdiction,—supposing, of course, the clerical character, at least the

tonsure. All temporal rights, such as administration, are included only in so far as they are strictly connected with the spiritual office.

If, therefore, *suspension from office* is inflicted without any further restriction,[7] it forbids the *exercise of any act of the power of order or jurisdiction, and of mere administration attached to the office itself*. But the administration of one's benefice is not withdrawn. Besides, it should be noted that the office itself is not lost, for the effect touches only the exercise of rights. Consequently, a suspended priest cannot lawfully say Mass, or administer the Sacraments, except as far as canons 2284 and 2261 permit (of which see below). Neither can a suspended prelate grant indulgences or inflict censures, under the same restriction (*i. e.*, can. 2284), for these are acts of jurisdiction.

As to acts of administration accruing to the office itself, such are mentioned under can. 262; 691, §1; 1489; 1520 f. Thus the administrators and rectors of pious associations, provided they are clergymen, lose the right of administration if suspended. Exception is made of the administration of one's own benefice, which means that a pastor may retain control of the revenues of his benefice. But if suspended, he could not administer the benefice of another pastor. Assistance at marriage is invalid only after a declaratory or condemnatory sentence,[8] or according to can. 2284.

Since, however, a *suspension from office may be only partial*,— which fact should be duly stated in the decree or sentence,— the Code distinguishes *various degrees or cases* of suspension from office.

---

[7] For instance, if the bishop should say: "I hereby suspend you from your office," the office which the addressed cleric holds is meant.

[8] See can. 1095, § 1, n. 1.

1. Suspension from jurisdiction *(a iurisdictione)*, in general, forbids the exercise of every act of ordinary as well as delegated power of jurisdiction in the external and internal forum; hence every grant of faculties or indulgences made by a superior thus suspended is forbidden, nay, may even be invalid, according to can. 2284, also every exercise of judiciary or administrative power and every act of preaching or teaching is forbidden; and from the moment the suspension takes effect every delegation is ineffective.[9]

2. Suspension *a divinis forbids every act of the power of order which one may have received in virtue either of sacred ordination or of a privilege.* Hence all acts based upon the power of order are forbidden, *e. g.,* the administration of Sacraments and sacramentals, the celebration of holy Mass, and all the acts of order which one may exercise in virtue of a special indult or privilege, such as conferring minor orders, confirmation, consecration or blessings.[10]

3. Suspension from orders *(ab ordinibus)* forbids every act of the power of orders received by ordination. Consequently this more general prohibition includes what is specifically stated under n. 4. But powers granted by privilege or indult, *e. g.,* that of conferring minor orders, are not included in this prohibition.

4. Suspension from sacred orders *(a sacris ordinibus)* forbids every act of the power of sacred or higher orders, *i. e.,* from subdeaconship onward (can. 949).

5. Suspension from *exercising* a certain specified order *(a certo et definito ordine exercendo)* forbids only the exercise of that order. But the cleric thus suspended is

---

9 Attention should, however, be called to can. 209.

10 See can. 951; can. 782; can. 1147, § 1;—but no privilege is involved in can. 964.

not allowed to confer or to receive a higher order, nor to exercise a higher order after suspension. Thus a priest suspended from the priesthood may not say Mass or impart the blessings reserved to priests, but he may impart the blessings which deacons can give. This is also true of blessings which he may impart by a special indult.[11] Thus a priest under such a suspension may lawfully distribute holy Communion, since deacons may perform this function; he may also confer Baptism, but not solemnly.[12] But a priest thus suspended may not licitly be promoted to the episcopate, or, if promoted, exercise episcopal functions. A bishop suspended from the exercise of the episcopal order cannot licitly consecrate a bishop. But a bishop suspended from the priestly order may exercise and confer all orders, with the sole exception of the sacerdotal order.

6. Suspension from conferring a certain and specified order (a certo et definito ordine conferendo) forbids administering only that order and none other, either higher or lower.

7. Suspension from a certain and specified ministry or office (a certo et definito ministerio vel officio) forbids the exercise of acts attached to that specific ministry or office. Thus if a confessor, teacher, or preacher is suspended, it means that he cannot hear confessions, or teach in an ecclesiastical capacity, or preach the word of God.[18] If a chancellor is suspended, it signifies that he cannot exercise these offices as long as the suspension lasts;[14] if a priest is suspended from the care of souls, every act con-

---

11 Can. 1147, n. 1, 2–4. For the necessary order is not lost, neither is the indult taken away by suspension of n. 5.

12 Can. 742, § 2.
13 See can. 2317.
14 See can. 373, § 5.

nected with that office is forbidden, such as hearing confessions, visiting the sick, etc.[15]

8. Suspension *ab ordine pontificali* forbids the exercise of acts belonging to the episcopal order, *e. g.*, the conferring of orders, Confirmation, the consecration of churches or altars, etc.[16]

9. Suspension *a pontificalibus* forbids the exercise of pontifical acts for which mitre and crozier are required according to the liturgical laws; for these two emblems always go together.[17] Is this suspension identical with the preceding one? It would seem that if all acts proper to the episcopal order are comprised by the name pontificals, as Thesaurus and Benedict XIV expressly state,[18] the difference seems to be very slight. Thus Thesaurus says: Among these acts are enumerated: the conferring of orders,[19] the consecration of sacred vessels, churches, virgins, and chrism, Confirmation, blessing of vestments and corporals, sacerdotal acts usually performed with mitre and crozier; also the conferring of the tonsure. Some of these acts belong strictly to the episcopal order, *viz.*: the conferring of holy orders, Confirmation and consecration. How, then, is n. 8 to be distinguished from n. 9? Reference to can. 337, §2 does not solve the difficulty. To us it seems that by acts of the episcopal order are understood all acts which require, at least *per se*, the episcopal character; whilst the term " pontificals " includes purely ceremonial functions, or, as Thesaurus says, the priestly acts performed with mitre and crozier.

---

15 See can. 462, 464, 892.

16 See can. 951; 782, § 1; 1147, § 1.

17 *Caeremoniale Episcop.*, l. I, c. 17, nn. 4, 8.

18 *De Poenis Eccl.*, P. II, c. 5

(*ed. cit.*, p. 180); Bened. XIV, "*Ad audientiam*," Feb. 15, 1753, § 8.

19 Bened. XIV, *l. c.*, distinctly adds: also of minor orders.

If this should be too restrictive, it may also be said, without doing violence to the text, that n. 9 comprises all acts performed with mitre and crozier, and therefore is more comprehensive than n. 8. The former interpretation appears more probable because it clearly distinguishes the two suspensions and minimizes the penalty.[20]

10. *Suspension from benefice* is the subject of can. 2280. By benefice is understood a juridical entity established by competent authority, consisting of an office and the right to receive the revenues attached to the same. As insinuated elsewhere,[21] there may be a doubt as to our country and other countries where benefices in the sense attached to that term before the promulgation of the Code are almost unknown. However, it appears that the wider range of endowment and the less strictly defined subjective perpetuity of beneficiaries clearly perceptible in the Code render it necessary to apply the term benefice to our parishes, as our pastors actually hold canonical parishes in the sense of the Code. Besides, there can hardly be any doubt that, even in our country, the income or salary of the pastor can be really distinguished from the office he holds. This suffices to assume that the term *fructus beneficii* comprises all the revenues accruing from an office which one holds. Consequently, suspension from benefice is applicable also to our country and other countries similarly situated.

The effect of *suspension from benefice* consists in *privation of the fruits or revenues of the benefice.* By this name *(fructus beneficii)* is understood all the material

---

20 There is only one difficulty: Are *abbots*, if suspended *a pontificalibus*, allowed to confer tonsure and minor orders on their own subjects? The answer should be affirmative; although we really doubt it, because the two emblems are, according to the Pont. Rom., required, and abbots do not possess the episcopal order.

21 See Vol. VI, can. 1411.

or temporal income derived from the benefice, whether in specie or natural offerings, tithes, interest, produce, etc. *Not included* in these are manual Mass stipends, (to some extent) daily distributions,[22] much less patrimonial and quasi-patrimonial possessions, revenues which were due at the moment the suspension was incurred, pensions, government subsidies.

Our *Code exempts from these fruits*:

a) the dwelling or *living in the residence of the beneficiary, i. e.,* the actual accupation of the parsonage for the purpose of dwelling therein: this can in nowise be taken away from the clergyman, even though he be suspended by a declaratory or condemnatory sentence;

b) the *right of administering the benefice,* which means that he can continue to perform all legal acts required for the lawful administration, improvement, and safeguarding of his benefice.[23] However, this right, says the Code, may be taken away by a decree or sentence and given to another. But the decree or sentence must expressly state this fact. If the suspended cleric himself administers the benefice, he is entitled to an adequate remuneration for his expenses and labor.[24]

§2 of can. 2280 obliges a cleric suspended from his benefice *to make restitution of the fruits received during the time of suspension.* He has unjustly acquired something to which he was not entitled.[25] Therefore, says the text, *if he should refuse to make restitution, he may be compelled to do so by penal measures, even censures, if*

---

22 Cfr. can. 394 f.; but to some extent daily distributions may constitute a benefice as per can. 1410; thus also stole fees (but not in our country, where the stole fees are properly distinguished from salary).

23 The old law also took away this right; cc. 1, 16, 6°, I, 6.

24 Cfr. Hilarius a Sexten, *l. c.,* p. 73.

25 Suarez, *De Cens.,* disp. XXVII, sect. 1, n. 7.

necessary. It is evident that, since a benefice is considered to be a juridical entity, restitution must be made to the very benefice or to the church to which it is attached. Neither can a suspended cleric dispose of the revenues at will. The obligation in conscience is retroactive up to the moment when the censure was incurred, though with the benefit mentioned in can. 2232, §1.

Since suspension from a benefice is adequately distinguished from suspension from an office, it follows that the acts forbidden to one suspended from office are not the same as those forbidden in virtue of suspension from a benefice. Consequently, not only the rights, but also the duties, attached to the office remain intact, even though the remuneration may fail. This punishment was intended, that the delinquent may, by receding from contumacy, obtain absolution and rehabilitation. But the fruits lost during the time of suspension cannot be reclaimed, unless the sentence has been declared invalid or its unjustice becomes manifest afterwards.[26]

EXTENT OF SUSPENSION

Can. 2281

Suspensio generaliter lata vel suspensio *ab officio* aut *a beneficio* afficit omnia officia aut beneficia, quae clericus habet in dioecesi Superioris suspendentis, nisi aliud appareat.

Can. 2282

Loci Ordinarius nequit clericum suspendere a determinato officio vel beneficio quod in aliena dioecesi

---

[26] Suarez, *l. c.*, disp. XXVII, sect. 2, n. 6; Wernz, *l. c.*, VI, n. 211, p. 220.

reperiatur; sed suspensio latae sententiae, iure communi irrogata, afficit omnia officia vel beneficia in quacunque dioecesi possideantur.

Can. 2283

Quae de excommunicatione can. 2265 statuuntur, etiam suspensioni sunt applicanda.

There is implied in the first two canons a distinction which is common to all censures, viz.: a iure and ab homine, either ferendae or latae sententiae (see can. 2217). Besides this, another distinction is hinted at, viz.: that between ius commune and ius particulare. Both may again be latae or ferendae sententiae. Thus a particular community may enact suspension ipso iure, i. e., particulari; and the Ordinary, or judge, or religious superior of an exempt organization may also inflict a sentence of suspension (ab homine, ferendae sententiae). The suspensions iure communi irrogatae are contained in the Code, and besides these, no others of common law are to be heeded (can. 6, n. 5). Thereby, of course, the supreme legislator or a general council is not bound, in the sense that they could not, iure communi, either decree or inflict a suspension not contained in the Code.

The general principle, "Extra territorium jus dicenti impune non paretur" [27] is applicable here, provided the distinction between common and particular law be duly noted.

1. *A suspension that is generally worded and inflicted, concerns all offices and benefices which the cleric holds in the diocese of the superior who inflicts the suspension from office or benefice, unless the contrary is evident.*

[27] C. 2, 6°, I, 2.

This general suspension does not apply outside the diocese, for it is supposed to be inflicted either by a particular law or by the superior, *ab homine*. Consequently if one holds an office or benefice in a strange diocese, the exercise of that office or benefice would not be curtailed by such a general suspension. The contrary intention would have to be made known by the Ordinary of the strange diocese.[28]

2. A *total suspension from office* comprises all the offices — but not the benefices — one holds in the diocese of the superior who inflicts the suspension, unless the contrary is apparent.

3. A *total suspension from benefice* extends to all the benefices—but not to all the offices—one holds in the diocese of the superior who suspends, unless, again, the contrary intention of the superior is obvious.

4. The *local Ordinary*, according to can. 2282, *cannot suspend* a clergyman *from a specified office or benefice* that belongs to *another diocese*. For this suspension supposes either a particular law or a sentence inflicted by the superior, the effect of which cannot be extended to the territory where the jurisdiction of the suspending superior ceases.[29] The contrary opinion held by some is, therefore, wrong.[30]

5. A suspension *latae sententiae* inflicted by common law, *iure communi, affects all offices and benefices,* no matter in what diocese the suspended cleric may hold them. Of course, this suspension is here supposed to be general and total without restriction.[31]

---

28 See c. 37, 6°, I, 6: a suspension of three years inflicted *ipso iure,* yet binding only for the diocese for which the *compromissarii* elected an *indignus,* not for the benefices he held in a strange diocese.

29 Ballerini-Palmieri, *l. c.,* Vol. VII, n. 501 ff.; p. 284 ff.; Wernz, *l. c.* VI, n. 208, p. 215.

30 This opinion was held by Suarez and Thesaurus, cfr. Wernz, *l. c.*

31 Ballerini-Palmieri, *l. c.;* Wernz *l. c.*

According to the common opinion of canonists, a cleric suspended *ab ordine* is obliged to observe the suspension everywhere, because suspension is a personal penalty which the common law desires and demands to see respected.[32] Since in the suspension *ab ordine* is included the suspension *ab officio* or a *divinis*, it follows that a cleric suspended from office, or a *divinis*, even though suspended only *ab homine,* or by a particular law, cannot exercise his order anywhere. Consequently, can. 2280, as stated above, must be understood as follows: The suspension *ab officio* inflicted by a diocesan superior must be observed in the diocese and elsewhere, and the suspension *ab ordine* is implicitly included in the suspension *ab officio*. Otherwise we should have to give up the teaching of the school, stated above, that suspension *ab o dine* obliges everywhere, and simply state that suspension, unless decreed or inflicted by common law, is merely local, *i. e.*, diocesan.

It may be asked: How can one suspended *ab officio* in diocese A, and holding an office in diocese B, where he is not suspended, exercise his office in diocese B, since the exercise of the power of order is taken away from him by his superior? The answer is that the effects are separable, and therefore jurisdiction is not taken away in diocese B. Besides, what one cannot do by himself, he may do through a substitute, and a benefice is not affected by suspension from office.

Can. 2283, perhaps too briefly, *applies the effects of excommunication also to suspension.* The suspended cleric loses the active and passive voice and cannot be promoted to orders, as stated in can. 2265 with regard to excommunication. This is quite clear. But not so

---

32 Ballerini-Palmieri, *l. c.,* n. 502, p. 285.

evident is the answer to the question whether the legislator means to attach these effects only to *general suspension*. Ancient [33] as well as modern commentators disagree on this point. A modern writer says: " Some
canonists held, against the common opinion, that these
effects are produced only by general suspensions from
benefice; but the present law does not distinguish, and
assimilates suspended clerics to excommunicated ones in
this matter." [34]   Therefore, according to this author, the
effects enumerated in can. 2265 follow each and every
kind of suspension, because the law does not distinguish.
But this reasoning is not exactly to the point.   For can.
2278, §2 *does distinguish* between various suspensions,
and only to the *suspensio generaliter lata* must be applied
all the effects enumerated in article III, ch. II, title VIII
of this fifth book.   Hence the argument *ex silentio* proves
nothing in this matter.   There is also an essential distinction between excommunication and suspension, because the effects of the former, unlike the effects of the
latter, are inseparable.   Therefore, only a general suspension can be assimilated to excommunication, but
never a special one, be it total or partial.   Besides, since
penalties must be interpreted benignly and, if the text
is obscure, the least must be assumed,[35] we cannot help
accepting the interpretation that general suspension only
is accompanied by the effects mentioned in can. 2265.   A
last observation may confirm this statement.   Can. 2265
commences with *quilibet excommunicatus*, every excommunicated person.   Analogously we should say in can.

---

33 Wernz, *l. c.*, VI, n. 209, p. 216,
calls the opinion which holds that
every suspension produces the
effects mentioned in can. 2265, *communior*, although he himself does
not share it.

34 Ayrinhac, *l. c.*, p. 149; V. Cappello, *l. c.*, p. 167 is silent; Eish-
mann, *l. c.*, p. 104, accepts the view
of Wernz.

35 See *Reg. Iuris* 49, 30, *in 6°*.

2283: every suspended cleric — which would mean, concretely speaking, that every cleric suspended *ab ordine pontificali, a pontificalibus,* or *a divinis* would also lose the active and passive voice.[36] This sounds untenable and improbable, and consequently we hold that, in can. 2283, only a *general suspension is intended, i. e.,* one worded and inflicted in general terms, comprising office and benefice, to the exclusion of every special suspension, either total or partial.[37]

MITIGATION OF THE EFFECTS

Can. 2284

Si incursa fuerit censura suspensionis quae vetat administrationem Sacramentorum et Sacramentalium, servetur praescriptum can. 2261; si censura suspensionis quae prohibet actum iurisdictionis in foro seu interno seu externo, actus est invalidus, ex. gr., absolutio sacramentalis, si lata sit sententia condemnatoria vel declaratoria, aut Superior expresse declaret se ipsam iurisdictionis potestatem revocare; secus est illicitus tantum, nisi a fidelibus petitus fuerit ad normam mem. can. 2261, §2.

Here the modification stated in can. 2261 is extended to suspension.

1. If a suspension is incurred that forbids the *administration of Sacraments and sacramentals,* as is the case in suspensions *ab officio* and *a divinis,* the suspended cleric

---

[36] The loss of the active voice was not denied by Schmalzgrueber; V, tit. 39, n. 298.

[37] The texts quoted in Card. Gasparri's edition for can. 2283 mention suspension, but leave it doubtful whether a general or special suspension had been incurred; this is especially the case with c. 8, X, I, 4. We do not, however, deny that the text apparently favors the opinion rejected above.

may lawfully administer them only in case he is legitimately requested by the faithful; nor is he obliged in this case to ask for the reason of the demand. This favor, however, supposes that no condemnatory or declaratory sentence has been pronounced against him. For after such a sentence the faithful could not lawfully demand of him the administration of the Sacraments or sacramentals, nor could he lawfully accede to the request, except in case of danger of death, when other ministers were wanting.

2. When the suspension, *e. g., ab officio, a iurisdictione, a definito et certo ministerio (audiendi confessiones)* forbids an *act of jurisdiction* either in the internal or external forum, the act performed under such censure is *invalid,* if a condemnatory or declaratory sentence has been pronounced or if the superior has expressly declared that the power of jurisdiction is withdrawn; but if no such sentence or such express declaration has been made, the act of jurisdiction is valid, even though *illicit.* Nay, it even becomes lawful if the minister has been legitimately asked by the faithful. In danger of death the act of jurisdiction which is exercised in the form of sacramental absolution is valid and licit, even though other priests or ministers are available (can. 2261.).

SUSPENSION OF COMMUNITIES

Can. 2285

§1. Si communitas seu collegium clericorum delictum commiserit, suspensio ferri potest vel in singulas personas delinquentes vel in communitatem, uti talem, vel in personas delinquentes et communitatem.

§2. Si primum, serventur huius articuli canones.

§3. Si alterum, communitas prohibetur exercitio iurium spiritualium quae ipsi, uti communitati, competunt.

§4. Si tertium, effectus cumulantur.

History proves that a community may be suspended.[88] That it is juridically possible follows from the fact that a community, as such, may be guilty of crimes and, consequently, liable to punishment. Special rights are attached to corporate bodies and may be suspended for a time. As a crime (for instance, appropriation or embezzlement of church property or disobedience to lawful authority) may be perpetrated by single members of a community, as members, or by the community as such (for instance, by a capitular decree), or by single members *and* the community simultaneously, it follows that a community or corporation can be suspended in three different ways.

1. If *single members* of a community (also male religious [89]) are suspended, all the effects which that suspension involves, follow, and therefore what has been stated in connection with canons 2278-2284 must here be applied.

2. If the *community or corporation* as such is suspended, all its spiritual corporate rights, *i. e.*, spiritual rights which the community as such enjoys, are suspended. To this class belong especially the rights of

88 Cathedral, collegiate, and religious chapters, *sede vacante*, proved detrimental to the property of the prelates or church, and were therefore suspended; c. 40, 6°, I, 6; c. un. 6°, III, 8.

89 Of female chapters the Canon Law says nothing, although some abbesses overstepped the limits of their power, examples of which may be found in c. 10, X, V, 38; c. 12, X, I, 33, in which latter chapter an abbess is said to have suspended her clerics from office and benefice. Neither are female religious suspended.

election, presentation, nomination; also, we presume,
that of corporate representation at processions, and therefore also the right of precedence.   All these are suspended (see can. 2275) ; but the right to administer property is not stopped.   It also appears logical to deny
the right of exercising pontifical functions, if such belong
to a suspended community.

3. If *single members and the community as such* are
suspended, the effects are bulked, according to can. 2275.

TITLE IX

VINDICTIVE PENALTIES

Can. 2286

Poenae vindicativae illae sunt, quae directe ad delicti expiationem tendunt ita ut earum remissio e cessatione contumaciae delinquentis non pendeat.

Can. 2287

Ab inflictis poenis vindicativis datur appellatio seu recursus in suspensivo, nisi aliud expresse in iure caveatur.

Can. 2288

Exceptis poenis degradationis, depositionis, privationis officii aut beneficii, et nisi urgeat necessitas reparandi scandalum, prudentiae iudicis remittitur, si reus talis sit ut prima vice post vitam laudabiliter peractam deliquerit, poenae ordinariae per sententiam condemnatoriam inflictae exsecutionem suspendere, ea tamen conditione ut, si reus intra proximum triennium aliud delictum eiusdem vel alterius generis commiserit, poenam utrique delicto debitam luat.

Can. 2289

Poena vindicativa finitur eius expiatione vel dispensatione ab eo concessa qui legitimam habeat dispensandi potestatem ad norman can. 2236.

Can. 2290

§1. In casibus occultis urgentioribus, si ex obser-
vatione poenae vindicativae latae sententiae, reus
seipsum proderet cum infamia et scandalo, quilibet
confessarius potest in foro sacramentali obligationem
servandae poenae suspendere, iniuncto onere recurrendi saltem intra mensem per epistolam et per
confessarium, si id fieri possit sine gravi incommodo,
reticito nomine, ad S. Poenitentiariam vel ad
Episcopum facultate praeditum et standi eius
mandatis.

§2. Et si in aliquo casu extraordinario hic recursus
sit impossibilis, tunc ipsemet confessarius potest dispensationem concedere ad normam can. 2254, §3.

Every society is instituted for the welfare of its members, but also for the sake of its own existence and weal.
This lies in the nature of society. The Church, too, must
necessarily provide for the salvation of souls, this being
her supreme law. But as a human society consists of
men, not of angels, it is evident that the Church has to
wield a sword in order to exact obedience if other means
fail. This privilege belongs to her as an autonomous
society. Self-respect and self-preservation prescribe
means that savor of atonement and public reparation.
Such means are called vindictive penalties, because their
primary end is to avenge the public order. It is not
necessary to recall the penitential system, which had very
much of a public character up to the twelfth century.
Neither is it necessary to remind the reader of the
historical fact that, during the time of religious union,
the vindictive measures were more numerous and more

effectively enforced than now, and that in the course of later centuries they became fewer and more spiritualized. Still the present number is far from insignificant.

1. *Vindictive penalties,* says can. 2286, *are intended directly for the expiation of crimes, and consequently their relaxation does not depend on the mere cessation of contumacy.* The reason for this statement has been given above. These penalties are called *vindictive* because their object is to avenge the social and juridical order of the Church. They are *penalties* because inflicted by lawful authority by way of privation, as plainly appears in all the penalties enumerated in canons 2291 and 2298.

Note that vindictive penalties may be either *latae* or *ferendae sententiae.* Those *latae sententiae* require no judiciary trial.[1] A declaratory sentence is indeed required, *i. e.,* one to ascertain the criminal fact, but this does not mean that the delinquent would not be obliged to execute the sentence on himself if he knew himself to be guilty of a crime on which the law puts a certain penalty. Can. 2232, § 1, expressly says that vindictive penalties have the same obligation attached to them as corrective penalties. There are, however, exceptions to this self-execution; see can. 2290.

2. *Appeal* or *recourse from vindictive penalties is admitted,* and this appeal has a *suspensive,* not merely a devolutive effect, unless the law contains an express provision to the contrary. This, of course, must be understood of such penalties as are inflicted *ab homine* or *a iure,* but *ferendae sententiae;* because when the law

---

[1] Can. 2223 f. and can. 2290, § 1 distinctly mention a vindictive penalty *latae sententiae;* wherefore we cannot agree with Eichmann, *l. c.,* p. 109, that vindictive penalties can be inflicted only after a trial; see also Thesaurus-Giraldi, *l. c.,* p. 1, c. 5, p. 5, who admits such a penalty *latae sententiae;* especially ineligibility for office.

declares a penalty to be incurred *ipso iure*,[2] there is no recourse or appeal with suspensive effect possible.[3] The suspensive effect, to repeat what was said before, means that, pending the recourse or appeal, the delinquent is not bound to consider or to conduct himself as convicted or guilty, either in the internal or in the external forum.

3. *Suspension of the sentence* is a mitigation introduced in legal terms by the Code. It may be called a conditional pardon, such as is granted by judges on condition of good behaviour in future, and has been used in civil codes.[4] In our can. 2288 it is called a *suspension of the execution of a condemnatory sentence* by which an ordinary penalty is inflicted. An ordinary penalty is one which is determined in law or by custom[5] and does not exceed the proportion of imputability, scandal, and damage (see can. 2218). The judge may prudently apply this benefit of the law to a delinquent who had led an irreproachable life before, but now has committed a punishable crime for the first time. Suspension of sentence

a) Is a *conditional* suspension or pardon, for *if the delinquent commits the same or a different crime within three years* (from date of the conditional pardon) *he has to pay the penalty originally decreed as well as the penalty determined for the new crime.* But the suspended penalty is not retroactive; or, at least the text is silent about its retroactive character.

b) *The benefit of conditional pardon cannot be applied* by the judge if : 1°. the penalty of degradation, deposition, privation from office or benefice has been inflicted, or

---

2 See can. 2343, § 1, n. 2: *est ipso iure infamis.*

3 Thesaurus-Giraldi, *l. c.,* p. 39; p. 1, c. 25.

4 Thus the *Regolamento* of Gregory XVI, art. 36, § 4; art. 49; Wernz, *l. c.,* VI, n. 85, p. 93.

5 Schmalzgruber, V, 37, n. 11.

if 2°. there is need of repairing public scandal, because vindictive penalties are intended for the maintenance of the public order.

4. *Cessation of penalties.* Since the object just mentioned can be obtained by atonement or *expiation,* it is evident that, if satisfaction is made, the penalty should cease. This is readily understood if the penalty was a fixed one, as happens when a fine is imposed, or if the penalty is limited to a certain time, after the lapse of which it ceases.[6] Prescription cannot be alleged, inasmuch as criminal action only, not penalty, is liable to prescription.[7] But in many cases expiation has a relative meaning, which depends upon the acceptance of the ecclesiastical authority, who must decide whether atonement is sufficient.

Therefore, besides expiation, can. 2289 mentions a more specific manner of releasing the penalty; *viz.: by dispensation.* As dispensation in general is a relaxation of the law, so here it is the remission of a penal law or sentence. Such a relaxation can proceed only from the authority which has the power to enact penal laws or inflict vindictive penalties.[8] This, however, must be judged according to can. 2236. Consequently:

a) *A dispensation can be granted only by the prelate* who inflicted the penalty and, therefore, a penalty inflicted by *common law* can be remitted only by the *Pope;* a penalty inflicted by a *particular law* or statute can be remitted by the one who enacted that particular law,

6 Thesaurus-Giraldi, *l. c.,* p. 41.
7 See can. 1703–1705.
8 Of little practical value is the distinction between *absolution* and *dispensation,* as if the former proceeded from the judiciary, the latter from the legislative power (thus Hollweck, *l. c.,* p. 141 according to Thesaurus-Giraldi, *l. c.,* p. 21); yet there is a difference between the two, inasmuch as absolution is an act of justice *(actus iustitiae),* whereas dispensation is a favor *(actus gratiae).*

i. e., concretely speaking, by the local Ordinary,[9] or in the case of exempt religious communities, by the competent superior who enjoys this power according to the constitutions.

b) A penalty inflicted by a superior *ab homine* can be dispensed with by himself;

c) And, since the *successor* in office has equal power, he, too, can dispense; the same, of course, is to be said of *delegates.*

d) But a *judge* who merely applies the penal law or precept cannot dispense from penalties, since his office ceases with the sentence and his power is thereby exhausted.[10]

All other extensions of these principles, proposed by authors,[11] must be limited to the rules stated above; but the Code has adopted some of the modifications providing for urgent cases (see can. 81).

5. *Extended power* is given to confessors for *more urgent occult cases.* What occult or secret crimes are has been explained in can. 2197, 4°. This power is limited as follows:

a) It is not only *conditioned* upon *secrecy and urgency,* but the observance of the vindictive penalty, which is supposed to be *latae sententiae,* must, at least probably, cause the loss of good name to the delinquent and scandal to the people. Of the existence of this condition the petitioner may judge, and his testimony must be believed. Take, *e. g.,* suspension from office for a certain time, or refusal to accept a dignity offered, of which the confessor might know nothing.

9 Not by the metropolitan, nor even by the Apostolic Delegate, unless the latter has obtained delegated power; but his delegation generally concerns only matters *a iure,* not *ab homine.*

10 Wernz, *l. c.,* VI, n. 88 f.; p. 93.

11 Thesaurus-Giraldi, *l. c.,* p. 29 ff.

b) The power granted to confessors is *limited* also in this sense, that the confessor in the confessional—therefore not merely *in foro interno*—can only *suspend* the obligation of observing the vindictive penalty imposed by law, and must hold the penitent to the duty of *having recourse* to the proper authority in writing, through the confessor, within *one month* from the date of confession, if this can be done without serious inconvenience. This recourse must be had, without mentioning names, to the S. Poenitentiaria or to the bishop, if he enjoys the necessary faculties. The penitent must then abide by their orders.

c) *If in an extraordinary case recourse is impossible,* the confessor is empowered to grant the dispensation, according to can. 2254. §3.

CHAPTER I

Can. 2291

Poenae vindicativae quae omnes fideles pro delictorum gravitate afficere possunt, in Ecclesia praesertim sunt:

1°. Interdictum locale et interdictum in communitatem seu collegium in perpetuum vel ad tempus praefinitum vel ad beneplacitum Superioris;

2°. Interdictum ab ingressu ecclesiae in perpetuum vel ad tempus praefinitum vel ad beneplacitum Superioris;

3°. Poenalis translatio vel suppressio sedis episcopalis vel paroecialis;

4°. Infamia iuris;

5°. Privatio sepulturae ecclesiasticae, ad normam can. 1240, §1;

6°. Privatio Sacramentalium;

7°. Privatio vel suspensio ad tempus pensionis quae ab Ecclesia vel ex bonis Ecclesiae solvitur, vel alius iuris seu privilegii ecclesiastici;

8°. Remotio ab actibus legitimis ecclesiasticis exercendis;

9°. Inhabilitas ad gratias ecclesiasticas aut munia in Ecclesia quae statum clericalem non requirant, vel ad gradus academicos auctoritate ecclesiastica consequendos;

10°. Privatio vel suspensio ad tempus muneris, facultatis vel gratiae iam obtentae;

11°. Privatio iuris praecedentiae vel vocis activae et passivae vel iuris ferendi titulos honoris, vestem, insignia, quae Ecclesia concesserit;

12°. Mulcta pecuniaria.

Can. 2292

Poenalis suppressio aut translatio sedis episcopalis est Romano Pontifici reservata; sedis autem paroecialis, a locorum Ordinariis decerni nequit, nisi cum consilio Capituli.

Can. 2293

§1. Infamia est vel iuris vel facti.

§2. Infamia iuris illa est quae casibus iure communi expressis statuitur.

§3. Infamia facti contrahitur, quando quis, ob patratum delictum vel ob pravos mores, bonam existimationem apud fideles probos et graves amisit, de quo iudicium spectat ad Ordinarium.

§4. Neutra afficit delinquentis consanguineos aut affines, firmo praescripto can. 2147, §2, n. 3.

Can. 2294

§1. Qui infamia iuris laborat, non solum est irregularis ad normam can. 984, n. 5, sed insuper est inhabilis ad obtinenda beneficia, pensiones, officia et dignitates ecclesiasticas, ad actus legitimos ecclesiasticos perficiendos, ad exercitium iuris aut muneris

ecclesiastici, et tandem arceri debet a ministerio in
sacris functionibus exercendo.

§2. Qui laborat infamia facti, repelli debet tum a
recipiendis ordinibus ad normam can. 987, n. 7, dignitatibus, beneficiis, officiis ecclesiasticis, tum ab exercendo sacro ministerio et ab actibus legitimis ecclesiasticis.

Can. 2295

Infamia iuris desinit sola dispensatione a Sede
Apostolica concessa; infamia facti cum bona existi-
matio apud fideles probos et graves, omnibus perpensis
adiunctis et praesertim diuturna rei emendatione,
fuerit, prudenti Ordinarii iudicio, recuperata.

Can. 2296

§1. Si agatur de rebus ad quas assequendas capa-
citas iure communi statuitur, inhabilitatis poenam
infligere una Sedes Apostolica potest.

§2. Iura iam quaesita non amittuntur ob superveni-
entem inhabilitatem, nisi huic addatur poena privationis.

Can. 2297

Mulctas pecuniarias iure communi inflictas, quarum
erogatio non sit eodem iure praefinita, aliasque iure
peculiari statutas vel statuendas, Ordinarii locorum
erogare debent in pios usus, non vero in commodum
mensae episcopalis aut capitularis.

This chapter enumerates,— *demonstrative*, not *taxative*,
as the word *praesertim* indicates,— some vindictive pen-

alties which may be imposed on any delinquent Catholic in proportion to the gravity of his crime (see can. 2218).

Four species of penalties are explained in special canons: transfer, infamy, disability, and fines.

1. The *interdict,* as far as it is imposed upon a community or corporation, is either local or personal, but it is to be considered as a vindictive penalty only if inflicted *either forever, or for a certain time,* or *ad beneplacitum superioris.* For if it is imposed merely for the time being, namely, until contumacy ceases, it is a censure. For the rest, the effects do not differ in either case.

2. The interdict *ab ingressu ecclesiae* forbids, according to can. 2277, entering the church, but only when divine offices are celebrated; during the sermon or at other times the church may be entered.

3. *Penal transfer* or *suppression of an episcopal see* or *parochial residence* differs from the administrative transfer of benefices mentioned in can. 1421 f. Besides stress must be laid on see, or residence, for it means a transfer from one place to another, not extinction. Suppression, however, involves extinction, and in that case a union with another diocese or parish would have to follow; this is called *unio extinctiva* (can. 1419 f.).

According to can. 2292 penal suppression or transfer of an *episcopal* see is reserved to the *Roman Pontiff, i. e.,* the S. C. Consistorialis (can. 248). But a *parochial residence* may be transferred or suppressed by the *local Ordinary,* provided he has asked the advice (he does not need the consent) of his chapter (with us, the diocesan consultors).

4. There is a twofold infamy distinguished in can. 2293: one of law, the other of fact.

a) *Infamy* of law *(iuris)* is that expressly stated in

common law as a penalty for certain crimes;[12] it is legal conviction of a crime.

b) Infamy of fact *(facti)* exists when one, by reason of a crime committed, or on account of bad character, has lost his good reputation with upright and serious Catholics. Whether and when this is the case, is for the Ordinary to decide. Generally speaking, apostates, bigamists, adulterers contract *infamia facti*. But the facts must be proved, not merely asserted, and, as in criminal cases, at least two trustworthy witnesses are required.[18]

c) The effects of *legal infamy* are stated as follows:

1°. Legal infamy may be inflicted as a *penalty*, as per can. 2291, n. 4.

2°. Legal infamy involves *irregularity* according to can. 984, n. 5, and therefore no layman affected by it can receive the tonsure or any order without an apostolic dispensation.

3°. Legal infamy entails *disability* or disqualification for any ecclesiastical benefice, pension, office, dignity; if conferred, the act is invalid (can. 2391).

4°. It *disqualifies* the infamous person from performing any *legal ecclesiastical act* of the kind mentioned in can. 2256, n. 2, especially sponsorship.[14]

5°. It *disqualifies* the infamous person from *exercising any ecclesiastical right or charge*, e. g., the right of election, presentation, or nomination,[15] or such charges as are involved in the offices of notaries, defenders, pro-

---

12 These crimes are mentioned in canons 2314, § 1, n. 2, 3; 2320; 2328, 2343, § 1, n. 2; § 2, n. 2; 2351, § 2; 2356; 2357, § 1; 2359, § 2.

18 Cfr. I Tim. 5, 19; can. 1939-1946.

14 See canons 765, n. 2; 766, n. 2; 795, n. 2; 796, n. 3.

15 See canons 167, § 1, n. 3; 1470, § 4.

curators or attorneys, counsel, administrators,[16] and, we suppose, also church trustees.

6°. An infamous person must be prevented from *coöperating in sacred functions*, such as serving at Mass, carrying the canopy, cross, or censer, playing the organ at divine service, etc.

d) *Infamia facti* produces the following effects:

1°. It constitutes a canonical *impediment* for receiving orders, but does not render one irregular (can. 987, n. 7).

2°. It *disqualifies* one from *lawfully* (not validly) *accepting ecclesiastical dignities, benefices, or offices.*

3°. Infamous persons may not *exercise any function of the sacred ministry* which may ordinarily be performed by laymen, as stated above.

4°. They must be repelled from exercising *actus legitimi* as explained under can. 2256, n. 2. Those who are manifestly infamous must also be refused the Holy Eucharist (can. 855, §1).

Note that *neither legal infamy* nor *infamy of fact affects the blood relations or legal relations of the infamous subject.* Therefore, the *consanguinei* and *affines* of an infamous person are not included in this penalty, nor do the effects of infamy affect them. On the other hand, a pastor may incur the infamy of his *familiares* and blood relations and be removed in an administrative way on this account (can. 2293, §4; can. 2147, §3, n. 3.).[17]

e) *Cessation of infamy.*

---

[16] See canons 373, § 3; 1571, § 3; 1589, § 1; 1657, § 1; after a condemnatory or declaratory sentence they are excluded from being witnesses or experts; can. 1757, 1795, 1931; but not from being plaintiffs, at least no such exclusion is stated; Eichmann, *l. c.*, p. III.

[17] Can. 1755, § 2, n. 2, must be applied to both kinds of infamy, and hence a witness who is afraid of causing infamy to himself or to his relatives is not obliged to answer on the witness stand.

1°. Legal infamy or *infamia iuris* can be removed only by an *Apostolic dispensation;* this is true with one exception, *viz.:* occult urgent cases, for in these can. 2290 may be applied.[18]

2°. Infamy of fact *(infamia facti)* ceases by *rehabilitation* of one's good name, *i. e.,* by regaining one's lost reputation with upright and serious Catholics. This depends upon particular circumstances, continued good behavior, and, above all, on the judgment of the Ordinary.

An observation on *civil infamy* may not be superfluous. The Roman law [19] branded several crimes with infamy *(infamia notati).* Its regulations were partly adopted and partly modified by the common law.[20] However, the modern civil legislation on this subject, though based upon the Roman law, at least in Latin countries, has never been formally adopted by the Church. Consequently, when we speak of *infamia iuris* in ecclesiastical language, this must be strictly understood of Canon Law only. It does not follow, however, that civil infamy, which generally consists in the withdrawal of civic rights, at least for a time, does not produce canonical infamy of fact *(infamia facti).*[21] Therefore bishops, as custodians of discipline, should not lose sight of the particular laws of their respective countries. In England and many States of the U. S., all disqualifications, such as disability to serve as witness or juror, have been abolished.[22] Notwithstanding this abolition of the effects of infamy, however, certain crimes are still known as infamous and should therefore be taken as a directive norm for

---

18 See also can. 1948, § 1: *correptio iudicialis* cannot be substituted in case of infamy.

19 Cfr. Dig. 3, 2, *de his qui infamia notantur.*

20 Cfr. cc. 2, 17, C. 6, q. 1; c.

5, Dist. 51; c. 4, x, IV, 21; c. 5, 6°, V, 9.

21 Wernz, *l. c.,* VI, p. 112, n. 105.

22 *New International Encycl.,* 1904, Vol. X, *s. v.* "Infamy."

ecclesiastical presumption, more especially when admission to the clerical state is in question.

5. *Privation of ecclesiastical burial,* according to the rules laid down in can. 1240, §1.

6. *Privation of the sacramentals,* for instance, churching of women, nuptial blessing, blessing of homes.

7. *Privation or temporary suspension of pensions* which the Church is wont to pay, or which come from ecclesiastical property; also *withdrawal of some other ecclesiastical rights or privileges.* Therefore, state pensions or pensions paid by private persons or companies, although they may have an ecclesiastical name or be under ecclesiastical guidance, do not fall under the heading of ecclesiastical pensions.[28] A right that may be withheld is that of presentation, a privilege, that of a private oratory or a special seat in church.

8. *Exclusion from legal ecclesiastical functions,* such as sponsorship, proxy, lawyer (see can. 2256, n. 2).

9. *Disability* to obtain: (a) ecclesiastical favors, for instance, dispensations or privileges; (b) charges which do not presuppose the clerical state, for instance, notary, administrator, beadle, sexton, etc.; (c) academic degrees which are conferred by church authorities, either by ecclesiastical institutes [24] in the ordinary way, or by favor, *i. e., honoris causa.*

Can. 2296, on disability, has two sections. The first supposes that disability may be established by common law *(iure communi)* or by a particular law, as also *ab*

28 Eichmann, *l. c.,* p. 112.

24 Degrees conferred by secular universities are not excluded; nor are academic degrees which are conferred by ecclesiastical institutions, but in virtue of civil or State authority, for the text says: *auctoritate ecclesiastica.* Hence if a college or university has obtained a State diploma enabling it to grant B.A. or M.A. or Ph.D., etc., it may be legitimately acquired and retained.

homine. Disability by common law, as, for instance, with regard to orders and advowson,[25] can be inflicted only by the Apostolic See. But if a particular law or diocesan statute should attach special qualities to a certain charge held in the diocese (for instance, church trustee), the disqualification can be established by the local Ordinary.[26]

§*2 of can. 2296* states that *rights* already acquired, *e. g.,* the right of a private oratory, *are not taken away by a supervening disability.* Disqualification, therefore, concerns only the future, not the past. However, the text adds quite logically: "*Nisi huic addatur poena privationis*"; for if the penalty of privation is added and doubled, it is evident that charges, rights, favors, academic degrees may also be taken away; for it lies in the nature of privation that a man cannot be deprived of what he does not possess.

10. *Privation or temporary suspension of a charge, faculty,* or *privilege already obtained.* Concerning cases in which the Ordinary may dispense, see can. 2237. If privation requires a declaratory sentence, infamy excuses from its observance (can. 2232, §1), unless the crime is notorious. If the sentence of privation has been validly issued and carried out, the office becomes vacant (can. 183, §1).

11. *Withdrawal of the right of precedence, of the active and passive voice,* of the right of using honorary titles, of wearing robes and insignia granted by the Church, for instance, pontifical emblems and prelatical garb.[27]

12. *Pecuniary fines* began to be imposed in the seventh century and became quite frequent after the Germanic

---

25 Can. 948 ff., 1453, 2383, 2394.   27 See canons 325; 349, § 1, n. 2;
26 See can. 2237 concerning   405; 407; 409.
public and occult cases.

laws were applied.[28] But abuses soon crept in and became so scandalous that the Council of Trent thought it necessary to limit such fines.[29] The Code admits them for canons, for ecclesiastical judges, lawyers, and pro-curators, against unlawful alienators, unjust copyists or officials of diocesan courts who have to do with official documents, and those who overcharge in demanding taxes.[30]

The Code (can. 2297) regulates the *use* of fines as follows: Pecuniary fines inflicted by *common law*, but not determined by the same as to the manner in which they are to be employed, also fines established or to be inflicted by *particular law*, must be spent by the Ordinaries for *charitable purposes*, never for enriching the episcopal or capitular fund. Although payment could be enforced by ecclesiastical censures (can. 2198), the secular arm would hardly lend its aid in the matter.

28 Kober, in the *Tübinger Quar-talschrift*, 1881, p. 3 ff. On pecuni-ary fines see c. 41, X, V, 3; c. 14, X; V, 6; c. 2, X, V, 26; c. 7, X, V, 36; Hollweck, *l. c.*, p. 154, § 85.

29 *Trid.*, Sess. 25, c. 3, *de ref.*
30 See canons 395, § 2; 413; 1625, § 2; 1666; 2347, n. 2; 2406, § 2; 2408.

CHAPTER II

Can. 2298

Poenae vindicativae quae clericis tantum applicantur, sunt:

1°. Prohibitio exercendi sacrum ministerium praeterquam in certa ecclesia;

2°. Suspensio in perpetuum vel ad tempus praefinitum, vel ad beneplacitum Superioris;

3°. Translatio poenalis ab officio vel beneficio obtento ad inferius;

4°. Privatio alicuius iuris cum beneficio vel officio coniuncti;

5°. Inhabilitas ad omnes vel ad aliquot dignitates, officia, beneficia aliave munera propria clericorum;

6°. Privatio poenalis beneficii vel officii cum vel sine pensione;

7°. Prohibitio commorandi in certo loco vel territorio;

8°. Praescriptio commorandi in certo loco vel territorio;

9°. Privatio ad tempus habitus ecclesiastici;

10°. Depositio;

11°. Privatio perpetua habitus ecclesiastici;

12°. Degradatio.

Can. 2299

§1. Si clericus beneficium inamovibile obtineat,

eodem in poenam privari potest solum in casibus iure expressis; si amovibile, etiam ob alias rationabiles causas.

§2. Clerici obtinentes beneficia, officia, dignitates, possunt etiam aliquo tantum ministerio cum iisdem coniuncto, ex. gr., ministerio praedicandi, confessiones audiendi, etc., prohiberi ad certum tempus.

§3. Nequit clericus privari beneficio aut pensione cuius titulo ordinatus fuit, nisi aliunde eius honestae sustentationi provideatur, salvo praescripto can. 2303, 2304.

Can. 2300

Si clericus gravia scandala praebeat et monitus non resipiscat, nec scandalum queat aliter removeri, potest interim privari iure deferendi habitum ecclesiasticum; quae privatio, dum perdurat, secumfert prohibitionem exercendi ministeria quaevis ecclesiastica et privationem privilegiorum clericalium.

Can. 2301

Ordinarius nequit praescribere ut clericus certo in loco, extra fines suae dioecesis, commoretur, nisi accedat consensus Ordinarii illius loci vel agatur de domo poenitentiae seu emendationis clericis non solum dioecesanis, sed etiam extraneis destinata, aut de domo religiosa exempta, Superiore eiusdem consentiente.

Can. 2302

Tam praescriptio quam prohibitio certo in loco commorandi et collocatio in domo poenitentiae aut in domo religiosa, praesertim si diu duraturae sint, imponantur tantum in casibus gravibus, in quibus, prudenti Ordinarii iudicio, eae poenae necessariae sint ad clerici emendationem aut scandali reparationem.

Can. 2303

§1. Depositio, firmis obligationibus e suscepto ordine exortis et privilegiis clericalibus, secumfert tum suspensionem ab officio, et inhabilitatem ad quaelibet officia, dignitates, beneficia, pensiones, munera in Ecclesia, tum etiam privationem illorum quae reus habeat, licet eorum titulo fuerit ordinatus.

§2. Sed hoc ultimo in casu, si clericus vere indigeat, Ordinarius pro sua caritate, quo meliore modo fieri potest, ei providere curet, ne cum dedecore status clericalis mendicare cogatur.

§3. Poena depositionis infligi nequit, nisi in casibus iure expressis.

Can. 2304

§1. Si clericus depositus non det emendationis signa et praesertim si scandalum dare pergat monitusque non resipiscat, Ordinarius potest eum perpetuo privare iure deferendi habitum ecclesiasticum.

§2. Haec privatio secumfert privationem privilegiorum clericalium et cessationem praescripti can. 2303, §2.

Can. 2305

§1. Degradatio in se continet depositionem, perpetuam privationem habitus ecclesiastici et reductionem clerici ad statum laicalem.

§2. Haec poena ferri solummodo potest propter delictum in iure expressum, aut si clericus, iam depositus et habitu clericali privatus, grave adhuc scandalum per annum praebere pergat.

§3. Alia est *verbalis* seu *edictalis*, quae sola sententia irrogatur, ita tamen ut omnes suos effectus iuridicos statim habeat sine ulla· exsecutione; alia *realis*, si serventur sollemnia praescripta in Pontificali Romano.

Some penalties formerly employed, even against clerics, such as branding, bodily chastisement *(fustigatio)*, exile, imprisonment and permanent confinement in monasteries, are not mentioned in the Code.[1]

This enumeration of twelve species of penalties seems not to be complete, but applies to clerics only *(clericis tantum)*.

1°. Prohibition of exercising the sacred ministry except in a *specified church*. Thus a clergyman may be told to say Mass in a certain chapel or church only, or preach only in a certain church of a city, whilst all others are forbidden to him.

2°. *Perpetual suspension*, or *suspension for a specified term* or *ad beneplacitum superioris*, in which latter case the superior may shorten or lengthen the time.

3°. *Transfer* from a better office or benefice to an inferior one, which is always odious and, therefore, savors

---

[1] Perforation of the tongue and the galleys (after degradation, especially of the so-called *disconi selvaggi)* were also sometimes used. Such are not exactly in accordance with our present, rather sentimental, notions of the penal code, and are, therefore, discarded. On the other hand, it must not be forgotten that bishops and popes, and also abbots, as *temporal lords* of their respective territories, when employing such penalties, acted like other monarchs according to the custom of *their* times; Hollweck, *l. c.*

of degradation and, of course, involves loss of jurisdiction in the territory from which the transfer is made.[2]

4°. *Privation of one or the other right* connected with a benefice, *e. g.*, administration of the same, or with an *office, e. g.*, the exercise of preaching or hearing confessions, or, for bishops, the granting of faculties or free appointment to offices.

5°. *Disability for all or certain dignities, offices, benefices, and clerical charges,* which also extends to religious offices.[3] Here can. 2296, §2 must be applied, although one may find there an analogy which is inadmissible in penal matters. The analogy, however, consists not in the application of the penalty, but only in the competency to inflict it. Consequently the Ordinary cannot decree disability for holding offices already possessed or acquired,[4] but only disqualify the delinquent for the future, *i. e.*, debar him from obtaining other dignities, offices, benefices, charges which may be held by clergymen. Besides, also in case of clergymen, can. 2296, §1, must be applied, so that only the Apostolic See can inflict this penalty if it is stated in common law. Only the Apostolic See can dispense in public cases of *inhabilitas latae sententiae*.[5]

6°. *Privation* of benefice or office, with or without pension, which is followed by a vacancy in the office or benefice itself, provided it be decreed *ipso iure* or after a regular trial.[6] This is called *penal* privation, because there is another, viz., the administrative one, treated in can. 2147 ff. Here *can. 2299* must be added, which

---

2 See canons 2162-2167: 183; 873, § 3.

3 See can. 2413.

4 Here it may be added that the *ius ad rem*, for instance, by accepting an election, is a real right and consequently included.

5 Can. 2237, § 1, n. 3; Thesaurus-Giraldi, *l. c.*, P. I, c. 28 (*ed cit.* p. 49)

6 See can. 183, § 1; can. 192.

further determines the penalty in question as follows:

a) An *irremovable beneficiary* — our irremovable rectors are here included — can be deprived of his benefice (or pastorship) only in cases expressly stated in law;[7] a *removable beneficiary*, on the other hand, may be deprived of his benefice also for other reasonable causes, such as protracted disobedience or neglect of pastoral duties, and those mentioned in can. 2182.

b) Clergymen who are in possession of benefices, offices, or dignities may be forbidden to exercise part of their *ministerial functions for a special term;* for instance, they may have to abstain from preaching or hearing confessions, or from administering their benefice, or from exercising the functions of their dignity. Of course, this must be clearly expressed, for instance, by withdrawing the faculty of hearing confessions, etc. That with the total withdrawal of all faculties the office also is withdrawn, is evident.

c) A *cleric cannot be deprived of the benefice or pension which constitute his titulus ordinationis,*[8] *except in the cases mentioned in can. 2303 and 2304.* If the Ordinary should deprive a cleric of the benefice or pension to which he has been ordained, the Ordinary must provide a decent support, for instance, by offering the cleric another position or pension, or maintaining him in a charitable house. In cases of deposition this latter obligation on the part of the Ordinary ceases to be one of

---

7 *Latae sententiae;* see canons 2396, 2397, 2398, 2366.

Ferendae sententiae; canons 2314, § 1, n. 2; 2331, § 2; 2340, § 2; 2343, § 2; n. 3, 2354, § 2; 2359,

§ 2; 2368, § 1; 2345; 2346; 2350, § 2; 2381, n. 2.

Facultative; canons 2324, 2336, § 1, 2; 2355; 2359, § 2; 2360, § 2; 2394 n. 2, 2403; 2405.

8 See can. 979.

justice and becomes one merely of charity (can. 2303, §2). In cases of degradation both titles, of justice as well as charity, cease to oblige the Ordinary (can. 2404).

7°. *Prohibition to live in a certain place or territory.*

8°. *Command to stay in a certain place or territory.* Concerning these two penalties canons 2301 and 2302 must be consulted.

a) The Ordinary *cannot order such a cleric to live in a certain place outside his own diocese.* For his jurisdiction is territorially circumscribed, and only if the Ordinary of the other diocese gives his formal consent, may the clergyman thus ordered to live in a strange diocese remain there. If there should be an *interdiocesan house of correction or detention,* the Ordinary may send a cleric there, because it is supposed that all the bishops concerned have an agreement among themselves to that effect. If the Ordinary wishes to inflict on a cleric the punishment pronounced in n. 8, with the command to stay, for the time being, in a *religious house that belongs to an exempt institute,* he can do so only with the *consent of the respective superior.* For with regard to this matter the local Ordinary has no power over exempt houses in his diocese, though with *non-exempt houses* he can deal more imperiously, although it would not be against the dictates of natural equity if he would first consult the religious superior, for religious houses are not reform schools or houses of correction.

b) The command to stay in a certain place or in a house of correction or a religious house, especially for a considerable time, *should not be imposed except for weighty reasons,* such as the necessary amendment of the clergyman or the repairing of scandal. The Ordinary is the judge, but he should give the cleric a fair hearing and not simply "shut him off," as one Archbishop did in a case brought before the S. Congregation.[9]

9°. *On prohibition to wear the ecclesiastical dress* enough has been said under can. 136. It refers, of course, to the usual clerical garb and tonsure (can. 213, §1), not the vestments used in the sacred ministry.

Concerning this penalty, can. 2300 makes the following regulations:

a) *Temporary privation* of this right *can only be inflicted* if the scandal given by the cleric is really serious, after admonition has proved useless,[10] and the scandal[11] cannot be removed in any other way.

b) As *long as the privation lasts,* its effects are:

α) The clergyman thus punished is not allowed to perform any act of his ecclesiastical ministry. The text does not declare the invalidity of such acts, *e. g.,* of jurisdiction exercised in the confessional, or assistance at marriage, nor the loss of the respective office; therefore, the least is to be taken.

β) This privation entails the loss of the clerical privileges or rights mentioned in can. 118-123.

10°. *Deposition,*[12] one of the oldest and at the same time, heaviest ecclesiastical penalties, consists in the pri-

9 S. C. EE. et RR., March 6, 1841 (Bizzarri, *l. c.,* p. 532) instructed the archbishop to leave the priest in peace or give him a fair hearing. A kind of long exile or prohibition to stay in one's diocese might cause a conflict with the civil authorities; for ordinaries have no right to forbid one to stay in a certain place from the viewpoint of civil law.

10 On admonition, see can. 2143.

11 Notice the plural *scandala,* which may mean diverse or protracted or repeated scandals.

12 See Kober, *Die Deposition und Degradation,* 1867: formerly deposition and degradation were identical, and entailed loss of office and benefice together with disqualification, but the privileges *fori* and *canonis* remained. After the XIIth century, however, deposition was clearly distinguished from degradation, which later only implied loss of the clerical privileges, see c. 10, X, II, 1; c. 7, X, V, 40; c. 27, X, V, 40.

vation of all the titles that a clergyman may possess,
except the clerical state itself and its essential privileges.
Its effects are more minutely described in can. 2303 as
follows:

a) The *obligations* inherent in the order received, as
well as the clerical *privileges remain*. Therefore, even a
deposed cleric, if he has been ordained subdeacon,
must recite the Breviary and remain unmarried (can. 132,
135), and retains the prerogatives mentioned in can. 118-
123.

b) A deposed cleric is *ipso facto suspended* from office;

c) He is *disqualified* for any office, dignity, benefice,
pension or any ecclesiastical charge *(munus);*

d) He is *deprived of all the offices, dignities, benefices,
pensions, and charges that he holds, even though he has
been ordained on the title of benefice or pension.* However, in case of the benefice or pension being the title on
which the clergyman was ordained, the *Ordinary should
act charitably towards a needy cleric* and provide
him with the necessary support, so that he may not be
compelled to beg his living and so disgrace the clerical
state.

No juridical claim can be asserted against this charitable support. Even if the clergyman belongs to a clerical aid society, which is based on mutual agreement and
contributions, he can in justice claim diocesan support,
because he still belongs to the clergy and is supposed to
be still incardinated. For our text, can. 2303, §2, only
mentions the two canonical sources of support: benefice
and pension. These, however, are essentially distinct
from a clerical aid society. On the other hand, it must
also be noted that the Ordinary, in case such a society
should furnish the means for an indigent clergyman,

would not be obliged to exercise charity towards him. Besides, the by-laws or constitutions might contain other regulations precluding a deposed clergyman from the benefit of support.

The *mode of inflicting* the penalty of deposition is indicated in can. 2303, §3: "*It cannot be inflicted except for crimes expressly stated in the Code.*" However, the Code knows no penalty which would be incurred *ipso iure* or *latae sententiae.*[18] But cases *ferendae sententiae* are mentioned.[14] If the Ordinary wishes to depose a clergyman, he has to proceed in the judiciary way, and constitute a collegiate body of five judges,—otherwise the trial is null and void.[14a] In cases where deposition is inflicted, can. 1948, §1 and can. 2288 must be applied.

11°. *Perpetual privation of the clerical garb* is a more serious penalty than even deposition. For, as can. 2304, §2 states, *it implies privation of all clerical privileges and releases the Ordinary from even the charitable obligation of providing the necessary support for an indigent cleric.* But, as the same can. 2304, §1 says, this penalty can only be inflicted,

a) If the cleric has been previously deposed;

b) If he shows no signs of repentance, but rather continues to give scandal;

c) If he does not heed the admonitions addressed to

---

[18] The Decretals are ambiguous, so that some, for instance, Thesaurus-Giraldi (P. I, c. 27), could speak of a deposition *latae sententiae;* see c. 3, X, V, 27; c. 1, § 2, 6°, V, 4; c. 5, 6°, V, 9; c. un. Extrav. Comm., V, 6. Hollweck, *l. c.*, p. 158, § 91, note 1, denies that such a penalty *latae sent.* can be read into the old law.

[14] See can. 2314, § 1, n. 2; 2320; 2322, n. 1; 2328; 2350, § 1; 2354, § 2; 2359, § 2; 2379; 2394, n. 2; 2401; a canonically deposed cardinal loses the active voice: "*Vacante Sede,*" n. 31.

[14a] Can. 1576, §1, n. 2.

him.[15] All these conditions must concur in order to permit the Ordinary to inflict this penalty. The trial must be conducted in the same way as for deposition.[16] This also applies to religious superiors who have to proceed in such cases.[17]

12°. *Degradation*, the last and severest of all clerical penalties, consists in the *reduction of a cleric to the lay state*. This seems to be impossible on account of the indelible character imprinted by the Sacrament of Holy Orders, but since a real distinction was introduced between deposition and degradation in the XII century, it was but logical to maintain the severest penalty for those who had juridically degraded themselves.

a) The *effects* of .degradation, according to can. 2305, §1, are: deposition, perpetual privation of the clerical dress, and reduction to the lay state. These effects follow *both kinds* of degradation, the verbal as well as the real *(verbalis seu edictalis et realis)*, as the difference between the two lies only in the mode of application. *Verbal* degradation requires merely a judicial sentence, whereas *real* must be accompanied by the ceremonies described in the Roman Pontifical.[18] Note that even a degraded cleric is bound to observe celibacy.[19]

b) This penalty is *ferendae sententiae* only, since no case of *latae sententiae* is mentioned in the Code. Therefore the text (can. 2305, §2) says: "*ferri potest,*"

---

15 Can. 2143.

16 Can. 1576, § 1, n. 2.

17 Can. 670.

18 P. III: "*Degradationis Forma,*" which contains the doleful ceremonies of degradation, commencing with the rite for degrading a Pope and ending with that for tonsured clerics. This ceremony, as stated in the Pont. Rom., presupposes that the clergyman was tried and sentence was given, and, besides, that he is offered to the local ordinary for this act of humiliation.

19 Cfr. can. 213, § 2; but the obligation of reciting the Breviary ceases; can. 138.

it may be inflicted for crimes mentioned in the law; [20] or
if the cleric, being already deposed and deprived of the
clerical garb, continues for one year to give scandal.
Attention must again be drawn to can. 1576, §1, n. 2,
which requires five judges to pronounce sentence, and
to can. 1948, §1, which forbids substituting the judicial
warning in this case, and to can. 2288, which excludes
a suspension of the execution of the sentence.

20 These cases, besides the one
mentioned in the second clause of
can. 2305, § 2, are canons 2314, § 1,
n. 3; 2343, § 1, n. 3; 2354, § 2;
2368; 2388, § 1.

TITLE X

PENAL REMEDIES AND PENANCES

The title is divided into two chapters, the first of which treats of penal or preventive remedies, the other of penances. This order is logical, since penal remedies are more closely related to penalties proper than the so-called penances. For penal remedies cause some deprivation or pain to normally constituted persons, and this is essential to any penalty. All such remedies leave a stain upon the moral character of the person subjected to them. They presuppose a punishable crime or at least blameworthy conduct, which might lead to more serious breaches of the penal laws. Therefore penal remedies, as stated, partake of the nature of penalties. This applies also to the mode by which they are inflicted. Some of them are mentioned in the decrees of the Council of Trent,[1] others were introduced by later disciplinary laws and now appear formally sanctioned in the Code.[2] To each of the penal remedies we shall add the respective canons referring to them.

[1] Trid., Sess. 13, c. 1, *de ref.*
[2] S. C. EE. et RR., June 11, 1880 (*Coll. P. F.*, n. 1534); see also Wernz, *l. c.*, VI, p. 257, n. 253 f.; Eichmann, *l. c.*, p. 121.

CHAPTER I

Can. 2306

Remedia poenalia sunt:
1° Monitio;
2°. Correptio;
3°. Praeceptum;
4°. Vigilantia.

Can. 2307

Eum qui versatur in proxima occasione delictum committendi vel in quem, ex inquisitione peracta, gravis suspicio cadit delicti commissi, Ordinarius per se vel per interpositam personam moneat.

Can. 2308

Si ex alicuius conversatione scandalum vel gravis ordinis perturbatio oriantur, est locus correptioni, ab Ordinario per se vel per interpositam personam, etiam per epistolam faciendae, peculiaribus accommodatae conditionibus personae et facti de quo agitur.

Can. 2309

§1. Tam monitio quam correptio potest esse vel publica vel secreta.

a) The warning or rebuke may be either *public* or *secret*. If secret, it is rather paternal and generally given in writing or through an intermediary,[4] who, however, must be commissioned by the Ordinary, *i. e.*, by the diocesan bishop, or the prelate *nullius*, or the exempt religious superior, but not the vicar-general, unless he has received a special commission for this purpose. The reason is that penal remedies partake of the nature of penalties, concerning which, according to can. 2220, §2, the vicar-general is not competent in virtue of his office. He may, however, like the dean or pastor, be employed as *persona interposita*.

b) *Public correction* or admonition must be made either before a notary, who in this case may also be the chancellor,[5] or in the presence of two witnesses, who may be discreet laymen, or by letter, which should be registered. If by letter, a record must be kept, showing that it was delivered,[6] and an abstract of the contents must be preserved in the diocesan chancery or court.

c) A *public rebuke* — not a warning — can be served only when the delinquent has been convicted of, or confessed, a crime. It is a judiciary rebuke *(correptio iudicialis)*[7] if administered by the judge sitting in tribunal or by the Ordinary (not the vicar-general unless he has a special mandate) before the criminal procedure has taken a legal turn.

d) A *judiciary rebuke* may take the place of a criminal penalty or may be added to the criminal penalty, especially in case of relapse.

e) Both *admonition and correction*, if made *secretly*, must be recorded in writing and an abstract of the records

4 S. C. EE. et RR., June 11, 1880, n. 6.
5 Can. 372, § 3.
6 The receipt for the registered letter should be inserted *in actis*.
7 See can. 1947–1953.

kept in the secret archives of the diocesan court, because they may be needed as documents for criminal procedure.

f) Both *warning and rebuke* may be administered once or oftener, as the superior shall judge prudent. Although the word *peremptory* should be employed for the sake of greater efficacy, yet the rebuke or warning could not be impugned if this term were omitted, because the Code contains nothing to that effect, but insists only on registration.

3. A *precept,* order, or injunction *is a special command of the bishop, accompanied by threats of punishment in case of disobedience.*[8] It may be served after a warning or a rebuke has proved ineffective or if it is likely that these two, warning and rebuke, will not produce the desired effect. Therefore, in this latter case, the warning and rebuke may be omitted, and the bishop — not the vicar-general — may proceed at once to issue an injunction. This, no doubt, depends on the psychological condition of the delinquent (obstinacy, hot temper) and on the nature of the delinquency, whether the scandal or neglect is great and wide-spread or not. The precept must *contain* as clear and distinct a statement as the case permits, of what the *praeventus*[9] must do or avoid.

4. *Surveillance or vigilance,* as a separate and distinct penal remedy, is entirely new,[10] though the well known *Motu proprio* of Pius X, " *Sacrorum antistitum,*" Sept. 1, 1910, appointed a vigilance committee against modernistic tendencies. Here it has the character of a special penalty, and according to the order of enumeration, is the severest

---

8 S. C. EE. et RR., *l. c.,* n. 1, 1880, n. 7, which furnished the substance of our text.

9 *Praeventus* in the text implies that one has been served with an anticipated or informal accusation.

10 S. C. EE. et RR., *l. c.,* n. 1 says: "*Ordinario iudici pastorale onus incumbit . . . super eorundem vitae rationem vigilando*"; but this is a general obligation, not a penal remedy.

of the penal remedies. It is doubtless the most disagreeable one, especially in our country, although even the civil law employs police vigilance.

Can. 1311 says that a *very serious case may demand vigilance, especially if a person is exposed to the danger of relapse into the same crime.* Under such conditions the Ordinary may place the person in question, whether he be a layman or a cleric, under special supervision. But he may also increase the penalty, particularly for *recidivi.*

It may be added that, since injunction and surveillance are severer penal remedies than warning and rebuke, the procedure required for the latter *a fortiori* also applies to the former.

CHAPTER II

PENANCES

Can. 2312

§1. Poenitentiae in foro externo imponuntur ut delinquens vel poenam effugiat, vel poenae contractae absolutionem aut dispensationem recipiat.

§2. Ob delictum aut transgressionem occultam nunquam poenitentia publica imponatur.

§3. Poenitentiae non tam secundum quantitatem delicti, quam secundum poenitentis contritionem moderandae sunt, pensatis qualitatibus personarum et delictorum adiunctis.

Can. 2313

§1. Praecipuae poenitentiae sunt praecepta:

1°. Recitandi determinatas preces;

2°. Peragendi piam aliquam peregrinationem vel alia pietatis opera;

3°. Servandi peculiare ieiunium;

4°. Erogandi eleemosynas in pios usus;

5°. Peragendi exercitia spiritualia in pia aut religiosa domo per aliquot dies.

§2. Poenitentias Ordinarius pro sua prudentia addere potest poenali remedio monitionis et correptionis.

Penance, in the external forum, means penal satisfaction and may be compared, to some extent, to an apology.

The Code first determines the effect or object of penances and then enumerates some special kinds.

1. *Penances are imposed, in the external forum, in order that the delinquent may escape a canonical penalty, properly so-called, or that he may obtain absolution or dispensation from a penalty already imposed.*

Hence a penance may be decreed,[11] even if no censure *latae sententiae* has been incurred on account of ignorance. Besides the willing assumption of a penance is indicative of willingness to recede from contumacy [12] and renders one worthy of a dispensation, even though the latter depends entirely on the superior's good pleasure. In former times public penances were applied quite frequently; but they could be redeemed,[13] and this led to many abuses, so that, about the thirteenth, and especially in the fourteenth century, public penances fell entirely into desuetude. However, although public sacramental penances are abolished, yet some public penances may even now be imposed. But the Code clearly states (can. 2312, §2) that no *public penance can ever be imposed for an occult crime or transgression*, even though the penitent should be willing to undergo it. This text is negatively worded and therefore admits of a conversion of terms, *scil.*: A public penance may be imposed for a public crime.[14]

The kind of penance imposed should be *proportionate,* not so much to the gravity of the crime, as to the disposition of the delinquent. And in meting it out, due regard should be paid to the *qualities* of the *person* concerned and the *nature of his crime.*[15]

11 Can. 2229, § 3, n. 1.
12 Can. 2224, § 3.
13 See X, V, 38 of the Decretals and the commentators thereon.

14 For instance, apologizing to a congregation for marrying before a non-Catholic minister.
15 See cc. 7, 8, X, V, 38.

2. The principal *penances*, though not the only ones, are:

a) To recite certain prayers, *e. g.*, the penitential psalms, or the Stations of the cross, or the Rosary;

b) To make a pilgrimage to a certain shrine—provided the penitent has the means to do so and is physically able,— or to perform other devotional works, such as taking care of the church or altar;

c) To observe special fasts, if one's work or family permits;

d) To give alms for charitable purposes;

e) To retire for some days into a religious house.

These penances may be imposed by the Ordinary (but not by the vicar-general) and they may be inflicted either judicially or extra-judicially.[16]

16 See can. 1933, § 4.

PART III

PENALTIES FOR INDIVIDUAL CRIMES

The Code now proceeds to the consideration of the penalties to be inflicted for specified crimes. The nature of the latter furnishes a basis for classifying the former. It is not the kind of penalty, as was the case in the Constitution "*Apostolicae Sedis*," of 1869, but the character of the transgression that constitutes the formal basis of division. The Code contains all the penalties now applied, whilst the aforesaid Constitution only dealt with censures: excommunication, suspension, and interdict. This exhaustive treatment of ecclesiastical penalties [1] renders a return to former sources as such (though not, of course, as historical and interpretative aids) quite superfluous. Therefore we shall refer to former laws in the footnotes rather than in the text, except in as far as they contribute to a clearer understanding of the present discipline. Note that some terms and subjects, which seem to require an explanation, have been treated in former volumes of this Commentary.

[1] See can. 6, n. 5; can. 2219; can. 2226, § 2, 3.

TITLE XI

CRIMES AGAINST FAITH AND UNITY

It is quite natural that a society which claims to be the one Church instituted by Christ, should direct its first penalty against crimes that subvert its very foundation, *i. e.*, divine and Catholic faith. Belief in the divine mission and the dogmas of the Church is attacked and shattered by apostasy, heresy, and schism, to which must be added every suspicion uttered publicly and the denial of propositions which, though not formally dogmas, are closely connected with the deposit of faith. Special danger to the faith arises from the perusal of writings that attack the Church and her teachings. Finally, the practice of faith is relaxed, and faith itself jeopardized, by too free intercourse with non-Catholics, either in sacred things or socially.

APOSTASY, HERESY, AND SCHISM

Can. 2314

§1. Omnes a christiana fide apostatae et omnes et singuli haeretici aut schismatici:

1°. Incurrunt ipso facto excommunicationem;

2°. Nisi moniti resipuerint, priventur beneficio, dignitate, pensione, officio aliove munere, si quod in Ecclesia habeant, infames declarentur, et clerici, iterata monitione, deponantur;

275

3°. Si sectae acatholicae nomen dederint vel publice adhaeserint, ipso facto infames sunt et, firmo praescripto can. 188, n. 4, clerici, monitione incassum praemissa, degradentur.

§2. Absolutio ab excommunicatione de qua in §1, in foro conscientiae impertienda, est speciali modo Sedi Apostolicae reservata. Si tamen delictum apostasiae, haeresis vel schismatis ad forum externum Ordinarii loci quovis modo deductum fuerit, etiam per voluntariam confessionem, idem Ordinarius, non vero Vicarius Generalis sine mandato speciali, resipiscentem, praevia abiuratione iuridice peracta aliisque servatis de iure servandis, sua auctoritate ordinaria in foro exteriore absolvere potest; ita vero absolutus, potest deinde a peccato absolvi a quolibet confessario in foro conscientiae. Abiuratio vero habetur iuridice peracta cum fit coram ipso Ordinario loci vel eius delegato et saltem duobus testibus.

§1. All apostates from the Christian faith and all heretics and schismatics:

1°. Incur excommunication *ipso facto,* and

2°. Unless they repent, *shall be deprived* of any benefice, dignity, pension or other charge which they may hold in the Church, and be declared *infamous;* clerics, after repeated warning, *shall* be deposed;

3°. If apostates, heretics or schismatics have joined a non-Catholic sect, or publicly professed themselves members thereof, they are by this very fact *(ipso facto)* infamous; clerics, after having been warned without result, must be degraded and their offices thereby become vacant.

1) What the terms apostates, heretics, schismatics mean, has been explained in can. 1325, §2. All three presuppose valid baptism. By *apostates* are here understood all who have gone astray from the Christian faith *(devii a fide).*[2] For the rest it matters not whether the apostate has espoused Paganism, Judaism, Mohammedanism, or atheism, or whether he is a mere unbeliever. Therefore also *Freethinkers* must be included in the term, because they reject all authority in matters of faith.[3] Concerning *Spiritists* there is room for doubt. For although it is quite evident that Spiritism as a sect is heretical,[4] or rather tantamount to apostasy, because it retains hardly anything specifically Christian, yet it is possible, nay probable, that some of its followers may persuade themselves that they are Catholics, and can not, therefore, be classified among those mentioned in can. 2205, §3. The benefit of doubt may be applied to them (can. 209).

Heretics, according to can. 1325, §2, are such as deny obstinately one or more articles of faith. It is not necessary to join a non-Catholic sect in order to be a heretic in the sense of §1, n. 1.

Schismatics refuse obedience to the Roman Pontiff and therefore are outside the communion of the faithful.

[2] *Apost. Sedis*, I, 1: "*Omnes a christiana fide apostatas, et omnes ac singulos haereticos, quocumque nomine censeantur, et cuiuscumque sectae existant, eisque credentes, eorumque receptores, fautores ac generaliter quoslibet illorum defensores.*"—I, 3: "*Schismaticos, et eos, qui a Romani Pontificis pro tempore existentis obedientia pertinaciter se subtrahunt, vel recedunt.*" S. Thom., II-II, q. 12,

art. 1: "*a fide christiana recessio*"; Paul III, "*Cum ex apostolatus,*" Feb. 15, 1559, § 2.

[3] Thus also Avanzini, *De Constitutione Apostolicae Sedis*, ed. 6, 1883, p. 4; Ballerini-Palmieri, *Opus Theol. Morale*, Vol. VII, n. 422, p. 219 (ed. 2).

[4] S. O., July 28, 1847; Aug. 4, 1856 (*Coll. P. F.,* nn. 1018, 1128); Pennacchi, *Commentaria in Const. Ap. Sedis*, 1883, Vol. I, p. 83.

This separation, too, may take place with or without forming or clinging to schismatic doctrines. Since the Vatican Council, schism is generally connected with heresy. For pure schism, *i. e.*, mere disobedience to the lawful head of the Church, without at least a speculative positive doubt in her divinity, is not easily possible, except in individuals.[5]

The crime of *apostasy, heresy, or schism* must be *exteriorly manifested*, either in words, writings, or acts which betray defection from the Christian Church, denial of some article of faith, or separation from the unity of the Church, according to can. 2195, §1; because merely internal apostasy, heresy, or schism do not belong to the external forum and therefore are not intended here.[6] From merely internal transgressions, even though they be grievously sinful, any confessor may absolve.

2) The *penalties here enunciated are twofold*: censure and vindictive penalties; besides, a distinction is drawn, according to can. 2207, n. 1, by reason of dignity, between laymen and clerics.

a) The *censure inflicted is excommunication incurred ipso facto*, which *per se* requires not even a declaratory sentence. Only if, in the prudent judgment of the superior, the public welfare should require such a sentence, it must be pronounced.[7] The *bonum publicum* certainly demands it in the case of clergymen. Note that the term *moniti* (§1, n. 2) does not refer to the in-

---

[5] Thus the Greek schismatics, the Jansenists, and the "Old Catholics" are no less heretics than schismatics; also the National Italian Catholics; see D'Annibale, *In Constitutionem Ap. Sedis*, ed. 1894, p. 34.

[6] See Hollweck, *l. c.*, p. 162;

D'Annibale, *l. c.*, says it does not matter whether the words or facts betraying the crime were heard or witnessed by bystanders; they are public if they *could* have been heard or seen (*l. c.*, p. 24).

[7] See can. 2223, § 4; also can. 2232.

curring of the censure. Consequently, no canonical warning or admonition is required.[8]

b) The *vindictive penalties* inflicted are:

For *laymen: privation of all offices and pensions* they may hold in the Church, and *infamy*.

For *clerics: privation* of every benefice, dignity, pension, office, or charge which they may hold; also *infamy* and, after a fruitless warning, *deposition*.

A *warning* must precede these vindictive penalties, and we suppose the warning must be administered according to can. 2143, *i. e.*, before an official of the diocese or two witnesses, or by registered letter. The *infamy* inflicted on both laymen and clergymen, and the *deposition* pronounced against clerics, are *ferendae sententiae*.[9]

Deposition requires a second warning after the first one has been served, with the threat of privation and infamy.

3). The vindictive penalties are rendered *more severe* in two cases, which may be distinct, but may also occur by one and the same act: *sectae acatholicae nomen dare* or *publice adhaerere*.

A *sect* means a religious society established in opposition to the Church, whether it consist of infidels, pagans, Jews, Moslems, non-Catholics, or schismatics.[10] To become a member of such a society *(nomen dare)* means to inscribe one's name on its roster. Of course, it is presumed that the new member knows it is a non-Catholic society, otherwise he would not incur the censure. If he hears of the censure after he has become a

---

8 Pennacchi, *l. c.*, I, p. 101 f.
9 See can. 2223, § 3. Formerly these penalties were incurred *ipso iure*, Hollweck, *l. c.*, p. 162 f.
10 D'Annibale, *l. c.*, p. 79.

member, and promptly severs his connection, the penalty is not incurred.[11]

The text also provides for cases of informal membership. *Publice adhaerere* means to *belong publicly* to a non-Catholic sect. This may be done by frequenting its services without any special cause or reason, or by boasting of being a member, though not enrolled, by wearing a badge or emblem indicative of membership, etc. Those guilty of such conduct, whether laymen or clerics, render themselves infamous *(infamia iuris latae sententiae)* and consequently can. 2294, § 1 must be applied to them.[12] A *cleric must, besides, be degraded* if, after having been duly warned, he persists in being a member of such a society. All the offices he may hold become vacant, *ipso facto*, without any further declaration. This is tacit resignation recognized by law,[13] and therefore the vacancy is one *de facto et iure*. It need hardly be added that excommunication follows in each case, although the vindictive penalties only are mentioned in 2° and 3°.

It may not be amiss to add that the penalties decreed for apostasy, heresy, and schism, presuppose malice *(dolus)* as explained above in can. 2200. Consequently, if one would retain the Christian faith interiorly, but act exteriorly as an apostate or heretic,— which would be detestable hypocrisy,— he would not incur the penalties *in foro interno*,[14] but *in foro externo* the presumption

---

11 Can. 2202, § 1; Hollweck, *l. c.*, p. 170.

12 Privation of benefices, etc., mentioned in can. 2314, § 1, n. 2, is not repeated in n. 3, because included in the *infamia iuris*. Note

that *irregularity* is attached to this infamy; can. 984, n. 5.

13 Can. 188, n. 4.

14 Therefore any confessor may absolve him in the sacramental forum; Hollweck, *l. c.*, p. 163, note 5.

would be against him, and the proof of his internal defection would be incumbent on the one who asserted it, according to can. 2200, §2.

§2 Treats of absolution in the internal and external forum, and of abjuration.

1°. *Absolution from excommunication,* mentioned in §1, is *reserved to the Apostolic See speciali modo,* as far as it is to be imparted in the *court of conscience* only. Concerning this absolution, the rules laid down in can. 2248–2254 must be consulted; in cases of reasonable doubt, can. 209. Ordinaries need a special faculty to absolve from this censure.[15]

2°. Absolution in the *external forum* may be imparted by the *local Ordinary* (but not by the vicar-general, without special commission) *in the following circumstances:*

a) If the crime of apostasy, heresy, or schism has been in any way brought before the external court of the local Ordinary;

b) If the delinquent is repentant, and

c) If he abjures his error in juridical form and complies with all other prescribed conditions.

Ad a) Juridically the crime is before the external court of the local Ordinary if a summons has been duly issued. However, since the Code adds: " *quoquo modo ad forum deductum,* " we may adopt the opinion of St. Alphonsus, that it would be sufficient if the crime had been proved to the ecclesiastical judge by at least one witness.[16] This is all the more acceptable since our text admits *voluntary confession,* which certainly can be made in writing or

---

15 Apostolic Delegates enjoy this faculty; see *Index Facultatum,* May 6, 1919, n. 4.

16 Putzer, *Comment. in Facult. Apost.,* ed. 4, p. 24, n. 17.

through another person. This is nothing else but the
sponte comparere, to appear of one's own accord, before
the Holy Office or the local Ordinary,— a formula found
in former decisions.[17]

Ad b) Repentance is supposed to be effected by a spon-
taneous accusation, but it also means that a relapse should
be dealt with more severely, although the Code does not
make it a condition of absolution.[18]

Ad c) Abjuration must be made according to the
formula contained in the Roman Pontifical and Ritual.[19]
It is a *juridical* abjuration if made before the local
Ordinary or his delegate *and* at least two witnesses.
Hence the vicar-general, or the rural dean, or any other
priest may be delegated for the purpose. Note, however, that religious superiors, as such, even though exempt, cannot receive this juridical abjuration, because
it appertains to matters of faith, in which they are not
competent,[20] though, of course, they may act as delegates
of the local ordinary.

Here it may be proper to call attention to the regulations issued by the Holy Office concerning the manner
of absolution in cases of doubtful baptism.[21] The same
S. Congregation has ruled that boys and girls under four-
teen years of age need not pronounce the abjuration, but

---

17 S. O., June 21, 1672; Jan. 3,
1648 (*Coll. P. F.,* nn. 31, 98).
Hence, in case of converts being
received, the priest (pastor or assistant, curate) may simply take
down in writing the confession of
the convert and write a letter to
the bishop, informing him that he
witnessed the voluntary confession
and asking for delegation to receive
the abjuration in the presence of
two witnesses.

18 S. O., Jan. 21, 1627, *l. c.*
19 *Pont. Rom.,* P. III, tit. "*Ordo
ad Reconciliandum Apostatam,
Schismaticum vel Haereticum.*" *Rit.
Rom.,* tit. III, cap, 3; S. O., Aug.
28, 1861 (*Coll. P. F.,* n. 1221).

20 Can. 501, § 2.

21 S. O., July 20, 1859 (*Coll. cit.,*
n. 1178); also to be found in the
priest's New Ritual, published by
various editors, under the title
Reception of Converts.

should make a simple profession of faith, after which they may be reconciled to the Church.[22]

These are the *servanda de iure, viz.:* assurance of Baptism, sacramental confession, and a wholesome penance.[23]

4) *After being absolved in the external forum, the penitent may be absolved from his sin by any confessor in the court of conscience* [24] (can. 2251). *Why absolution in foro externo is required,* can be gathered from certain decisions of the Holy Office. The reason is that the penitent might otherwise, if his crime became notorious or public, be prosecuted by the Holy Office or the local Ordinary. Hence he should be given a certificate of absolution.[25] This is all the more important, since the other penalties are not lifted by this absolution, which refers only to excommunication. Therefore a *dispensation* from the vindictive penalties should be imparted, according to can. 2289.[26] A layman, for instance, who held a title or decoration or order of knighthood from the Pope, would have lost that dignity, and therefore a dispensation would be required. However, it appears conformable to the mind of the legislator that the Ordinary, who can absolve from the heavier penalty (excommunication), should also be entitled to dispense from the vindictive penalty.

---

[22] S. O., March 8, 1882 (*Coll. cit.,* n. 1566.)

[23] S. O., July 30, 1806 (*ib.,* n. 688).

[24] It is hardly necessary to add that the local Ordinary may do all this personally. Attention may be drawn to can. 199, § 1, concerning *delegation;* for the power mentioned in can. 2314, § 2, is ordinary, and may therefore be delegated. Where-fore the Ordinary may habitually delegate any priest to receive so-called juridical abjurations before two witnesses. This may be done at a synod or when issuing the so-called faculties.

[25] S. O., Jan. 3, 1640; May 7, 1822 (*Coll. P. F.,* nn. 98, 771).

[26] Said canon refers to can. 2236, which requires papal dispensation.

SUSPICION OF HERESY

Can. 2315

Suspectus de haeresi, qui monitus causam suspicionis non removeat, actibus legitimis prohibeatur, et clericus praeterea, repetita inutiliter monitione, suspendatur a divinis; quod si intra sex menses a contracta poena completos suspectus de haeresi sese non emendaverit, habeatur tanquam haereticus, haereticorum poenis obnoxius.

Suspicion, in the psychological sense, is doubt, coupled with a positive leaning to one side; — in our case, towards a heretical doctrine. In law it may be expressed by presumption or circumstantial evidence. It is, therefore, a judgment formed about some one without sufficient evidence on the ground of certain *indicia*.

Three kinds of suspicion are generally distinguished: light, vehement, and violent. *Light* suspicion admits of no conclusion, because it is based on absolutely insufficient *indicia*. *Vehement* suspicion rests on effective signs and conclusions. *Violent* suspicion amounts to morally certain proof.[1]

The Decretals,[2] from which the notion "suspicion of heresy" is taken, have in view vehement suspicion, and no doubt this is here to be understood. Light suspicion often amounts to no more than rash judgment, whilst violent suspicion is to be considered as a positive proof, and therefore rather falls under can. 2314. That the

[1] Suarez, *De Fide*, disp. XXIV, sect. 2, n. 1 (*ed. Paris.*, 1858, t. 12, p. 592).

[2] See c. 14, X, II, 23; c. 10, X, V, 34.

limits between vehement and violent suspicion cannot be very clearly set off, is owing to the nature of circumstantial evidence.

Formerly jurisprudence used to resort to an expedient which seemed to ward off vehement as well as violent suspicion. It was the so-called *purgatio canonica,* or canonically admitted proof of one's innocence of an imputed crime. The reception of Holy Communion or the celebration of Mass were accepted as such proofs. But these means gave way to a more juridical means of purging oneself of suspicion, the *iuramentum purgatorium,* an oath administered by the judge in order to disperse a suspicion.[3]

Our canon, too, mentions a removal of heresy, or rather of the cause that gave rise to suspicion. But in what this removal consists, is not expressly stated. This is quite natural, for the different cases of suspected heresy permit a different way of removing suspicion.

The Code declares the following persons as suspect of heresy:

1. The propagators of heresy and those who participate with non-Catholics *in divinis* (Can. 2316);

2. Those who contract marriage under the condition of having their offspring educated in a non-Catholic sect and those who have their children baptized by non-Catholic ministers or educated in a non-Catholic denomination (can. 2319);

3. Those who desecrate sacred hosts or species (can. 2320);

4. Those who appeal from the Pope to a general council (can. 2332);

---

[3] Reiffenstuel, C. V, tit. 34, n. 1 ff.

5. Those who remain under sentence of excommunication for more than a year (can. 2340);

6. Those who administer or receive the Sacraments simoniacally (can. 2371).

As may be seen from this list, each species of suspicion here enumerated may be removed in a different way: by formal retraction, by withdrawing the condition and complying with Catholic principles, or by protesting against what was done or received, for instance, returning the money received from simony, or giving up the sacred species. We do not, however, hesitate to say that the judge may in each case demand a guarantee of genuine amendment, in fact, he should do so, unless he is convinced of the sincerity of the penitent. Neither would the judge exceed his power if he would require an oath or a statement in presence of two witnesses.

We now proceed to the penalties the Code inflicts on those suspected of heresy.

a) They must, first, be *warned,* according to can. 2307, to remove the cause of suspicion. A reasonable time should be granted for this purpose in the canonical warning.

b) If the warning proves fruitless, the suspected person must be *forbidden* to perform any ecclesiastical *legal acts,* according to can. 2256. If he is a cleric, he must be suspended *a divinis,*[4] after a *second warning* has been left unheeded.

c) If, *after the lapse of six months,* to be reckoned from the moment the penalty has been contracted, the person suspected of heresy has not amended, he must be *regarded as a heretic, amenable to the penalties set forth in can. 2314.* Whilst the penalties enumerated under

4 See can. 2279, § 2, n. 2.

(b) are *ferendae sententiae*, to be inflicted according to can. 2223, §3, the penalties stated under (c) are *a iure* and *latae sententiae*.[5]

Note that, since the *ferendae sententiae* penalties require a canonical warning and a clear statement of the time granted, the moment from which the penalty is contracted can be almost mathematically determined.

COÖPERATION IN HERESY

Can. 2316

Qui quoquo modo haeresis propagationem sponte et scienter iuvat, aut qui communicat in divinis cum haereticis contra praescriptum can. 1258, suspectus de haeresi est.

This crime is singled out as a species for itself, and the penalty is taken partly from older sources and partly from the Bull "*Apostolicae Sedis*.[1]" Two distinct cases are contained in our canon, and the penalty is the same as for those suspected of heresy.

1. Whosoever *spontaneously and knowingly assists in any way in the propagation of heresy, is himself suspected of heresy.* Under this heading fall, according to "*Apostolicae Sedis*," all those who believe the errors of heretics, or who receive, protect, and defend heretics. There is little doubt[2] that our text includes all these,

---

5 See can. 2217, § 1, 2. Where the phrase *similia verba* indicates that though the terms *a iure* or *latae sententiae* are not expressly used, equivalent terms, as in our canon 2315: *habeatur tanquam haereticus,* *haereticorum ponis obnoxius*, mean the same.

1 L. c., see note under can. 2314.

2 This seems to be indicated also in the notes of Card. Gasparri to this canon.

provided, of course, they act of their own accord and knowingly. Hence

a) *Credentes* are such as externally profess the errors of heretics, *e. g.*, by asserting that Luther or Döllinger were correct in their views, even though they may not know the particular errors of these leaders.[8]

b) *Receptores* are those who receive and shelter heretics, especially with the intention of hiding them from the ecclesiastical authorities.[4]

c) *Fautores* are such as favor heretics because of their heresy, by omitting to denounce them when required or demanded by their office, or by giving support to non-Catholic propaganda. This latter way of propagating heresy is followed by public and private persons who write for heretics, praise their methods and objects, recommend their work and give it material support, always provided that the heresy itself is the object of their mental and material favors.[5]

d) *Defensores* means those who defend heretics for the sake of heresy, orally, in writing, or by acts of defence proper. All such persons are suspected of heresy if they act of their own accord and knowingly. *Sponte* is opposed to compulsion and fear, and therefore implies full deliberation and a free will not hindered by any extrinsic or intrinsic impediment, such as fear of losing an office, or one's reputation, or customers. *Scienter* is opposed to ignorance, the object of which here is heresy, and means that these promotors or propagators of heresy must be

---

8 D'Annibale, *l. c.*, p. 24; Avanzini, *l. c.*, p. 8, n. 5, who justly observes that they may not be heretics if they profess these errors only in a mechanical way.

4 D'Annibale, *l. c.*, p. 12, n. 12;

this was important in former times on account of the office of inquisitors; Hollweck, *l. c.*, p. 165.

5 D'Annibale, *l. c.*, p. 24, n. 32: "*intuitu haeresis*"; Hollweck, *l. c.*, p. 164 f.

aware that they are helping *heresy as such*. Besides, as *iuvare propagationem* seems to imply an effective propaganda, it may be said that these *fautores*, etc., must produce an effect. However, this is rarely wanting if the support is a material one.[6]

2. Those *who communicate with heretics in divinis* are themselves suspect of heresy. Here we refer to can. 1258, where the necessary explanation has been given.[7]

3. These and all others suspected of heresy incur the penalty stated in can. 2315.

TEACHING AND DEFENDING CONDEMNED DOCTRINES

Can. 2317

Pertinaciter docentes vel defendentes sive publice sive privatim doctrinam, quae ab Apostolica Sede vel a Concilio Generali damnata quidem fuit, sed non uti formaliter haeretica, arceantur a ministerio praedicandi verbum Dei audiendive sacramentales confessiones et a quolibet docendi munere, salvis aliis poenis quas sententia damnationis forte statuerit, vel quas Ordinarius, post monitionem, necessarias ad reparandum scandalum duxerit.

This canon is a modified repetition of a passage in the Constitution *Apostolicae Sedis*.[1] We say modified, because the penalty of excommunication *latae sententiae*

---

6 *Ibid.* an example: those who contribute to non-Catholic propaganda are guilty of coöperation.

7 See Vol. VI of this Commentary, p. 192 ff.

1 § II, 1: "*Docentes vel defendentes sive publice, sive privatim propositiones ab Apostolica Sede damnatas sub excommunicationis* poena latae sententiae; item docentes vel defendentes tanquam licitam praxim inquirendi a poenitente nomen complicis, prouti damnata est a Benedicto XIV. in Const. Suprema 7. Julii 1745; Ubi primum 2. Julii 1746; Ad eradicandum 28. Septembris 1746."

is changed into another. Besides our canon mentions *doctrine,* while the aforesaid papal constitution referred to *propositions.* Materially speaking there can hardly be any difference between doctrines and propositions, except that the former is a somewhat wider term comprising formulated propositions as well as errors which have not yet been cast into theses.

The text says: *All who obstinately teach or either publicly or in private defend a doctrine that has been condemned by the Apostolic See or by an ecumenical council, but not as a formal heresy, are to be excluded from the ministry of preaching the word of God or hearing confessions, and from the office of teaching. This in addition to the penalties which the sentence of condemnation decrees against them and the penalties which the Ordinary, after a due warning, may consider necessary in order to repair the scandal given.*

1. The *persons* here intended are those who *teach* or *defend* condemned doctrines. To *teach* means to communicate something to others who are ignorant thereof, with the intention of convincing them.[2] To *defend* signifies to take some one under one's protection, especially if he is attacked. Hence a mere assertion, proposal or profession of a condemned doctrine would not be a defence.[3] The defence, however, must be of the false doctrine itself; to protect a person who was condemned would not be a defence in the sense of our canon.

2. A false doctrine may be taught or defended either in public or privately. The defence is *public* if done in a public place, such as a pulpit, or a school, or an open

---

[2] Thus Hollweck, *l. c.,* p. 166, note 3. D'Annibale, says (*l. c.,* p. 71): "*docere est, nescientibus tradere*"; but this is too wide a definition.

[3] Hollweck, *l. c.;* D'Annibale, *l. c.;* Pennacchi, *l. c.,* I, 458 f.

meeting. It is *private* if individuals are approached in conversation by chance or appointment. It makes no difference whether the teaching or defending is done in writing or orally.[4]

3. The *object* of this teaching or defence must be a *doctrine condemned by the Apostolic See or by a general council,* though not as a formal heresy. By *Apostolic See,* of course, is understood the whole Roman Court, consisting of the Sacred Congregations, Tribunals, and Offices (can. 7), more especially the Holy Office, which is the competent judge in matters of faith. A *general council,* according to can. 222, must have the Roman Pontiff as its head.

The term *doctrine,* as already observed, is somewhat wider than "propositions," used in the "*Apostolicae Sedis.*" Propositions are brief sentences, generally taken from the works of suspected authors, cast into the form of a canon, and accompanied by a theological censure or note, the grading of which has become almost stereotyped, which is a great advantage because it admits of a precise theological-moral classification [5] of objectionable doctrines.

A proposition is *haeretica* if opposed to a truth clearly proposed by the Church as *de fide.*

A proposition is *erronea* if opposed to the theological teaching commonly held in the Church, though not proposed as *de fide.*

---

4 Hollweck, *l. c.;* D'Annibale, *l. c.* p. 71. *Public* may also imply a person in a public capacity, and *private* a person in private position, although this significance is not directly intended in the text; but neither is it excluded, for, as a rule, a public person exercises more influence than a private person.

5 See Franzelin, S. J., *Tractatus de Divina Traditione et Scriptura,* ed. 4, 1896, p. 141 ff., sect. II, scholion to thes. XII; Pennacchi, I, 149 ff.

A propositio temeraria differs from an *erronea* only in degree; it is less offensive than an erroneous proposition because less repugnant to the teaching of the Church.[6]

A proposition is called *male sonans* if its wording may be taken in a good sense, yet, according to common parlance within the Church, sounds very suspicious.[7]

Piarum aurium offensiva is a proposition which is opposed to the common belief or sentiment of the faithful.

We may safely say that all these propositions,— with the exception of *haeretica,* which belongs to heresy proper, — are included in the text. But as the term *doctrine* is employed, it should be clearly understood that, when a doctrinal system as such, like Modernism, is condemned, no specific propositions need be mentioned as condemned.

In chronological [8] order the following propositions and doctrines fall under can. 2317:

a) The errors of Wiclif and Hus, as censured in the Constitution of Martin V, "*Inter cunctas,*" of Feb. 22, 1418;

b) The errors of Luther — in so far as they are not formally heretical — as condemned by Leo X, "*Exsurge Domine,*" of June 15, 1520;

c) The proposition condemned by Clement VIII, June 20, 1602, styling as false, rash, and scandalous the assertion that confession and absolution could be made by letter or message;

d) The 45 propositions condemned by the Holy Office in its decrees of Sept. 24, 1665 and March 18, 1666;

---

6 Cfr. *"Auctorem fidei,"* prop. 26.

7 *Ibid.,* prop. 44, 45.

8 See Avanzini, *l. c.,* p. 117 ff.; they are also found in Denzinger's *Enchiridion.*

e) The 65 propositions condemned by the Holy Office on March 4, 1679, as "scandalous and pernicious in practice";

f) The 68 propositions of Michael de Molinos, condemned by the Constitution of Innocent XI, "*Coelestis Pater,*" of Nov. 20, 1687, partly as heretical, partly as suspected, erroneous, scandalous, etc.;

g) One proposition condemned by Alexander VIII, Aug. 24, 1690, and 31 condemned by the same Pope, Dec. 7, 1690;

h) The 101 propositions of Paschasius Quesnel, condemned by Clement XI, in the Bull "*Unigenitus,*" Sept. 8, 1713 and again in the "*Pastoralis Officii,*" Aug. 28, 1718;

i) Five propositions condemned by Benedict XIV, "*Detestabilem,*" Nov. 10, 1752;

k) 85 propositions of the Synod of Pistoja, condemned by Pius VI, "*Auctorem fidei,*" Aug. 28, 1894;

l) Finally, the errors of the Modernists, in so far as they are not formally heretical.[9]

The errors censured in the Syllabus of Pius IX and Pius X's "*Lamentabili*" must be judged according to the censure attached to each.[10]

4) The *penalties* attached to the transgression of this law, for clergymen, consists *in the withdrawal of their faculties.* Laymen guilty of this delinquency must be removed from the teaching office *(a quolibet docendi*

---

[9] Pius X, "*Praestantia Scripturae,*" Nov. 18, 1907 (*Anal. Eccl.,* XV, 435); "*Sacrorum Antistitum,*" Sept. 1, 1910 (*A. Ap. S.,* II, 701 ff.).

[10] Concerning the Syllabus of Pius IX,—which Card. Gasparri omits from his notes,—the question whether it is a dogmatic definition belongs to the theologians; here it enters only in as far as a doctrine condemned by the Apostolic See is concerned.

munere), which includes all professorships in schools, colleges, universities, etc.

The clause *" salvis aliis poenis quas sententia damnationis forte statuerit "* concerns the future, not the past. The *" Exsurge Domine "* of Leo X (§4) enumerates several such penalties, and the Motu proprio of Pius X, *" Praestantia scripturae, "* contains the same clause in almost identical words. But these penalties must be considered as abrogated, according to can. 6, n. 5, otherwise there would be a flagrant contradiction, and hence *statuerit* must be taken as the future.

If the *Ordinary* deems it necessary to add other penalties, he must *first issue an admonition,* according to canons 2143 and 2309. He is not obliged to inflict other penalties, but may do so if he deems it expedient (see can. 2223).

PENALTIES IN REGARD TO FORBIDDEN BOOKS

Can. 2318

§ 1. In excommunicationem Sedi Apostolicae speciali modo reservatam ipso facto incurrunt, opere publici iuris facto, editores librorum apostatarum, haereticorum et schismaticorum, qui apostasiam, haeresim, schisma propugnant, itemque eosdem libros aliosve per apostolicas litteras nominatim prohibitos defendentes aut scienter sine debita licentia legentes vel retinentes.

§ 2. Auctores et editores qui sine debita licentia sacrarum Scripturarum libros vel earum adnotationes aut commentarios imprimi curant, incidunt ipso facto in excommunicationem nemini reservatam.

§ 1. Those who *publish books written by apostates, heretics, or schismatics, incur the excommunication reserved speciali modo to the Holy See, after the book has been effectively published.* The same penalty is incurred by those who defend such books or others nominally forbidden by Apostolic letter, or who knowingly read or retain them without due permission.

§ 2. *Authors and publishers who print books of Sacred Scripture, or annotations and commentaries thereon, without due permission, incur the excommunication reserved to no one.* After what was said elsewhere[1] a few remarks may suffice.

1. The *persons* who incur this penalty are:

a) The *editores* of the books named, by which term are to be understood the author himself as well as the publisher, but not the printers and their co-workers. The editors, whether they undertake the publication in their own name, or under an assumed name, or anonymously, incur the penalty only after the edition is complete and for sale, *opere publici iuris facto.*

b) Those who *defend*[2] books forbidden under this canon or *read or retain* them *without the necessary permission and knowingly, i. e.,* being aware that they are forbidden.

2. The *books* forbidden here under the penalty stated in §1, are those of *apostates, heretics,* and *schismatics,* which not merely propose, but defend apostasy, heresy, or schism. The defence may concern only one heretical doctrine. The term "*book*" must here be strictly interpreted and hence can. 1384, § 2 cannot be applied.

---

1 See Vol. VI of this Commentary, p. 428 ff.

2 By defending the contents, or protecting the book from being destroyed or given up; Eichmann, *l. c.,* p. 132.

Consequently pamphlets, magazines, leaflets, papers, etc., are not comprised under this penal sanction. Besides, the "books" must be forbidden by *Apostolic letter*, wherefore decrees of the Holy Office or any other S. Congregation forbidding certain books do not fall under this heading, even though the decree may have been issued "*facto verbo cum SSmo.*" On the other hand it does not matter whether these Apostolic letters are issued in the form of a brief, or bull or encyclical letter, or any other.

3. The *penalty* is excommunication reserved *speciali modo* to the Apostolic See; it is incurred *ipso facto, i. e.*, by the fact of having published such a forbidden book, or defended, read, or retained it, according to the explanation given in Title XXIII, Book III.

Here it may be added that the Ordinary may, in virtue of can. 1402, grant permission to read and retain books forbidden by common law (can. 1399) or by a decree of the Apostolic See (Holy Office), but he cannot grant permission to read and retain books forbidden by Apostolic letter.

§ 2. Another category of books is mentioned in § 2 of can. 2318: the *authors* and *publishers* of books of *Sacred Scripture* or of annotations and commentaries thereon,[3] if printed without due permission.[4] All these incur *excommunication* reserved to no one, from which any confessor may absolve, according to can. 2253, 1°.

MIXED MARRIAGES AND NON-CATHOLIC EDUCATION

Can. 2319

§ 1. Subsunt excommunicationi latae sententiae Ordinario reservatae catholici:

---

[3] Cfr. can. 1385, § 1, n. 1; 1391; 1399; 1400.

[4] This means to have them printed for publication or sale, not

1°. Qui matrimonium ineunt coram ministro acatholico contra praescriptum can. 1063, § 1;

2°. Qui matrimonio uniuntur cum pacto explicito vel implicito ut omnis vel aliqua proles educetur extra catholicam Ecclesiam;

3°. Qui scienter liberos suos acatholicis ministris baptizandos offerre praesumunt;

4°. Parentes vel parentum locum tenentes qui liberos in religione acatholica educandos vel instituendos scienter tradunt.

§2. Ii de quibus in § 1, nn. 2-4, sunt praeterea suspecti de haeresi.

This canon states four different cases, all of which have to do with family life in relation to the Catholic faith. Common to all four is the penalty of *excommunication latae sententiae, reserved to the Ordinary.* Three of them, besides, fall under the *suspicion of heresy,* which must be judged according to can. 2316.

1. Those who *contract marriage before a non-Catholic minister,* against can. 1063, §1, *incur the aforesaid excommunication,* but do not become suspected of heresy. It is, of course, immaterial whether one or both parties belong to the Catholic faith. For the rest, we refer to can. 1063 and its explanation.

2. *Those who contract marriage with the implied or express agreement that all or some of the children shall be educated outside the Catholic Church, incur the aforesaid excommunication and, besides, are suspected of heresy.* This crime is against can. 1061, §1, n. 2, which requires a promise that all the offspring shall be

for one's own use; in the latter case, the censure would *not* be incurred.

educated in the Catholic Church in case of a mixed marriage. Of course, if two Catholics should marry under the same condition, they, too, would incur the penalty.

The text mentions a twofold agreement (*pactum*), one express and the other implied. *Express* contracts or agreements are those the terms of which are openly uttered and avowed at the time of the making. *Implied* are such as reason and justice dictate, and which, therefore, the law presumes that every man undertakes to perform, and upon this presumption makes him answerable to those who suffer from his non-performance. This distinction refers only to the mode of proof.[1] Yet it will serve our purpose; for the agreement must be either a legal or an informal one, *i. e.*, a mutual promise or consent by two or more persons. An express agreement would be one made in legal and written terms, as the so-called reversals usually are. An implied contract would be an agreement or promise made by one of the parties to comply with the conditions, though iniquitous, of the civil law that the boys should follow the religion of the father and the girls that of the mother.[2]

A mere reluctant silence on the part of the Catholic party, inspired by the desire not to cause a disturbance, could not be styled an agreement. On the other hand, regret after the promise was made would not save the Catholic party from incurring the censure. Neither would the promise made to have only the first-born boy educated in a non-Catholic sect offset the effects of this canon. Finally, it may be observed that the text says:

[1] See Harriman, *Contracts*, 1901, § II.

[2] Pius VIII, *"Litteris altero,"* March 25, 1830 (*Coll. P. F.*, n. 811).

"*extra catholicam Ecclesiam,*" which implies total exclusion of the Catholic religion and its principles. It involves either omission of Catholic education, *i. e.*, indifferentism, or a positively sectarian or infidel training.

3°. *Those who knowingly dare to offer their children to non-Catholic ministers for baptism incur excommunication reserved to the Ordinary and, besides, are suspected of heresy.*

a) Here the parents are intended, because the text says: "*suos liberos,*" *their* children. Therefore, if a midwife or nurse should commit this crime without the knowledge of the parents, the latter would not be subject to this penalty. On the other hand, the word "*suos*" cannot be interpreted as if the parents would not incur the penalty if they commanded or even permitted such an act. Here Regula Iuris 72 in 6° finds application: "What one does through another, is as if he did it himself." Can. 2209, §3, also applies and consequently the coöperation must be judged according to this canon. But a nurse or midwife would not incur the penalty, even though she was guilty of such an unqualified interference with parental rights of her own accord.

b) The words "*scienter praesumpserint*" must be interpreted according to can. 2229, §2. Therefore any notable lessening of responsibility, either on the part of the intellect or of the will, would render one immune from incurring the penalty *latae sententiae*. A case to the point is that mentioned in a decision of the Holy Office.[3] Some Irish mothers, for fear of pecuniary fines, had presented their children to Protestant ministers. They committed a grievous sin, but did not incur the

[3] S. O., Nov. 29, 1672, ad 2 (*Coll. P. F.*, n. 205).

penalty stated in our canon.[4] If the parents were deceived as to the true denomination of an intruding
sectarian, imputability would be wanting, and consequently the penalty would not be incurred.

4. *Parents or those who hold their place, if they knowingly offer children to be educated or brought up in a
non-Catholic denomination, incur the aforesaid penalty
of excommunication and are suspected of heresy.*

a) Here not only parents, but also *guardians or tutors,*
are included. It is irrelevant whether the guardians are
legally appointed, or have assumed authority over the
children of their own accord, or with the connivance and
approval of the parents.

b) The *act* which is here declared punishable, is that
of *educating* or bringing up the child *in a non-Catholic
religion.* This may be done either in sectarian schools,
properly so-called, or by means of private tutors and
teachers, either systematically or without method. The
public schools of our country are not supposed to be
sectarian.

c) The adverb *scienter* presupposes that the anti-
Catholic tendency of the school or teacher was known to
the parent or guardian.[5]

4 We know of tricks played on
poor Italian mothers by unscrup-
ulous proselytizing ministers, who
offered twenty lire to be allowed
to baptize a baby.

5 See can. 2229, § 2.

TITLE XII

CRIMES AGAINST RELIGION

The delinquencies enumerated in this title are directed partly against the Catholic faith and partly against the religious sentiments common to all whose religious and, we might add, natural instincts are not entirely perverted. All of them offend against the inborn respect of the faithful for the sacred things which are closely connected with religion.

DESECRATION OF CONSECRATED SPECIES

Can. 2320

Qui species consecratas abiecerit vel ad malum finem abduxerit aut retinuerit, est suspectus de haeresi; incurrit in excommunicationem latae sententiae specialissimo modo Sedi Apostolicae reservatam; est ipso facto infamis, et clericus praeterea est deponendus.

The crime here mentioned was perpetrated by fanatics imbued with the heretical tendencies of the Manichæans, against whom the papal inquisitors proceeded severely, but not without encountering difficulties on the part of some Catholics. These outcasts abused the sacred hosts for magic and diabolical purposes, trying them on products and animals.[1] But the Inquisition alone could not

1 Hadrian VI, "*Dudum*," July 20, 1522 (*Bull. Luxemb.*, 1727, I, 625).

eradicate this evil. Hence the popes decreed severe penalties against all such malefactors of whatever dignity, condition, or age, provided they had attained the twentieth year.[2] The penalty of being delivered to the secular authority, which generally inflicted capital punishment, was at first condoned if the culprits confessed the crime of their own accord. But Clement XIII abolished this mitigation.[3] Clerics were formerly degraded and then delivered up to the secular power. Our Code decrees as follows: *Whoever throws away the sacred species, or carries them away for evil purposes, or retains them, is suspected of heresy, incurs excommunication latae sententiae, reserved modo specialissimo to the Apostolic See; he is ipso facto infamous, and, if a cleric, shall be deposed.*

In explaining this canon we shall follow the Constitution of Benedict XIV.

1. Whoever *(qui)* means any person, layman or ecclesiastic, of the highest as well as lowest rank or dignity, and no privilege, exemption, or indult shall protect one guilty of such a crime.[4]

2. The text says, furthermore, that the crime must be committed with *consecrated species.* The aforesaid Constitution mentioned sacred hosts, thereby intimating that consecrated wine, *i. e.*, the Sacred Blood, is not so easily exposed to sacrilege. Our text includes both bread and wine, provided they are consecrated. When consecration may be legitimately presumed, Benedict XIV de-

---

[2] Innocent XI, "*Ad nostri Apostolatus,*" March 12, 1677; Alexander VIII, "*Cum alias,*" Dec. 22, 1690, embodied in Bened. XIV, "*Ab augustissimo,*" March 5, 1744.

[3] "*Gravissimum,*" March 6, 1759, § 6 (*Continuatio Bull., ed. Prati, 1842, I, 114*).

[4] From this excommunication are exempted cardinals, but not bishops; see can. 2227, § 2.

scribes as follows: if hosts or particles are preserved in a repository, tabernacle, pyxis, or ostensorium, the legal presumption is that they are consecrated. The same presumption holds if a communicant should take a particle of the host out of his mouth after Holy Communion. Against this presumption conclusive and evident proofs are admitted, which means that at least two first-class sworn witnesses must prove the contrary, *viz.*, that the hosts were not consecrated. Such a proof, unless the minister who presumptively consecrated the sacred species should testify under oath to the contrary, could hardly be furnished; and therefore the presumption might just as well be called *iuris et de iure*.[5]

3. The acts by which this penalty is incurred are described as: *abiicere, abducere, retinere*. The first designates the act of intentional throwing away or spitting out. Accidental vomiting, sickly or sudden jerking or coughing does not, of course, constitute irreverence. The second term (*abducere*) denotes a carrying away of the sacred host, either violently (by robbery) or secretly, together with the sacred vessels or without them. The sacred species may be *retained* in places where they should not be kept, *i. e.*, in private homes, on one's own person, always supposing that this, like *abducere*, is done for an evil purpose. For the *abiicere* no evil purpose is required; the act alone is sufficient to constitute the crime in question. An *evil purpose* is legally presumed if the sacred species are carried away or retained. If these two acts are proved it is not necessary to prove

5 See can. 1825 f.

6 The purpose would also be evil if the sacred species were stolen or retained in order to hand them over to heretics, infidels, Free- masons, etc., or if they were used for superstitious purposes, for witchcraft or magic; Hadrian VI, "*Dudum*."

the bad intention.[6] Therefore the defendant himself must prove conclusively that he had no bad intention. Thus Benedict XIV in the aforesaid Constitution.

4. The *penalties* are somewhat mitigated, inasmuch as the delivering up of the culprit to the secular arm is not mentioned, and degradation (in case of clergymen) is changed into deposition *ferendae sententiae*. The infamy mentioned in our Canon is that of law *(infamia iuris)*, with all the effects mentioned in can. 2294, §1.

VIOLATION OF THE LAWS OF BINATION AND FASTING

Can. 2321

Sacerdotes qui contra praescripta can. 806, § 1, 808 praesumpserint Missam eodem die iterare vel eam celebrare non ieiuni, suspendantur a Missae celebratione ad tempus ab Ordinario secundum diversa rerum adiuncta praefiniendum.

Priests who dare to say Mass twice a day against the ruling of can. 806, §1, or who presumptuously say Mass without fasting, contrary to can. 808, should be suspended by the Ordinary from saying Mass for a time, the duration of which should be determined by circumstances.

Enough has been said concerning bination and fasting in connection with previous canons. As to the penal character, we may add:

1°. The term *presumption* is attached to both transgressions, and consequently can. 2229, §2 must be here applied. Any reason, therefore, of (not affected) ignorance, or fear, or physical incapacity, would diminish imputability. But since the penalty is not *latae sententiae,* these reasons do not entirely exempt one from incurring it. One decision of the Holy Office indeed reads that fear of scandal or astonishment would not justify a priest in saying a second Mass if he had broken the fast.[1] However, since our text expressly adds the term *praesumpserint*, it evidently admits a diminution of imputability and implies that the transgression must be a rash one.

2°. Suspension, even though only temporary, belongs to the class of *vindictive* penalties (can. 2298, n. 2), and consequently requires a judiciary procedure.[2] Its *duration* is to be measured by circumstances. These may be serious, on account of scandal or bad example, but may also depend on the need of priests, local conditions, etc.[3]

SAYING MASS AND HEARING CONFESSIONS BY PERSONS NOT PRIESTS

Can. 2322

Ad ordinem sacerdotalem non promotus:

1°. Si Missae celebrationem simulaverit aut sacramentalem confessionem exceperit, excommunicationem ipso facto contrahit, speciali modo Sedi Apostolicae reservatam; et insuper laicus quidem privetur pensione aut munere, si quod habeat in Ecclesia, aliisque poenis pro gravitate culpae puniatur; clericus vero deponatur;

2°. Si alia munia sacerdotalia usurpaverit, ab Ordinario pro gravitate culpae puniatur.

Persons not in sacerdotal orders, who pretend to say Mass or hear sacramental confession, ipso facto incur the excommunication reserved speciali modo to the Apostolic See.

1 S. O., Dec. 2, 1874 (*Coll. P. F.*, n. 1425).

2 Can. 1933, § 4; however, it may

3 If avarice were the motive of form a reason for suspension *ex informata conscientia*.

A layman performing such acts must, besides, be deprived of any pensions and offices he may hold in the Church, and be punished with other penalties, according to the gravity of the crime; a cleric is to be deposed.

Benedict XIV, in his Constitution "*Sacerdos in aeternum,*" mentions several papal documents (of Paul IV, Sixtus V, Clement VIII, and Urban VIII) which contain penalties decreed against such atrocious sacrileges. It is a usurpation of the highest power given to man, and is deservedly punished with great severity, not only with excommunication, but also with the delivery of the culprit to the secular arm, and degradation.[1] Our Code has modified the penalties according to the exigencies of the times.

1°. The persons intended here are all *who have never been promoted to the order of the priesthood.* Hence all laymen who are not of the clerical rank, as well as all clerics from the first tonsure to deaconship, inclusively.

The question may arise: How are we to prove that one is not of the priestly order? This, according to the aforesaid Constitution of Benedict XIV, may be settled by demanding of the incriminated person the testimonials of his ordination. For, according to our Code, can. 1010, §2, every cleric must be given a paper certifying the order he has received. Besides, the episcopal court must keep the records. Consequently, information, even in a private or confidential (*i. e.,* extrajudicial way) may furnish the necessary proof for ordination required in our case. If no such written proof could be found, at least two witnesses would have to testify under oath to

---

bination, or intemperance of breaking the fast, the circumstances would be serious.

1 Of these, Bened. XIV, "*Quam grave,*" Aug. 2, 1757, treats *in extenso.*

the ordination or the fact that the defendant is a priest.[2]

3°. The *acts* here punished are two: pretending to say Mass and hearing sacramental confession.

a) *Simulatio* is an act by which one pretends to be what he is not. A Mass said by any person lacking the priestly power is no Mass at all,[3] no matter whether the person has the intention to say Mass or not. However, as Benedict XIV says, the sacrilegious act must have proceeded at least as far as the elevation of the host and chalice, or one of these acts inclusively. Whether or not the words of consecration were pronounced does not matter. Neither does it constitute a diminution of criminal imputability if Mass was said only once.

b) *Hearing sacramental confession* is also included in our canon. The text does not say: *simulaverit;* hence the mere act of hearing sacramental confession is sufficient to constitute the crime. What is a sacramental confession? It is the penitent's accusation of his sins made to a competent priest in order to obtain absolution. A confession made for the sake of obtaining consolation or counsel would not be sacramental, nor would it be sacramental if the penitent knew that the person to whom he made his confession lacked the priestly character.[4] But the formula of absolution need not be pronounced.[5]

---

[2] Whether an *invalidly ordained* priest would incur this censure, is not quite certain; hence the benefit of doubt may at least be admitted in favor of non-incurrence.

[3] See Lehmkuhl, *l. c.*, II, n. 44:" *fictum esse actum, qui externe ita ponatur, ac si omnia ad valorem requisita adsint, sed animo, seu* *sine interna voluntate et intentione.*" But here the intention is lacking objectively or fundamentally, not subjectively, at least not *in recto.*

[4] Arregui, *Summarium Theological Moralis,* 1919, ed. 4, p. 367.

[5] Bened. XIV, " *Sacerdos in aeternum,*" § 8.

4°. The *penalties* inflicted are: (a) excommunication *latae sententiae* reserved *speciali modo* to the Holy See. The phrase here is not accompanied by any extenuating or modifying word, such as *praesumpserit, scienter,* etc.; (b) all the other penalties are *ferendae sententiae.* This is also true of the punishments to be inflicted arbitrarily, *i. e.,* proportionately to the seriousness of the criminal act, when persons who are not priests *usurp the exercise of other priestly functions.* Of this kind would be blessings reserved to priests if given by laymen. [6]

BLASPHEMY AND PERJURY

Can. 2323

Qui blasphemaverit vel periurium extra iudicium commiserit, prudenti Ordinarii arbitrio puniatur, maxime clericus.

Whoever blasphemes or commits perjury, outside of an ecclesiastical trial, may be punished according to the prudent judgment of the Ordinary, especially if the culprit is a cleric.

Two religious crimes, blasphemy and perjury, are here connected, because both are an offense against the immediate object of religion.

1. Blasphemy is defined as contumelious speech against God. It is *heretical* if His existence or His attributes are impugned or denied. It is simple if the contumelious utterance consists of mere imprecations. Blasphemous words may also be uttered against the Saints, because, as God is praised in his Saints, so also

---

6 See can. 1147, § 3; 1342, § 1.

may He be blasphemed in his Saints.[1] But it is controversial among theologians whether blasphemy, in the proper sense, can be committed by gestures, signs, or acts, for instance, spitting against heaven, treading on the crucifix, etc.[2]

a) Our text appears to include every species of contumelious utterance, whether by speech or gesture, provided the intention of blaspheming can be deduced from the act according to the common usage of the people and country.[3] An indication may be found in the expression "*absque contumelia Creatoris*," which doubtlessy includes gestures and acts.

b) The *penalty is left to the Ordinary*, who may decree a public penance or any other ecclesiastical penalty, provided, of course, the offense was an external and a public act.[4] For although it is not essential to the notion of crime that it be public, yet a public penance could not be imposed for an occult crime.

Heretical blasphemy belongs exclusively [5] to the ecclesiastical court. *Simple blasphemy* belongs to the mixed forum, *i. e.*, the ecclesiastical as well as the secular courts may prosecute it. In England and in most of the United States blasphemy is still a statutory crime, but prosecutions for the offence have become very rare.[6]

2. *Perjury* is here understood as the contrary of an oath, and, therefore, a violation of truthfulness as well as a breach of a promise made under oath (see can.

---

1 C. 2, X, V, 26; Reiffenstuel, *ib.*, n. 15.

2 C. 2 just quoted only mentions: *linguam in blasphemiam relaxare;* thus also S. Thom., II-II, q. 13, art. 2; Ballerini-Palmieri, *l. c.*, II, n. 370.

3 Thus Hollweck, *l. c.*, p. 193; Arregui, *l. c.*, n. 202; Eichmann,

l. c., p. 136; see also Rom. II, 14; I Tim. VI, 1; Tit. II, 5.

4 Cfr. can. 1933, § 1; can. 2312, § 2; for former penalties, see c. 2, X, V, 26; Pius V, "*Cum primum*," April 1, 1566, § 33.

5 Reiffenstuel, V, 26, n. 27.

6 Blackstone-Cooley, *Commen-*

1316 ff). There is no doubt that both kinds of perjury are here included and intended, provided only that the oath be *extrajudicial*, *i. e.*, not taken with reference to an ecclesiastical trial.

Experts, witnesses, counsel, proxy, judges, who take the oath before or at the trial, therefore, are punishable in case of perjury according to can. 1743, §3; 1757, §2, n. 1; 1795, §2. Any other perjury, committed either by private persons or officials, except in reference to an ecclesiastical trial, is also punishable. If it occurs in a secular court, and the latter metes out a sufficient penalty, the ecclesiastical court may be satisfied.[7] The secular courts punish perjury if at least two trustworthy witnesses attest the falsity of the perjured statement.[8] This procedure may serve as a norm for Ordinaries in proceeding against perjurers. The penalty, being vindictive, requires some sort of judiciary trial.

Clerics should, of course, be tried in the ecclesiastical court and be punished more severely than laymen. Formerly penalties against laymen guilty of perjury were of varying severity. Thus a fast of forty days on bread and water, and seven years of ordinary penance, which meant at least two fast-days a week, were to be meted out according to a Pseudo-Fabian decree.[9] Clergymen were to be deposed, and in case of obstinacy, degraded.[10] These severe penalties show how the Church abhors this crime, which is not only an offense against religion, but undermines public trust and confidence.

taries, IV, 59; *New International Encyclopedia*, 1904, Vol. III, 163.
7 Can. 1933, § 3.
8 Kenny-Webb, *Outlines of Criminal Law*, p. 280 ff.

9 C. 18, C. 6, q. 1.
10 C. 7, Dist. 50; c. 9, C. 3, q. 5; c. 10, X, II, 1.

TRAFFICKING IN MASS STIPENDS AND DEFRAUDATION

Can. 2324

Qui deliquerint contra praescriptum can. 827, 828, 840, § 1, ab Ordinario pro gravitate culpae puniantur, non exclusa, si res ferat, suspensione aut beneficii vel officii ecclesiastici privatione, vel, si de laicis agatur, excommunicatione.

What canons 827, 828, 840, §1, forbid has been explained elsewhere,[1] and we have nothing to retract. We only add that (a) every species of trafficking in Mass stipends, (b) every curtailment of the number of Masses offered and accepted, (c) every fraudulent subtraction from the alms given for Masses when sending the intentions to others, is here included. The *penalty is left to the judgment of the Ordinary, who shall take into consideration the seriousness of each case,* especially the number and amount of stipends, the scandal given, and whether or not the culprit is a habitual offender. If the case is important and the transgressor is a *clergyman, suspension or privation of benefice or ecclesiastical office would not be an exorbitant penalty.* Hence the Ordinary could suspend the clergyman from both office and benefice. But the vindictive penalty of privation could only be *either* of benefice *or* of office, not of both together. *Laymen* who transgress these laws, *e. g.,* booksellers and other merchants, can be punished by excommunication.

What we said elsewhere [2] concerning pious frauds we

---

1 See Vol. IV of this Commentary, p. 186 ff.

2 See Vol. VI of this Commentary, p. 614, note 1.

here repeat, but with a restriction. If $100 are offered for Masses, without any further determination, 100 Masses must be said; neither would the priest satisfy his obligation if he said or sang twenty high Masses of his own accord. Only in case of a parish—this is our restriction—where the priest sings a Mass every day of the week and the donors know that the ordinary stipend for such a Mass is five dollars, might the priest be justified in saying only twenty Masses for $100.

SUPERSTITION AND SACRILEGE

Can. 2325

Qui superstitionem exercuerit vel sacrilegium perpetraverit, pro gravitate culpae ab Ordinario puniatur, salvis poenis iure statutis contra aliquos actus superstitiosos vel sacrilegia.

Whoever practices superstition or perpetrates a sacrilege, shall be punished by the Ordinary in proportion to the gravity of the offense. The penalties provided by law against certain superstitious acts and sacrileges are not touched by this canon.

1. *Superstition* is defined by St. Thomas [1] as an excess of religious worship or a vicious, ignorant, and abnormal form of belief and practice. Our canon considers not so much the speculative or purely mental excess as its practical expression, *i. e.,* superstitious observance. This may be defined as an inadequate means to produce certain effects in a more or less preternatural way, generally by invoking the assistance of creatures or the

[1] *Summa Theol.,* II–II, q. 92, art. 1; S. C. P. F., Feb. 9, 1760 (*Col*. n. 424).

powers of darkness. In the Decretals[2] a special title was devoted to this subject under the name of *sortilegia*. This is subsumed under divination or manifestation of secret and hidden things by means of signs and with the help of demons. A long list of various species, divided according to the signs or means employed, is given by the commentators: *geomantia,* if the earth was consulted, *aeromantia,* if the air; *hydromantia,* if water; *pyromantia,* if fire; *haruspicium,* if the entrails of animals; *auspicium,* if the flight of birds; *augurium,* if the twittering and chirping of birds; *pedomantia,* if the feet, and *chiromantia,* if the hands were inspected; *omina,* if the voices of men; *onyrocritica,* if dreams; *physiognomia,* if the whole body was inspected; *spatulamantia* if the *spatula;*[3] *metoposcopia,* if the forehead; *pythonia,* if the demon tells something through living men who are his tools; *necromantia,* if dead bodies are consulted; *astrologia,* if heavenly bodies are observed, not in a scientific, but superstitious way. We quote these names to show that the number of fools has not yet decreased. For all these forms of witchcraft, sorcery, magic, etc., are more or less practiced to-day by *Spiritists.* We may include here the use of the *ouija board,* unless it is handled for mere pastime—a most dangerous diversion.[4] Also certain medical practices which promise health to those who use certain signs or apply certain herbs in a specified way. As to *hypnotism,*

---

[2] Lib. V, tit. 21; see the commentators on the same, especially Reiffenstuel and Schmalzgrueber.

[3] The term is not quite clear; *" in spatula divinare "* (Du Cange, *Glossarium,* VI, 632) seems to signify to divine from the shoulder or hips or brawn of a pig.

[4] See the works of J. Godfrey Raupert: *Modern Spiritism, The Dangers of Spiritualism, The New Black Magic* (last chapter on the Ouija Board); J. Liljencrants, *Spiritism and Religion;* T. F. Coakley, *Spiritism, the Modern Satanism;* Lapponi-Gibbs, *Hypnotism and Spiritism,* 1915.

it is not forbidden in itself, nor can it be styled a superstitious observance if practiced by scientific and conscientious physicians, and if no extraordinary effects are expected or promised. The *penalty* for these transgressions is arbitrary, but must be inflicted according to the rules laid down in can. 2223.

2. *Sacrilege* is a violation of sacred things, *i. e.*, things destined for divine worship either by consecration or blessing (can. 1497, §2). It is *personal,* if a sacred person is violated externally;[5] *local,* if a sacred place is subjected to irreverence or scorn, such as suffices to desecrate a holy place (can. 1154); *real,* if sacred things are violated, such as the sacred species, consecrated utensils or images, etc.

3. All these sacrileges are here intended. The *penalty is left to the Ordinary,* though, as our canon says, *the penalty for crimes specified* in the Code remains intact, *e. g.:*

a) *Personal* sacrilege against clerics is procecuted by our Code in can. 2241, 2243, as far as the clerical privileges are concerned. The *sacrilegium carnale* is punished, especially as far as illicit or invalid marriage is concerned, in can. 2358, 2388.

b) *Sacrilegium locale* is especially punished in can. 2320, 2328, 2329. But the *ius asyli* is no longer[6] prosecuted by a special penalty, and therefore the first clause only of our canon takes effect;

c) *Sacrilegium reale* has special punishments assigned to it in can. 2320, 2345, 2346 (ecclesiastical property). The clause " *salvis poenis,*" etc., means that the Ordinary should not inflict arbitrary punishment. He may, but

---

5 External action is required in order to constitute a crime; can. 2195, § 1.

6 "*Apostolicae Sedis,*" n. 18;

" *Immunitatem asyli ecclesiastici, ausu temerario, violare iubentes aut violantes*"; (*exc. latae sent. R. P. reservata*).

is not bound to punish in cases where the law has not
provided a special penalty.

TRADING IN FALSE RELICS

Can. 2326

Qui falsas reliquias conficit, aut scienter vendit, distribuit vel publicae fidelium venerationi exponit, ipso facto excommunicationem Ordinario reservatam contrahit.

Those who manufacture false relics or knowingly sell or distribute them or have them exposed to the public veneration of the faithful, ipso facto incur excommunication reserved to the Ordinary.

The preliminary questions as to the authenticity of
relics have been explained under can. 1283-1285. No
doubt the sad experiences made in Italy, especially since
1870, contributed to the making of this penal canon.

1. *Manufacturers* of relics are persons who make
relics of common bones or other things pertaining to the
Saints.[1] It does not matter whether these relics are
direct (from the body) or indirect (from objects related to the Saints). It seems probable that, if part of a
genuine relic were mixed with common things, there
would be no manufacture of false relics in the sense of
our canon, at least it would be doubtful and the benefit of
doubt should be sustained.

2. Those who *knowingly sell false relics* are such as
are fully aware that no authentic document exists
or has ever existed. If can. 1285, §1 would have to be

---

[1] Selling of true relics is forbidden as simony and sacrilege and to be punished according to can. 2325; but no excommunication is attached.

applied, because of social disturbance, the relics could not be simply styled false; but in that case the local Ordinary should be consulted; excommunication, however, would not follow.

3. Those who *distribute* false relics *knowingly, i. e.,* knowing that they are not genuine. It does not matter whether this is done by official or private persons. Thus a *custos s. supellectilis* may be as guilty as a simple-minded woman.

4. Those who *knowingly expose or cause such false relics to be exposed* may be the ecclesiastical or the civil authorities, who command such exposition. If an inferior, say a sexton or lay-brother, were ordered to expose them, his coöperation would have to be judged according to can. 2209. If he does not know the relics are false, he is entirely excused; but if he has doubts, he should try to make sure, though while in doubt he would escape excommunication, according to can. 2229, §2.

TRAFFICKING IN INDULGENCES

Can. 2327

Quaestum facientes ex indulgentiis plectuntur ipso facto excommunicatione Sedi Apostolicae simpliciter reservata.

Those who make profit from indulgences incur the ipso facto excommunication simply reserved to the Apostolic See.

The history of this canon runs back to the Reformation, but the traffic in indulgences and other spiritual favors is as old as the term simony. Pius V made special efforts to eradicate this evil,[1] and yet it lives on;

---

1 "*Etsi Dominici,*" Feb. 8, 1567; "*Quam plenum,*" Jan. 2, 1570.

else the "*Apostolicae Sedis*"[2] and the Code would not
have deemed it necessary to provide a special penalty for
the modern followers of Simon Magus. The Code
has considerably modified the former text; for, while
the constitution of St. Pius V ("*Quan plenum*")
and Pius IX included all kinds of spiritual favors, the *Code strictly limits the penalties to indulgences.*

The penalty provided in our canon is incurred by all
who derive material profit from indulgences. Hence the
mere announcement or promise of indulgences is sufficient, if money or other material profit, such as promotion, protection, aid, has been received and accepted.
The essential thing is the simoniacal intention; whether
the indulgence was really gained, does not matter. The
mere fact that a *questus* (lucre, gain) was obtained by
promulgating, preaching, or promising an indulgence,
either papal or episcopal, is sufficient to establish the
criminal fact.

It does not matter whether one does it himself or
through another, or whether the purpose is good or bad,
or the cause charitable.[3]

It was held before the promulgation of the Code
that bishops do not incur this penalty.[4] This view must
now be abandoned; for, according to can. 2227, §2,
bishops are declared immune only from suspension and
the interdict *latae sententiae*, but not from excommunication. Therefore, with the exception of Cardinals, all
prelates may incur this censure. Neither is there any

---

where other spiritual favors besides
indulgences are mentioned.

2 II, 11: "*Omnes qui quaestum
facientes ex indulgentiis aliisque
gratiis spiritualibus, excommunicationis censura plectuntur Constitu-*

*tione S. Pii V. Quam plenum, a.
Januarii, 1569.*"

3 This is expressly stated in the
aforesaid Constitution of Pius V.

4 Thus D'Annibale, *l. c.*, p. 92,
n. 137.

reason why they should be exempt, since indulgences
are granted or promulgated by prelates.

DESECRATION OF GRAVES AND CORPSES

Can. 2328

Qui cadavera vel sepulcra mortuorum ad furtum vel
alium malum finem violaverit, interdicto personali
puniatur, sit ipso facto infamis, et clericus praeterea
deponatur.

*Whosoever desecrates corpses or graves to commit
theft, or from some other evil motive, is to be punished
with the personal interdict, is ipso facto infamous, and if
a cleric, should be deposed.* The Christian religion as
well as nature inculcate reverence for the dead and
their resting places. The violation of a tomb was regarded as a crime under the Roman law and visited with
the severest penalties. Those convicted of removing a
body or digging up human bones were, if persons of the
lowest rank, condemned to capital punishment; if of
higher condition, they were banished to an island or condemned to work in the mines.[1] A chapter of the Decree
of Gratian declares them infamous.[2] This *penalty* is
here repeated and involves *infamia iuris.* The other
two penalties, *viz.,* the *personal interdict,* which may be
inflicted on laymen and clerics, and deposition for
clergymen, are *ferendae sententiae.*

No distinction is made between kinds of bodies or
graves. Consequently, the body of a criminal is as
sacred, in this respect, as that of a respectable citizen.

---

1 L. 11, Dig. 48, 12 *de sepulchro*   2 C. 17, C. 6, q. 1.
violato; infamy stated in h 1, *ibid.*

Neither is it necessary that the grave be blessed. To violate it is a crime against a universal religious sentiment. The motive must be *theft* (for instance, to steal the appurtenances of a corpse, such as jewelry or precious metal) or some other wicked purpose, such as revenge, hatred, or superstition. While the keeping of bodies for anatomical purposes is legitimate,[3] stealing them, even though done for the sake of science, is an indictable offence[4] and falls under our canon.

DESECRATION OF CHURCHES AND CEMETERIES

Can. 2329

Ecclesiae vel coemeterii violatores, de quibus in can. 1172, 1207, interdicto ab ingressu ecclesiae aliisque congruis poenis ab Ordinario pro gravitate delicti puniantur.

Those who cause a church or cemetery to be desecrated or violated by acts described in canons 1172 and 1207, *should be punished by the Ordinary with the interdict forbidding them to enter the church and with other penalties proportionate to the gravity of the crime.*

The acts referred to are set forth in canons 1172 and 1207 and need no repetition. The penalty is *ferendae sententiae*, but stated preceptively, which means that the Ordinary is not entirely free to inflict it or not (can. 2223).

In connection with this canon and can. 2326, we may add that our Code is silent on an excommunication

---

3 Eichmann, *l. c.*, p. 144.

4 Blackstone-Cooley, *Comment.*, II, 429, note 7: "It being considered a practice contrary to common de-cency, and shocking to the general sentiments and feelings of mankind."

latae sententiae simply reserved to the Holy See which was formerly imposed for carrying away relics from the catacombs of the City of Rome without the permission of the Cardinal Vicar.[1]

[1] This penalty was mentioned in the *"Apostolicae Sedis,"* II, § 15, but it has now a merely historical value. The curious reader is referred to the commentaries on said Constitution.

TITLE XIII

CRIMES AGAINST ECCLESIASTICAL AUTHORITIES, PERSONS AND THINGS

The term *ecclesiastical* comprehends whatever the Church makes use of by constitutional provision, either divine or human, and whatever she holds by legitimate titles. Constitution spells authority and therefore is here treated first (can. 2330-2340). Then comes the inviolability of clerical persons, including religious, or rather a specially privileged class of religious (can. 2341-3344), and, lastly, ecclesiastical property, which is safeguarded against unjust usurpation and incompetent administration (can. 2345-49).

TRANSGRESSIONS OF LAWS CONCERNING PAPAL ELECTION

Can. 2330

Quod attinet ad poenas statutas in delicta quae in eligendo Summo Pontifice committi possunt, unice standum const. Pii X *Vacante Sede Apostolica*, 25 Dec. 1904.

All laws touching papal election are abrogated except the Constitution of Pius X, "*Vacante Sede Apostolica*," Dec. 25, 1904, which remains in full force.[1] This Constitution also regulates the penalties decreed against offenders.

---

[1] See the text in Card. Gasparri's (large) edition, pp. 685 ff., cap. VI. To this may be added "*Commissum Nobis*," Jan. 20, 1904, concerning

1. Those who commit *simony* [2] in the election of a Pope *ipso facto* incur *excommunication,* reserved to the future Pope, who shall declare the fact that the penalty has been incurred and who alone can absolve from this crime. However, the validity of the election can not be assailed on this score.

2. The same penalty is incurred by those, either cardinals, clerics, or laymen, who during the *lifetime of the Pope* and without his advice,[3] enter into negotiations with regard to *the election of his successor,* or promise to give their vote (with or without effect or counter promise) or dare to hold private meetings in order to deliberate and decide on the subject of the election.

3. The same penalty (excommunication) is incurred by cardinals, the secretary of the sacred college, and conclavists or others who in any way take part in the conclave, who under whatever pretext accept from any civil power the charge of proposing the so-called *Veto* or *Exclusiva,* even in form of a mere wish, or manifest it either to the S. College as a body or to single cardinals, whether in writing or orally, directly or indirectly, by insinuation or hints, or in any manner whatsoever, as long as the conclave lasts. This penalty extends to every kind of intervention or intercession or any form of interference that may come from any lay power of whatever rank or condition.

4. Cardinals who *enter into ante-election agreements,* or hold meetings or pledge themselves to give their vote to a certain person, henceforth incur the sentence of excommunication.

---

the *Veto* or *ius exclusivae,* and the Motu proprio "Cum proxime" of Pius XI (*A. A. S.,* XIV, 6).

2 See can. 727.

3 *Tractare* means systematic negotiation with serious intent, not mere gossip or passing remarks.

5. *During the conclave* the following transgressions are punished:

a) Cardinals who are not present at the balloting *(scrutinium)* after the bell has rung, incur the penalty of *excommunication latae sententiae* unless they are sick.[4]

b) *Epistolary intercourse* with the outside world is strictly forbidden during a conclave, more especially any communication through newspapers or magazines. The transgressors of this law incur *excommunication latae sententiae.* This penalty concerns not only the cardinals, but all conclavists.[5]

c) Every *violation of the secrecy of the ballot* is forbidden under the same penalty. This affects the cardinals only, and covers every communication, whether direct or indirect, that concerns the balloting or transactions of the congregation of cardinals, or the acts and decrees of the same, either before or during the conclave.[6]

DISOBEDIENCE AND CONSPIRACY

Can. 2331

§ 1. Qui Romano Pontifici vel proprio Ordinario aliquid legitime praecipienti vel prohibenti pertinaciter non obtemperant, congruis poenis, censuris non exclusis, pro gravitate culpae puniantur.

§ 2. Conspirantes vero contra auctoritatem Romani Pontificis eiusve Legati vel proprii Ordinarii aut contra eorum legitima mandata, itemque subditos ad inobedientiam erga ipsos provocantes, censuris aliisve poenis coerceantur; et dignitatibus, beneficiis aliisve muneribus, si sint clerici; voce activa et passiva atque officio, si religiosi, priventur.

---

[4] "*Vacante Sede,*" n. 37.   [6] *Ibid.,* n. 52.
[5] *Ibid.,* n. 50.

This canon regards two crimes which differ from each other not specifically, but in degree, namely disobedience and conspiracy.

1. *Disobedience. Those who obstinately refuse to obey the Roman Pontiff or their own Ordinary, when these authorities legitimately command or forbid something are to be punished in proportion to the gravity of their guilt, censures not excluded.*

a) *Obedience* presupposes the right to command and the obligation to obey. Hence there must be a tie or relation between superior and inferior. This is established either juridically or morally. In the *juridical order* the Roman Pontiff is the head and ordinary pastor of all the faithful, clergy and laity; the local Ordinary is the ecclesiastical governor of his territory and of those subject to him by reason of domicile or quasi-domicile. The superiors of exempt religious orders wield their power over those who are subject to them by reason of profession. In the *moral* order there are still other superiors, who govern their subjects by reason of the domestic power, but these are not considered in our canon.[1] For although the vow of obedience binds religious to their superiors, yet it is the moral power rather than the juridical (exercised in the external forum) that establishes the mutual relationship. But all religious, superiors and inferiors, are alike subject to the Roman Pontiff (can. 499, §1).

b) By *Roman Pontiff* there must be understood the supreme head of the Church as a religious and supernatural society. Consequently, disobedience to the Pope

[1] The text says *ordinarius*, which must be understood according to can. 198, § 1, and can only be applied to superiors of exempt clerical institutes. Therefore, this canon does not concern non-exempt religious organizations with regard to their own superiors, but may concern them with regard to the local ordinary or prelate regular.

as a temporal ruler is not included.[2] The supposition here is that the Pope is the legitimate occupant of St. Peter's chair.[3]

c) *Ordinarius proprius*, as stated above, means one who has subjects of his own. The clergy are especially obliged to exhibit reverence and obedience to their bishops (can. 127). The faithful living in the diocese are also obliged to obey the bishop, as their pastor. Exempt religious here are those subject to their own prelates or to the superiors of autonomous communities. To strange bishops and strange prelates or superiors the clergy and religious pay respect, but not obedience.[4]

d) Like a law, a precept, too, may be *positive* or *prohibitive*, according as it commands men to do or to omit something. The objective norm for all precepts is that what they order *must be legitimate.*

Legitimacy is measured, not by personal qualities or powers, but by the object of the precept. Since, however, every law is a participation in the eternal law, and every exercise of human power is therefore confined within the limits of that law, it follows that even the papal power has certain boundaries:

α) The *Pope* can command nothing that runs counter to the natural and divine law, though he may interpret or determine it. But he is not bound by the common law of the Church, although it is commonly presumed that he will order nothing that would exceed his power.

β) *Ordinaries*, including *exempt religious superiors*, cannot command anything that would clash with the common law. Neither are they allowed to command beyond what is established by particular law; at least, they are supposed to keep within proper limits.[5] *Re-*

2 D'Annibale, *l. c.*, p. 33, n. 44.
3 Hollweck, *l. c.*, p. 196.

4 C. 11, C. 11, q. 3.
5 Politics do not fall under the

ligious superiors are not allowed to command anything against the common law of the Church, and a religious would not act disobediently if he refused to obey a command contained neither in the rule nor in the Constitutions of his order.

γ) Disobedience must be *obstinate*, which presupposes knowledge and free will, and, besides, a warning, according to can. 2307 or 2143; for obstinacy must be proven.

δ) The penalty is arbitrary, *pro gravitate culpae*, and *ferendae sententiae*.

2. A *conspiracy* is an agreement by two or more persons to effect an unlawful object, whether as the ultimate aim or only as a means to the same.[6]   The aim of conspiracies as a rule is twofold: subversion of the ecclesiastical authority and incitement to rebellion against it.

a) This canon is aimed at those who enter into a *conspiracy against the authority of the Roman Pontiff, or his legate, or their own Ordinary, or against the lawful commands of these authorities,* as far as their power reaches, either legislative, or judiciary, or coercive, and as far as these authorities keep within the limits of their power.   For such conduct is subversive of the hierarchic order and spells resistance to God.

Personal invectives, libelous writings, and defamation of the person as such, do not constitute a conspiracy. If a cathedral or religious chapter proposes amendments to its statutes or constitutions, this is not conspiracy.   The *Gravamina Nationis Teutonicae*[7] were not considered a conspiracy, although they very closely resembled one. But if the threefold power named above is attacked by mutual agreement, and resisted, there is a conspiracy.

list of objects to which the power of the ordinary extends. Neither can superiors forbid their subjects to have recourse to the Holy See.

6 Kenny-Webb, l. c., p. 273.
7 See Funk, *Manual of Church History*, II, 88, 165.

b) *Provoking or inciting subjects to disobey the aforesaid authorities also constitutes the crime here mentioned.*
But those who provoke or incite others to disobedience
may be single individuals, agreement or conspiracy not
being required. How far guilt may be imputed to them
is to be determined according to can. 2209.

c) The *penalty* for conspiracy and incitement to disobedience is: the conspirators must be restrained by censures and other penalties; *clerics* must be deprived of their
dignities, benefices, and other charges; *religious* must be
deprived of the active and passive voice, and of their
offices. Formerly clerics guilty of this crime were deposed and delivered to the *curia*.[8]

APPEAL TO A GENERAL COUNCIL

Can. 2332

**Omnes et singuli cuiuscunque status, gradus seu
conditionis etiam regalis, episcopalis vel cardinalitiae
fuerint, a legibus, decretis, mandatis Romani Pontificis pro tempore exsistentis ad Universale Concilium
appellantes, sunt suspecti de haeresi et ipso facto contrahunt excommunicationem Sedi Apostolicae speciali modo reservatam; Universitates vero, Collegia,
Capitula aliaeve personae morales, quocunque nomine
nuncupentur, interdictum speciali modo Sedi Apostolicae pariter reservatum incurrunt.**

The theory that a general council is above the Pope
now appears absurd. It was called ridiculous by Pius

8 Cfr. c. 18, C. 11, q. 3; a
horrible imprecation is contained in
c. 14, C. 11, q. 3 (Pseudo-Anterus):
"*inobediens spirituali animadver-*
sione truncatur, et eiectus ab
Ecclesia rabido daemonum ore
discerpitur."

II [1] — not by Aeneas Silvius Piccolomini —, but in those sad times of schism even well-meaning men like Gerson looked upon it as the only anchor available on a troubled sea. To-day, of course, the error is neither excusable nor intelligible. It was proscribed several times [2] and our Code fixes its penalty.

1. The *persons* who incur the penalty here stated are:

a) Single *individuals,* of whatever state (lay or clerical), rank or condition, even royal persons, bishops, and cardinals.

b) *Corporations,* such as universities (also faculties), colleges, chapters, and other artificial persons, no matter what their name (congress, senate, parliament).

2. It makes no difference whether the *general council* appealed to, is in session, or to be held in future.[3] For appeal means recourse to a higher instance, and the fundamental error involved here is that there exists a higher tribunal than the Pope, and the injury is therefore committed against the supreme judge.

3. The *appeal must be made from laws, decrees, or ordinances issued by a Pope* actually governing the Church. The text includes *laws,* which the "*Apostolica Sedes*" had omitted: therefore all *laws,* also privileges and favors, *decrees,* either dogmatical or disciplinary, *ordinances,* for instance, provisions or appointments, or judiciary sentences in particular cases, provided these have emanated from the Roman Pontiff, as such, not as

---

1 "*Execrabiltis,*" Jan. 18, 1459.

2 Julius II, "*Suscepti regiminis,*" July 1, 1509; Bened. XIV, "*Altissimo,*" June 26, 1745, § 1; "*Apostolicae Sedis,*" § 1, n. 4:

"*Omnes et singulos, cuiuscumque status, gradus seu conditionis fuerint, ab ordinationibus seu mandatis Romanorum Pontificum pro tempore existentium ad universale futurum Concilium appellantes, nec non eos, quorum auxilio, consilio vel favore appellatum fuerit.*" Conc. Vatic., IV, 3.

3 Since the text of the "*Apostolicae Sedis*" had "*future,*" a council held *hic et nunc* seemed to be excluded; Pennacchi I, 412.

a temporal ruler [4] or an international judge. The canon does *not* include decisions or ordinances issued by the S. Congregations and Tribunals.

Some [5] have raised a difficulty concerning an appeal from a law, decree, or ordinance of a Pope who has died after having issued said law, etc., and therefore seems not to exist any more. However, this is a rather subtle interpretation and certainly nullifies the intention of the lawgiver. Besides, it entails the absurdity that after the death of a Pontiff his laws, decrees, and ordinances could be appealed. Finally, such laws, etc., are intended not only for the lifetime of the Pope. Most probably the phrase *"pro tempore exsistentis"* was inserted in view of a possible resignation. An appeal from laws, decrees, or ordinances already abrogated would be senseless.

4. The *penalties* are:

For the *individuals* mentioned in the first clause (1, a), *excommunication* incurred *ipso facto* and reserved *speciali modo* to the Apostolic See; besides, suspicion of heresy.

b) For *corporations,* as such, mentioned in the second clause (1, b), the interdict *ipso facto,* reserved to the Apostolic See. Single members of the corporation, however, do not incur this censure. [6] If they are partakers or accomplices, they, as individuals, incur excommunication, but not the interdict. [7] Thus the members of a parliament or senate may vote against appeal to a council, and in that case they would not incur the penalty, even though the minority had appealed in their name; the single members

4 D'Annibale, *l. c.,* p. 34, n. 47.   note 8; Eichmann, *l. c.,* p. 150.
5 Pennacchi *l. c.,* I, 409 f.   7 See can. 2209; can. 2219: a
6 Thus Hollweck, *l. c.,* p. 197,   more benign interpretation.

would be excommunicated, not interdicted, nor would the whole body be interdicted.

CIVIL INTERFERENCE WITH PAPAL COMMUNICATIONS (PLACET)

Can. 2333

Recurrentes ad laicam potestatem ad impediendas litteras vel acta quaelibet a Sede Apostolica vel ab eiusdem Legatis profecta, eorumve promulgationem vel exsecutionem directe vel indirecte prohibentes, aut eorum causa sive eos ad quos pertinent litterae vel acta sive alios laedentes vel perterrefacientes, ipso facto subiaceant excommunicationi Sedi Apostolicae speciali modo reservatae.

The kings of England and France in the XIIth century, constitutional monarchies and free republics alike were afraid and jealous of the papal power and endeavored to blockade its influence by submitting documents emanating from the Roman Curia to their personal inspection and approbation.[1] This is called the royal *placet,* although the text here has a somewhat wider meaning.

Three kinds of offenders incur the penalty here named: those who recur in order to impede, those who prohibit, and those who by word or deed terrify others.

1. The *recurrentes* are those who seek or ask the

1 Paschal II (1099-1118) already complained against the King of England that he would admit neither papal nuncios nor letters without his royal *placet;* see E. Friedberg, *Die Grenzen zwischen Staat und Kirche,* Tübingen, 1872, p. 729. Friedberg is strong in denouncing "papal absolutism," yet he does not defend the retention or introduction of the *placet,* because it does not fit in with the modern State (*Rechtsstaat*) and renders clashes with the Church more frequent; *ib.,* p. 799 f.

service and aid of others. The mode of recourse is not determined. It may be formal or informal, *i. e.*, by appeal in civil law or by a mere petition.[2] All Catholics, whether laymen or ecclesiastics, are here included, excepting the Cardinals (can. 2227, §2).

The *terminus ad quem* of the *recursus* is the lay or civil power *(laica potestas)*. This term supposes real power, as wielded in our country by the president, governors, congress, and judges.[3]

The *terminus a quo* is recourse calculated "*to impede letters and documents (acta) coming from the Apostolic See or from its legates.*"[4] Apostolic letters are bulls, briefs, or motu proprios, or letters of recommendation, such as we often read in the *Acta Apostolicae Sedis*. *Acta* are decisions, decrees, admonitions, summonses, or any kind of rescripts issued either by the Pope himself or by the Roman Court,[5] according to can. 7.

Impedire means to impede or prevent some one from doing or obtaining something. The term implies that the one thus impeded is unwilling to bear the obstacle.[6] Since this word is connected with Apostolic letters, etc., which are already issued *(profecta)*, it can only refer to the reception or transmission of such.

2. The *prohibentes* are not clearly determined, and the term itself is somewhat ambiguous. For *prohibere* in Latin may mean to *prevent* or *impede* as well as to *prohibit* or *forbid*. It appears to us that Pennacchi[7] has stated the correct meaning when he says that the act of

---

2 D'Annibale, *l. c.*, p. 42, n. 61; Hollweck, *l. c.*, p. 198.

3 Hollweck, *ibid.*

4 By legates are understood *nuntii, internuntii, delegati apostolici*, as the title of ch. V, tit. VI,

book II, indicates; see can. 265-267.

5 S. O., Jan. 13, 1892 (*Coll. P. F.*, n. 1777).

6 D'Annibale, *l. c.*, p. 41, n. 60.

7 *Comment.*, I, 285 f.; also D'Annibale, p. 49, n. 74.

prohibition must proceed from some one in power. The prohibition of *promulgating and executing papal documents* may be direct or indirect. It is *direct*, if the competent magistrate forbids divulgation of such documents by a formal law, decree, bill, or sentence. It is *indirect*, if effective means are employed to hinder the promulgation or execution in a round-about way, for instance, by forbidding a courier to enter a city or town, or by commanding a postmaster not to transmit or deliver a papal document.

Promulgation may here be taken in the juridical sense, *i. e.*, the making known of a papal letter in the usual form, which is now by insertion in the *Acta Apostolicae Sedis*. However, this interpretation appears to us improbable, since in that case only the Vatican Printing Office, or, at most, the Roman civil authorities would be concerned. Therefore we believe that promulgation here has the meaning of divulgation or making known. The Vatican Press, where the *Acta Apostolicae Sedis* are printed, is extra-territorial and the Italian government is supposed to respect the Law of Guarantees.

Execution means carrying into effect, and must be more particulary referred to the *Acta* of the Apostolic See. Here the "*placet*" might enter; for it means inspection and approval of a papal document by the civil government before it may be published and carried into effect. It is called "*exequatur*" if it concerns appointments. Of course, where both *placet* and *exequatur* are ratified by concordats, the penalty is not incurred.[8]

3. Those who, on account of papal letters or documents, *injure or intimidate persons concerned in these documents, or other persons*, are called *laedentes*. The

[8] D'Annibale, l. c., n. 73.

injury must be real, not merely verbal, and the insults serious, *e. g.*, beating.

The *perterrefacientes* are those who grievously and seriously scare the interested persons into disobedience. The fear must be such as would influence a man of strong character.[9] The *persons concerned* are those for whom the documents are intended,— bishops, clerics, laymen, as well as others who are concerned with the publication and execution of the same.[10]

4. The *penalty* provided for such offenders against papal, *i. e.*, sovereign authority, is *excommunication reserved speciali modo to the Apostolic See and incurred ipso facto*. The question is: *When is the fact verified so that excommunication is incurred?*

As to the *recurrentes*, D'Annibale[11] says, the excommunication is not incurred by them unless the lay or civil power has published a bill impeding the publication or execution of papal documents, because a recourse is an attempt and must be judged as such. This is according to our Code, can. 2212-2213.

As to the *prohibentes*, the same author says that the controversy among canonists exempts them from incurring the penalty, in case of a doubt of law or fact, because the benefit of doubt is always favorable to the defendant or guilty.[12]

As to *laedentes* and *perterrefacientes*, their guilt depends on the fact; if the injury is done or the fear ex-

---

9 *Ibid.;* thus threats of damage or defamation may scare a normally firm person.

10 *Ibid.*

11 *L. c.*, p. 50, n. 74.

12 The *prohibentes*, therefore, would not incur the censure if the effect did not follow (*effectu non secuto*). Lehmkuhl, on the other hand, says: " *Recursus sufficit, etsi recurrens passus sit repulsam* " (II, 933). Hollweck (*l. c.*, p. 198) distinguishes: If the recourse was rejected *a limine*, the penalty is not incurred; but if the motion is made and seconded, though it does not carry, the effect is verified and therefore the penalty is incurred.

ercised, with the intent mentioned, *viz.*: to forbid the promulgation or execution of papal documents, this suffices to incur the penalty, no matter whether the effect intended did or did not follow. Neither is there any contradiction involved here, for the three classes are quite distinct from one another.

VIOLATION OF THE LIBERTY AND RIGHTS OF THE CHURCH

Can. 2334

Excommunicatione latae sententiae speciali modo Sedi Apostolicae reservata plectuntur:

1°. Qui leges, mandata, vel decreta contra libertatem aut iura Ecclesiae edunt;

2°. Qui impediunt directe vel indirecte exercitium iurisdictionis ecclesiasticae sive interni sive externi fori, ad hoc recurrentes ad quamlibet laicalem potestatem.

This canon comprises two rather inadequately distinguished violations of ecclesiastical liberty and rights. The one is a positive violation of any kind of rights, comprising the whole range of ecclesiastical liberty explained below. The other is a specific kind of violation, *viz.*: of jurisdiction *(appellatio ab abusu)*. [1]

---

[1] The *appel comme d'abus* cannot be clearly traced historically; but the fact is that, after the Pragmatic Sanction of 1438, it became a juridical institute of the French Parliament and appeared in the Gallican Articles (1682) as well as in the Organic Articles of Napoleon (1802); see Friedberg, *l. c.*, p. 486 ff. *England*, too, had its *Praemunire*, the statutes of which were framed by Edward I (1272-1307) and sharpened by Richard II (1377-1399); see Blackstone-Cooley, *Comm.*, IV, 103 ff. On the *Writs of Prohibition*, which are similar to the *appellatio ab abusu*, see Blackstone, III, 113; Friedberg, *l. c.*, 738 ff.

1. *Those who issue laws, ordinances or decrees against the liberty and rights of the Church incur excommunication latae sententiae reserved speciali modo to the Apostolic See.*

a) *Edere* means to pass a law; in this country any bill that passes both houses of Congress and is not vetoed by the President, is a law. An ordinance *(mandatum)* is an order issued by a particular court or magistrate, especially for the arrest or capture of a criminal; also a summons, warning, or injunction. A *decree* may be taken as a decision issued by a court, for instance, a supreme or district court, also a municipal ordinance either commanding or forbidding something. However, these decrees and ordinances must have a general character, and not refer merely to a particular case,[2] unless this should form a precedent.

All those, then, who coöperate in issuing or effectively enacting laws and decrees detrimental to the Church, must be considered guilty of the crime here denounced. But, in parliamentary language, several acts are required to make a law: the bringing in of a bill, seconding the motion, voting on it, passing it through the house or houses and, finally, signing or vetoing it. Are all these equally guilty? The answer is that, if the bill becomes a law, all are guilty who have in any effective way contributed to this end.[3]

Concerning decrees and ordinances, all those are guilty who shape and issue them, but not minor officials who

2 D'Annibale, *l. c.*, p. 46, n. 68. Read, for instance, St. 16, Ric. 2, c. 5: "If any one shall purchase or pursue in the court of Rome or elsewhere, any translations of prelates, processes, sentences of excommunication, bulls, instruments, or any other things whatsoever against the King, his crown, his dignity, or his realm . . . he shall be put out of the King's protection and his lands and goods forfeited to the King," etc.

3 Hollweck, *l. c.*, p. 206; D'Annibale, *l. c.*, p. 46, n. 68.

merely write or typewrite, print or publish the text, or sheriff or marshals who serve it.

b) The *liberty and rights of the Church* must be curtailed or set at naught in these laws, ordinances or decrees. The *Church* here is the *universal Church*, as such, although, as one distinguished commentator truly says,[4] it may happen that the whole Church is affected if a particular church is injured, for instance, by forbidding certain religious to exist in a certain province or diocese, or prohibiting processions and missions in a country. The *liberty* of the Church means her right to exist and to spread according to her nature and constitution (can. 100). Violations of this liberty are enumerated in can. 2333, 2334, 2336. Of course, there can hardly be serious talk about liberty where the *native and independent rights* of the Church are either entirely taken away or curtailed. Native rights are the right to preach the Gospel, can., 1322; to educate and train the clergy, can. 1352; to found and maintain her own schools, can. 1375; to possess her own cemeteries and property, can. 1206 and can. 1495; to enjoy the judiciary and coercive power, canons 1553 and 2214. These are essential rights. Acquired rights, if not directly connected with these native rights, are necessary only *ad melius esse*.

2. Those *who, in order to impede the exercise of ecclesiastical jurisdiction in the internal as well as external forum, either directly or indirectly have recourse to any secular* (lay) *power, incur excommunication latae sententiae reserved modo speciali to the Apostolic See.*

As is evident from the text, there is but one leading thought in it; or, in other words, one compound sentence,

4 Hollweck, *l. c.,* p. 206, § 137,   5 Hollweck, *l. c.,* p. 207.
note 1.

not two, as in the "*Apostolicae Sedis.*" [6] Dissecting this one statement the following salient points may be distinguished.

a) The leading subject is "*recourse to any lay power.*" What *recourse* means has been explained above: it is to seek help, or redress, or protection against real or imaginary wrongs. However, the recourse must produce an effect, *viz.*, the act of impeding. If, therefore, the secular power refuses to entertain the recourse, the penalty is not incurred. But if the lay power would issue an injunction, even though it remained without effect, the penalty would follow.[7]

The term *quaelibet laicalis potestas* is wider here than in can. 2333, and may signify not only public, but also private power,[8] in as far as this really has power in the juridical sense, be it legislative, judiciary, executive or administrative. Whether this includes the domestic power, such as a father has over his children, a husband over his wife, seems doubtful; all the more so since the *appellatio ab abusu*, which is here intended, was addressed to the magistrates. Yet even private power may really impede the exercise of ecclesiastical jurisdiction, especially in the internal forum, and whenever it does so, it is undoubtedly included.

b) The subject or aim of such recourse must be *to impede the exercise of ecclesiastical jurisdiction.* The power of *jurisdiction* extends over all acts that emanate from, or presuppose, this government, as far as

---

6 § I. " 6. *Impedientes directe vel indirecte exercitium iurisdictionis ecclesiasticae sive interni, sive externi fori, et ad hoc recurrentes ad forum saeculare eiusque mandata procurantes, edentes, aut auxilium, consilium vel favorem praestantes.*"

7 Hollweck, *l. c.,* p. 200, note 10.
8 See c. 4, 6°, III, 27; however, what we state in the text may be doubtful, although D'Annibale (*l. c.,* p. 42, n. 60) sets it forth as *sententia communior.*

they are distinguished from the power of order. All
acts of order, strictly speaking, are therefore to be
eliminated from this text, such as the celebration of
Mass, the holding of religious services, saying public
prayers; in fact, we believe, all acts of divine office.
Our canon refers only to acts of jurisdiction, though
these may, of course, presuppose the power of order.
It does not matter whether the jurisdiction is *ordinary*
or *delegated*, of the internal or the external forum,
sacramental or non-sacramental, exercised criminally or
civilly, or by way of administration, such as appointment
to, or removal from, offices or benefices.

To *impede* means to cause one to quit working
against his will. An obstacle may be put in the way in
the very beginning, or when the sentence is to be executed. Take, for instance, the case of the removal of
a pastor under can. 2156. If the investigation is prevented *in limine* by lay interference, the procedure is
nipped in the bud; whereas, if the sentence of removal
has been given, and the pastor does not move nor leave
his residence, the execution only is stopped.

An impediment may be placed in the way of a process
either directly or indirectly. *Direct* interference is that
used against one who is entitled to exercise jurisdiction,
by either resisting or nullifying his acts. *Indirect*
intervention is that used against the Ordinary or others
who exercise jurisdiction by threatening or molesting
their relatives, friends, dependents, agents, servants, in
order to intimidate, prevent or stop the giving or carrying out of a sentence.[9]

c) The *penalty* for such interference is *excommunication* for laymen as well as clerics of every degree and
rank, with the exception of cardinals (can. 2227, §2).

9 D'Annibale, *I. c.*, p. 41 f.; n. 60.

Clerics and religious who transgress the penal laws of can. 2334 and 2335 are, besides, subject to the following penalties.

Can. 2336

§ 1. Clerici qui delictum commiserunt de quo in can. 2334, 2335, praeter poenas citatis canonibus statutas, poena suspensionis vel privationis ipsius beneficii, officii, dignitatis, pensionis aut muneris, si qua forte in Ecclesia habeant; religiosi autem privatione officii et vocis activae ac passivae aliisque poenis ad normam constitutionum plectantur.

§ 2, see *infra*, p. 346.

This penalty is *ferendae sententiae,* but does not supersede or supplant the excommunication stated in can. 2334. Those who inflict it, are obliged to do so according to can. 2223, and there is no choice except between general suspension and privation of benefice, office, dignity, pension, or any position the culprits may hold in the Church. *Religious* must be deprived of their office and of the active and passive vote; they should also be punished according to the penal rules of their own constitutions.

FREEMASONRY

Can. 2335

Nomen dantes sectae massonicae aliisve eiusdem generis associationibus quae contra Ecclesiam vel legitimas civiles potestates machinantur, contrahunt ipso facto excommunicationem Sedi Apostolicae simpliciter reservatam.

Those who enlist in Masonic sects or other associations of the same kind, which plot against the Church or against lawful civil authority, ipso facto incur the excommunication simply reserved to the Apostolic See.

The text distinguishes two kinds of pernicious societies, although both have the same purpose, and the purpose alone is sufficient to merit the penalties decreed in the text.

1. *Freemasons* are here understood as a sect with compact organization and set rules or constitutions. Their origin, to judge from their own writings, seems to be rather obscure, but is generally assigned to the year 1717. England is the birthplace of Freemasonry.[1] There is no doubt that secrecy is the essence of this institution, that symbols and allegories which are traced to the beginning of religion are conspicuous in the genuine sect of Freemasons. It is also admitted that their outspoken advocacy of a sort of freedom which brooks no law except the ego has prompted civil governments to forbid them long [2] before Clement XII issued his Constitution " *In eminenti,*" April 28, 1738, which Benedict XIV ratified and renewed in " *Providas,*" March 18, 1751, and other papal constitutions and decrees repeated or modified, as will be seen in the course of these comments.

By *Masonic sects* were understood societies whose members were bound by an oath to keep everything secret, and who had their own ritual as well as organization. Their aim was clearly characterized by their underground activities. However, though the first papal constitutions, up to the time of Pius IX, stress secrecy,

---

[1] A. Preuss, *A Study in American Freemasonry,* 1908, pp. 346 ff.

[2] Thus its lodges were proscribed in 1735 by an edict of the States of Holland, and Louis XIV forbade them in France, 1737; Preuss, *l. c.,* p. 372.

we find a departure from this "essential" element of Masonry in 1846. For a decree of the Holy Office, Aug. 5, 1846, reads thus: When secret societies are spoken of in the papal constitutions, all those are to be understood which pursue a special aim against the Church or government, no matter whether or not they demand an oath of secrecy.[3] Henceforth this practice was adhered to by the Roman court, as later decisions prove. Consequently, the dependent clause in our text which begins with "*quae contra Ecclesiam*—" must be referred to Masonic sects, as a distinctive note. It is implied that every Masonic sect has this aim in view. But this is a mere presumption, which can be overthrown by facts. And the facts can be ascertained only by an inspection of the resp. constitutions and by-laws; for the ritual alone would barely give a satisfactory answer. This we thought necessary to state in order to avoid confusion. It goes without saying that the "*Grand Lodges*" of America, the English Lodges of the York and Scottish Rite, as well as the Grand Orient and Supreme Council of France and Italy and elsewhere[4] belong not only to the Masonic sect, as here intended, but are condemned sects. For there can be little doubt that they aim at subverting Church and State. The nations involved in the world war need have no doubts as to this sad and well-established fact.

2. Which are the other *associations of the same kind* mentioned in our text? Note the word *association*, which is different from sect, the term employed in the "*Apostolicae Sedis.*"[5] Association admits of a wider

---

3 *Coll. P. F.*, n. 1350, note 2.
4 Preuss, *l. c.*, p. 378 ff.
5 § II. 4. "*Nomen dantes sectae Massonicae, aut Carbonariae, aut aliis eiusdem generis sectis, quae contra Ecclesiam vel legitimas potestates seu palam, seu clandestine machinantur, nec non iisdem sectis favorem qualemcumque praestantes;*

range. It does not necessarily mean a "closed" or compact society, with statutes or by-laws, but merely a union of individuals for a definite purpose. From this viewpoint *l'Internationale*, Communists, Nihilists, Bolshevists, etc., may be included in the term.

3. The aim or end of these societies must be, as the text says, "*plotting either against the Church or the legitimate civil power.*" Therefore, if by a happy inconsistency any Masonic sect would reverse this aim, it would not incur the penalty provided by this canon.

a) *Machinari* signifies to contrive, but is generally used in the bad sense of plotting or contriving with an evil design, scheming maliciously, as we say in the impediment of crime: *uno machinante*. Here it means any written, oral or actual agitation or concerted propaganda and incitement against Church or State.[6] However, it must be understood that such plotting must be the aim of the society or association as such, not merely of individual members. For no society can be held responsible for acts which single members perform as private citizens. Therefore, the constitutions or statutes or by-laws or a secret oath or simple promise must bind — not oblige, for no obligation can arise from illicit promises — the members to pursue that aim.

b) The plotting must be directed *either* against the Church *or* against the lawful civil authority,— one of them being sufficient.

The *Church* is plotted against if the whole Church, not merely particular parts of it, is attacked in her dogmas and disciplinary or administrative laws, in her hierarchy and ministers.[7] One plots against the *lawful civil power*

---

earumque occultos coryphaeos ac duces non denunciantes, donec non denunciaverint."

[6] Hollweck, *l. c.*, p. 171, note 7.
[7] Leo XII, "*Quo graviora,*" March 13, 1825. For instance, the book of

by stirring up the people and overthrowing the legitimate government, as was the case in Portugal of late. The question when a government is *lawful*, may cause some trouble to the international, national, and individual conscience. The international and national consciences — if there is such a thing — are closely interwoven.

Broadly speaking, a government must be held legitimate if it is recognized by other nations, either formally by an act of declaration, or informally by establishing or re-establishing diplomatic relations.[8] But the individual conscience cannot be settled by a " League of Nations " or by diplomatic relations or commercial treaties. Take, for instance, the case of the Portuguese or the French Royalists, or the Castilian-Catalonian pretensions, not to speak of the former Papal States.[9]

4. Which sects or associations are intended by our canon?

a) There can be no doubt that the *Masonic* lodges, as they originated in England and were transplanted to the U. S., in 1729, *i. e.,* the " Ancient and Accepted Scottish Rite " as well as the " Grand Orient of France," have all the earmarks of a sect, as here intended. And by the way it may be stated that *Orientals* also, (Ruthenians, Greeks, Armenians, Syrians, etc.), who belong to such a sect incur the censure here mentioned.[10]

b) What about the *" Independent Order of Good Templars "?* If it is true that this society is closely allied with the Freemasons, nay even presupposes Masonry of a high degree,[11] there can be no doubt that

---

J. D. Buck. *The Genius of Freemasonry,* 1907 (Preuss, *l. c.,* p. 423 ff).

[8] See Westlake, *International Law,* 1910, Part I: Peace, pp. 50 ff.

[9] In such cases the benefit of doubt should be accorded, and therefore the censure is not incurred.

[10] S. O., Aug. 6, 1885 (*Coll. P. F.,* n. 1640).

[11] See Preuss, *l. c.,* p. 421, note.

it is included in the name of Masonic sects, provided its aim is plotting against Church and State. It may be added that the Holy Office,[12] although severely forbidding them, has not declared the Good Templars liable to the excommunication pronounced in the "*Apostolicae Sedis.*"

c) The same is true with regard to the "*Odd Fellows,*" the "*Sons of Temperance*" and the "*Knights of Pythias.*"[13] But although these four lodges are not formally condemned, and therefore do not constitute "condemned sects," yet if they either secretly or openly pursue a subversive aim, as defined in our canon, they certainly incur censure.

d) To the associations with a pernicious aim of plotting must now[14] be reckoned the Nihilists, the Communists, the radical Socialists, and others of the same kind.

e) The *Fenians* of Ireland and England were especially singled out as falling under the censure.[15]

5. The last-named sect gave rise to several questions concerning *absolution*. The bishops were advised as follows:

a) They should gravely enjoin on *confessors* the duty of admonishing the penitents not to enroll in secret societies, nor to frequent the meetings of these societies, nor to favor them in any way.

b) The confessors should refuse absolution to the obstinate *(pertinacibus)*, *i. e.*, those who insist on remaining members of the secret society in question.

---

12 S. O., Aug. 9, 1893 (*Coll. P. F.*, n. 1845): "*Dilata*" but the answer never came.

13 S. O., Aug. 20, 1894 (Putzer, *Comment.*, ed. 4, p. 235).

14 D'Annibale, *l. c.*, p. 79, n. 117 excludes: Old Catholics (of course!),

Communists, Socialists, the so-called Internationale, Nihilists.

15 S. O., July 2, 1845; July 5, 1865; Jan. 12, 1870 (*Coll.*, nn. 998, 1870), also cremation societies if affiliated with Freemasons; S. O., May 19, 1886, ed. 1 (*ib.*, n. 1657).

c) Those genuinely repentant should be absolved from the excommunication incurred.[16]

There are difficulties in demanding the *eiuratio* or abjuration of secret societies, on account of the serious temporal disadvantages often involved. The Bishop of St. Hyacinth petitioned the Holy Office *in casu*,[17] and received the following answer:

Repentant members of such societies may be admitted to the Sacraments if: 1°. they really withdraw from the secret societies in question; 2°. if they promise never to take part in any secret or public act and not to pay the dues or fees; 3°. if they repair the scandal given as well as they can; 4°. if they are really disposed to withdraw their name from the roster as soon as it can be done without serious loss.

d) A later decision of the Holy Office [18] again touched the question. The *eiuratio*, it says, may be performed before the confessor, no matter whether the fact of membership be notorious or not, provided the members of forbidden societies actually withdraw from membership, forswear and reject the sect at least in presence of the confessor, and repair the scandal they have given as well as they can.

Since the censure is one *simply reserved*, Ordinaries need a general faculty to absolve from it.[19] This may be imparted to confessors. But *regulars* cannot absolve from this censure in virtue of their privileges.[20]

Concerning *occult cases*, see can. 2237, §2, which permits Ordinaries to absolve from occult cases. This

16 S. O., Aug. 1, 1858 (*Coll. P. F.*, n. 1116).

17 S. O., March 7, 1883 (*ib.*, n. 1593); the decision of Jan. 19, 1896, is not inserted in this collection, probably on account of its very particular character.

18 S. O., Aug. 3, 1898 (*Coll.*, n. 2014).

19 Can. 2253, n. 3.

20 S. Poenit., Dec. 5, 1873 (*Coll. P. F.*, n. 1409).

faculty may be communicated to others (see can. 199, §1).
A case is occult as long as the name is not published or
the membership publicly known, or known only to a
few reticent persons. But those who frequent Masonic
meetings, wear Masonic emblems, and show themselves
as adepts in Masonry,[21] cannot be called secret Masons.
Since the *very fact* that *they have enrolled in such a sect* is
sufficient for incurring the censure, it may be that one
would say: I did not know the true character of this
society. He may be looked upon as penitent and may be
really penitent. However, be it as it may in rare individual cases, such ignorance seems hardly possible after
all the papal constitutions and warnings that have been
published. On the other hand, since a general rule can
hardly be stated, the benefit of doubt may be accorded to
one who asserts that he was really ignorant and is now
penitent.[22] Hence can. 209 and can. 2247, §3 may be
applied.[23]

Can. 2336

For § 1 see *supra*, p. 339.

§ 2. Insuper clerici et religiosi nomen dantes sectae
massonicae aliisque similibus associationibus denun-
tiari debent Sacrae Congregationi S. Officii.

Clerics and religious who join (*nomen dantes*) the
Masonic sect and other similar associations must be denounced to the Holy Office. Consequently religious
superiors are not allowed to meddle in such cases, because
they concern matters of faith, according to can. 501, §2.

---

21 S. O., June 27, 1838 (*ib.*, n.
868).
22 S. O., Aug. 1, 1855 (*ib.*, n.
1116).

23 That can. 2254 may also be
applied is evident.

But they may denounce delinquents either to the local Ordinary or to the Holy Office directly, provided there is proof, not mere suspicion based on gossip. No canonical warning or judiciary hearing of witnesses is permitted.

INCITEMENT OF PRIESTS TO INSUBORDINATION

Can. 2337

§ 1. Si parochus, ad impediendum exercitium ecclesiasticae iurisdictionis, ausus fuerit turbas ciere, publicas pro se subscriptiones promovere, populum sermonibus aut scriptis excitare aliaque similia agere, pro gravitate culpae, secundum prudens Ordinarii iudicium, puniatur, non exclusa, si res ferat, suspensione.

§ 2. Eodem modo puniat Ordinarius sacerdotem qui multitudinem quoquo modo excitet ad impediendum ingressum in paroeciam sacerdotis legitime nominati in parochum aut oeconomum.

The proximate source of §1 of this canon is the decree "*Maxima cura*," of Aug. 20, 1910, which formerly regulated the administrative removal of pastors. The material source is nothing less than the documents which protested against the "appeal from abuses." There is a chapter in the Pseudo-Decretals which forbids under severe penalty the inciting of a congregation against its pastor and says the disturber should be punished like a revolutionary, *i. e.*, "expelled from the whole people.[1]" The custom of appealing to the civil court became common in France and was imitated in other countries, as

---

[1] C. 7, C. 11, q. 3 (*Capitula Martini Brag.*, Migne, 130, 584).

may be gathered from Innocent VIII's complaint.[2] The so-called Liberal clerics of the time of Pius IX followed the same tendency. It was but natural, therefore, that the "*Maxima cura,*" which facilitated the removal of pastors, should contain a penal paragraph for such as would not obey the command of removal. Hence the wording of can. 18, §1 in the "*Maxima cura*" commences with "*ad renunciationem et amotionem impediendam*" and ends with "*puniantur,*" — to which our canon adds: "*non exclusa, si res ferat, suspensione.*"

A pastor who, in order to impede the exercise of ecclesiastical jurisdiction, dares to perpetrate the following or similar acts must be punished in proportion to the gravity of his guilt by the Ordinary according to his own prudent judgment, if necessary, even with suspension. The acts thus punishable are:

    a) Exciting the people;

    b) Promoting public subscriptions for himself, or

    c) Rousing the people by sermons or writings, etc.

The *intention* must therefore be to place an *obstacle in the way of the exercise of ecclesiastical jurisdiction.* The text does not say that the exercise must be just. Of course, if jurisdiction has ceased, there can be no attack against it. Thus if a resigned or suspended[3] bishop should attempt to exercise jurisdiction, this canon would not apply. On the other hand, no matter how unjust the exercise or its motive may be, obedience is required. For to adjust matters in a revolutionary way is worse than the suffering of one innocent person. Besides, there are plenty of legal ways and means to get justice done, such as recourse, appeal, etc.

<hr />

[2] "*Officii nostri,*" Jan. 25, 1491, [3] See can. 2284: after a declaratory or condemnatory sentence.
[2] (*Bull. Luxemb.,* I, 449).

"*Ausus fuerit*" supposes full knowledge and approval, according to can. 2229, §2. Therefore, if a pastor was mentally depressed, the penalty should not be meted out. Also, if others perpetrated the forbidden acts against his will. But if the others acted thus at his instigation or with his approval, either public or secret,[4] he would be liable to punishment.

The *acts* forbidden include all kinds of demagogic demonstrations. Worst of all is *turbas ciere*, for this means to set a large and promiscuous crowd into commotion. The *penalty* for this crime is arbitrary and *ferendae sententiae*. *Suspension* both from office and benefice may be applied in more serious cases unless the Ordinary limits it to one (can. 2279).

This section of canon 2337 is strictly limited to *pastors,* and to all who go by that name, either irremovable or removable, including *quasi parochi,* etc., according to can. 451, §2. The *"Maxima cura"* (can. 30) excepted *oeconomi* and temporary vicars, but the Code undoubtedly includes *vicarii paroeciales,* provided they have full parochial powers.[5]

§ 2 of can. 2337 establishes the penalty to be meted out by the Ordinary to offending *priests.* This is a wider term, including any priest of the secular clergy as well as of religious orders. *Priests, then, who in any way stir up the populace to impede or prevent a fellow-priest who has been lawfully appointed as pastor or oeconomus from entering the parish, must be punished in like manner.* Here the incitement to insubordination is described

---

4 Innocent VIII, "*Officii nostri*," § 2; *Reg. Iuris 72 in 6°.* Collecting "affidavits," as such, in order to prove one's innocence, is not, we believe, forbidden by this law; but if the affidavits would amount to a great number and be accompanied by a protest against removal, "promoting public subscriptions" would certainly be verified.

5 This seems to follow from § 2 of our canon.

rather indefinitely *(quoquo modo)*, without reference to the effect.

Ingressus means the taking possession of an office to which one has been appointed. If accompanied by ceremonies, it is sometimes called *installation*. But the appointment must have been lawfully *(legitime)* made. The legitimacy may be affected by the person who makes the appointment. Thus an appointment made by a Vicar-General without special commission from the Ordinary would be illegitimate (can. 152). A suspended or resigned bishop could not legitimately appoint a pastor or curate. Again, validity may suffer on account of the office not being vacant by law, concerning which see canons 150, §1, 151 and 183. The lack of a written document (can. 159) does not invalidate an appointment.

The *penalty* stated is the same as in §1. Hence it is arbitrary, but obligatory, in the sense of can. 2223. Suspension, either general or special, total or partial, may be inflicted.

Religious, too, may be thus punished, provided they be pastors or priests, according to can 616, §2.

DISREGARD OF RESERVATION AND OF PENALTIES

Can. 2338

§ 1. Absolvere praesumentes sine debita facultate ab excommunicatione latae sententiae specialissimo vel speciali modo Sedi Apostolicae reservata, incurrunt ipso facto in excommunicationem Sedi Apostolicae simpliciter reservatam.

§ 2. Impendentes quodvis auxilium vel favorem excommunicato vitando in delicto propter quod excommunicatus fuit; itemque clerici scienter et sponte in divinis cum eodem communicantes et ipsum in divinis officiis recipientes, ipso facto incurrunt in excommunicationem Sedi Apostolicae simpliciter reservatam.

§ 3. Scienter celebrantes vel celebrari facientes divina in locis interdictis vel admittentes ad celebranda officia divina per censuram vetita clericos excommunicatos, interdictos, suspensos post sententiam declaratoriam vel condemnatoriam, interdictum ab ingressu ecclesiae ipso iure contrahunt, donec, arbitrio eius cuius sententiam contempserunt, congruenter satisfecerint.

§ 4. Qui causam dederunt interdicto locali aut interdicto in communitatem seu collegium, sunt ipso facto personaliter interdicti.

Three of these four sections repeat in a somewhat modified form parallel enactments of the *Apostolicae Sedis.*"[1]

1. The first section punishes with excommunication *ipso facto* and *simply reserved to the Apostolic See* all who without the necessary faculty *dare* to absolve any one from excommunication *latae sententiae,* either most especially or especially reserved to the Apostolic See.

---

[1] *Absolvere autem praesumentes sine debita facultate, etiam quovis praetextu, excommunicationis vinculo Romano Pontifici reservatae innodatos se sciant, dummodo non agatur de mortis articulo, in quo tamen firma sit quoad absolutos obligatio standi mandatis Ecclesiae, si convaluerint.*

§ *II. 16. Communicantes cum excommunicato nominatim a Papa in crimine criminoso, ei scilicet impendendo auxilium vel favorem.*

§ *II. 17. Clericos scienter et sponte communicantes in divinis cum personis a Romano Pontifice nominatim excommunicatis et ipsos in officiis recipientes.*

§ *VI. 2. Suspensionem ab Ordine suscepto ipso iure incurrunt, qui eumdem ordinem recipere praesumpserunt ab excommunicato vel interdicto nominatim denunciatis, aut ab haeretico vel schismatico notorio: eum vero, qui bona fide a quopiam eorum est ordinatus, exercitium non habere ordinis sic suscepti, donec dispensetur, declaramus.*

Here the phrase "*quovis praetextu*" is omitted, and instead of it there is inserted "*sine debita facultate.*" This involves contempt or disregard of the *papal authority*,[2] which is entitled to limit the power of inferior prelates. Notice the word *praesumentes* and compare can. 2229, §2, also can. 2247, §3, concerning ignorance of reservation, except of censures *specialissimo modo* reserved to the Apostolic See. Of course the cases of necessity and death, mentioned in canons 2252 and 2254, are excepted from the penalty here stated.

2. The second section regards the *communicatio cum vitandis* and implies disregard for the coercive power, contempt of the common penal law, and coöperation in crime. The first clause of the paragraph concerns all, laymen as well as clerics, whilst the second is directed to clerics only.

a) Those *who offer any aid to or favor an excommunicatus vitandus in the crime for which he was excommunicated, ipso facto incur the excommunication simply reserved to the Apostolic See.* To lend a helping hand *(auxilium impendere)* properly means to assist in committing a crime,[3] but this cannot be the meaning here, as the crime is supposed to have been already committed. What is meant, therefore, is participation in a crime for which one was excommunicated, or, as it used to be called, *in crimine criminoso.* Furthermore, the help must be given to one who was nominally declared *vitandus* by the Apostolic See. Hence we are dealing with a clearly determined case,[4] and consequently, the aid here intended is confirmation in evil, assisting in publishing a defence of the crime denounced, or material

2 See c. 1, Clem. V, 7.

3 Cfr. cc. 3, 6, 17, C. 11, q. 3; c. 29, X, V, 39.

4 Such were the cases of Hubert Reinkens (1873) and Romolo Murri.

support in order to enable the culprit to escape from the ecclesiastical court.

Favor is a somewhat wider term and includes any favor, either spiritual or temporal, by vote, recommendation, presence, also negatively, *e. g.,* the omission of a denunciation to which one is in duty bound. In this sense also counsel or advice is included.[5] But all that is, as we said, strictly to be referred to the reason for which one was nominally declared *vitandus.* Hence mere social intercourse, as described in can. 2267, is not forbidden; nor would those otherwise not allowed to have intercourse with a *vitandus* incur the penalty here stated for this act, even though it were forbidden. Hence the *excommunicatio minor* is entirely obsolete.

b) The second clause of §2, can. 2338, punishes with the same excommunication incurred *ipso facto* and *simpliciter* reserved to the Apostolic See all *clerics who knowingly and of their own accord communicate with a vitandus in divinis and receive him in divinis officiis.*

This text is a modified reproduction of older sources.[6]

1°. By *clerici* are understood all clerics,[7] religious as well as secular, of every rank and dignity. There is no reason [8] whatever why prelates inferior to the Pope should not be included, except cardinals.

2°. The *vitandus* here mentioned must be a *cleric,* for mere participation *in divinis* is not sufficient to incur the penalty, but *admission* to the performance of divine office is required. Therefore, if the rector of a church

---

5 D'Annibale (*l. c.,* n. 152) and Pennacchi (I, 1045, ff.) hold otherwise; yet D'Annibale (*l. c.*) says: "*Excommunicato propter furtum persuadeat* [*sic!*] *ne restituat.*" This is called in Italian *battibecchio* — a hair-splitting, unfounded altercation about a word or phrase.

6 See c. 18, X, V, 39; "*Apostolicae sedis*" (quoted above).

7 Can. 2227, § 2.

8 Weak is the reasoning of Pennacchi I, 1053. What we say is upheld also by D'Annibale, p. 99, n. 152; Hollweck, *l. c.,* p. 337 note 2.

would administer holy communion to a *clericus vitandus*,
or would bury him, or admit him to hear Mass, the
penalty would not be incurred. But if he would admit
him to say Mass, or to administer the Sacraments, he
would be amenable.[9]

3°. The text clearly states admission to, and participation in, *divinis officiis*. This removes all doubt[10]
as to the nature of the offices intended. They are the
divine offices mentioned in can. 2256, n. 1. Consequently
mere official acts, such as administrative or judiciary
functions, are not included. Preaching, though an act
emanating primarily from jurisdiction, presupposes the
clerical character, and is therefore, at least indirectly,
enumerated among the divine offices.[11] It follows that
clerici vitandi should not be allowed to preach.

4°. The participation and admission here forbidden
must be rendered knowingly and spontaneously (*scienter
et sponte*). Therefore can. 2229, §2 must be consulted.

§ *3 of can. 2338* punishes disregard of the local interdict
and of the ecclesiastical censures incurred by clerics.
The wording of our text, which is based on ancient
sources[12] and on the "*Apostolicae Sedis*," is less liable
to misinterpretation than the older laws on the subject.

1. The *local interdict* (can. 2268 ff.) is first safeguarded. Those *who knowingly celebrate or have others
celebrate divine offices in interdicted places, ipso iure
incur the interdict prohibiting them from entering any
church until they have given due satisfaction to him
whose sentence they have disregarded.*

a) The *persons* to be understood here are *clerics* only,
as all commentators maintain, because clerics alone are

9 D'Annibale, *l. c.*

10 *Ib.*, note 8; Hollweck, *l. c.*, p.
337, note 7.

11 Can. 2259, § 1.

12 See c. 7, C. 11, q. 3; c. 18,
X, V, 39; c. 18, 6°, V, 11.

supposed to be celebrants.[13] *All* clerics are included, also exempt religious.[14] Exception, of course, must be made in favor of *bishops,* but not of Ordinaries as such, in virtue of can. 2227, §2. Bishops therefore do not incur this penalty.

b) By *officia divina* are understood the offices named in can. 2256, n. 1.

c) The *penalty* is not incurred if *ignorance* can be pleaded, *i. e.,* any kind of ignorance except affected.[15] Nor is the penalty incurred when the celebration and permission of the celebration occur in places, though interdicted, where celebration is allowed according to common law, as stated in can. 2270 f. On the other hand, it does not matter whether the local interdict was imposed by law, by the Apostolic See, or by the bishop.

d) Consequently, the judge as to whether *the satisfaction is sufficient or not,* is the authority who has pronounced the interdict; he may also *absolve* from this penalty.

2. *Those who admit to the celebration of divine offices forbidden under censure such clerics as have sustained a declaratory or condemnatory sentence of excommunication, interdict or suspension,* incur the same interdict from entry into the church, under the same condition of sufficient satisfaction.

a) The term *admittentes* includes all clerics, higher or lower, with the exception of bishops (can. 2227, §2). Prelates regular or their subjects, also chaplains, and custodians of clerical rank, are also included.[16]

b) Those *admitted* are clerics under *censure.* Hence

---

13 D'Annibale, *l. c.,* p. 135, n. 218; see can. 1260.

14 C. 8, 6°, V, 7. Regulars caused trouble in regard to maintaining the interdict.

15 Can. 2229, § 2; but *sponte* must not be read into the text except as far as the canon quoted allows.

16 D'Annibale, *l. c.,* p. 136, n. 220; Hollweck, *l. c.,* p. 338, note 2.

a vindictive penalty is excluded. Besides, the censure of either excommunication or (personal) interdict or suspension must have been either *declared* or incurred by a *condemnatory sentence*. On the other hand, it matters nothing whether this sentence was declared or issued in a condemnatory way by the Pope, or by the bishop, or by a religious superior.

c) *Scienter* must be connected with *admittentes*, and therefore can. 2229, §2 is applicable. But light fear or compulsion would not be sufficient to escape the penalty.[17]

b) The *penalty* for both transgressions enumerated in §3 of our canon is the interdict *ab ingressu ecclesiae*, as defined in can. 2277.

If the cases mentioned in can. 2261, §2 and §3, or in can. 2270, are verified, a cleric may be admitted to the administration of the sacraments without incurring a penalty.

§4 of can. 2338 states that those *who were the cause of a local interdict, or of an interdict laid upon a community or corporation, are ipso facto personally interdicted*. The cause or reason is described in a Decretal of Boniface VIII as identical with, or at least correlated to, guilt, malice, or fraud.[18] Hence the persons affected are the principals in a crime, or the instigators or ringleaders, for instance, in a parish disturbance interdicted by the bishop. The consequence, of course, is that the privation attached to the personal interdict, as stated in can. 2275, takes effect. This is so true that, even if a privilege had been granted of not observing the interdict, it would not avail the person privileged if he were the cause of the interdict.[19]

17 C. in 6°, V, 7.
18 C. in 6°, V, 7: c. 24 *Alma*, 6°, V, 11.
19 What "*causam dare*" implies, see above page 214; it undoubtedly refers to the author or originator or ringleader of procedure forbidden by the Church under penalty of interdict.

EXTORTION OF CHRISTIAN BURIAL

Can. 2339

Qui ausi fuerint mandare seu cogere tradi ecclesiasticae sepulturae infideles, apostatas a fide, vel haereticos, schismaticos, aliosve sive excommunicatos sive interdictos contra praescriptum can. 1240, § 1, contrahunt excommunicationem latae sententiae nemini reservatam; sponte vero sepulturam eisdem donantes, interdictum ab ingressu ecclesiae Ordinario reservatum.

What a Christian burial consists in is explained in can. 1204. It comprises the transfer of the corpse to the church, the exequies held in church, and burial in the graveyard. The principle that governs Christian burial is this: With those with whom we have had no communication in life, we should not communicate in death.[1] Since the Church honors those who died in her communion, and punishes those who despised her in life, it is an attempt against her authority to extort a favor which she refuses. A ceremonious or at least decent burial has ever been coveted by all whose sense of honesty and decency has not been entirely stifled. Therefore, societies, confraternities, and guilds surround the burial rite with much splendor. The Church is plainly entitled to show her respect for her faithful members and to refuse the honors of a Christian burial to those who disobeyed her. The privation of Christian burial is a penalty. Our canon says:

Those who dare to command or to compel (the Church authorities) *to give a Christian burial to infidels,*

---

1 C. 2, X, III, 28.

*apostates from the faith, heretics, schismatics, or other ex-
communicated or interdicted persons, contrary to the
rule laid down in can. 1240, §1, incur the excommunication latae sententiae reserved to no one in particular.*

1. The terms "*mandantes*" and "*cogentes*" are taken
from the "*Apostolicae Sedis,*" where, however, the phrase
ausi fuerint is omitted. Commentators on the aforesaid
Constitution are divided as to the intent of this command
— whether it exclusively affects persons in authority,
more particularly the public power, or private persons
also.[2] A *mandans*, broadly speaking, is one who begs
or orders some one else to do something in his name.[3]
This, however, does not necessarily suppose public authority; any one may be a *mandans*, as any one may be a
mandatarius, unless forbidden by law. Besides, there is
no question here of protecting or defending a right,
which was forfeited *a priori*. Therefore no appeal or
recourse, as in can. 2333, is required or supposed, as if
a violation of one's right had taken place.

Note that the text is not disjunctive, *i. e.*, either — or.
The word *seu* may just as well be taken in the sense of
juxtaposition or opposition.[4] Therefore, the *cogentes*
are closely related to the *mandantes* and may even be
taken as differing from them merely by the means they
employ. For whilst *mandare* means begging or commanding one to do something in another's name, *cogere*

---

[2] § *IV. I. Mandantes seu cogentes
tradi ecclesiasticae sepulturae haereticos notorios aut nominatim excommunicatos vel interdictos. ..*

§ *VI. 2. Scienter celebrantes vel
celebrari facientes divina in locis
ab Ordinario, vel delegato iudice,
vel a iure interdictis, aut nominatim
excommunicatos ad divina officia,
seu ecclesiastica sacramenta, vel
ecclesiasticam sepulturam admittentes, interdictum ab ingressu Ec-*
*clesiae ipso iure incurrunt, donec
ad arbitrium eius, cuius sententiam
contempserunt, competenter satisfecerint. (Apost. Sedis).*

[3] Pennacchi, *l. c.*, II, 65 f.;
Hollweck, *l. c.*, p. 214, note 31;
D'Annibale, *l. c.*, p. 12, n. 12.

[4] Disjunctive are *vel—vel; aut—
aut; seu* or *sive*, in classical language, denotes *and if, or if, even
if, although.*

signifies to induce or impel one to do something by compulsion, grave fear, or serious threats.[5] Therefore, the
mandantes or cogentes may be public or private persons,
for instance, an assistant commanded or compelled by
the pastor, dean, vicar-general, or bishop, or a mayor or
governor, or a patron or private citizen, especially of the
influential kind.[6] The term *ausi fuerint* presupposes
knowledge and free will.[7]

2. The *object* of this command or compulsion must be
ecclesiastical burial, which, as stated above, comprises
three acts.

The question arises: Are all three acts equally
essential to the burial service, so that if one of them
were omitted, the penalty would not be incurred? It
is an ancient controversy, which act precisely was forbidden or intended by the penal law. The more common opinion accepted the burial place as intended by the
legislator, not the liturgical ceremonies and prayers.
However, notwithstanding this being the common
opinion before the promulgation of the Code, it must now,
we think, be abandoned. For can. 1204 is decidedly
against such an interpretation, and we cannot depart
from the significance of a term so clearly defined by the
legislator himself and then used without any further explanation. Therefore, we take Christian burial as defined in can. 1204, but will add an explanation. In our
country the transfer of the body under liturgical prayer
is not in vogue. Besides, it not infrequently happens
that the body is not buried from the church. It may
even be that it is buried in a non-Catholic cemetery, and

---

5 Pennacchi, *l. c.,* II, p. 68. Thus
also Eichmann, *l. c.,* p. 159; what
Cappello, *l. c.,* p. 137, says, is mean-
ingless.

6 Gravediggers, pallbearers, and
other participants are not included.

7 Pennacchi, *l. c.,* II, p. 68 ff.;
Hollweck, *l. c.,* p. 214, note 5.

though this is contrary to the will of the Church (can. 1205, §1), no penalty is imposed. Consequently nothing remains of ecclesiastical burial but the exequies, or funeral services strictly so-called, *i. e.,* the blessing before Mass, the Mass, and the *absolutio.* This no doubt constitutes the essence of Christian burial.[8] If only the grave can be blessed, as is the case where all are buried in a common graveyard, the *locus sepulturae* cannot be understood in our text. Times are different now, and unless we wish to maintain that this canon applies only to Catholic countries under normal conditions, we must admit that Christian burial here signifies merely the exequies, *i. e.,* the blessing of the corpse before and after Mass, and the exequial Mass itself.

3. The persons *whose bodies are not allowed to be given Christian burial,* are:

a) *Unbaptized persons* or infidels. Concerning babies to be buried with their mother, we believe that the benign interpretation can safely be held, without incurring the penalty. The phrase *ausi fuerint* at least permits such an assumption.

b) *Apostates from the faith,* provided their apostasy was notorious;

c) *Heretics and schismatics,* provided they notoriously belonged to a non-Catholic sect or schismatic body;

d) Other *excommunicated* or *interdicted persons,* after a condemnatory or declaratory sentence.

According to canons 19 and 2219, § 1, the interpretation of such laws as this is both strict and benign. Therefore the burial of the other persons named in can. 1240, §1, n. 3-6 would not fall under the penal sanction of can. 2339. However, if, *e. g.,* a Freemason had pro-

8 Thus also Eichmann, *l. c.,* p. 159. Note should be taken of can. 1212 and 1241.

voked a declaratory sentence, according to can. 2335, not only the prohibition, but the penalty also would take effect. Otherwise it is a mere prohibition.

4. Whilst so far only the *mandantes seu cogentes* were considered in connection with Christian burial, the second clause of can. 2339 *punishes also those who, of their own accord, give a Christian burial to the persons enumerated above.* These, being *clerics,* incur the *interdict which prohibits them from entering any church,* and it is *reserved to the Ordinary.*

The Ordinary of exempt clerical religious may here be understood to be their superior or the local Ordinary, inasmuch as burial concerns divine worship. Hence can. 616, § 2, is applicable here, but the penalty is incurred only if the ecclesiastical authority has granted ecclesiastical burial (*i. e.,* funeral rites, as stated above, not merely interment) *sponte, i. e.,* with full knowledge and freely, without being compelled by any one; therefore, even light fear would excuse him from the penalty.

PERSEVERANCE IN CENSURE

Can. 2340

§ 1. Si quis, obdurato animo, per annum insorduerit in censura excommunicationis, est de haeresi suspectus.

§ 2. Si clericus in censura suspensionis per semestre perseveraverit, graviter moneatur; et si, exacto a monitione mense, a contumacia non recesserit, privetur beneficiis aut officiis, si qua in Ecclesia forte habeat.

This canon contains two sections, one of which concerns excommunication, the other suspension.

1. *Whoever stubbornly remains under a sentence of excommunication for one year, is suspected of heresy,*[1] because it may be presumed that he spurns the Church, more especially the power of the keys, and therefore doubts an article of faith.[2] However, it is a simple presumption, not one *iuris et de iure,* and therefore any plausible reason, or an offer to prove that he was prevented from asking for absolution, would suffice to purge the culprit from the suspicion of obstinacy.

Obduracy also supposes a warning, which must take the form of a canonical admonition.[3] The law does not distinguish between an excommunication *a iure* and one *ab homine,* much less between a *vitandus* and a *toleratus.* Can. 2385 provides that an apostate from a religious organization, after a year or 13 months,[4] becomes suspect of heresy, if he does not return or take steps to be dispensed from his vows, or have himself secularized.

2. *A cleric who remains for six months under the censure* (not vindictive penalty) *of suspension, must be seriously admonished; if he does not give up his contumacy within a month from the date of the warning, he is to be deprived of his benefice or the offices he may hold in the Church.*

Although this text mentions only suspension, and, therefore, concerns only clerics, yet the penalty stated in §1 is not thereby quashed. Consequently, if a cleric should have contracted excommunication besides suspension, he would also incur the suspicion of heresy. The text requires a canonical warning, to be given according to can. 2309; otherwise contumacy cannot be presumed.

---

1 See *Trid.,* Sess. 25, c. 3, *de ref.;* C. 7, 6°, V, 2.
2 Reiffenstuel, V, 39, n. 7.
3 Schmalzgrueber, V, 39, n. 195; see can. 2309.
4 See can. 642, § 1, 2.

A doubt may arise as to what kind of suspension is here intended, general or special. Can. 2278, § 2 seems to point to a general suspension, and therefore, a special suspension from either office or benefice, or a partial one, would not seem to fall under this canon.[5]

VIOLATION OF THE PRIVILEGIUM FORI

Can. 2341

Si quis contra praescriptum can. 120 ausus fuerit ad iudicem laicum trahere aliquem ex S. R. E. Cardinalibus vel Legatis Sedis Apostolicae, vel Officialibus maioribus Romanae Curiae ob negotia ad eorum munus pertinentia, vel Ordinarium proprium, contrahit ipso facto excommunicationem Sedi Apostolicae speciali modo reservatam; si alium Episcopum etiam mere titularem, aut Abbatem vel Praelatum *nullius*, vel aliquem ex supremis religionum iuris pontificii Superioribus, excommunicationem latae sententiae Sedi Apostolicae simpliciter reservatam; demum si, non obtenta ab Ordinario loci licentia, aliam personam privilegio fori fruentem, clericus quidem incurrit ipso facto in suspensionem ab officio reservatam Ordinario, laicus autem congruis poenis pro gravitate culpae a proprio Ordinario puniatur.

The *privilegium fori* has been explained under can. 120. Here the penal sanction is stated, which concerns only the actual violators, not the framers or makers of laws contrary to the personal immunity of the clergy.[1] The latter are comprised by can. 2334, n. 1.

---

[5] Thus Eichmann, *l. c.*, p. 160; c. 8, X, I, 14 as well as other commentators; Schmalzgrueber (V, 39, n. 197) simply says suspension, without further determination.

[1] The *"Apostolicae Sedis,"* I, 7.

The present canon distributes the clergy into three classes, with a special penalty for the aggressors of each.

I. *Excommunication reserved modo speciali to the Holy See is incurred ipso facto by those who dare to drag before a lay judge (civil court) cardinals, legates of the Apostolic See or higher officials of the Roman Court concerning affairs which belong to their office, or their own Ordinary.*

1. "*Trahere ad iudicem laicum*" means to compel one to appear before a lay judge, who has no jurisdiction over clerics, who have a judge of their own. But *trahere* (to drag) must not be understood literally, as if it required physical compulsion, *e. g.*, by a policeman.

The act declared punishable in this canon begins with the summons and ends with the final sentence and its execution. However, the term also has the definite meaning of an accomplished fact. Therefore, a mere judiciary summons, if unheeded or retracted, would not constitute the crime here intended. Even if a subpoena [2] should have been issued, the crime would not be established if the defendant would not appear. [3] Denouncing a clergyman to the State's attorney would not fall under this canon, though it might be classified as an inchoate crime. [4] On the other hand, the mere fact of being called and compelled to take the witness stand, is sufficient, [5] for this is a judiciary act and supposes a tribunal. Neither does it matter whether the clergy-

says: "*Cogentes sive directe, sive indirecte iudices laicos ad trahendum ad suum tribunal personas ecclesiasticas praeter canonicas dispositiones: item edentes leges vel decreta contra libertatem aut iura Ecclesiae.*"

[2] A subpoena is a judicial writ commanding a party or witness to appear in court under penalty; *Stimson's Law Dictionary, s. v.*

[3] This is evident from the "*Quantavis diligentia,*" of Pius X, Oct. 9, 1911 (*A. Ap. S.,* III, 555): "*qui ad tribunal laicorum vocent ibique adesse publice compellant.*"

[4] See can. 2212; Eichmann, *l. c.,* p. 164.

[5] See Vol. II, p. 63 f. of this Commentary.

man wins or loses the suit, or is remunerated or compensated.

The Code here again employs the words " *ausus fuerit,*" which suppose a knowledge of the unlawfulness of the act proscribed. One must know that the person thus called to court is a cleric in possession of his clerical privileges;[6] also that there is a privileged court for Catholic clergymen. If inculpable ignorance existed on this point, the plaintiff would not incur the penalty. If he knew of the *privilegium fori,* but not of the penalty here stated, his responsibility would be diminished.[7] From this it may logically be deduced that lower officials who arrest a cleric and hale him into court because the laws of the country demand it, are immune from this penalty. But private citizens, who effectively denounce, summon, subpoena or bring suit against a clergyman cannot escape the penalty, *suppositis supponendis,* as just stated. It makes no difference whether the judge before whom a cleric is haled sits in the civil or in the criminal court, for no distinction is made.

2. The *persons* who must not be brought into the civil courts are:

a) The *cardinals* of the Holy Roman Church, because they are of princely rank and constitute the immediate senate of the Pope;

b) The *legates of the Apostolic See,* whether nuncios, internuncios, or Apostolic delegates; for can. 265 appears to include this threefold class as representatives of the Pope;

c) The *higher officials of the Roman Court.* These are not specifically determined, but may be described as follows:

6 See can. 123, 2304, 2305.   7 See can. 2202.

For the Holy Office, the *assessor* and the *commissarius;*

For the Congregatio Consistorialis, the *assessor* and the *substitutus;*

For the Congregatio de Sacramentis, the *praelatus a secretis* and the three *subsecretarii;*

For the Congregatio Concilii, the *praelatus a secretis* and the *subsecretarius;* and similarly for the other congregations, which are made up in the same way. If we do not mention the Cardinal Prefect, who also belongs to the higher officials, it is because cardinals are expressly exempted as such.

The *Tribunals* of the Holy See comprise:

The *Poenitentiaria,* with the cardinal Poenitentiarius, the regent, the secretary, and the substitute;

The *Signatura Apostolica* with its secretary;

The *Romana Rota* with its auditors, *promotor iustitiae,* and *defensor vinculi.*

The *Offices* comprise:

The *Cancellaria Apostolica* with its regent and substitute;

The *Dataria Apostolica* with its subdatary and prefect;

The *Camera Apostolica* with the vice-camerlengo, auditor general, and treasurer general.

None of these higher officials may be brought before a lay court *on account of affairs which pertain to their office.* This phrase does not refer to the cardinals or legates, but to the officials just named. The importance of the matter and their close relation to the Pope requires a higher sanction for their immunity.[9]

---

8 The "*Sapienti consilio*" of Pius X, June 29, 1908 refers to *administri maiores,* who are identical with the *officiales maiores (A. Ap. S., I,* 78 ff.).

9 If these higher officials were cited before a lay judge for matters of a private character, inheritance, property, affairs of relatives,

d) One's own *Ordinary* is here classed with the highest persons, and offenders against this enactment are threatened with severe penalties because the Ordinaries are immediate representatives of the Pope, upon whom their jurisdiction depends. Therefore an attack against them is a qualified offence by reason of the implied contempt of a higher authority.[10] Note that the text simply says "*Ordinary,*" *without the addition:* "*local.*" Therefore, if a religious of an exempt clerical order should dare to hale his own superior into a civil court, he would incur the penalty stated above. To bring any of these personages before a lay court requires permission from the Apostolic See.[11]

II. *Excommunication latae sententiae, simply reserved to the Apostolic See,* is incurred by those who dare to drag before a lay judge *another bishop* (*i. e.,* not their own Ordinary), or *a titular bishop, or an abbot nullius or prelate nullius, or one of the major superiors of religious of papal institutes.* Who these major superiors are, is plainly stated in can. 488, n. 8. If such persons are to be brought into court, the permission of the Apostolic See must be obtained.[12]

III. Those who dare to bring before a lay court *any other persons endowed with the clerical privilege, the privilegium fori,* are, if permission has not been obtained from the local Ordinary, to be punished as follows:

1. A *cleric* who dares to bring another cleric before the lay court *ipso facto* incurs *suspension from office reserved to the Ordinary;*

2. A *layman* must be punished by his own Ordinary according to the gravity of the guilt.

the penalty stated in the first clause would not be incurred, but one of the following (2) clauses would be applicable according to the hierarchical rank: titular bishops, clergymen, (to which latter also belong monsignori).

10 See can 2207, n. 1.
11 See can. 120, § 2.
12 *Ibid.*

The *other persons* here meant are those not specially mentioned under I and II; hence all clerics of secular rank, from vicar-general down to those who have received the first tonsure; of *religious* superiors all those who do not go by the name of higher superiors (generals, provincials and those who hold power equal to provincials), *i. e.*, all religious except those mentioned, of male as well as female organizations, and their novices.

A difficulty remains concerning *exempt clerical religious*. These must obtain permission from the *local* — not the religious — superior in order lawfully to hale either a secular or religious cleric into court. But to whom is the suspension reserved? As the text does not here repeat the "*loci*" of the first clause, it follows that the Code means their own superior, not the local Ordinary, to whom they are not subject. There is no contradiction in this. For the obtaining of permission is a matter of public discipline for the whole diocese, but a reservation that belongs to the Order is of mere ecclesiastical jurisdiction. The suspension from office is to be understood according to can. 2279, §1.

What we have said elsewhere [13] concerning concordats and custom, can safely be applied to our country.

PAPAL ENCLOSURE

Can. 2342

Plectuntur ipso facto excommunicatione Sedi Apostolicae simpliciter reservata:

1°. Clausuram monialium violantes, cuiuscunque generis aut conditionis vel sexus sint, in earum monasteria sine legitima licentia ingrediendo, pariterque

---

13 Vol. II, p. 64.

eos introducentes vel admittentes; quod si clerici sint, praeterea suspendantur per tempus pro gravitate culpae ab Ordinario definiendum;

2°. Mulieres violantes regularium virorum clausuram et Superiores aliique, quicunque ii sint, eas cuiuscunque aetatis introducentes vel admittentes; et praeterea religiosi introducentes vel admittentes priventur officio, si quod habeant, et voce activa ac passiva;

3°. Moniales e clausura illegitime exeuntes contra praescriptum can. 601.

This whole canon concerns regulars and nuns only; therefore, even exempt religious of male congregations, and all female religious with simple, even though perpetual, vows are not affected by it. The text treats first of the enclosure of nuns, then of that of regulars, and, finally, of nuns unlawfully leaving the cloister.[1]

I. Those *who, no matter of what rank or condition or sex they be, violate the enclosure of nuns by entering their monasteries without lawful permission; likewise those who introduce or admit such violators, ipso facto incur the excommunication simply reserved to the Apostolic See. If they are clerics,* they shall, besides, be *suspended* for a time to be determined by the Ordinary according to the gravity of the crime.

1. The *enclosure* is the whole space contained within the precincts of a monastery, and assigned as such.[2]

---

1 *Apostolicae Sedis*, § II, n. 6, 7: *Violantes clausuram monialium cuiuscumque generis aut conditionis, sexus vel aetatis fuerint, in earum monasteria absque legitima licentia ingrediendo; pariterque eos introducentes vel admittentes; itemque Moniales ab illa exeuntes extra casus ac formam a S. Pio V. in Constitutione "Decori" praescriptam. Mulieres violantes Regularium virorum clausuram, et Superiores aliosve eas admittentes.*

2 Gibalini, S. J., *Disquisitiones*

Note that the limits once drawn cannot be arbitrarily changed. The constant practice of the Roman Court demands that the bishop superintend the enclosure of nuns;[3] to him also must be referred any change of the limits.

2. The *violantes* are here determined, first, as *ingredientes*, which means that the law[4] of enclosure is trespassed by one entering the limits or threshold with his whole body, and without *the necessary permission*. This is given and determined by can. 600, which permits the local Ordinaries and superiors regular, the confessor or his substitute, the actual rulers and their wives and suite, and Cardinals to enter the precincts for certain reasons there stated. Besides, the superiors may also admit, if necessary and with the permission of the local Ordinary, physicians, surgeons, and workingmen. These, therefore, are permitted to enter and do not incur the penalty of this canon, provided the conditions set forth in can. 600 are verified. Where there is a case of violation of the enclosure, *neither descent* (birth), nor *social condition*, or *sex* makes any difference. But age does. For the Code does not add *aetatis* and therefore *impuberes*, according to can. 2230, do not incur the penalty here mentioned, although they, too, are forbidden to enter the enclosure.

3. *Introducentes* or *admittentes*. The former term signifies effective invitation, or leading the way by opening the gate (private entrance), provided the introducing person (one of the nuns) is on the inside and

---

Canonicae de Clausura Regulari, Lugduni 1648, p. 51; D'Annibale, *l. c.,* p. 82, n. 123.

[3] We could allege many decrees of the S. C. EE. et RR., which we have perused in Rome; but the papal constitutions suffice.

[4] Older laws; Carth. III, can. 33 etc., (Gibalini, *l. c.,* p. 5; Hollweck, *l. c.,* p. 221 f.); c. un. 6°, III, 16; *Trid.,* Sess. 25, c. 5, *de regg.*

really coöperates in the induction of a forbidden person.

To *admit* means: not to prohibit or not to close the entrance if this is necessary and can easily be done. This, some authors say, is the duty of the superioress and portress only.[5] Others extend it to all persons (nuns) who can and may easily prevent an unlawful entrance.[6] Of course, the rules of politeness, shyness, and circumstances may keep one from mentioning the law of enclosure if this has already been trespassed, and in this case certainly the censure would not be incurred.

Those who merely counsel or command the violation, for instance, an Ordinary who would unjustly order it, would not incur excommunication.[7]

II. The *enclosure of* regulars is violated by *women entering it, by superiors and others, whoever they be, who introduce or admit women of whatever age.* All these incur the *ipso facto excommunication simply reserved to the Apostolic See.* The *religious who introduce or admit women, must be deprived of the office they hold and also of the active and passive vote.*

1. What is to be understood by the name of enclosure has been stated above.[8] However, what Suarez says, seems to be very reasonable and more adapted to the real condition existing in monasteries of male religious: " What is to be understood by the name of cloister, and where it ends, must be judged from the locality, form,

---

5 Gibalini, *l. c.*, p. 165; D'Annibale, *l. c.*, p. 83, n. 123.

6 Pennacchi, *l. c.*, I, 742; Hollweck, *l. c.*, p. 225, note 12.

7 D'Annibale, *l. c.* However, this must be rightly understood; for religious superiors who would command it, would not escape the penalty; such an interpretation would render the law ridiculous and nullify its effect.

8 Ferraris, *Prompta Bibliotheca,* s. v. " *Conventus,*" art. III, n. 9 f; cemeteries, courtyard, cells, dormitories, refectory, infirmary, kitchen, also gardens if joined to the monastery, the sacristy if it has only an entrance from the enclosure, but not the choir of the church; thus also D'Annibale, p. 85, n. 127.

and custom, and especially from the *declaration of the prelate,* which must be in conformity with the respective constitutions and religious discipline."[9]   This, we say, is a very reasonable interpretation, because not all monasteries are built the same way, or surrounded by the same conditions.   But one thing is certain, *viz.:* that the prelate is not at liberty to change the limits of the enclosure arbitrarily.   They must be determined once for all and may be changed only in case of real necessity, and then permanently, not *ad hoc, i. e.,* merely to escape the law. Such a procedure would render the supreme legislator ridiculous and the object of enclosure nugatory.[10]   An enclosure for regulars, no matter how small it be, must be definitely assigned.   This is the will of the lawgiver, and it is most reasonable.

2. The violators here intended are *women,* not men. Exempted from this rule are the wives of actual rulers and their suite.   In the U. S. there are no such rulers *(qui supremum actu tenent principatum;* can. 598, §2); if any come as visitors from foreign countries, a president's or governor's wife accompanying them might be admitted.[11]

3. Here again the *introducentes* and *admittentes* are mentioned, and the term is more clearly explained. They are the *superiors and others.*   The name *superior* comprises all superiors, whether higher or lower, general, provincial or local.   The procurator and other officials go here by the name of " others. "   By *alii* were formerly understood only religious,——— clerics, lay brothers, or

<hr>

9 *De Relig.,* c. I, c. 7, n. 2 (*ed. Paris.,* 1860, Vol. XVI, 41).

10 The purpose is: *servanda castitas, scandalum praecavendum et necessarius spiritus recollectionis.*

11 Yet it would be no rigorous interpretation to say that since such rulers do not actually rule in our country, their wives may therefore be excluded.

novices, not outsiders.[12] This interpretation was justified
by the text of the "*Apostolicae Sedis.*" But as the
Code adds: "*quicunque ii sint*," we believe that a wider
interpretation is now justified, *i. e.*, any one who knowingly and freely introduces or admits women into the enclosure, whether he be a lay janitor or a hired man, or an
employee of the monastery. Those, however, who
have nothing to do with the monastery, are excluded, because they have no right either to introduce or to admit
others.

Note the phrase *cuiuscunque aetatis*, no matter of what
age these women be, old or young; also those between
twelve and seven years of age; and, we believe, also in-
fants, *viz.*, girls who have not yet reached the age of seven.
It is quite true that the commentators on the "*Apostolicae
Sedis*" exempted those not yet seven years of age, because
not capable of guilt.[13] But it should be noted that said
Constitution employs the clause " of whatever age " under
the enclosure of nuns, but omits it under the enclosure of
men. Our text on the other hand connects this clause
with the *introducentes*, and hence we maintain that it was
done purposely, so that no women or girls of whatever
age may be introduced by the religious under penalty of
excommunication. Neither does the fact that these in-
fants (*septennio minores*) are not capable of guilt affect
the merit of the question; for the guilt is referred to the
introducentes. Of course, if the *introducentes* can not distinguish a boy from a girl — which mistake is possible —
no censure is incurred.

Note that the *purpose* of entering, introducing or admitting any one to the enclosure, whether good or bad,

12 Thus D'Annibale, *l. c.*, p. 85, n.
128; Hollweck, *l. c.*, p. 229, note 5.
13 Thus, we say, by general interpretation; for the S. C. EE. et
RR. included also *pueros et puellas;*
March 16, 1593; June 10, 1650:
Regesta of the respective years, Reg.
fol. 118, fol. 260; see can. 2230.

does not change the nature of the law or quash the penalty.

The *penalty* for *religious* is privation of their offices and of the active and passive vote. This also concerns the superiors, of whatever rank, as is evident from former papal Constitutions.[14]

But since it is *ferendae sententiae*, which certainly requires a declaratory sentence, it follows that concerning exempt religious the declaration would have to be given by their respective immediate superior, otherwise by the Congregatio Religiosorum, to which such cases might be brought.

Simple religious *must* be deprived of their office and ballot by their immediate superior.

Concerning dispensation and absolution in occult cases see can. 2237, §3.

III. *Nuns with solemn vows*, who *leave the enclosure* against the law, as stated in can. 601, *ipso facto incur the excommunication simply reserved to the Apostolic See.*

To leave the enclosure means to put the whole body outside the limits assigned, no matter for how long a time or for what purpose.[15] The reasons which permit this are imminent danger of death or fear of a very serious evil. The former law mentioned as reasons: fire leprosy, and epidemics.[16] This may safely be extended to

---

14 Pius V, "*Regularium,*" Oct. 24, 1506, § 4; Gregory XIII, "*Ubi gratiae,*" June 13, 1575, § 3; Bened. XIV, "*Regularis disciplinae,*" Jan. 3, 1745, § 5.

15 We read many and curious cases of leaving brought to the S. Congregation; a nun gathering apples on a tree, a limb of which she climbed and thus happened to find herself outside the wall;— *acquiescent;* a nun climbing the house-top, which seemed more serious;— at least provisional absolution. But *unlawful* here implies acting knowingly against the law, and therefore cases like those just mentioned should not cause scruples.

16 Epidemic may be justly taken for a contagious or even infectious disease, such as consumption, even influenza; there is also the necessity of undergoing an operation.

earthquakes and sudden invasions, or serious danger to virtue.

Absolution in occult cases may be granted by the local Ordinary according to can. 2237, §2. But in public cases bishops can absolve only if they have a general faculty (can. 2253, n. 1).

VIOLATION OF THE PRIVILEGIUM CANONIS

Can. 2343

§ 1. Qui violentas manus in personam Romani Pontificis iniecerit:

1°. Excommunicationem contrahit latae sententiae Sedi Apostolicae specialissimo modo reservatam; et est ipso facto vitandus;

2°. Est ipso iure infamis;

3°. Clericus est degradandus.

§ 2. Qui in personam S. R. E. Cardinalis vel Legati Romani Pontificis:

1°. In excommunicationem incurrit latae sententiae Sedi Apostolicae speciali modo reservatam;

2°. Est ipso iure infamis;

3°. Privetur beneficiis, officiis, dignitatibus, pesionibus et quolibet munere, si quod in Ecclesia habeat.

§ 3. Qui in personam Patriarchae, Archiepiscopi, Episcopi etiam titularis tantum, incurrit in excommunicationem latae sententiae Sedi Apostolicae speciali modo reservatam.

§ 4. Qui in personam aliorum clericorum vel utriusque sexus religiosorum, subiaceat ipso facto excommunicationi Ordinario proprio reservatae, qui praeterea aliis poenis, si res ferat, pro suo prudenti arbitrio eum puniat.

This canon contains two censures which the "*Apostolicae Sedis*"[1] placed under distinct headings. Here they are combined under the one species of personal inviolability, or the so-called *privilegium canonis*, the historical basis of which has been explained elsewhere.[2]

"*Violentas manus inicere*" is a remnant of the famous old canon, "*Si quis suadente diabolo.*" Malicious intent is presumed if the action is such as to hurt and offend the person against whom it is directed.

1. *Violent* implies that the person be really injured.

a) A bodily offence is one committed against the physical nature or constitution of a man *(in corpus)*. To this class belong all acts of felonious murder, manslaughter, maiming,[3] assault, battery and wounding. Tantamount to felonious assault would be the administration of poison or other noxious things which inflict grievous bodily harm.[4] As to wounding, the skin must be broken; a mere scratch is no wound.[5]

b) Personal, physical injury may also be committed by interfering with one's liberty *(in libertatem)*. Thus capturing or imprisoning or detaining a person against his will must be styled violence. For "to deprive another person of his liberty will usually involve either

---

1 § 5. "*Omnes interficientes, mutilantes, percutientes, capientes, carcerantes, detinentes, vel hostiliter insequentes S. R. C. Cardinales, Patriarchas, Archiepiscopos, Episcopos, Sedisque Apostolicae Legatos, vel Nuncios, aut eos a suis dioecesibus, territoriis, terris seu dominiis eiicientes, necnon ea mandantes vel rata habentes seu praestantes in eis auxilium, vel favorem.*" § II, 2: "*Violentas manus, suadente diabolo, injicientes in Clericos, vel utriusque sexus Monachos, exceptis quoad reservationem casibus et personis, de quibus iure vel privilegio permittitur, ut Episcopus aut alius absolvat.*"

2 See Vol. II, p. 58 of this Commentary.

3 Maiming from mayhem; thus to cut off a finger or even to knock out a front tooth would be mayhem; Kenny-Webb, *l. c.*, p. 135.

4 *Ibid.*, p. 137; D'Annibale, *l. c.*, p. 35, n. 50.

5 Kenny-Webb, *l. c.*

touching or threatening to touch him." [6] Detention may be such as to shut one up in his room or home. [7]

c) A person may also suffer bodily harm in his *dignity*, or official condition, or social position. Thus pursuing a man, ejecting him from his own property, house or premises constitutes a physical injury, provided it is done in a hostile spirit, even though no immediate contact is involved between the assailant and the assailed. Thus merely spitting at a person, or bespattering him with mud or rotten eggs, etc., would constitute an indictable offence; also stopping a horse or automobile with hostile intent or striking the horse or shaking the vehicle so as to throw out the rider, would be considered a hostile act. [8]

2. The action must not only be violent, but also *injurious, i. e.*, affect the person contumeliously against his own will and be perpetrated with knowledge of the injury done. Consequently:

a) *Self-defence* is not injurious, for the injured must impute it to his own conduct if he is injured in the act of aggression. Hence self-defence is permitted if practiced *hic et nunc* and the amount of force used does not exceed the immediate need. This is also extended to the defence of one's wife, mother, sister, and daughter. [9]

b) *Knowledge of injury* is absent if the violence is committed against a cleric who is not known as such. Therefore, if a cleric has been reduced to the lay state, [10] the penalty would not be incurred, even though he would

6 *Ibid.*, p. 143.

7 D'Annibale, *l. c.*, p. 71, n. 109; p. 35, n. 50.

8 Kenny-Webb, *l. c.*, p. 142; D'Annibale, *l. c.*, p. 35, n. 50.

9 C. 3, X, V, 39. Defence of one's property (Kenny-Webb, *l. c.*, p. 144) is not acknowledged in Church law; Hollweck, *l. c.*, p. 219, note 3.

10 See can. 136, § 3; 141 § 2; 211, § 1, 2; 640; 2305, § 1; 2387.

wear the clerical dress with a big tonsure on his head. If one would try to strike at James, a cleric, but hit Brutus, also a cleric, he would incur the penalty, because the privilege is not individual, but attached to the clerical state.[11] But no penalty is attached to the corrective striking or beating of children, provided the chastisement is reasonable and the instrument one not likely to inflict serious bodily harm, and provided the *percussus* be not *in sacris*.[12] Some authors [13] also exempt the case of sudden anger or wrath; which may be accepted, provided can. 2206 is verified. An involuntary striking or wounding or even killing of a cleric must be judged according to can. 2203, §2, and is generally immune from penalty. Finally, it may be stated that only the actual perpetrator is punishable and instigators or counselors are not included in this penalty.

After this somewhat lengthy exposition we have but to explain the penalties, which are graded according to the dignity of the offended person, as per can. 2207, n. I.

1. Those who lay violent hands on the *person of the Roman Pontiff:*

a) incur the *excommunication latae sententiae reserved modo specialissimo to the Apostolic See* and are *ipso facto vitandi* (can. 2285);

b) they are also *infamous ipso iure* (see can. 2293, 2294, §1), but this infamy no longer [14] passes to the relatives and descendants of the offender.

c) A *cleric* guilty of this crime must be *degraded,* which is *ferendae sententiae.*

11 Thus also D'Annibale, p. 74, n. 110.

12 C. 54, X, V, 39; Kenny-Webb, p. 100.

13 S. Alphonsus, VII, 575; D'Annibale, *l. c.*

14 Formerly it did; see c. 17, C. 6, q. 1; c. 22, C. 11, q. 1; c. 5, 6°, V, 9; c. 1, Clem. V, 8, because it was treated as treason; the histories of Leo III, Gregory VII, and Boniface VIII furnish examples.

2. Those who lay violent hands on a *Cardinal or legate of the Roman Pontiff (or Apostolic delegate)*

a) incur *excommunication latae sententiae* reserved *speciali modo* to the Apostolic See;

b) are *ipso iure infamous,*

c) *must be deprived of their benefices, offices, dignities,* pensions, and every ecclesiastical charge they may hold.

3. Those who lay violent hands on a *patriarch, archbishop, bishop (diocesan or titular)* incur *excommunication latae sententiae* reserved *modo speciali* to the Apostolic See.

4 Those who lay violent hands on the person of *other clerics* or religious of either sex *ipso facto* incur the *excommunication* reserved to their *own Ordinary,* who may inflict additional penalties if in his prudent judgment he should deem it proper or if the case demands it.

This last section calls for a few remarks.

1. *Clerics* are all men dedicated to the divine mysteries by at least the first tonsure (can. 108, §1), unless, as already stated, they have been reduced to the lay state.

2. *Religious,* in the sense of the Code (can. 488, n. 7), are all those who have taken the three vows and live in an approved religious institute. The same privilege is also accorded to religious associations, according to can. 680. The novices (but not the postulants) of both kinds of organizations enjoy the same favor, but not *hermits,* who live for themselves, though with the approval of the ecclesiastical authority and wear a religious habit, nor secular tertiaries.[15]

---

15 D'Annibale, p. 73, n. 108, expresses a doubt concerning such hermits as had received the religious habit at the hands of a bishop; but these are not religious.

3. Whether the so-called *percussio* be *enormis*, or *mediocris*, or *levis*, the Ordinary may absolve from it. And the Ordinary of exempt religious is their superior major general, provincial, guardian, rector, or conventual prior, all of whom may absolve from any kind of *violatio canonis*. If the superior himself should be guilty of such an excess, he may give his confessor the faculty to absolve him. In case of non-exempt religious, the Ordinary in whose diocese the *percussor* lives as a member of a religious family, is competent to absolve him.[16]

PUBLIC VERBAL INJURIES

Can. 2344

Qui Romanum Pontificem, S. R. E. Cardinalem, Legatum Romani Pontificis, Sacras Congregationes Romanas, Tribunalia Sedis Apostolicae eorumque Officiales maiores, proprium Ordinarium publicis ephemeridibus, concionibus, libellis sive directe sive indirecte, iniuriis affecerit, aut simultates vel odia contra eorundem acta, decreta, decisiones, sententias excitaverit, ab Ordinario non solum ad instantiam partis, sed etiam ex officio adigatur, per censuras quoque, ad satisfactionem praestandam, aliisve congruis poenis vel poenitentiis, pro gravitate culpae et scandali reparatione, puniatur.

Pseudo-Isidore ascribes to Pius I a text resembling our canon.[1] This Decretal was to protect bishops against insidious attacks, contumelies, calumnies and all kinds

---

[16] If the case should be brought to a trial before the ordinary, the latter would become competent to absolve also exempt religious *ratione deliciti.*

[1] C. 18, C. 11, q. 1.

of verbal injuries. Clement III (1187-1191) complained of a cleric who deprecated the " office and benefice "(sic!) of the Roman Pontiff or the Roman Church in the presence of many.[2] No doubt this latter Decretal is the material source of our canon. But the Roman law, too, contained a title " *De Iniuriis et Famosis Libellis*," and punished especially injuries against higher personages.[3] The English law treats the *scandalum magnatum* as a heinous crime.[4] It is but natural that the Code should protect dignitaries of the Church against possible and probable attacks.

1. The *persons* here mentioned are: the Roman Pontiff, the Cardinals, the papal legates, the Roman Congregations, the Tribunals of the Roman Court and their higher officials, as explained above,[5] and one's own Ordinary; therefore also the superiors of exempt clerical institutes, provided the attack comes from one of their own members.

2. The *acts* which are declared liable to punishment are: *inuriis afficere* or *simultates aut odia excitare* against their acts (documents), decrees, decisions, sentences.

a) *The word injuries* is here to be taken strictly in the sense of verbal injuries. An injury is an act done against law or right.[6] An injury, says Labeo, may be inflicted either by deeds or words. To the latter class the Roman lawyers gave the name *convicium*, either singular or plural. The canonists speak of them under the title *De Maledictis*[7] and divide *maledictum* into detraction, calumny, and blasphemy. The last-named crime, however, does not concern the present subject,

2 C. 1, X, V, 26.
3 Dig. 47, 10.
4 Blackstone-Cooley, *l. c.*, III, 123.

5 See can. 2341.
6 L. 1, Dig. 47, 10: *iniuria es eo dicta est, quod non iure fiat.*
7 Tit. 26, lib. V.

for blasphemy is a strictly religious crime. There is a slight difference of opinion between canonists and moralists as to the definition of detraction and calumny. The commentators[8] on the above-named title define detraction as any defamation of a person in his absence, and calumny as an insult made in the face of the person. The moralists[9] define detraction in general as an unjust violation of the good name of a neighbor who is absent. Under this general notion they subsume simple detraction, which they call imputation of a real but unknown crime; calumny they call imputation of a false crime or a crime not committed by the person to whom it is attributed. In English we style all detractions slanders if spoken, and libels if written. A libel is a writing or picture which either defames an individual or injures religion, government or morals. Defamatory or private libel is a crime which not only is a tort, but is often treated as such in actual practice.[10] Since the Church has doubtless taken the body of her criminal law from the old Roman law, it is not too much to say that the civil law, as understood at present, should be consulted as to the constituent elements of slander and libel.[11] Therefore we may assume that the injuries in question should be of an actionable character, and it is the function of the judge to decide whether the deed, word or writing impugned is capable of bearing the alleged defamatory meaning.

b) *Simultates vel odia excitare* are wider terms and difficult of precise definition. The former properly means aversion, a secret grudge, or animosity. But how

---

8 See Reiffenstuel, V, 26, n. 3. Blackstone-Cooley, *l. c.*, III, 112 ff.
9 See Arregui, *l. c.*, n. 427. 11 Hollweck, *l. c.*, p. 277, note 1.
10 Kenny-Webb, *l. c.*, p. 297;

a judge can determine secret thoughts is hard to understand. *Odia* is more tangible, because it signifies the manifestations of hatred, for instance, imprecations, threats, outbursts of irreverent speech, etc. However, no objective criticism on the value and truth of these documents is here intended. Neither would ridicule or a jocose travesty constitute an offence. Notice well that animosity and hatred are connected with official documents issued by the above-named persons, while *iniuria afficere* may be referred only to distinguished persons, because dignity or official character is impaired by injuries.

3. The *means* by which slander and libel may be conveyed to others are: magazines, speeches, pamphlets, etc.

a) *Ephemerides* are periodicals published regularly, *i. e.,* at stated times, principally magazines; newspapers are not comprised in the term.

b) *Conciones* may be either lectures, or discourses, or sermons, or catechetical instructions, in which a subject is treated systematically.

c) *Libelli* are pamphlets of some size, *i. e.,* booklets, not mere leaflets.

d) All these may contain an injury, or excite animosity or hatred, either directly or indirectly. Directly if a specified person or body, for instance, a congregation, is assailed; *indirectly* if, *e. g.,* the Roman Court would be called corrupt or immoral, or if a diocese or episcopal see were insulted. Directly may also refer to a specified crime imputed, for instance, bribery; indirectly would then mean by *innuendo* a certain tendency or class of crimes.

4. The *penalty* is stated as follows: the Ordinary should not only proceed upon complaint or indictment,

but should prosecute offenders officially (criminally) by
censures if necessary. He may also inflict other suitable
penalties and penances, as the gravity of the crime and
the reparation of scandal may demand.

USURPING AND RETAINING PROPERTY AND RIGHTS
OF THE ROMAN CHURCH

Can. 2345

**Usurpantes vel detinentes per se vel per alios bona
aut iura ad Ecclesiam Romanam pertinentia, subiaceant excommunicationi latae sententiae speciali modo
Sedi Apostolicae reservatae; et si clerici fuerint,
praeterea dignitatibus, beneficiis, officiis, pensionibus
priventur atque inhabiles ad eadem declarentur.**

The Roman Church from the earliest times possessed
property, which went by the name of patrimony of St.
Peter, and was scattered over the Italian peninsula,
Sicily and Sardinia, nay even in Spain and France. In
the course of the eighth century this property received
the form of a Roman Duchy and was enriched by
Pippin's donations. Civil and political strifes of the
Roman, Tuscan, and Spoletan nobility and the interference of the Teutonic rulers in Italian and ecclesiastical affairs shaped the Duchy on the Tiber into a poli-
tico-ecclesiastical State, for which the popes, the born defenders of forsaken Rome, fought tenaciously against
foreign invaders. Thus out of the material patrimony
of St. Peter, conjointly with the civil-ecclesiastical authority of the Roman pontiffs, grew what is known as the
temporal dominion of the popes. This is the immediate
object of our canon, which is taken in a modified form

from the *"Apostolicae Sedis."*[1] A year after the promulgation of this Constitution (1870) *Italia Unita* became a *fait accompli* at the cost of the Papal States. *The Law of Guarantees* was devised to smooth the worst features of that inexcusable usurpation. Under its provisions the Pope was to continue to enjoy the Apostolic Palaces of the Vatican and the Lateran, with all the buildings, gardens, and plots connected with them, as well as the Villa of Castel Gandolfo with all its appurtenances and dependencies; also the museums, library, and artistic and archæological collections therein contained.[2] Of the *iura* or sovereign rights the law guaranteed the inviolability of the person of the Sovereign Pontiff, also his right, active and passive, of embassy with all the privileges (extraterritoriality and immunity) attached thereto; also, if he pleases, to have his own post office and telegraph service or to entrust it to the Italian government, free of charge. This is the condition of the papacy at present, at least on paper. Remonstrances, of course, were not wanting, and the present canon, although modified, is a reminder to the royal and parliamentary offenders. We shall not attempt to enter into an interpretation of this canon, as it deals with a delicate subject, which the Roman Court alone can handle adequately. Only one observation: the term *bona et iura Romanae Ecclesiae* may have a wider sense, inasmuch as all property and all rights, wherever found, may be concerned, provided they are held in the name of the Roman Church, as a legal corporation.[2]

1 § I, 12. *Invadentes, destruentes, per se vel per alios civitates, terras, loca aut iura ad Ecclesiam Romanam pertinentia; vel usurpantes, perturbantes, retinentes supremam iurisdictionem in eis nec non ad singula praedicta auxilium, concilium, favorem praebentes.*

2 Art. 6; see Prior, *Is the Pope Independent? or Outlines of the*

Those who usurp or detain, personally or through others, property or rights belonging to the Roman Church,[3] *incur excommunication latae sententiae, reserved modo speciali to the Apostolic See.* If the guilty ones are *clerics* they *must be deprived of their dignities, benefices, offices, and pensions, and be declared incapable of holding such.* This clerical penalty is *ferendae sententiae.*

The question has been asked: Does the present King of Italy fall under the excommunication formulated in this canon? He is not a usurper, but merely one who detains or holds or occupies property that was usurped by another, and in this sense authors maintain that "to retain" means the same as "not to restore,"[4] But is there a moral imputability? We hardly believe so; for the King alone could not restore the Papal States.[5] Deputies and senators are not responsible as individuals.[6]

USURPATION AND SECULARIZATION OF CHURCH PROPERTY

Can. 2346

Si quis bona ecclesiastica cuiuslibet generis, sive mobilia sive immobilia, sive corporalia sive incorporalia, per se vel per alios in proprios usus convertere et usurpare praesumpserit aut impedire ne eorundem fructus seu reditus ab iis, ad quos iure pertinent, percipiantur, excommunicationi tandiu subiaceat, quandiu bona ipsa integre restituerit, praedictum im-

Roman Question, 1907, p. 127 f.

3 But it would be improper to identify this property with the Roman See (Ayrinhac, p. 275); our text means only the *Roman* Church, understood as a political and ecclesiastical corporation, distinct from the Catholic Church at large.

4 Thus D'Annibale, p. 67, n. 100, note 6.

5 Thus also Eichmann, *l. c.,* p. 170.

6 D'Annibale, *l. c.*

pedimentum removerit, ac deinde a Sede Apostolica absolutionem impetraverit; quod si eiusdem ecclesiae seu bonorum patronus fuerit, etiam iure patronatus eo ipso privatus exsistat; clericus vero, hoc delictum committens vel in eodem consentiens, privetur praeterea beneficiis quibuslibet, ad alia quaelibet inhabilis efficiatur et a suorum ordinum exsecutione, etiam post integram satisfactionem et absolutionem, sui Ordinarii arbitrio suspendatur.

This canon aims at protecting the right claimed in can. 1495. It is not necessary to repeat what we said there. The spoliation of Church property forms an old and oft-recurring chapter in the annals of secular and ecclesiastical history from the time of the Merovingians to the wholesale secularization of churches and monasteries towards the end of the eighteenth and the beginning of the nineteenth century. The cupidity of men is insatiable, but its exercise against the Church has ever been followed by visible, though perhaps slow, punishment, inflicted either on individuals or on whole nations. The law inflicts a severe punishment (1°) *on those who, either personally or through others, dare to appropriate to their own use and usurp ecclesiastical property of whatever kind, be it movable or immovable, corporeal or incorporeal* and (2°) upon *those who dare to prevent either individual or corporate ecclesiastical persons from receiving the fruits or income due to them.*

1. The first class is that of *convertentes* and *usurpantes.* The text is essentially a repetition of the Tridentine[1]

1 *Trid.,* Sess. 22, c. 11: " *Si quem clericorum vel laicorum . . . bona, census ac iura . . . fructus, emolumenta, seu quascumque obventiones, quae in ministrorum et pauperum necessitates converti debent, per se vel alios, vi vel timore incusso, seu etiam per suppositas personas clericorum aut laicorum, seu quacumque arte aut quocumque quaesito

anathema against the unrightful holders of ecclesiastical property. We should expect that usurpation would be mentioned first and then appropriation; for *usurpare* means to occupy something as owner after having taken it away from the real proprietor. But the Council reverses the order, thus intimating that *convertere* and *usurpare* constitute one juridical act or criminal deed. This, indeed, appears to be the meaning of the Tridentine text, which emphasizes the alienation of ecclesiastical property from its real purpose. This may be embezzlement proper, or secularization, *i. e.*, turning ecclesiastical property to profane or worldly uses. *Embezzlement* is committed by a servant or employee. Hence it is clearly stated that only clerics may be guilty of this crime. *Secularisation* is proper to lay persons, especially the powerful and influential, who appropriate church goods to their own use.[2]

Whether this act of unlawful appropriation be committed by the usurpers *themselves* or *through others,* is immaterial. Therefore the *mandantes* are here concerned, who act through others.[3] *Per alios* may have another meaning. Take this case, for instance: A buys from B a piece of church property, which B had purchased at an auction from the government that had robbed a religious community, but turned the misappropriated property to public, not private, uses. Has A incurred the censure? Yes, answered the Holy Office.[4] Since these cases are not rare, it may be of

---

colore in proprios usus convertere, illosque usurpare praesumpserit, seu impedire, ne ab iis ad quos iure pertinent, percipiantur, is anathemati tamdiu subjaceat. . . ."

2 See D'Annibale, *l. c.*, p. 60, n. 91; Gallemart, *Conc. Trid.*, 1780, II,

654; Hollweck, *l. c.*, p. 238 takes *usurpantes* and *convertentes* as distinct terms.

3 But not the *consulentes.*

4 S. O., July 8, 1874 (*Coll. P. F.*, n. 1420).

interest to state the practice of the S. Poenitentiaria.[5] Its decisions turn about municipal authorities, mayors, and aldermen and naturally concern a country where wholesale spoliation of religious communities had taken place. The substance of these decisions is:

a) As long as these authorities do not appropriate such property to their own uses, they do not incur the censure, no matter how they may have coöperated in the unjust spoliation. Neither do those incur the censure who freely receive such property through the " liquidateur. "

b) Such authorities, mayor, aldermen, etc., are bound to make restitution *singillatim, i. e.,* each one for himself; as to the liquidators, it is not quite certain whether they are obliged to restitution.

c) Those who buy confiscated property and turn it to their own use, incur the censure;

d) With the exception of the last-named class (c) the confessor should not regard the aforesaid persons as public sinners;

e) Concerning the ecclesiastical burial of such persons, the local Ordinary must judge in each individual case.

f) The buyers *(emptores)* of church property illegitimately confiscated are bound to make restitution, but may easily obtain a " composition " or agreement with the Ordinary or Apostolic Delegate, who receive special faculties to this effect from the S. Poenitentiaria.

A kind of embezzlement no doubt forbidden under censure is keeping back, or occupying and retaining, money

---

5 Jan. 3, 1906; March 8, 1906; May 9, 1906; June 7, 1906; Sept. 17, 1906 (*Anal. Eccl.,* XV, 128 ff.) Apostolic Delegates enjoy the faculties to absolve in such cases (*Index Facult.,* n. 9).

and property belonging to the Holy Land, provided, of course, it is turned to one's own use.[6]

Clerics of every rank incur the censure if they misappropriate money or property destined for the maintenance of divine worship or the support of ministers.[7]

Bona ecclesiastica are defined in can. 1497 as such as pertain either to the universal Church, or to the Apostolic See, or to another artificial person, *i. e.*, ecclesiastical corporation, or which are under ecclesiastical ownership and control. This property may be *movable* (precious and sacred things), or *immovable* (such as lands). It may be *corporeal* or *incorporeal*. The former term comprises all goods which can be seen and handled, whilst *incorporeal* property is that which cannot be seen as such, for instance, leases, patent rights, literary or copyrights, incorporeal hereditaments.[8] An incorporeal property would also be the secret of manufacturing a certain trade article. All these properties, provided they belong to an ecclesiastical corporation or entity, are here included. It is not quite correct[9] to say that *loca pia* do not fall under this category. For such institutions (hospitals, orphanages, homes for the aged, the poor, etc.), if erected by the local Ordinary as a juridical person,[10] are ecclesiastical entities and the present canon applies to them.

2. The next class of fraudulent detainers of church property are the *impedientes* (see can. 2333), *viz.*:

6 S. O., June 28, 1876 (*Coll. P. F.*, n. 1457.)

7 Wernz, *l. c.*, VI, n. 336, p. 333. The amount required to incur the censure would certainly have to be considerable, $100 or $200; see Hollweck, p. 156, note 18. Thieves and robbers do not incur the censure under this heading; Pennacchi, *l. c.*, II, 368; but may be punished according to can. 2325.

8 Blackstone-Cooley, *l. c.*, II, 16; bonds and stocks rather belong to corporal property.

9 Thus Hilarius a Sexten, *l. c.*, p. 142.

10 Can. 1487, § 1.

those who authoritatively and effectively prevent others from coming into their own. When we say "authoritatively" we do not, however, mean to imply that only public authority in the strict sense is to be understood. Our church trustees, e. g., are not public authorities in the strict sense, but only representatives of private corporations, yet they exercise a certain authority and may, therefore, really "impede." The preventing may be done by threats, violence, sequestration, suspension of payment, lawsuits,[11] etc.

Fructus seu reditus are natural products, such as the tithes from animals, land, trees, etc., formerly paid to the clergy or the Church. *Reditus* refers particularly to revenues or salaries, such as the income from a benefice. Not comprised under this name or canon are the stole fees ·and the so-called *incerti, i. e.,* fees for dispensations, expediting documents, etc.[12] For these are especially mentioned under can. 2349.

But these fruits and revenues must belong *iure* to ecclesiastical persons. The legal title to them is established by the fact that one is a duly appointed minister of an ecclesiastical corporation and has not forfeited his right by illegal acts punishable in law by temporary or perpetual suspension or privation of one's benefice.

3. The *penalty* is

a) *Excommunication latae sententiae, reserved to the Apostolic See until full restitution has been made, the impediment removed, and absolution imparted.*

Since, as stated above, compensation or agreement is easily admitted, it is evident that such an act would

---

11 Hollweck, *l. c.*, p. 237, note 16. To this class belong also advowson and governmental retention of salaries.

12 Can. 463, § 1; can. 1507.

entitle one to absolution, provided the confessor has the necessary faculties.

b) The *patron of a church or property* who is guilty of acts forbidden by this canon, *is, besides, ipso facto deprived of the ius patronatus,* and his church or benefice becomes one of free appointment.

c) A *cleric* who has *committed the crime here mentioned or* [18] (by effective confiscation or detention) *has consented to the same, must be deprived of all his benefices and declared incapable of obtaining any benefice in future.* Besides, he must be *suspended from the exercise of his orders* for a period to be determined by his Ordinary, even after he has given full satisfaction and obtained absolution. All these clerical penalties, with the exception of excommunication, are now *ferendae sententiae,* and therefore require the usual admonition and sentence.

"*Ausus fuerit*" (can. 2229, § 2) implies knowledge that the property was an ecclesiastical one, and also freewill. Therefore, can. 2229, §2 must be consulted.

ILLEGAL ALIENATION

Can. 2347

Firma nullitate actus et obligatione, etiam per censuram urgenda, restituendi bona illegitime acquisita ac reparandi damna forte illata, qui bona ecclesiastica alienare praesumpserit aut in iis alienandis consensum praebere contra praescripta can. 534, § 1, et can. 1532:

1°. Si agatur de re cuius pretium non excedit mille

---

[18] The cleric, in virtue of his office, is obliged to protect the church property entrusted to him; a protest from him would be sufficient to render him immune from penalty; Hollweck, *l. c.,* p. 239, note 23.

libellas, congruis poenis a legitimo Superiore ecclesiastico puniatur;

2°. Si agatur de re cuius pretium sit supra mille,
sed infra triginta millia libellarum, privetur patronus
iure patronatus; administrator, munere administratoris; Superior vel oeconomus religiosus, proprio
officio et habilitate ad cetera officia, praeter alias con-
gruas poenas a Superioribus infligendas; Ordinarius
vero aliique clerici, officium, beneficium, dignitatem,
munus in Ecclesia obtinentes, solvant duplum favore
ecclesiae vel piae causae laesae; ceteri clerici suspendantur ad tempus ab Ordinario definiendum;

3°. Quod si beneplacitum apostolicum, in memoratis
canonibus praescriptum, fuerit scienter praetermissum,
omnes quovis modo reos sive dando sive recipiendo
sive consensum praebendo, manet praeterea excommunicatio latae sententiae nemini reservata.

Alienation has been explained elsewhere.[1] Here the
penalties are set forth. Those who *alienate church property, or consent to such alienation, despite the law laid
down in can.* 534, § 1 *and can.* 1532:

1°. Must be fittingly punished by the lawful ecclesiastical superior, if the value of the alienated property
does not exceed 1000 francs (lire);

2°. If the value *exceeds 1000 francs,* but does not
reach *30,000:*

a) The *patron* must be deprived of the *ius patronatus;*

b) The *administrator* must be removed from his office;

c) The *religious superior* or *oeconomus* (procurator)
must be deprived of his office and declared incapable
of holding any other office, and may also be otherwise
punished by his superiors in proportion to his guilt;

---

1 See can. 534, 1530–1533 (Vol. III and VI of this Commentary).

d) The *Ordinary* and *other clerics* who hold an office, benefice, dignity, or charge in the Church, are bound to pay the double amount to the church or charitable institution which they injured by alienation;

e) *Other clerics* must be suspended for a period to be fixed by the Ordinary.

3°. If, according to the aforesaid canons, the *beneplacitum apostolicum* was required, but was *knowingly neglected*, all those guilty of the crime, those who gave and those who received as well as those who merely gave their consent (if this was needed), incur the *excommunicatio latae sententiae* reserved to no one.

Our canon states that *no obligation* arises from an illegal alienation because the act is *null* and void in the internal as well as the external forum. Furthermore, those who *acquire* church property by illegal alienation, are bound to *make restitution* and *repair the damage* sustained by the ecclesiastical owner of the property.

But what about Ordinaries and clergymen (2, d) who have to pay the *duplum?* There is no doubt that *duplum* is here to be taken in comparison with the sum illegally alienated. Therefore, if 20,000 francs were illegally alienated, the Ordinaries guilty of the crime would have to repay 40,000 francs, and if the damage suffered by illegal alienation would not be covered by this latter sum, they would have to pay more.

But who shall enforce these penal laws, since, with the exception of the censure, they are all *ferendae sententiae?* The immediate superior, and therefore the Apostolic See with regard to autonomous prelates, and the local Ordinary with regard to the inferior clergy.

Attention must be drawn to the terms *praesumpserit* and *scienter praetermissum* (consult can. 2229, § 2).

Fear of loss, or deterioration, or real need, or any kind of ignorance would excuse one from the penalties above mentioned.

NEGLECT TO EXECUTE PIOUS BEQUESTS

Can. 2348

Qui legatum vel donationem ad causas pias sive actu inter vivos sive testamento, etiam per fiduciam, obtinuerit et implere negligat, ab Ordinario, etiam per censuram, ad id cogatur.

The Church always insisted upon the strict fulfillment of last wills (can. 1493, 1515) and considered it criminal to delay their execution. Those who retained pious offerings or bequests were cast out of the Church as infidels and called "killers of the poor" (*necatores pauperum*).[1] Our canon rehearses, though in a milder form, the ancient legislation by providing that *those who have received a legacy or donation for a pious cause, or a fiduciary bequest, be it inter vivos or by last will, and neglect to fulfill or execute it, should be compelled to do so, if necessary, even by censures.* One penalty mentioned in the Decretals is privation of the executorship and loss of every interest and commission accruing from such an office. But a canonical warning must precede. Another penalty is the use of censures, which also requires a canonical admonition.[2] The time within which the bequest must be executed or liquidated, is one year from the date of the last will or testament becoming known, or, as we would say, probated. This law concerns, as the sources clearly state, the secular as well as the

---

1 C. 9, 11, C. 13, q. 2.   2 Cc. 3, 6, 17, X, III, 26.

regular clergy.[3] Of course, as far as formalities are concerned, the civil law must be obeyed. But if that law would confiscate or forbid bequests for church purposes, the heirs would nevertheless be bound in conscience to do what they could to comply with the will of the testator.

REFUSAL TO PAY STOLE FEES AND TAXES

Can. 2349

Recusantes praestationes legitime debitas ad normam can. 463, § 1, 1507, prudenti arbitrio Ordinarii puniantur, donec satisfecerint.

Whilst it would be simony to demand a temporal remuneration for the administration of the Sacraments, as such, yet the legitimacy of stole fees for the support of the ministers has always been upheld by the Church, and the custom of paying such fees has been called praiseworthy.[1] Can. 2349 says these *stole fees* (for baptisms, marriages, funerals) and the *taxes* due according to law for civil or voluntary jurisdiction and execution of Apostolic rescripts must *be paid by the faithful.* Those who *refuse* to pay may be *punished by the local Ordinary* until they comply with their obligation. Of course, to those unable to pay, the sacred ministry must be rendered free of charge (can. 463, § 4).

---

[3] Thesaurus-Giraldi, P. II, *s. v.* "*Testamento,*" ed. cit., p. 423 f.).
[1] See c. 42, X, V, 3. Some refused to pay on account of heretical tendencies, most probably the Petrobrusians and followers of Arnold of Brescia.

TITLE XIV

CRIMES AGAINST LIFE, LIBERTY, PROPERTY, GOOD NAME

ABORTION AND SUICIDE

Can. 2350

§ 1. Procurantes abortum, matre non excepta, incurrunt, effectu secuto, in excommunicationem latae sententiae Ordinario reservatam; et si sint clerici, praeterea deponantur.

§ 2. Qui in seipsos manus intulerint, si quidem mors secuta sit, sepultura ecclesiastica priventur ad normam can. 1240, § 1, n. 3; secus, arceantur ab actibus legitimis ecclesiasticis et, si sint clerici, suspendantur ad tempus ab Ordinario definiendum, et a beneficiis aut officiis curam animarum interni vel externi fori adnexam habentibus removeantur.

This canon comprises two criminal acts, both related to homicide, *viz.:* abortion and suicide.

1. *Abortion* was widespread among the Greeks and Romans of pagan antiquity. The Christian Church treated it severely.[1] The Roman Law condemned persons of the lower ranks of society who committed abortion to the *metalla, i. e.,* the fiscal mines, and those of higher rank to exile.[2] The ecclesiastical law up to the sixteenth

---

[1] See Eschbach, *Disquisitiones Physiologico-Theologicae*, 1901, p. 277 ff. The synods of Elvira, Ancyra, etc., mention infanticide, which is identical with abortion in the popular sense.

[2] L. 8, Dig. 48, 8; l. 38, § 5, Dig. 48, 19: *"Qui abortionis aut*

century classified abortion with homicide.[3] A decisive
step in the penal legislation concerning this offense was
taken by Sixtus V, in his Constitution " *Effraenatum*, "
Oct. 29, 1588, which was modified considerably by
Gregory XIV in his Constitution, " *Sedes Apostolica*, "
May 31, 1691. Sixtus V had inflicted the excommunication reserved to the Apostolic See, made no distinction
between *foetus animatus* and *inanimatus*, *formis* or
informis, and included all accomplices. Gregory XIV
reserved the excommunication to the bishop, and restricted the crime to *foetus animatus*. This was the law
of the Church until 1869, when the " *Apostolicae
Sedis* " [4] was issued by Pius IX, which made no distinction between *foetus animatus* and *inanimatus*, whilst, on
the other hand, it condemned only the *procurantes* and
reserved the censure to the Ordinary.

But the question whether the mother was included
was left undecided and opinions continued divided on
this point. Our text settles *this* question by saying:
Those *who procure abortion,— the mother not excepted,
— after the effect has followed, incur the excommunication latae sententiae, reserved to the Ordinary; clerics
must, besides, be deposed.* This text is identical with
that of the " *Apostolicae Sedis* " except as to the clause:
" *matre non excepta*, " and in that it makes the penalty for
clerics *ferendae sententiae*.

1. Now, what is abortion? Authors differ in defining
this crime. We accept the following definition: Abortion is the expulsion of a human fetus from the womb

*amatorium poculum dant, etsi dolo
non faciant, tamen qui mali exempli
iis est, humiliores in metallum,
honestiores in insulam amissa parte
bonorum relegentur.*" The woman

is expressly mentioned in l. 8, *l. c.*
3 C. 20, C. 2, q. 5; c. 8, C. 32, q.
2; cc. 5, 20, X, V, 12.
4 § III, n. 2; "*Procurantes abortum, effectu sequuto.*"

before it is capable of living separately.[5]   This supposes
the existence of a human fetus, from the time it can
really be called a fetus, to about the seventh month of
pregnancy.   For after the seventh and up to the ninth
month the act of bringing forth a fetus is styled premature birth, not abortion proper, because the fetus at that
stage has viability, even though it be precarious.   But fetus
may also mean the embryonic stage of development from
the time of conception to about the sixth week of
pregnancy.[6]

The distinction between *foetus animatus* and *inanimatus*
had been given up since the *"Apostolicae Sedis"* with
regard to censure, but not as to vindictive penalties, and
especially irregularity.   Yet even now it is safely held
and taught that ejection of the semen immediately
after the copula does not fall under censure, because
conception is not as yet certain.   Neither would the
ejection of so-called molae (false conceptions) be subject
to censure, even though these were ejected with the intention of procuring abortion.   As a general rule it may
be stated that any act committed within twenty-four
hours of conception is not to be construed as abortion,
even though done with that intention.[7]

Abortion is called *accidental* when it is brought about
involuntarily, in consequence of a fall, overexertion, or
natural dislocation.   It is *criminal* when induced voluntarily for selfish reasons and by forbidden means.   It
is *artificial* when induced for medical-therapeutic reasons.
But the latter species may be criminal according to sound

5 See *Encyclopedia Americana*,
1920, I, 45; also Eschbach, *l. c.*,
p. 274; Pennacchi, II, 34.
  6 See Vol. IV of this Commentary, p. 50 f.
  7 Hilarius a Sexten, *l. c.*, p. 218;

Hollweck. *l. c.*, p. 252, note 8.
The consequence is that syringing
after the *copula*, though perhaps
done with criminal intent, does not
fall under censure.

moral principles,[8] and hence the above division is not fully adequate.

2. The different kinds of abortion must be judged by the act that produces abortion. This is called *procuratio* and its agents *procurantes*. To procure an abortion means to bring it about purposely and intentionally.[9] This may be done in a twofold way: (a) by seeking abortion directly and for its own sake, in which case it is purely and simply *criminal*, or (b) as a means to a higher end, for instance, to preserve the life of the mother. In both cases abortion is sought and intended directly as a means to an end.

Mandantes are those who order an abortion to be committed and in whose name it is perpetrated, for instance, the mother who commands the physician to perform an operation the direct effect of which is abortion; or the father or seducer, provided, of course, the woman consents; for it is she who has to give the final permission — always provided she is in a physically and mentally normal condition. The *mandantes* are without doubt to be reckoned among the *procurantes*.[10]

Whether the *mandatarius, i. e.,* he who executes the order or command, must be classed with the *procurantes*, is a controverted question. The executor of the will or command of another does not act in his own name, although, as one commentator most justly observes in our case, he truly and properly procures abortion.[11] We say

---

8 *Encyclopedia Americana, l. c;* Eschbach, *l. c.,* p. 274 ff. distinguishes an involuntary or casual and a voluntary abortion; this from a theological viewpoint. Hollweck, *l. c.,* says: directly philosophical and only indirectly physiological.

9 *Procurare est studiose et ex industria aliquid quaerere;* Pen-

nacchi, II, 34; D'Annibale, *l. c.,* n. 159.

10 Pennacchi, *l. c.,* II, 36; D'Annibale, *l. c.,* p. 103, n. 161; Hollweck, *l. c.,* note 6.— Misleading is the superficial statement: " Some deny it" (Ayrinhac, *l. c.,* p. 288).

11 *La Nouvelle Revue Théolo-*

the question is controverted, because such well-known commentators on the "*Apostolicae Sedis*" as Pennacchi [12] and D'Annibale [13] deny that the *mandatarius* incurs the censure. Therefore the benefit of a real doubt may safely be granted to such, thereby exempting them from the censure.

Those who *advise* or *favor abortion,* and druggists or physicians who prepare drugs conducive to abortion, do not incur excommunication. The same is true of those who beat a pregnant woman for any other motive except that of procuring abortion. [14]

3. *Effecto secuto* means that the attempt must be effective. Whether the effect (abortion) is procured by means of drugs or instruments, or by burdens imposed on the pregnant woman does not matter. [15] A moral cause, for instance, voluntary fright or fear intentionally brought to bear upon a woman, may produce an abortion. But there must always be a *causal connection* between the means used and the effect intended. Hence if an abortion were produced by a fall, or a scare, or by sickness, even though the woman had taken a drug to insure it, the censure would not be incurred. If it is doubtful what caused abortion, the fall, etc., or the drug, some authors deny [16] that the censure is incurred, while others [17] assert that it is.

These few comments may suffice to disperse at least some doubts. The principal fact to be kept in mind is that the *mother* is no longer exempt from incurring the

gique, Vol. XI, n. 350, quoted by Pennacchi, II, 36.

12 *L. c.*

13 *L. c.;* see also Hilarius a Sexten, *l. c.,* p. 219 f.

14 Pennacchi, *l. c.,* p. 35.

15 Sixtus V, *"Effraenatum,"* § 2;

D'Annibale, *l. c.,* p. 102, n. 159.

16 D'Annibale, *l. c.,* p. 102, n. 160; Hilarius a Sexten, *l. c.,* p. 220.

17 Lehmkuhl, *l. c.,* II, n. 970. The state of doubt permits can. 209 to be applied.

censure. She may, however, be immune from censure, if can. 2205, § 2 is verified. For grave fear would render her immune from censure, inasmuch as a censure is a purely ecclesiastical penalty.

Now a brief remark concerning *artificial abortion.* It has become almost a dogma among authors [18] that craniotomy and embryotomy, though grievously unlawful and forbidden, do not fall under the censure of can. 2350. Craniotomy consists in crushing the fetus and taking it out piecemeal. Another kind of artificial abortion is called *medical* and consists in the expulsion of an immature fetus on account of a too narrow pelvis. All authors hold as theologically certain that it is never allowed to procure or intend an abortion as such *(uti finis)* or as means to an end, for instance, to preserve the life of the mother, if the means cause abortion directly *(per se)* and cannot preserve the life of the mother except by causing abortion.[19] Two, or rather three, decisions of the Holy Office confirm this view: "It cannot be safely taught in Catholic schools," says one of them, "that any kind of surgical operation is allowed which will directly kill the fetus; even if acceleration of birth is not possible on account of the narrowness of the female organs, it is never allowed to cause or provoke an abortion." [20] But where is the censure? We answer: If the physician performs the operation of his own accord, without being commanded or asked by those concerned, he certainly incurs excommunication.[21] But if he merely acts as *mandatarius,* he does not incur the censure.

18 Hilarius a Sexten, *l. c.,* p. 218 calls it *fere communis theologorum sententia.*

19 Eschbach, *l. c.,* p. 390 ff.; Coppens, *Moral Principles and Medical Practice,* 1897, p. 65 ff.

20 S. O., May 28, 1884; July 24, 1895; May 4, 1898 (*Coll. P. F.,* nn. 1618, 1906, 1997).

21 Thus also Eichmann, *l. c.,* p. 176.

II. *Suicide.* Those who *deliberately commit suicide,* are *to be deprived of ecclesiastical burial,* according to can. 1240, § 1, n. 3, where the necessary remarks have been made on funerals. Those who command the ecclesiastical burial of a suicide do not incur excommunication, because they are not mentioned in can. 2339. If there is doubt whether a suicide was accidental or deliberate, the former is to be presumed. But if there is doubt whether the suicide was committed with deliberation or in the state of mental aberration, malice or intentional suicide should be presumed, according to can. 2200, § 2. However, the statement of a physician or of relatives as to the physical condition of the deceased may safely be accepted. [22]

If one who attempts to commit suicide survives, *he must be denied all legal ecclesiastical acts* (can. 2256, n. 2). *Clerics* guilty of such an attempt *must be suspended* for a period to be fixed by the Ordinary, and, besides, *must be removed from any benefice or office connected with the care of souls, both in the internal and external forum.* Therefore such clerics, after a declaratory sentence issued by the Ordinary, can no longer function as chaplains, confessors, assistants or curates, pastors or Ordinaries.

DUELLING

Can. 2351

§ 1. Servato praescripto can. 1240, § 1, n. 4, duellum perpetrantes aut simpliciter ad illud provocantes vel ipsum acceptantes vel quamlibet operam aut favorem

22 See Hollweck, *l. c.,* p. 253, note 2; Eichmann, *l. c.,* p. 177. The same is true if the suicide gave signs of repentance before dying; can. 1240, § 1.

praebentes, nec non de industria spectantes illudque permittentes vel quantum in ipsis est non prohibentes, cuiuscunque dignitatis sint, subsunt ipso facto excommunicationi Sedi Apostolicae simpliciter reservatae.

§2. Ipsi vero duellantes et qui eorum patrini vocantur, sunt praeterea ipso facto infames.

A duel is a combat with deadly weapons, without or with fatal result, between two persons who have deliberately agreed on the conditions of the fight.[1] A duel is *private* if it takes place by private agreement between the parties and their friends: *public,* if sanctioned by the lawful authority for a public purpose. The purpose may render it lawful or unlawful. If the purpose is a good one, as the prevention of an impending war, for instance, the duel could not be styled unlawful. If held only to satisfy public curiosity, however, like the gladiatorial combats of the Romans, it is wrong and forbidden.

Here we are concerned with *private duels.*[2] Our text, in terms almost identical with that of *" Apostolicae Sedis,"* *subjects to ipso facto excommunication, simply reserved to the Apostolic See,* the following persons:

1. *Those who participate in a duel, i. e.,* a single combat fought according to rules laid down by private agreement as to time, place, and weapons, no matter whether the intended result is fatal or not. Therefore, the so-called *Mensuren* of students and officers are included.[3]

---

1 Hill, *Ethics,* ed. 8, p. 210 — except the clause, "with or without fatal result," which had to be added on account of the so-called *Mensuren.*

2 Public duels are no longer in vogue.

3 § III, 3. *Duellum perpetrantes aut simpliciter ad illud provocantes, vel ipsum acceptantes, et quoslibet complices, vel qualemcumque operam aut favorem praebentes, nec non de industria spectantes, illudque permittentes, vel quantum in illis est, non prohibentes, cuiuscumque dignitatis sint, etiam regalis vel imperialis.*

2. Those *who challenge* others to a duel, as just described, no matter whether the duel takes place or not or whether the challenge was accepted or not, provided only it was meant seriously.[4]

3. Those *who accept a challenge* thus issued.

4. Those *who offer any assistance or favor* to duellists, for instance, by acting as seconds, witnesses, physicians,[5] and those who rent a place, or carriage, or automobile for that purpose.

5. Those *who purposely witness* a duel as spectators. The penalty is not incurred if they merely pass by, or watch the duel from a nearby place, provided they are not hired for that purpose.[6]

6. Those *who, no matter of what dignity they be, permit or fail to prevent a duel as far as lies within their power.* To this class belong the rulers of peoples, if they can impede duels; the magistrates as individuals, under the same condition; and, we believe, also policemen, if the law prohibits duelling; nay, even private citizens, if they can interfere without serious inconvenience; the latter, however, may easily be excused on account of the odium they might expose themselves to.

Note that the *provocantes* and *acceptantes* incur excommunication even though the duel does not take place; whilst the others named in numbers 4 to 6 incur it only if the duel really comes off.[7]

The duellants and their seconds (*duellantes et patrini*) also incur the *infamy of law*, and hence contract *irregularity* with regard to orders (can. 984, n. 5; 985, n.

4 S. C. C., Aug. 9, 1890 (*Coll. P. F.*, n. 1739).

5 If the physician is present by chance, he does not incur the censure, but if he is hired for the purpose, he does; S. O., May 28, 1884 (*Coll. cit.*, n. 1617, ad 1).

6 *Ib.*, ad 2 et 3. No confessor is allowed to be purposely present; *ib.*

7 D'Annibale, *l. c.*, p. 77; n. 115; Pennacchi, *l. c.*, I, 549 f.; Hollweck, *l. c.*, p. 254 f.

5). *"Mensuren"* are not excepted from this rule.[8]

Lastly, *ecclesiastical burial must be denied to those who die in a duel or from a wound received in a single combat,* unless they give signs of repentance before they die (can. 1240, § 1). But those who command or extort ecclesiastical burial for duelists do not incur excommunication; but those who would grant such a request freely and of their own accord, would incur the interdict, as per can. 2339.

COMPULSION IN REGARD TO THE CLERICAL OR RELIGIOUS VOCATION

Can. 2352

Excommunicatione nemini reservata ipso facto plectuntur omnes, qualibet etiam dignitate fulgentes, qui quoquo modo cogant sive virum ad statum clericalem amplectendum, sive virum aut mulierem ad religionem ingrediendam vel ad emittendam religiosam professionem tam sollemnem quam simplicem, tam perpetuam quam temporariam.

Excommunication reserved to no one is ipso facto incurred by:

1. *All, no matter what their dignity, who in any way compel a man to embrace the clerical state;*

2. *All who in any way compel a man or a woman to enter the religious state or to make religious profession, be it solemn or simple, perpetual or temporary.*

This law, substantially taken from the Council of Trent,[1] guarantees the freedom of clerical and religious vocation.

8 S. C. C., Aug. 9, 1890 (*l. c.,* n. 1739).

1 Sess. 25, c. 18; see Bened. XIV, *"Si datam,"* March 4, 1748.

1. The *persons* here intended are all Catholics of the male or female sex, parents or strangers, of the highest and lowest civil or ecclesiastical dignity [2] or condition: parents, relatives, pastors, confessors, teachers, chaplains,[3] superiors, superioresses, etc., etc.

2. *Cogentes quoquo modo* means to compel or force one in any way, directly or indirectly, by threats, reverential fear, compulsion, persuasion, promises, etc., whether these means be used directly or through intermediary persons.[4]

3. The *purpose* must be to compel the other to choose a state for which he or she has or feels no vocation.

a) The *clerical* state begins with the first tonsure (can. 108, § 1), and hence the excommunication is incurred when that order is received.

b) The *religious state* is entered at the beginning of the novitiate, not postulancy, because this latter is not required for clerical organizations, and, besides, only novices enjoy the privileges of religious. To compel any one to *make profession* of any kind here mentioned, renders one liable to the penalty.

ABDUCTION OF WOMEN

Can. 2353

Qui intuitu matrimonii vel explendae libidinis causa rapuerit mulierem nolentem vi aut dolo, vel mulierem

---

2 Except Cardinals, on account of can. 2227, § 2.

3 If a chaplain of Sisters preaches to academy girls that the only salvation for them is the convent, he is certainly not far from incurring the censure, and should be removed at once.

4 If a girl is sent to a convent to be educated, there is no harm in that; but if the avowed purpose is to make her a nun against her will, the excommunication is incurred after she has entered.

minoris aetatis consentientem quidem, sed insciis vel
contradicentibus parentibus aut tutoribus, ipso iure
exclusus habeatur ab actibus legitimis ecclesiasticis
et insuper aliis poenis pro gravitate culpae plectatur.

This and the next four canons deal with crimes *mixti
fori, i. e.,* such as fall also within the competency of the
lay court and are prosecuted by the same. Exception,
of course, should be made of clerics, on account of the
privilegium fori.

*Any man who abducts a woman against her will,
by violence or deceit, either with the intention of marrying her or for the sake of gratifying his sensuality; or
who abducts a girl not yet of age, even though she is
willing, without the knowledge and against the will
of her parents or guardians, is ipso iure excluded from
legal ecclesiastical acts (can. 2256, n. 2) and should be
punished in proportion to his guilt.*

It is evident that this penal enactment, *latae sententiae,*
not only regards abduction (*raptus*) as an impediment,
but abduction in general, the condition being, however,
that the abductor be a man. The purpose of the law is
to protect the liberty and security of women.

MIXED CRIMES

Can. 2354

§ 1. Laicus qui fuerit legitime damnatus ob delictum
homicidii, raptus impuberum alterutrius sexus, vendi-
tionis hominis in servitutem vel alium malum finem,
usurae, rapinae, furti qualificati vel non qualificati in
re valde notabili, incendii vel malitiosae ac valde notabilis rerum destructionis, gravis mutilationis vel vul-

nerationis vel violentiae, ipso iure exclusus habeatur ab actibus legitimis ecclesiasticis et a quolibet munere, si quod in Ecclesia habeat, firmo onere reparandi damna.

§ 2. Clericus vero qui aliquod delictum commiserit de quibus in § 1, a tribunali ecclesiastico puniatur, pro diversa reatus gravitate, poenitentiis, censuris, privatione officii ac beneficii, dignitatis, et si res ferat, etiam depositione; reus vero homicidii culpabilis degradetur.

1. *Laymen* are *ipso iure excluded from legal ecclesiastical acts* and *any charge* they may hold in the Church, save the *obligation of indemnity,* if:

a) They have been lawfully condemned for *homicide;*

b) Or for the *abduction* of *impuberes* of either sex;

c) Or for *slavery* proper or white slavery;

d) Or for *usury,* as far as punishable by civil law;

e) Or for *rapine* or violent theft;

f) Or for *theft,* either qualified (for instance, in churches or public buildings: burglary) or unqualified (fraudulent misappropriation against the will of the owner) [1] *in re valde notabili,* that is, of a thing of considerable value, either materially or by reason of art or antiquity;

g) Or for *arson* or *malicious destruction* of considerable property, either out of a spirit of wanton cruelty or wicked revenge;[2]

h) Or for serious *mutilation,* wounding, or battery.

2. If a *clergyman* has committed any of the aforementioned crimes, he *must be punished by the ecclesiastical court* in proportion to the gravity of his guilt

[1] Cfr. Kenny-Webb, *l. c.,* p. 220.   [2] *Ib.,* p. 163.

with penances, censures, privation of office and benefice, and, in more serious cases, with deposition; if he is guilty of culpable homicide, he must be degraded.

Note, however, that these penalties are to be meted out only after the culprits have been *condemned* by a *legitimate court,* after a trial conducted according to the laws and customs of the country, and after the time for appeal has elapsed.

PRIVATE VERBAL INJURIES

Can. 2355

Si quis non re, sed verbis vel scriptis vel alia quavis ratione iniuriam cuiquam irrogaverit vel eius bonam famam laeserit, non solum potest ad normam can. 1618, 1938 cogi ad debitam satisfactionem praestandam damnaque reparanda, sed praeterea congruis poenis ac poenitentiis puniri, non exclusa, si de clericis agatur et casus ferat, suspensione aut remotione ab officio et beneficio.

Can. 2344 punishes libelous and oral injuries directed against higher dignitaries as public persons. Here these injuries are punished if committed against laymen or clerics by the persons just mentioned. But here a *tort* is committed, rather than a crime, which in secular law would be prosecuted in the civil, not in the criminal court. Those who *inflict* (not real but) *verbal injuries* by *word or writing*[1] *or in any other way, for instance,* by offensive gestures, on anyone, whether a *cleric of inferior rank or a layman,* or *who defame any of the aforesaid persons, may be compelled to give satisfaction*[2]

---

[1] To these belong insulting pictures or caricatures.

[2] Satisfaction is generally made by offering an apology or inserting

and to repair eventual damage, provided the offended party insists upon such punishment, according to can. 1618 (a civil trial) or a denunciation to the fiscal promotor has been made according to can. 1938 (a criminal trial in the ecclesiastical sense).

Besides, *other proportionate punishments and penances may be meted out;* and if the offenders are *clerics, they may,* if necessary (for instance, if the scandal or damage was of a very serious nature) *also be suspended or removed from office and benefice.*

Thus a slanderous cleric, according to the IVth Synod of Carthage, should be made to apologize, and if he demurs, may be degraded.[3] Laymen who slander a priest, orally or in writing should be excommunicated.[4] Laymen who commit the same offence against one of their own class, should be scourged and compelled to do public penance.[5]

The penalties are now fixed by the civil courts. Laymen who wish to bring suit against a cleric in such cases need the permission of the local Ordinary.[6] Prescription for such offences runs one year (*v.* can. 1703, n. 2).

BIGAMY

Can. 2356

Bigami, idest qui, obstante coniugali vinculo, aliud matrimonium, etsi tantum civile, ut aiunt, attentaverint, sunt ipso facto infames; et si, spreta Ordinarii monitione, in illicito contubernio persistant, pro

---

an article in a specified newspaper.
3 C. 2, Dist. 46.
4 C. 8, C. 5, q. 6.

5 C. 18. C. 5, q. 1.
6 See can. 120; can. 2341.

diversa reatus gravitate excommunicentur vel personali interdicto plectantur.

1. *Bigamists, i. e., persons who, though validly married, attempt another (though perhaps only civil) marriage are infamous by law,* and *if they spurn a warning given by the Ordinary and continue their unlawful relation, should be punished by excommunication or personal interdict, according to the grievousness of their guilt.*

A bigamist, as here understood, is a man who has two or more wives at the same time. Bigamy, therefore, is identical with polygamy. It is punishable only when it is *subjective,*[1] *i. e.,* when one knows that the former marriage tie was and is still valid and not dissolved in an ecclesiastically legal form. Unfortunately the State sometimes grants a divorce for reasons nugatory in the eyes of the Church, and without regard to her laws.

2. Polygamy is punishable only if a *second marriage has been attempted.* We say: attempted, not contracted, because the object of the marital contract has not only been promised, but delivered up to another party still living. But there must be a *semblance* of a second marriage, that is, the culprit must go through a legally recognized marriage ceremony with another person to incur the censure.[2] It is hardly imaginable that a Catholic minister would assist at a marriage without having inquired into the free state of the parties. Therefore, *civil marriage* is especially mentioned.

3. *Equally punishable* is the woman who, though free,

---

[1] A man who marries (invalidly) a woman whilst his first wife is still alive, but *bona fide* believed to be dead, would not commit bigamy subjectively, but objectively; and, therefore, could not be punished as a bigamist in the ecclesiastical court.

[2] Kenny-Webb, *l. c.,* p. 286 ff.

marries a bigamist, provided, of course, she knows of the married state of her supposed husband. The individual contract and the attempt against the unity of matrimony in this case require equal punishment.[3]

4. The penalty for bigamy is *legal infamy* with all its consequences (can. 2294, § 1). Besides, says the text, the *seriousness of the guilt* should be properly considered. For the rank of the parties (can. 2207, n. 1.) may set an exceptionally bad example or cause great scandal.[4] But the severer penalties are to be inflicted only *after a warning*, which should be a canonical one (can. 2309), because the penalty to be inflicted (*ferendae sententiae*) is the heaviest, namely, excommunication or the personal interdict.

CRIMES OF LAYMEN AGAINST GOOD MORALS

Can. 2357

§ 1. Laici legitime damnati ob delicta contra sextum cum minoribus infra aetatem sexdecim annorum commissa, vel ob stuprum, sodomiam, incestum, lenocinium, ipso facto infames sunt, praeter alias poenas quas Ordinarius infligendas iudicaverit.

§ 2. Qui publicum adulterii delictum commiserint, vel in concubinatu publice vivant, vel ob alia delicta contra sextum decalogi praeceptum legitime fuerint

---

[3] The secular law would have her indicted for bigamy as a principal in the second degree (*ib.*, p. 291). " It is no defence that the defendant was a member of a religious sect [Mormons of the original type are here meant], which professed to extol polygamy as a virtue, and that he conscientiously believed he was doing no wrong in contracting a plural marriage " (*ib.*, p. 292).

[4] Former penalties were excommunication and public penance; c. 19, C. 24, q. 3; cc. 8, 9, C. 32, q. 7; Urban VIII, "*Magnum in Christo*," June 20, 1637, § 2, condemned bigamists to the galleys or public whipping post and perpetual prison.

damnati, excludantur ab actibus legitimis ecclesiasticis, donec signa verae resipiscentiae dederint.

§ 1 declares laymen *legally infamous* and otherwise
punishable by the Ordinary:

1. If they have been *lawfully convicted of crimes
against the sixth commandment committed with minors,
i. e.,* persons of either sex who have not yet completed
the sixteenth year of age; or

2. If they have been *lawfully condemned for fornica-
tion, sodomy, incest,* or *panderage.*

As to the requisites for incurring this penalty, it may
be observed that the act must amount to a *copula perfecta; actus inconsummati* would not constitute the
crime,[1] wherefore *tactus, oscula, amplexus* are not here
intended. Minors may be of either sex, whence a *coitus
viri cum viro* would indeed be sodomy, but even more
punishable on account of the moral seduction and responsibility involved.[2]

Stuprum is here to be understood as violent forni-
cation, otherwise the text would have employed *forni-
catio.* Properly speaking it is the violent defloration of
a woman still a virgin.[3] But common doctrine has accepted it as a violation of any woman, married or single,
whose character was not ruined by immoral conduct.
However, if we say *violent,* this term must be understood also of deceit, fraud, threats, and fear.[4]

Sodomia is unnatural sexual gratification by an act
committed with a person of the same sex. It also includes *bestiality.* Not included under this penal law is

---

1 See Hollweck, *l. c.,* p. 267, note 4.

2 Pius V, " *Cum primum,*" April 1, 1566, § 11; it need not be habitual.

3 Civil law styles it seduction with a widely different definition; Kenny-Webb, *l. c.,* p. 294 f.

4 Reiffenstuel, V, 16, n. 43 f.

sodomia imperfecta or *coitus viri cum femina, non servato vase naturali.*[5]

Incestus is sexual intercourse between persons related within the degrees of consanguinity or affinity wherein they may not lawfully marry. The former[6] penalty of illicit affinity and loss of marital rights *(ius petendi debitum conjugale)* is now abolished. The fact of incest or the intention or agreement to commit incest in order more easily to obtain a dispensation need not be mentioned in the petition for the dispensation.[7]

Lenocinium is panderage for filthy lucre's sake, according to the Roman Law, *i. e.*, as a canon of the synod of Elvira (313, n. 3) states, the sale of another person's body for the purpose of unlawful gratification, no matter whether the mother, or the father, or another commits the crime.[8] Hence keepers of houses of ill fame fall under this heading and, therefore, incur infamy (can. 2294, § 1).

§ 2 considers the public crimes of *adultery* and *public concubinage*, as also other crimes against the sixth commandment, provided the perpetrators have been lawfully convicted of such crimes or misdemeanors, or whatever else they be styled, in civil law. The latter has not even a clear view of what constitutes adultery.[9] According to ecclesiastical law, adultery is sexual intercourse of a married person with another person than his or her consort.[10] It does not require the *copula perfecta* and may be committed with a married or a single person.

On *concubinage* see can. 1078.

The *penalty* for these crimes is *exclusion* from *legal*

---

5 Schmalzgrueber, V, 16, n. 117.
6 C. 1, X, IV, 13.
7 S. O., June 25, 1885 (Coll. P. F., n. 1635).
8 L. 4, § 2, Dig. 3, 2; Hollweck, l. c., p. 271, note 2.

9 See Kenny-Webb, l. c., p. 292 f.
10 "*Adulterium est alieni thori violatio*"; *Gratiani dictum*, § 3 ad c. 2, C. 36, q. 1.

ecclesiastical acts as long as no signs of repentance are given.[11]   But the penalty is *ferendae sententiae,* conditioned by a previous civil conviction.

CLERICAL OFFENDERS CONTRA SEXTUM

Can. 2358

Clerici in minoribus ordinibus constituti, rei alicuius delicti contra sextum decalogi praeceptum, pro gravitate culpae puniantur etiam dimissione e statu clericali, si delicti adiuncta id suadeant, praeter poenas de quibus in can. 2357, si his locus sit.

Can. 2359

§ 1. Clerici in sacris sive saeculares sive religiosi concubinarii, monitione inutiliter praemissa, cogantur ab illicito contubernio recedere et scandalum reparare suspensione a divinis, privatione fructuum officii, beneficii, dignitatis, servato praescripto can. 2176-2181.

§ 2. Si delictum admiserint contra sextum decalogi praeceptum cum minoribus infra aetatem sexdecim annorum, vel adulterium, stuprum, bestialitatem, sodomiam, lenocinium, incestum cum consanguineis aut affinibus in primo gradu exercuerint, suspendantur, infames declarentur, quolibet officio, beneficio, dignitate, munere, si quod habeant, priventur, et in casibus gravioribus deponantur.

§ 3. Si aliter contra sextum decalogi praeceptum deliquerint, congruis poenis secundum casus gravitatem coerceantur, non excepta officii vel beneficii privatione, maxime si curam animarum gerant.

---

11 Whether the signs are sufficient is to be decided by the one who issued the penal sentence in the ecclesiastical court.

These two canons have one and the same object in view, *viz.:* to punish more severely the crimes referred to in can. 2357, which are punished gradually, *i. e.*, according to the degree of the clerical state.[1] But what was stated as to consummate acts, by way of explanation of the preceding canon, etc., also applies here.

1. Clerics *in minor orders* who are proved guilty of an offense against the sixth commandment, are to be punished in proportion to the seriousness of the transgression, even with dismissal from the clerical state if necessary, *i. e.*, if the circumstances demand it; besides, the penalties stated in can. 2357 must be applied if the crime is such as to call for them.

2. Clerics *in sacris, i. e.*, from subdeaconship upward, either secular or religious, who *live in concubinage*, must first be canonically warned.[2] If the warning proves fruitless, they are to be compelled to give up the unlawful relation and to repair the scandal by suspension *a divinis* (see can. 2279, § 2, n. 2), privation of the income from office, from benefice, and from dignity. But the procedure stated under can. 2176-2181 must be observed.

3. Clerics *in sacris,* secular or religious, who have committed a crime against the sixth commandment with a person of either sex who has not completed the sixteenth year, or who have committed adultery, rape, bestiality, sodomy, panderage, incest with blood or legal relatives in the first degree,[3] shall be suspended, declared infamous, deprived of every office, benefice, dignity, and charge they may hold, and, in more serious cases, shall be deposed.[4] All these penalties, though preceptive (see

---

[1] Former penalties: deposition, removal from office, imprisonment in a monastery; see cc. 6, 28, C. 27, q. 1.

[2] See can. 2176.

[3] That is to say; with mother, daughter, stepmother, stepdaughter, sister, stepsister, sister-in-law.

[4] See can. 2278, § 2; 2291, n. 4; 2298, n. 6; 2298, n. 10.

can. 2223), are *ferendae sententiae* and, therefore, require a canonical warning (see can. 2233).

4. Clerics *in sacris,* either secular or religious, who have committed a delinquency *contra sextum* not mentioned in the preceding two sections, must be punished in proportion to the grievousness of the sin. Such delinquents, especially if they are entrusted with the care of souls, may also be deprived of their office or benefice.

TITLE XV

CRIMEN FALSI OR FORGERY

Under this heading were formerly reckoned not only the crimes mentioned in can. 2360 and 2362, but also forgery of weights, measures, and money, and the substitution of children *(suppositio partus alieni)*. [1] Our text retains only two of the former subjects classed in this category, namely, forgery of papal documents and forgery of ecclesiastical documents and acts. But it adds obreptitious and subreptitious rescripts, and above all the act of falsely accusing a confessor of solicitation in the confessional.

FORGERY OF PAPAL DOCUMENTS

Can. 2360

§ 1. Omnes fabricatores vel falsarii litterarum, decretorum vel rescriptorum Sedis Apostolicae vel iisdem litteris, decretis vel rescriptis scienter utentes incurrunt ipso facto in excommunicationem speciali modo Sedi Apostolicae reservatam.

§ 2. Clerici delictum de quo in § 1 committentes aliis poenis praeterea coerceantur, quae usque ad privationem beneficii, officii, dignitatis et pensionis ecclesiasticae extendi possunt; religiosi autem priventur omnibus officiis quae in religione habent et voce activa

---

1 See the commentators on X, V, 20, *de crimine falsi.*

ac passiva, praeter alias poenas in propriis cuiusque constitutionibus statutas.

The canon mentions three classes of criminal tamperers with official documents of the *Apostolic See*.

1. *Fabricatores* are forgers. To forge a document means to make a false imitation of it. The document may be drawn from pre-existing material, as, for instance, the Pseudo-Isidorian Decretals. The idea of forgery in the strict sense embraces the document as a whole; a document is a forgery when it purports to be what it is not; or, in other words, when it not only tells a lie, but tells a lie about itself.[2] That such a document cannot be called genuine, is evident. It is the task of diplomatics — as this art is called since the time of Mabillon — to determine the genuineness of documents. In the Middle Ages the seal appended to or impressed upon a diploma was considered a decisive proof of its genuineness.[3]

2. *Falsarii* are those who partly forge a document by interpolating, changing or correcting it[4] with the intention of defrauding *(cum dolo et jactura)*. Our canon does not exclude this malicious intention, for there can be no reasonable doubt that *falsarii* is used here in the same sense as in the "*Apostolicae Sedis*,"[5] where the commentators

---

2 Kenny-Webb, *l. c.*, p. 240.

3 Bresslau, *Urkundenlehre*, 1889, p. 5 ff. The diplomaticists distinguish internal and external marks of genuineness.

4 Cfr. c. 5, X, V, 20: appending a genuine bull or seal to false documents, changing the string of hemp or silk, using erasure, caustics, etc.

5 § I, 9. "*Omnes falsarios Litterarum Apostolicarum, etiam in forma Brevis ac supplicationum gratiam vel iustitiam concernentium per Romanum Pontificem vel S. R. E. Vice-Cancellarios seu Gerentes vices corum aut ae mandato eiusdem Romani Pontificis signatarum: nec non falso publicantes Litteras Apostolicas, etiam in forma Brevis, et etiam falso signantes supplicationes huiusmodi sub nomine Romani Pontificis, seu Vice-Cancellarii aut Gerentis vices praedictorum.*"

unanimously understood it in the sense of intentional fraud. We can hardly imagine that any one would tamper with papal documents just for fun. But the *fabricatores,* as distinguished from falsifiers, need not have an evil intention. The crime is committed if a false document is made.[6] It is an outrage to public authority, especially since such a document may be passed on to others. Therefore, the penalty is incurred as soon as the document is completely manufactured. As to the *falsifiers,* a *dolus* or malicious purpose is certainly required, but it does not matter whether the effect intended is or is not produced.

3. Those who *knowingly use* (or rather abuse) such forged and falsified documents, are also mentioned. The word *uti,* to make use of or enjoy, may mean by exhibition or offer either to benefit oneself or another, although the intention may have been frustrated by discovery. But mere reading, although knowingly done, would certainly not constitute the act of " using."

4. The *documents* here intended are letters, decrees, or rescripts of the Apostolic See,[7] *i. e.,* documents emanating either from the Pope himself or from some department of the Roman Court.

5. The *penalty* for all fabricators and forgers of papal documents, and those who knowingly use them, is *excommunication incurred ipso facto and reserved modo speciali to the Apostolic See.*

Clerics, besides incurring this censure, *are to be punished otherwise, even with privation of benefice, office, dignity, and ecclesiastical pension. Religious* are to be punished with privation of all offices they hold in their institute (*including prelacies*) and of the active and

6 D'Annibale, *l. c.,* p. 53, n. 81.   7 See can. 7.

passive vote, besides other penalties established in their constitutions.

SUBREPTITIOUS AND OBREPTITIOUS RESCRIPTS

Can. 2361

Si quis in precibus ad rescriptum a Sede Apostolica vel a loci Ordinario impetrandum fraude vel dolo verum reticuerit aut falsum exposuerit, potest a suo Ordinario pro culpae gravitate puniri, salvo praescripto can. 45, 1054.

Those who fraudulently or deceitfully suppress the truth or state a falsehood in a petition for a rescript addressed to the Apostolic See or the local Ordinary, may be punished by the latter according to the grievousness of their guilt.

However, according to can. 45, *all rescripts are now valid,* even if some essential point has been suppressed, provided the final or motive cause has been truly stated. And rescripts for *matrimonial dispensations* are valid even if the motive or final cause has been misrepresented. Thus can. 1054.

The penalty is *optional* and may therefore be inflicted by the Ordinary according to can. 2223, § 2, or not, as he chooses. The *Ordinary* qualified to inflict the penalty is the one whose subject has obtained the rescript under false pretences; for *religious,* their immediate superior.

FORGERY OF OTHER ECCLESIASTICAL DOCUMENTS

Can. 2362

Litterarum vel actorum ecclesiasticorum tam publi-

corum quam privatorum fabricatores vel falsarii vel huiusmodi documentis scienter utentes, pro gravitate delicti coerceantur, firmo praescripto can. 2406, § 1.

Those who forge or falsify ecclesiastical letters or acts, either public or private, as well as those who knowingly make use of such spurious documents, shall be punished proportionately to the seriousness of their crime. Those who are charged with compiling, writing or keeping official acts shall, in case such acts are criminally tampered with, be punished according to can. 2406, § 1.

Can. 1813 defines the term *public ecclesiastical documents*. They are: acts of Ordinaries,— for instance appointments and regulations emanating from the diocesan chancery, instruments drawn up by an ecclesiastical notary, judiciary acts of every kind pertaining to ecclesiastical courts, the different parochial books, etc.

Private documents: private letters, contracts or deeds, or abstracts thereof, legacies and bequests, as far as they pertain to ecclesiastical persons as such, not as private persons.

The *penalty* is obligatory, but arbitrary and proportionate, inasmuch as it is left to the Ordinary (or superior of exempt religious), who must weigh the importance of the document, the condition of the delinquent, and the damage caused by the criminal act. Formerly the punishment was deposition, *i. e.*, reduction to the lay state, and perpetual penance in a monastery, for bishops as well as clerics of lower rank.[1]

---

[1] See c. 7, Dist. 50. Ecclesiastical corporations as well as individuals were guilty of such unqualified acts; see Bresslau, *l. c.*, p. 972 ff.

FALSE ACCUSATION OF SOLICITATION

Can. 2363

Si quis per seipsum vel per alios confessarium de sollicitationis crimine apud Superiores falso denuntiaverit, ipso facto incurrit in excommunicationem speciali modo Sedi Apostolicae reservatam, a qua nequit ullo in casu absolvi, nisi falsam denuntiationem formaliter retractaverit, et damna, si qua inde secuta sint, pro viribus reparaverit, imposita insuper gravi ac diuturna poenitentia, firmo praescripto can. 894.

One who either himself or through others *falsely accuses a confessor of the crime of solicitation to his superiors* —

1. Incurs *ipso facto* the *excommunication* reserved to the Apostolic See *modo speciali,*

2. From which he can *in no case be absolved,* unless

3. *He has formally retracted the* slanderous denunciation, and

4. Has *repaired,* as far as possible, the *damage* caused by his act.

Besides a grave and lasting penance must be imposed on him, and canon 894 be duly observed.

What solicitation is has been explained under can. 894. It is *provocatio ad turpia* in the act or under the species of sacramental confession.[1]

a) The *denunciation* must be made *judiciarily, i. e.,* either to the Holy Office or to the Ordinary, and must be effective,[2] *i. e.,* be accepted as a means of prosecution.

---

[1] See Vol. IV of our *Commentary,* p. 318 f.   [2] Hollweck, *l. c.,* p. 280, note 4.

The effect is assured when the summons is issued to the accused or to the witnesses.

A *false* denunciation is one based on (at least subjective) untruth. Falsity always supposes prevarication of the truth, done with malice *(dolus)*. However, it may happen that a penitent has misunderstood a question put to him by the confessor and construed it as a solicitation. In this case the malice or subjective untruth would be wanting. The confessor might be an innocent victim until the prosecution cleared up the mistake.

Denunciation may be made by the *penitent himself* for any motive, — hatred, anger, revenge, etc. — or *through others,* by means of impious advice, promises, flattery, threats, or even ambiguous insinuations.

b) The censure *can in no case* be absolved from unless the conditions mentioned are complied with; hence neither in the case of danger of death — which was excepted by Benedict XIV in the Constitution quoted below [3] — nor in the cases mentioned under can. 2254.[4] The condition next mentioned is

c) *Formal retraction,* which is to be made to the same authorities before whom the accusation was brought, and in a judiciary way. If this is impossible on account of the physical or mental condition of the culprit, the confessor may receive the retraction, absolve the penitent (immediately if required), and then report to the authorities.

The other condition of *repairing the damage* has *tractum temporis,* and therefore, in case of urgent necessity, a serious promise may be accepted.

The question may here be asked: Would the *ab-*

3 Bened. XIV, *"Sacramentum poenitentiae,"* June 1, 1741, § 3.
4 This seems to be implied by the term *nequit in ullo casu,* although not especially mentioned in can. 2254, § 3.

solution be valid if no formal retraction had been made? Provided the priest had the necessary faculty, or the circumstance was one mentioned in can. 2252 or 2254, we believe that the absolution would be valid. For the *nequit* can just as well be referred to illicit absolution, and therefore the minimum must be assumed. Besides, retraction and reparation certainly cannot be made at the moment of confession. Consequently, we would have to say that absolution would be valid only after the reparation was made, which would hardly be admitted by theologians. As to the *gravity* and *duration of the penance,* the general rules given by moralists may be consulted.[5]

A last remark, inspired by some magazine articles,[6] may be permitted. The sin mentioned here is reserved, not only by reason of the censure attached, but on its own account *(ratione sui)*, and it is the only one thus reserved. This is reservation pure and simple, or limitation of jurisdiction, which requires only the necessary matter and that the persons be subject to the power of jurisdiction. Since the sin as such is reserved, and is supposed to be complete in *genere suo*, it follows that a person by committing this sin is withdrawn from the jurisdiction of any one inferior to the Pope, and consequently neither ignorance nor doubt can excuse the delinquent.

Arregui (*Summarium Theol. Moralis,* 1919, ed. 4, n. 607, note 2, p. 388) insists on the wording of the "*Sacramentum Poenitentiae,*" which says, "*ut tam detestabile facinus metu magnitudinis poenae coerceatur.*" But does the *finis legis* fall under the law itself? The "*ut finale*" would indeed have weight if the context were not contradictory.

---

5 Hearing Mass, Litany of All Saints, five decades of the Rosary, are grave penances; Lehmkuhl, II, n. 357.

6 See *Eccl. Review,* Vol. 59, p. 458 ff.; Vol. 60, p. 61 ff.

Here we may add another observation provoked by some writers (see *Eccl. Review,* 1921, May, Sept., Nov.). The controversy concerns the extent to which the *" periculum gravis scandali vel infamiae"* may be stretched. Can. 2254, § 1, where this phrase occurs, has reference to a rather urgent case, *casus urgentior.* An objectively light reason would hardly be acknowledged as sufficient to absolve from censure. For the matter of censure is a serious one, and the confessor is therefore obliged in conscience not to make light of it. However, the confessor is judge and physician in the confessional and minister of God's justice and mercy (Can. 888, § 1). Therefore he is entitled to use his own judgment in the matter of absolution. He must consider the grievous faults and the serious penalty on the one hand, and the welfare of the penitent on the other. But the welfare of the individual must cede to the welfare of society. Hence, when the public weal would be jeopardized, human respect or the consideration of private benefit must give way. Therefore, when a notorious violation of a penal law is involved, we cannot convince ourselves of the permissibility of absolving for a light reason, such as devotional or even society communion would be. But when the transgression is not a notorious violation, and the public welfare not in danger, we do believe that any plausible reason which appears such to the confessor is sufficient.— The interpretation of *" quoquo modo,"* in can. 899, § 3, as if this could mean " for examples, *in synodo aut extra synodum,"* sounds to us very improbable. For can. 895 tells the Ordinary the conditions or methods he should observe in reserving cases; but this produces no effect on reservation itself. And the *" quoquo modo "* concerns the mode of reserving which is twofold: under sin only, or under censure.

TITLE XVI

UNLAWFUL ADMINISTRATION AND RECEPTION OF ORDERS AND OTHER SACRAMENTS

Two Sacraments are especially protected by penal sanctions: Penance and Orders. Extreme Unction is not mentioned, though formerly religious were forbidden under censure to administer it.[1] Four canons of this Title refer to the Sacrament of Penance, five canons to Orders, and one each to Confirmation and Matrimony. The first canon is devoted to the administration of the Sacraments in general.

ADMINISTRATION OF THE SACRAMENTS TO PERSONS FORBIDDEN BY LAW TO RECEIVE THEM

Can. 2364

Minister qui ausus fuerit Sacramenta administrare illis qui iure sive divino sive ecclesiastico eadem recipere prohibentur, suspendatur ab administrandis Sacramentis per tempus prudenti Ordinarii arbitrio definiendum aliisque poenis pro gravitate culpae puniatur, firmis peculiaribus poenis in aliqua huius generis delicta iure statutis.

Ministers who dare to administer the Sacraments to such as are forbidden to receive them by either divine or ecclesiastical law, should be suspended by the

[1] *"Apostolicae Sedis,"* II, 14.

428

Ordinary from administering the Sacraments, for a time to be determined by the same Ordinary according to his own judgment, and punished with *other penalties according to the gravity of the guilt.* Special penalties decreed for specified transgressions of this kind remain untouched.

The administration of a Sacrament is unlawful not only in case of *invalid,* but also of *illicit* reception, for the Code does not distinguish, but only states: *recipere prohibentur,* which may be applied to invalid as well as illicit administration.

The Code states that the prohibition may be dictated either by divine or by ecclesiastical law.

1. The *divine law* excludes

a) From *Baptism* those incapable of receiving it according to can. 745, § 1;

b) From the *other Sacraments* those *who are not baptized,*[2] as well as heretics and schismatics.[3] Note also can. 968, § 1, according to which only males can be validly ordained.

The *ecclesiastical law* excludes

a) From *any Sacrament* all those who are *excommunicated* and personally interdicted;[4]

b) From *Baptism* the children of non-baptized parents, and of heretics and schismatics; adults against their own will and *amentes;*[5]

c) From *holy Communion* public *indigni* and those who unlawfully break the natural fast;[6]

d) From *Extreme Unction* those who, being of the age of reason, are not sick, according to can. 940;

e) From *Orders* those who are irregular or subject to a simple canonical impediment.[7]

---

2 See can. 786; 853; 901; 940; 968; 1012, § 2.
3 See can. 731, § 2.
4 Can. 2260, § 1; 2275, n. 2.

5 Can. 750-752, 754.
6 Can. 855, § 1; can. 858.
7 Can. 984, 985, 987.

As to marriage, observe that the priest merely assists at, but does not administer, the Sacrament of Matrimony, and that, therefore, can. 2364 cannot be applied in this case.

The penalty is both *vindictive* and *preceptive,* and accompanied by irregularity if any act of the power of orders is exercised.[8] The text states: *firmis peculiaribus poenis, etc.* The act of unlawful administration may, besides, have a special penalty attached, by reason of a special circumstance, as in regard to can. 2338, § 3, admitting excommunicated, interdicted, or suspended persons to the reception of the Sacraments.[9] Attention is also drawn to the term, *ausus fuerit,* which must be understood in the light of can. 2229, § 1-2.

CONFIRMATION ADMINISTERED BY A PRIEST

Can. 2365

Presbyter qui nec a iure nec ex Romani Pontificis concessione facultatem habens sacramentum confirmationis ministrare ausus fuerit, suspendatur; si vero facultatis sibi factae limites praetergredi praesumpserit, eadem facultate eo ipso privatus exsistat.

A priest who, though he is empowered neither by law nor by Apostolic faculty to administer Confirmation, yet dares to administer this Sacrament, must be suspended. If he presumes to overstep the limits of a faculty which he actually possesses, *let him be deprived of this faculty ipso iure.*

1. Priests empowered by *law* to administer Confirmation

8 Can. 985, n. 7; 2223; 2298, n. 2.   Eichmann, *l. c.,* p. 198.
9 See also can. 2370, 2373, 2375;

are all cardinals, abbots *nullius*, and prelates *nullius*, vicars and prefects Apostolic.[1]

2. Priests empowered to confirm by an *Apostolic privilege or faculty*, are those who have obtained this privilege by papal delegation or subdelegation, as stated elsewhere.[2]

If any priest not empowered by law or by a papal faculty should dare (*ausus fuerit*)[3] to administer Confirmation, he is to be suspended either by his Ordinary or by higher authority. The suspension here worded in general terms must be taken as a *general suspension*.[4] Besides, if those endowed with the power of administering Confirmation should dare to exceed the territorial or personal limits assigned to them, or to extend it beyond the duration of their office or of the term granted in the indult, they *lose* the power or faculty.

HEARING CONFESSIONS AND GIVING ABSOLUTION FROM RESERVED SINS WITHOUT JURISDICTION

Can. 2366

Sacerdos qui sine necessaria iurisdictione praesumpserit sacramentales confessiones audire, est ipso facto suspensus a divinis; qui vero a peccatis reservatis absolvere, ipso facto suspensus est ab audiendis confessionibus.

This canon mentions two distinct transgressions:

I. A *priest who dares to hear sacramental confessions*

---

1 See can. 782, § 3; it is supposed that these dignitaries have not received episcopal consecration.

2 See Vol. IV of this *Commentary*, p. 102 f.

3 See can. 2229, § 2.

4 See can. 2278, § 2; see can. 782, § 3, 4, 5: formerly an Oriental or a Ruthenian priest confirming a Latin child was *ipso facto* suspended; S. C. P. F., Oct. 6, 1863 (*Coll.*, n. 1243).

*without the necessary jurisdiction, is ipso facto sus-
pended a divinis.*

1. The culprit is supposed to be a validly ordained
priest, not a layman or cleric who has not yet received
the priesthood. Of the latter can. 2322, n. 1, treats
under crimes against religion.

2. The priest may be either *secular* or *religious,* and
it matters not what kind of a privilege he may have obtained, provided he hears sacramental confession without being endowed with the necessary (ordinary or delegated) jurisdiction.[1]

3. Concerning *exempt religious,* if they wish to
hear confessions of lay persons or of Sisters with
either solemn or simple vows, they need a special faculty
or jurisdiction from the local Ordinary in whose diocese
the confessions are to be heard.[2]

4. This faculty now required according to can. 879,
§ 1, must be granted *expressly,* either in writing or
orally.

5. The act must concern *sacramental confession* according to can. 2322, n. 1. A confession is sacramental also if it involves only venial sins, and hence
a *simplex sacerdos* without jurisdiction or faculties can
not hear confessions the matter of which are only venial
sins.[3] If the confession was sacramental, it matters not
whether absolution was given or not, because the text
simply says: *to hear* sacramental confessions. The
same term also occurs in the papal constitutions quoted
below.

---

1 See can. 872, 873, 874, 878, § 1.
2 *Ibid.;* also Innocent X, *"Cum
sicut,"* May 14, 1648, § 3, 4, I, ad
10 (*Bull. Luxemb.,* 1727, t. V,
458 f.). Even the privileges of the
Cruciata are of no avail; Bened.

XIV, *"Apostolica indulta,"* Aug. 5,
1744, §§ 3, 5.
3 It may appear strange to state
this explicitly, but the S. C. C., Feb.
12, 1679 (*Coll. P. F.,* n. 219) had
occasion to emphasize it.

6. The *penalty* is suspension *a divinis* incurred *ipso facto* according to can. 2279, § 2, n. 2. However, note the term *praesumpserit*, which presupposes that the act was done with full knowledge and deliberation (can. 2229). It might easily happen that a pastor or priest would think that he could hear the confessions of female religious in virtue of his general faculties. If under such an impression he did so, he would not incur the censure. Neither would he incur this penalty if he were in doubt (can. 209), and much less if he would hear the confession of a person in danger of death (can. 882).

II. *Priests who dare to absolve from reserved sins are ipso facto suspended from hearing confessions.*

1. What was said above I, 1-4 also applies here.

2. This case supposes that *absolution* was "attempted," *i. e.*, pronounced by a priest who, though perhaps possessed of ordinary faculties, did not have the special faculty required for absolving from reserved sins.

3. The *reservation* concerns sins, not censures, these being mentioned under can. 2338, § 1, as a usurpation of authority. To this class, therefore, belong the case mentioned in can. 894 (false accusation of an innocent confessor), and those cases which the local Ordinary may, according to can. 895, reserve to himself. From the latter cases, however, any confessor may absolve according to can. 900. Can. 882 mentions a lawful excuse from incurring the censure.

If superiors of exempt clerical religious have reserved cases to themselves, according to can. 986, their subjects would incur the censure if they absolved from these cases without possessing any other faculty than that granted by their superior. However, if they possess faculties from the local Ordinary, and absolve from sins reserved in their institute, they do not incur the penalty. Neither would secular priests absolving religious from sins reserved in their order incur the penalty, according to can. 519. But confessors, secular or religious, who would absolve female religious from sins reserved by the local Ordinary would incur the penalty, and could be removed from office.[4]

ABSOLUTIO COMPLICIS

Can. 2367

§ 1. Absolvens vel fingens absolvere complicem in peccato turpi incurrit ipso facto in excommunicationem specialissimo modo Sedi Apostolicae reservatam; idque etiam in mortis articulo, si alius sacerdos, licet non approbatus ad confessiones, sine gravi aliqua exoritura infamia et scandalo, possit excipere morientis confessionem, excepto casu quo moribundus recuset alii confiteri.

§ 2. Eandem excommunicationem non effugit absolvens vel fingens absolvere complicem qui peccatum quidem complicitatis, a quo nondum est absolutus, non confitetur, sed ideo ita se gerit, quia ad id a complice confessario sive directe sive indirecte inductus est.

Those who *absolve, or feign to absolve, an accomplice in peccato turpi, ipso facto incur the excommunication reserved modo specialissimo to the Apostolic* See.

To what was said on this subject elsewhere[1] only a few remarks need be added:

---

4 S. C. EE. et RR., Sept. 3, 1746 (Bizzarri, *Collectanea*, p. 365).

1 See this Commentary, Vol. IV, p. 291 ff. Hearing (voluntarily and knowingly) the confession of an accomplice is forbidden by the natural law on account of the danger of temptation; D'Annibale, *l. c.*, p. 55, n. 85.

1. The act forbidden under censure and declared invalid by can. 884 is absolution, not merely hearing confession. Therefore, any manifest refusal to absolve ("I am not in a condition to absolve you," etc.) would be sufficient to ward off the censure.

2. *Feigning to absolve* would not render one immune from the penalty. To feign or simulate *(fingere)* is to make an act or thing appear real or true when it is not so. To absolve fictitiously, therefore, would be to act as if absolution were given and thus lead the penitent to consider himself absolved. Thus giving a penance and making the sign of the cross, or even omitting the penance and giving the blessing in a way which the penitent could construe as an absolution, would be simulation or fictitious absolution, provided there were a *dolus* on the part of the confessor.[2]

3. § 2 of can. 2367 states explicitly that *the censure is incurred even if the confessor absolves an accomplice who does not confess the sin of complicity from which he was not yet absolved, but conceals that sin, because he was induced by the confessor not to confess it either directly or indirectly.*

This text is taken verbally from a decision of the S. Poenitentiaria,[3] which also explains the terms *directly* and *indirectly.*

A confessor would induce an accomplice *directly* if he would previously tell him or her not to mention the sin of complicity, because he already knows of it or because its manifestation would be useless. He would induce the accomplice *indirectly* if he would persuade him or her that the *turpis actus* is no sin or not grievous enough

---

[2] Thus Eichmann, *l. c.,* p. 201; but the *dolus* is presumed, according to can. 2200, § 2.

[3] Feb. 19, 1896 (*Coll. P. F.,* n. 1916).

to scruple about, thus leading the penitent to conclude
that the sin of complicity need not be mentioned and
causing him not to mention it. It can no longer be
taught, therefore, as was the case before the promulgation of the Code, that simulating absolution would
render the confessor immune from censure.[4] For, as
the above-quoted decision of the S. Poenitentiaria clearly
states, such an admission would render the censure
almost illusory.

4. From the same decision,[5] as well as from our text
itself, we may indirectly deduce that if the sin of complicity had been properly and lawfully absolved by another confessor, the censure would not be incurred by the
guilty priest, even though the accomplice would mention
it to him in the confessional.[6]

5. The complicity must concern a *peccatum turpe*,
i. e., contra sextum, which amounts to a grievous sin.[7]
Besides, since complicity here refers to the act of absolution, it is evident that, if the confessor does not recognize the penitent as his accomplice *in peccato turpi*,
he may lawfully and validly absolve him. The same is
true in case of a positive and well-founded doubt about
the identity of the person.[8]

6. As to the *case of necessity,* can. 2254 must be consulted. But this very canon refers to our canon 2367,
which, in § 1, determines the *mortis articulus* as follows:
In point of death, i. e., when the danger of death is real

---

4 S. O., Dec. 5, 1883 (*Coll. cit.*, n.
1608).

5 S. Poenit, *l. c.*

6 D'Annibale, *l. c.*, p. 57, n. 87.

7 D'Annibale, *l. c.*, p. 54, n. 84:
" *Ut peccatum adsit ultro citroque,
ac ultro citroque grave in ipso opere
externo.*"—S. O., May 28, 1873:
" *Comprehendi nedum tactus, verum*
*omnia peccata gravia et exterius
commissa contra castitatem, etiam illa
quae consistunt in meris colloquiis
et aspectibus, quae complicitatem important* "; Hollweck, *l. c.*, 330, note
5.

8 D'Annibale, *l. c.*, p. 56, n. 86;
Hollweck, *ib.*, note 2.

and certain, *provided no other priest, whether endowed with jurisdiction for hearing confessions or not, can be called without serious infamy or scandal.* If another priest is available, he must be called, under penalty of censure, *unless the dying person should refuse to confess to another priest.*[9]

7. Concerning *ignorance* it has been declared that neither *ignorantia crassa* nor *supina*, much less, of course, *affectata*, excuses from censure.[10] Absolution from *occult* cases of this kind is not included in the power granted to the Ordinaries by the Code.[11]

8. Finally, it may be observed that members of the *Oriental rites* are also subject to this censure.[12]

SOLLICITATIO

Can. 2368

§ 1. Qui sollicitationis crimen de quo in can. 904, commiserit, supendatur a celebratione Missae et ab audiendis sacramentalibus confessionibus vel etiam pro delicti gravitate inhabilis ad ipsas excipiendas declaretur, privetur omnibus beneficiis, dignitatibus, voce activa et passiva, et inhabilis ad ea omnia declaretur, et in casibus gravioribus degradationi quoque subiiciatur.

§ 2. Fidelis vero, qui scienter omiserit eum, a quo sollicitatus fuerit, intra mensem denuntiare contra praescriptum can. 904, incurrit in excommunicationem latae sententiae nemini reservatam, non absolvendus

9 See Vol. IV of our Commentary, p. 292.

10 S. O., Jan. 13, 1892 ad 3 (*Coll. P. F.*, n. 1777); see can. 2229.

11 See can. 2237, § 2; S. O., Sept. 13, 1859, ad 2-3 (*Coll. cit.*, n. 1181).

12 S. C. P. F., Aug. 5, 1885 (*ib.*, n. 1640).

nisi postquam obligationi satisfecerit aut se satis-
facturum serio promiserit.

1. What *solicitation means* has been explained under
can. 894 and 904. The earliest document referring to
this crime is the Constitution of Pius IV, "*Cum sicut
nuper,*" of April 16, 1561, which was directly intended
for Spain. The Constitution of Gregory XV, "*Uni-
versi,*" of Aug. 30, 1622, had a general bearing, and is
more explicit as to the nature and extent of solicitation.
The source *par excellence* of our Code is the Constitution
of Benedict XIV, "*Sacramentum poenitentiae,*" of
June 1, 1741.

That feigned confession is also intended seems to
follow from the term *praetextus,* which indicates a
simulated act committed in order to accomplish the evil
intention more freely.[1]

2. The Code says *that those guilty of the crime of*

---

[1] Cfr. Thesaurus-Giraldi, *l. c.,* P. II, p. 413 f. The words of the constitution of Bened. XIV: "*vel etiam extra occasionem confessionis in confessionali,*" seem to indicate that simulation is included; see also Holl-weck, *l. c.,* p. 328, note 5. However, D'Annibale, *l. c.,* p. 117, n. 181 makes some noteworthy restrictions concerning simulation, which we will quote verbatim: "*Simula-tione confessionis, reus sollicitationis intelligitur, qui dum fingit confes-sionem audire, provocat ad turpia. Verum ut videatur simulare confes-sionem, opus est ut specie tenus, qua alii decipiantur, confessio agi videatur. Proinde necesse est, ut stet vel in confessionario, vel in loco destinato, aut electo ad audiendas confessiones; utque nedum in hoc, et in isto, quod nemo dubitat, sed in*

illo fingat se confessionem audire. Praetextu, qui v. c. aliquem ad con-fessionem invitat, ut provocet ad turpia, licet ad veram confessionem invitet: praetextus enim est quod intentionem obtegit facto aliquo seu apparenti, seu vero. Quocirca sol-licitatio cessat, si non ipse, sed poen-itens confessionem praetexuit; vel ipse quidem, sed ut alium, (non poenitentem) deciperet; vel uterque ex condicto ut alios fallerent. Verum si is cubiculum aegrotantis in-gressus, rogatu ipsius adstantes re-cesserint, et remanserit solus cum sola quasi confessionem excepturus, nonne videtur eam sollicitare simula-tione confessionis? Minime, quippe non sollicitat occasione confessionis, sed turpiter agit." (St. Alph., VI, 679).

solicitation, according to can. 904, (a) *are to be suspended from saying Mass and hearing confessions or
declared incapable of hearing sacramental confession,*
according to the grievousness of the crime; (b) *Should
also be deprived of all benefices and dignities and of
the active and passive vote, and be declared incapable of*
holding or exercising both; (c) *In more serious cases
they should be subjected to degradation.*

3. All these penalties are *ferendae sententiae,* and
therefore require a procedure in conformity with the
instructions alleged elsewhere.[2] According to the Constitution quoted above, the inquisitors and local Ordinaries are the guardians and executors of criminal procedure and sentence in cases of solicitation. The Constitutions except no *dignitary* from these penalties.
Cardinals, however, are clearly exempt under can. 2227,
§ 2. But to exempt *bishops* from them on the plea that
inquisitors would be incompetent to proceed against them
and for the reason that they are not wont to hear confessions,[3] is more than we can understand. For the Holy
Office can always be approached, and the Pontiff in
person could take cognizance of such a case, according
to can. 1557, § 1, n. 3. The other plea, that bishops are
not accustomed to hear confessions, has no foundation
in our country, where many a bishop takes his regular
turn in the confessional in the cathedral and elsewhere.

Degradation, according to the Constitution of Gregory
XV, was to be decreed only for *enormous* crimes of
solicitation, and after being degraded, the culprits were
to be handed over to the secular power.

[2] See Vol. IV of this Commentary, p. 343 ff.; S. O., March 18,
1863 (*Coll. P. F.,* n. 1237).

[3] Thus some authors quoted by
Hollweck, *l. c.,* p. 327 note 2, who,
however, with Berardi, leans to
the opinion stated above. Besides,
can. 2227, § 2, does not exempt
bishops from these penalties.

§ *2 of can. 2368* imposes the strict *obligation on every
person solicited by a confessor to denounce the latter.
Whoever knowingly omits such denunciation for a month,*
as prescribed by can. 904, *incurs excommunication latae
sententiae, reserved to no one, from which, however, he
cannot be absolved unless he has complied with, or
seriously promised to satisfy, his obligation.*

The duty of denouncing clearly binds whenever the
following circumstances [4] concur:

1. The person to be denounced must be a *priest;* he
may be of any rank or dignity, cardinals and, possibly,[5]
bishops, excepted.

2. The *solicitation* must be *ad inhonesta et turpia,
sive verbis, sive signis, sive nutibus, sive tactu, sive per
scripturam, tunc aut postea legendam, i. e.,* a mutual,
grievous, external sin against the sixth commandment,
committed with a person of the same or the other sex,
whether solicited for himself (the confessor) or for
another person; whether the solicited person consented
or not.[6]

3. The solicitation must, in one way or another, concern *confession,* either as occasion or pretext, either in
a place properly destined for confession or at least connected with the act of confession, — immediately before or immediately after. It is, however, immaterial
whether the penitent understood the solicitation at once
or only afterwards. But there can be no obligation of
denouncing the confessor if the solicitation was not
certain.[7] How long a time may intervene between the

---

[4] "*Sacramentum Poenitentiae*";
Thesaurus-Giraldi, *l. c.*, p. 413 f.;
D'Annibale, *l. c.*, p. 114 f., n. 179.
[5] Because of the controversy
stated above; besides there is another reason which renders the case

somewhat unlike, *vis.:* shyness in
denouncing a bishop.
[6] In the procedure the person
must not be asked whether he or
she consented to the solicitation.
[7] D'Annibale, *l. c.*, n. 182.

solicitation and the cessation of the obligation to denounce the culprit, is not definitely stated.[8]

4. As to *difficulties* arising from circumstances of time and person, especially in the case of women, it must be said that as long as such circumstances prevail, they are not obliged to denounce the culprit.[9]

5. The *time when the censure is incurred* is after one month, to be reckoned from the moment the penitent knew or became aware of his or her obligation and of the censure attached to the omission. Those who seriously promise to make denunciation — an oath is not required — may be absolved from the censure even after a month has elapsed.[10]

VIOLATION OF THE SEAL OF CONFESSION

Can. 2369

§ 1. Cofessarium, qui sigillum sacramentale directe violare praesumpserit, manet excommunicatio specialissimo modo Sedi Apostolicae reservata; qui vero indirecte tantum, obnoxius est poenis, de quibus in can. 2368, § 1.

§ 2. Quicunque praescriptum can. 889, § 2 temere violaverit, pro reatus gravitate plectatur salutari poena, quae potest esse etiam excommunicatio.

There are two ways of breaking the seal of confession, as described in the fourth volume of this Commentary.[1]

---

8 The "*Sacramentum Poenitentiae*" merely says: "*nec post longum tempus*," and hence triennial prescription is not admitted; Thesaurus-Giraldi, *l. c.*, p. 415; also can. 1703 excludes from prescription cases to be brought before the Holy office.

9 See Vol. IV of this *Commentary*, p. 342.

10 D'Annibale, *l. c.*, p. 119, n. 183.

1 Page 302; but the *or* in line 5 from above should be changed into *and*; for different cases see the moralists, especially Ballerini-Palmieri.

Violation is *direct* if, together with the matter confessed, the name of the penitent is revealed, either explicitly or by a description which reveals his identity. It is *indirect* if, from the confessor's way of acting or speaking there is danger that the sin of the penitent and his identity become known, thus rendering confession hateful.

Can. 889, § 2, obliges also interpreters and *all others* who may in any way have acquired knowledge of confession, to keep the seal.

1. A confessor, says our canon (§ 1), *who dares to break the seal of confession directly, remains under excommunication reserved modo specialissimo to the Apostolic See.*

a) The term *confessor* implies a *priest*[2]; as to others who are not priests, whether laymen or clerics, consult can. 2322. But whether the term supposes jurisdiction is not quite certain. Can. 2366 punishes such priests with suspension *a divinis*. Could it be a sacramental confession if made to a priest bereft of jurisdiction? To make such a confession, an accusation of sins in order to obtain absolution is required. On the other hand, the seal of confession was instituted in favor of the penitent and the Sacrament. From this we should conclude that even a priest destitute of jurisdiction would fall under this censure. Yet we candidly confess that the opposite view is just as probable. For the text, by employing the term *confessor*, supposes a priest having jurisdiction, — at least, as we say, general faculties. Besides, since this is a most grievous penalty, it should not be extended to any one not comprised under the name of confessor.

mieri, *l. c.*, Vol. V, p. 485 ff.; nn.   2 See Schmalzgrueber, V, 38, n.
899 ff.   80.

b) The text furthermore says, *sigillum sacramentale*, which naturally presupposes a sacramental accusation. Therefore a fictitious or jocose confession would not induce the obligation of keeping the seal, nor entail censure. Whether a sacramental confession is intended must be judged from the words or acts which surround the deed. However the mere lack of intention of absolving the penitent would not be sufficient to excuse the confessor from the obligation of keeping the seal, though if he were to say: " I don't wish to hear your confession," this would render the accusation non-sacramental, and no obligation would arise to keep the seal.[3] The general rule, therefore, may be stated thus: *The censure is incurred whenever the obligation of keeping the sacramental seal is violated.*

c) But there is a condition to be added, namely, *unless the penitent himself* — none other, not even the Pope, can do so — *has given permission to reveal something out of confession.* This permission would have to be given expressly and freely.[4]

Note that the revelation of something else than the matter of confession would not constitute a violation of the seal. Besides, most authors say that a revelation of merely venial sins, confessed in a general way, though by a definite person, would not constitute a serious violation of the seal involving censure.[5]

d) The penalty is excommunication *latae sententiae* reserved *modo specialissimo* to the Apostolic See, provided *presumption* is verified. Therefore inadvertency or

3 Schmalzgrueber, V, 38, n. 80; Ballerini-Palmieri, *l. c.*, V, p. 490 f.; n. 909 f.

4 Schmalzgrueber, *l. c.*, n. 62;

Hollweck, *l. c.*, p. 276, note 5.

5 Ballerini-Palmieri, *l. c.*, V, p. 499 ff.; n. 924 ff.

indeliberate revelation would not induce the penalty, which formerly was deposition and perpetual banishment of the culprit to a monastery.[6]

2. Those who *violate the seal of confession indirectly* are liable to the same penalties as those who are guilty of solicitation (see can. 2368, § 1) *ferendae sententiae.*

3. Those mentioned above and in can. 889, § 2, namely, interpreters and bystanders, who rashly *(temere) violate the seal of confession, are to be punished with wholesome penalties,* according to the seriousness of the crime, excommunication not excluded.

The following five canons treat of Orders; and the first of episcopal consecration, for which a papal mandate is required, as stated elsewhere.[1]

EPISCOPAL CONSECRATION WITHOUT AN APOSTOLIC MANDATE

Can. 2370

Episcopus aliquem consecrans in Episcopum, Episcopi vel, loco Episcoporum, presbyteri assistentes, et qui consecrationem recipit sine apostolico mandato contra praescriptum can. 953, ipso iure suspensi sunt, donec Sedes Apostolica eos dispensaverit.

A bishop who consecrates another, and the assistant bishops or the priests taking their place, as well as the one who receives episcopal consecration without having obtained an Apostolic mandate, are suspended *ipso iure* until the Holy See has granted a dispensation. This is a general suspension, but has the character of a vin-

---

6 See c. 2, Dist. 6, *de Poenit.;* e. 12, X, V, 38.

1 See Vol. IV of this Commentary, p. 414 f.; can. 953.

dictive penalty.[2]   An example of its effective application may be seen in a papal constitution of historical importance.[3]

SIMONIACAL ADMINISTRATION AND RECEPTION OF ORDERS AND SACRAMENTS

Can. 2371

Omnes, etiam episcopali dignitate aucti, qui per simoniam ad ordines scienter promoverint vel promoti fuerint aut alia Sacramenta ministraverint vel receperint, sunt suspecti de haeresi; clerici praeterea suspensionem incurrunt Sedi Apostolicae reservatam.

Simony is clearly defined in the Code itself, as explained elsewhere.[4]   Not only real simony, but also conventional simony, which requires no fulfillment of the simoniacal contract, is punishable, the only supposition being that a simoniacal agreement existed.   Suspicion of heresy is founded on can. 727, § 1.

1. *Those,* then, *who have knowingly ordained any one, as well as those who have been ordained through simony, are suspect of heresy,* and must consequently be treated according to can. 2315.

Note that by *ordo* is also understood the first tonsure, as per can. 950 and the Council of Trent.[5]   However, the act must be complete, *i. e.,* the order must have been

---

[2] See can. 2278, § 2; can. 2298, n. 2; 2227, § 2; 2236, § 1: "*dispensaverit.*"

[3] Pius VI, "*Charitas,*" April 13, 1791, § 15: the civil constitution of the French Clergy; three bishops had consecrated another without an Apostolic mandate, nay without as

much as consulting the local ordinary.

[4] Vol. IV of this Commentary, pp. 5 ff.

[5] Sess. 21, c. 1, *de ref.;* the oldest source is c. 8, C. 1, q. 1, taken from the Council of Chalcedon; see also c. 1. X. V. 3.

conferred before the penalty is incurred, even though the price agreed upon was not paid and perhaps never will be paid, provided only an agreement was made. Then, the act of simony must have been committed knowingly *(scienter)* as per can. 2229, § 2. If it was committed by a third person with the ordaining minister, but the one ordained knew nothing of it, he would not fall under this canon, even if simony was committed according to can. 727.

2. *Suspected of heresy are also those, bishops not excepted, who administer or receive other Sacraments simoniacally,* supposing always that an agreement to that effect has been entered into.

Purely mental simony, though it may be grievous, is not intended by the Code. Thus it may happen that one administers the Sacraments merely for the sake of the stole fee; but as long as he does not make a formal agreement or utter his intention in an unmistakable way, with the other's consent, no simony in the sense of the law is committed.

Bishops too, we said, are included; for the position of the clause at the beginning doubtless comprises them.

Is the *scienter* placed between *ordines* and *promoverint* to be supplied in the *ministraverint?* We hardly think so, because the position of the word makes it appear to have reference only to orders. The reason probably is because Orders are intended chiefly for the public good and the welfare of society at large, and therefore the legislator wished to spare prelates unnecessary scruples.[6] The other Sacraments are more or less of a

---

[6] Clement VIII, "*Romanum Pontificem decet,*" Feb. 28, 1595 (*Bull. Luxemburg.*, III, 60): "*ab ordinum collatione deterreri,*" on account of scruples and the fear of the severe penalties threatened by Sixtus V, "*Sanctum et salutare,*" Jan. 5, 1589, § 6, § 2 (*Bull. cit.*, II, 711 f).

private character and, therefore, left to the uprightness of individuals.

3. Clerics offending against this canon also incur *suspension reserved to the Apostolic See*. Are bishops included in this clause. Some deny,[7] others assert it,[8] There seems to be little doubt that they are. Can. 2227, § 2, cannot be quoted against this view, as bishops are especially mentioned at the very beginning of this canon, and, moreover, the Council of Trent subjected bishops to all the penalties inflicted by law,[9] and the papal constitutions subjected them to the censure here mentioned.[10] Lastly, it must be remembered that bishops are the ministers of orders. There would be no justice, since simony requires an accomplice, if the greater culprit were less punishable than the simple cleric. The bishops, therefore, according to our view, are also subject to this suspension, which is a general one (can. 2278, § 2).

RECEPTION OF ORDERS FROM CENSURED ECCLESIASTICS

Can. 2372

Suspensionem a divinis, Sedi Apostolicae reservatam, ipso facto contrahunt, qui recipere ordines praesumunt ab excommunicato vel suspenso vel interdicto post sententiam declaratoriam vel condemnatoriam, aut a notorio apostata, haeretico, schismatico; qui vero bona fide a quopiam eorum sit ordinatus, exercitio careat ordinis sic recepti donec dispensetur.

---

7 Thus Ayrinhac, *l. c.*, p. 331, without giving a reason.

8 Thus Eichmann, *l. c.*, p. 207.

9 See cc. 6, 8, 101, 107, 113, C. 1.

q. 1; c. 4, C. 2, q. 5; cc. 4, 5, 11, 13, X, V, 3.

10 Clement VIII *(l. c.,)* modified the Constitution of Sixtus V, but left the censure.

The older sources of this canon seem to be conflicting. Some insinuate that the order received from bishops mentioned in the text was invalid,[1] whilst the majority clearly state that it was valid, though illicit.[2] Yet even the former may be explained of the exercise of orders.[3] Our text is taken in a somewhat modified form from the "*Apostolicae Sedis*."[4]

1. *Those who dare to receive Orders from an excommunicated, suspended, or interdicted minister, provided he has been declared such or condemned to one of the three afore-mentioned penalties,* or *from a notorious apostate,* a notorious *heretic,* or a notorious *schismatic, ipso facto incur suspension a divinis, reserved to the Apostolic See.*

That *orders* includes episcopal consecration, seems to us evident from can. 950, even though the majority of authors[5] does not maintain this view.

The penalties must have been *declared,* or must have been incurred by a *condemnatory* sentence. Formerly a nominal or personal denunciation was required. *Notoriety* of fact is here intended (can. 2197, n. 3), not of law, the latter not being required, as per can. 2314, unless a declaratory sentence should be necessary in virtue of can. 2223, § 4. But the term *praesumunt* also requires full knowledge of the fact that the ordaining minister was under censure, or had been condemned,

1 C. 33, C. 24, q. 1; cc. 41, 73, III, C. 1, q. 1; c. 24, C. 1, q. 7.

2 C. 8, Dist. 19; cc. 24, 25, C. 1, q. 7; c. 2, X, V, 8; this latter settles the former controversy.

3 Kober, *Die Suspension,* p. 189; Hollweck, p. 295, note 1; D'Annibale, *l. c.,* p. 129, n. 205.

4 § V, 6: "*Suspensionem ab ordine suscepto ipso iure incurrunt, qui eundem ordinem recipere praesumpserunt ab excommunicato vel suspenso, vel interdicto, nominatim denuntiato, aut haeretico vel schismatico notorio: eum vero qui bona fide a quopiam eorum est ordinatus, exercitium non habere ordinis sic suscepti, donec dispensetur, declaramus.*"

5 Hollweck, *l. c.,* p. 295, note 3.

or that he is a notorious apostate, heretic, or schismatic.[6]

Besides, it is generally held that the order must have been received *validly,* and therefore the penalty would not follow if, for instance, a Protestant bishop would confer an order.[7] The penalty is *suspension a divinis* (can. 2279, § 2, n. 2), excluding the exercise of any act of the power of orders.

2. *Those who have been bona fide ordained by one of the above-named persons* forbidden by law to administer orders, *may not exercise the orders thus received, until they are dispensed.* This dispensation can be given by the Ordinary to whom the *ordinatus* is subject.[8] It is a vindictive penalty, but irregularity would follow unlawful exercise of the Order thus received.[9]

ILLEGAL ORDINATION

Can. 2373

In suspensionem per annum ab ordinum collatione Sedi Apostolicae reservatam ipso facto incurrunt;

1°. Qui contra praescriptum can. 955, alienum subditum sine Ordinarii proprii litteris dimissoriis ordinaverint;

2°. Qui subditum proprium, qui alibi tanto tempore moratus sit ut canonicum impedimentum contrahere ibi potuerit, ordinaverint contra praescriptum can. 993, n. 4, 994;

3°. Qui aliquem ad ordines maiores sine titulo ca-

---

6 Mere hearsay or knowledge received from unofficial sources is not sufficient.

. 7 D'Annibale, *l. c.,* p. 206.

8 *Ibid.* and Hollweck, *l. c.,* p. 296, note 7; cc. 1, 2, X, I, 13.

9 Can. 985, n. 7.

nonico promoverint contra praescriptum can. 974, § 1, n. 7;

4°. Qui, salvo legitimo privilegio, religiosum, ad familiam pertinentem quae sit extra territorium ipsius ordinantis, promoverint, etiam cum litteris dimissorialibus proprii Superioris, nisi legitime probatum fuerit aliquem e casibus occurrere, de quibus in can. 966.

This canon furnishes the proper sanction of the laws laid down concerning the *episcopus proprius* (n. 1-2), the canonical title (n. 3), and the competent Ordinary with regard to religious. We may be permitted to refer the reader to the canons mentioned.

Suspension from conferring orders for one year, to be reckoned from the date of ordination and *reserved to the Apostolic See, is ipso facto incurred*

1. By those who ordain a *subject of another Ordinary* without *dimissorial letters* from that Ordinary, as per can. 955;

2. By those who ordain *one of their own subjects,* but without testimonials from the Ordinaries in whose dioceses the ordinand has lived long enough to contract a canonical impediment, as prescribed by can. 993, n. 4, and can. 994;

3. By those who confer *major orders* without a canonical title, as per can. 974, § 1, n. 7 (see also can. 980, § 2, 3);

4. By those who *ordain a religious* who belongs to a religious family located outside of the ordaining minister's territory, even though the aforesaid religious have dimissorial letters from his own superior; unless the certificate of the episcopal chancery proves that the case was one admitted by can. 966 or the exempt religious

order has obtained a *privilege* permitting it to have its subjects ordained by any bishop.

ILLEGAL RECEPTION OF ORDERS

Can. 2374

Qui sine litteris vel cum falsis dimissoriis litteris, vel ante canonicam aetatem, vel per saltum ad ordines malitiose accesserit, est ipso facto a recepto ordine suspensus; qui autem sine litteris testimonialibus vel detentus aliqua censura, irregularitate aliove impedimento, gravibus poenis secundum rerum adiuncta puniatur.

1. *Ipso facto suspended from the exercise of an order (illegally)* [1] *received are those who maliciously present* [2] *themselves for Ordination*

a) *Without any dimissorial or with false dimissorial* letters (see can. 958). The term *false* letters includes such as are forged, and consequently can. 2362 applies here. But the term also means letters issued by incompetent authorities (can. 958). Thus the vicar-general needs a special commission and the vicar capitular or administrator can issue them only after a year of vacancy;

b) *Without having reached the canonical age,* as per can. 975, or not being duly dispensed from this impediment;

c) Without observing the order prescribed by can. 977 (ordinations *per saltum*).

---

1 The other orders, which the cleric has received properly, he may exercise; see *Trid.,* Sess. 6, c. 5, *de ref.;* Hollweck, *l. c.,* p. 297, n. 4.

2 *Accedere* means *to approach,*

and could therefore be construed as if the penalty were incurred, even though ordination did not actually follow; however, the text refers to *orders actually received.*

2. Those who maliciously present themselves for ordination *are to be punished grievously,* according to the circumstances of each case.

a) This class includes those who have not the required testimonials (see can. 993-1001), or

b) who are *under censure,* be it excommunication, or interdict, or suspension, or who are bound by an *irregularity* of defect or crime (can. 984, 985), or by a canonical impediment (can. 987).

UNLAWFUL MIXED MARRIAGES

Can. 2375

Catholici qui matrimonium mixtum, etsi validum, sine Ecclesiae dispensatione inire ausi fuerint, ipso facto ab actibus legitimis ecclesiasticis et Sacramentalibus exclusi manent, donec ab Ordinario dispensationem obtinuerint.

Catholics who dare to contract a mixed, even though valid, marriage without ecclesiastical dispensation, are ipso facto debarred from legal ecclesiastical acts and from the Sacraments, until they have obtained a dispensation from the Ordinary.

1. Mixed religion constitutes a prohibitive impediment, which does not invalidate a marriage, but requires a dispensation to make it licit.

2. If the form prescribed in canons 1094 and 1099 has been omitted, the marriage is invalid.

3. Can. 1098 permits the full form to be omitted when there is danger of death or when the pastor, or Ordinary, or a delegate, cannot be reached.

The *ausi fuerint* is verified if the Catholic party, knowing that a dispensation is necessary and possessing the necessary means of communicating with the ecclesiastical authorities, neglects to ask for the dispensation. Deception of the pastor or assisting priest is possible, though not likely to occur, except in cases of elopement.

4. Such parties, provided they give signs of true repentance and accept the required conditions, may be admitted to the Sacraments [1];

5. But they are *excluded from the ecclesiastical acts* enumerated in can. 2256, n. 2.

6. This penalty lasts until the Ordinary *dispenses* from it, because it is a vindictive penalty, and dispensation here refers to the penalty, not to the impediment of mixed religion. Besides, no dispensation is required after the marriage is contracted.[2]

---

1 S. O., Aug. 23, 1877; Feb. 10, 1892 (*Coll. P. F.*, nn. 1478, 1783).

2 See Vol. V of this Commentary, p. 159. We may be permitted to say a word here in defense of this volume against a review of the same in the October number of the *Irish Theological Quarterly*. We regret to say that the critic does not appear to be competent, having betrayed his incompetency in reviewing our first volume by putting a synodal decree on the same level with the Code. Besides mere platitudes and general aspersions, we believe, should be avoided by a conscientious critic. There are, as a well-known professor in Rome used to say, when he was attacked by some writers, "*boni viri, sed non tenentur scribere.*"

TITLE XVII

VIOLATION OF THE OBLIGATIONS PROPER TO THE CLERICAL OR RELIGIOUS STATE

Under this heading fall the obligations mentioned in Book II, which determines the duties of the clerical state as such (Title III) and of the religious state in particular (Title XIII, Ch. 1). But it must be understood that the obligations peculiar to the clerical state are also incumbent on religious who belong to the clerical state, unless the wording makes it plain that religious are not comprehended. This shall be indicated under each canon.

REFUSAL TO MAKE EXAMINATIONS

Can. 2376

Sacerdotes qui neque ab Ordinario dispensati neque legitimo impedimento detenti examen de quo in can. 130 facere renuerint, ab Ordinario congruis poenis ad illud cogantur.

Priests who, without a dispensation from the Ordinary or a lawful impediment, refuse to make the examination required by can. 130, *shall be compelled by suitable penalties to do so.*

1. The above-quoted canon 130 requires *yearly examination for a term of three years* after the completion of a priest's theological studies.

2. All *secular priests*, even though they have obtained a parochial office or a canonicate, must submit to this examination, unless they are exempted from it by the Ordinary. *Religious* are *not* bound by this canon, but by can. 590.

3. To *refuse* is a positive act *(facere renuerint)*, although mere failure to appear at the examination would amount practically to the same thing, provided the time and matter of examination had been duly appointed and made known. In case of a lawful impediment, the Ordinary or the diocesan chancery must be notified, which may be done through the rural dean.

4. The *penalty* is arbitrary but preceptive (can. 2223). Except in case of protracted stubbornness, censures should not be used (can. 2241, § 2).

STUBBORN ABSENCE FROM PASTORAL CONFERENCES

Can. 2377

Sacerdotes contra praescriptum can. 131, § 1 contumaces, Ordinarius pro suo prudenti arbitrio puniat; quod si fuerint religiosi confessarii curam animarum non gerentes, eos ab audiendis saecularium confessionibus suspendat.

This canon embodies the sanction for can. 131, which relates to the pastoral conferences that are to be held several times a year. At these all *secular priests* as well as all *religious* who have charge of souls should be present, and also those other religious who hold faculties for hearing confessions in the diocese, provided no such conferences are held in their monasteries or convents, according to can. 591. Therefore the local Ordinary is entitled to know of this fact, even in exempt monasteries, unless a special privilege exempts them from attendance at the diocesan conferences.[1]

1. *Priests who resist the law laid down in can. 131, § 1, should be punished by the Ordinary* according to his good judgment. The name *sacerdotes* here includes religious who are in charge of souls, whether as pastors or assistants (curates). These also may, therefore, be punished according to can. 616, § 2. But *contumacy* must precede, and this supposes a canonical, not merely a paternal, warning (can. 2307). Although such a warning is to be given to all who are engaged as pastors, curates, or confessors, yet, says one decision, against secular priests who have no such charge, the bishop should proceed with exhortations and admonitions rather than with penalties.[2]

2. *Religious* who, though not in charge of souls, are *confessors* of Sisters or transient helpers in the confessional must, in case of contumacy, *be suspended from hearing confessions,* provided, of course, no pastoral conferences are held at their religious house.

SERIOUS NEGLECT OF RITES AND CEREMONIES

Can. 2378

Clerici maiores qui in sacro ministerio ritus et caeremonias ab Ecclesia praescriptas graviter negligant et moniti sese non emendaverint, suspendantur pro diversa reatus gravitate.

---

[1] Regulars who neither have charge of souls nor enjoy the usual faculties, cannot be compelled to attend diocesan conferences; S. C. EE. et RR., Aug. 23, 1593; Oct. 13, 1593 (*Regesta,* fol. 265 d, fol. 309 e), implied in can. 131.

[2] S. C. EE. et RR., Aug. 2, 1594 (*Regesta,* fol. 224 b).

Clerics in higher orders who in the sacred ministry *grievously neglect the rites and ceremonies prescribed* by the Church, and, when admonished, do not amend their ways, should *be suspended* according to the seriousness of their guilt.

1. The books which contain the rites and ceremonies of the Church are the Roman Ritual, the Missal, the Pontifical, and the rules governing these rites are called *rubrics,* of which mention is made elsewhere.[1] The rubrics here especially intended are those governing the administration of the Sacraments and sacramentals as well as the celebration of Holy Mass.[2]

2. The *grievousness* of the offence is to be gauged by the importance of the rubrics, the scandal given, and the duration of the neglect. Rural deans are called upon to watch over the pastors of their districts and the pastors over their assistants.[3]

3. In proceeding against offenders, the Ordinary must first issue a *canonical* warning according to can. 2307 and then await amendment within the term stated.

4. If no amendment follows, *suspension must* be inflicted, and it may be either total or partial, for a definite or an indefinite time, either as a censure or a vindictive penalty.[4]

---

1 See Vol. IV of this Commentary, p. 157.

2 See can. 755–761; 814–819; 945–947; 1002–1004; 1148.

3 Can. 447, § 1, n. 4; 476, § 7; concerning chapters can. 415, § 3, n. 2. This, of course, does not mean that every new rubric must at once be applied and insisted upon, as if the salvation of souls depended on a Talmudic observance of rites.

4 See can. 1933, § 4; 2278, f.; 2298, n. 2.

REFUSAL TO WEAR THE CLERICAL DRESS

Can. 2379

Clerici, contra praescriptum can. 136, habitum ecclesiasticum et tonsuram clericalem non gestantes, graviter moneantur; transacto inutiliter mense a monitione, quod ad clericos minores attinet, servetur praescriptum eiusdem can. 136, § 3; clerici autem maiores, salvo praescripto can. 188, n. 7, ab ordinibus receptis suspendantur, et si ad vitae genus a statu clericali alienum notorie transierint, nec, rursus moniti, resipuerint, post tres menses ab hac ultima monitione deponantur.

The clerical dress spoken of in can. 136 is the one usually worn by clergymen. It differs in different countries. Everyone knows the habit and usage of our country, except perhaps foreigners.[1]

The present canon may be said to contain three clauses: one applying to clerics in general, the second to clerics in minor orders, the third to clerics in major orders.

1. *Clerics* who do not wear the clerical dress and tonsure, as prescribed by can. 136, are to be *seriously warned;* which means that a formal admonition must be addressed to them according to can. 2143 and 2307, and put on record.

2. As to clerics in *minor orders,* can. 136, § 3 says that they are *ipso facto* reduced to the lay state if the canonical warning just mentioned is unheeded for *one*

---

[1] Thus we lately heard of a foreign bishop who travelled through our country in cassock and prelatial colors.

month (30 days). Therefore such clerics lose the clerical rank and its privileges without a formal sentence. However, we believe that, since the public welfare [2] is here concerned, a declaratory sentence, according to can. 2223, § 4, should be issued.

3. Clerics in *higher orders* should be dealt with as follows:

a) If they do not put on clerical dress *within a month* from the date of the canonical warning, their *office becomes vacant* without any further declaration, just as if they had resigned,— provided, of course, they hold an office — and they *must*, besides, *be suspended from the orders* which they have already ·received.

b) If, besides refusing to wear the clerical dress and letting the canonical warning go unheeded, they *notoriously* take up a mode of life not compatible with the clerical state, they must *again be warned*. If this second canonical warning also goes unheeded, they must be *deposed after the third month* (or 90 days), to be reckoned from the day of the last warning.

A *state or vocation of life not becoming the clerical character* would be one of those mentioned under can. 139, 141, 142 (store or saloon-keeper, etc.). However, the fact of the cleric's having embraced this state must be *notorious, i. e., notorietate facti*, which supposes a knowledge of the higher clerical state.

The *penalty for clerics* in minor orders is *latae sententiae*, whereas those for clerics in major orders are *ferendae sententiae*. Consequently, if a cleric has never been suspended or deposed, even though he may have

---

[2] Because of the public character of the clergy and of the clerical privileges.

been for several years a public teacher, unknown to the people as a priest, no absolution or dispensation is required.[8]

Discarding the clerical dress does not *ipso facto* entail a censure for clerics in higher orders. The penalty is prescriptive, which is to be understood according to can. 2223.

Although this canon does not strictly apply to *religious* who wear a habit of their own, yet the Ordinary may, under can. 616, § 2, proceed also against religious who neglect to wear the clerical dress customary in their country.

TRADING FORBIDDEN TO CLERICS

Can. 2380

Clerici vel religiosi mercaturam vel negotiationem per se aut per alios exercentes contra praescriptum can. 142, congruis poenis pro gravitate culpae ab Ordinario coerceantur.

Clerics or religious who, contrary to can. 142, practice a trade or engage in business, either by themselves or through the medium of others, shall be punished by the Ordinary according to the gravity of their guilt.

To what we have said elsewhere [1] on this subject only a few remarks need be added here. The subject is really important, affecting as it does the entire clerical-religious state, and " notions " or consciences sometimes seem to be very much obscured. *Negotiatio* is generally defined as " the act of buying things with the intention of

---

[8] We were informed of such a case by a late friend of ours.

[1] Vol. II of this Commentary, p. 95 ff.

selling them unchanged for a higher price."[2] Thus buying land with the sole view of selling it again, is trading; buying shares in mines, railroads, oil, cotton, etc., and selling them at a higher price is styled trading, or in common parlance, at least in the U. S., speculating or even gambling. Buying prayer-books or devotional articles from a firm in order to sell them with profit to pupils or parishioners is trading. The same must be said of books, magazines, calendars, typewriters, etc. All that we can justify in the sale of such articles is that the priest, religious, or religious house may add the additional expense of freight, express or an eventual risk of storage, but nothing more. Religious houses, especially those chartered as benevolent corporations, are not allowed to undertake financial operations.

1. The penalties established by the Constitutions of Urban VIII, " *Ex debito*," Feb. 22, 1633, and Clement IX, "*Solicitudo*," June 17, 1669, against trading by *missionaries* either in or outside of Europe, and which were maintained even after the "*Apostolicae Sedis*" (1869),[3] are now *destitute of legal force,* as per can. 6, n. 5.

2. But the declaration given by Benedict XIV, ("*Apostolicae servitutis commissum,*" Feb., 25, 1741) remains in force. This declaration says that trading by commission *(alieno nomine)* is forbidden. Hence a cleric may not furnish money to, or hire a layman to trade or traffic for him. To do so would be an evasion of the law or a deception. If family affairs or an inheritance compel a cleric to engage in business against his will, the bishop may grant him permission to continue in

---

2 Wernz, *Ius Decret.*, II, n. 216 (1st ed., Vol. II, p. 310); also Santi-Leitner, *Decret.* l. III, tit. 50, n. 3.

(*Coll.*, nn. 1398, 1589).

3 S. O., Dec: 4, 1872; Jan. 17, 1883; S. C. P. F., March 29, 1873

business for a short time, provided a layman acts as the actual administrator and manager (*l. c.*, § 2).

3. The *penalty*, though preceptive, is arbitrary, but its arbitrary character is somewhat modified by the gravity of the guilt, which is diminished if there is need of temporary support, or if, as stated above, family relations require such conduct. Although deposition and other severe penalties of former laws[4] should not be employed, yet suspension in more stubborn cases would not exceed the bishop's power.

VIOLATION OF THE LAW OF RESIDENCE

Can. 2381

Qui officium, beneficium, dignitatem obtinet cum onere residentiae, si illegitime absit:

1°. Eo ipso privatur omnibus fructibus sui beneficii vel officii pro rata illegitimae absentiae, eosque tradere debet Ordinario, qui ecclesiae vel alicui pio loco vel pauperibus distribuat;

2°. Officio, beneficio, dignitate privetur, ad normam can. 2168-2175.

Those who hold an office, a benefice, or a dignity which obliges them to residence, are, if they unlawfully absent themselves:

1. *Ipso facto deprived* of the revenues of their office or benefice in proportion to the duration of their unlawful absence, and these revenues, which are of the nature of a fine or vindictive penalty, must be handed over to the Ordinary, who shall distribute them to churches or charitable institutions, or to the poor;

---

4 See cc. 2, 3, Dist. 88, c. 1, Clem. III, 1; for filthy lucre's sake.

2. They *shall be deprived* of their office, benefice, dignity, according to the rules laid down in canons 2168-2175.

We need not again enter into the subject of residence,[1] but merely note that the *bishops are not affected by* this canon, for the reason stated in can. 338, § 4, where the metropolitan is called upon to report negligent bishops to the Apostolic See.

Who, then, are the *dignitaries* referred to in this canon? The cathedral and collegiate dignitaries, and none other. Not the prelates *nullius* or abbots *nullius*, because they too must choose a metropolitan and have the same obligations as the bishops [2]; nor the vicars or prefects Apostolic, for they are subject to the Apostolic See.[3] Nor religious superiors, for the vow of poverty prevents their assuming any dignities.

Are dignitaries who fail to observe the law of residence *bound to give up the revenues* received or due during their unlawful absence? Official Roman decisions clearly indicate that they are obliged to make restitution and that the Ordinary may proceed against them according to law.[4] The *bishops* or Ordinaries obliged to residence, on the other hand, are *not* bound to surrender the revenues *pro rata absentiae*, because the text distinctly says that these must be handed to the Ordinary. Therefore deliverer and recipient would be the same person. The Apostolic See shall therefore state what is to be done. As to n. 2, we refer the reader to the canons quoted.

---

1 See Vol. II of our Commentary, p. 98 f.; p. 358 ff.; p. 545 f.
2 See can. 285; can. 323.
3 See can. 301.
4 S. C. C., *Cathac.*, Nov. 14, 1671

(Richter, *Trid.*, p. 358, n. 71 f.); the procedure against non-resident canons, S. C. C., *Vercell.*, 1573 (*ib.*, n. 71).

NEGLECT OF PASTORAL DUTIES

Can. 2382

Si parochus graviter neglexerit Sacramentorum administrationem, infirmorum assistentiam, puerorum populique institutionem, concionem diebus dominicis ceterisque festis, custodiam ecclesiae paroecialis, sanctissimae Eucharistiae, sacrorum oleorum, ab Ordinario coercetur ad normam can. 2182-2185.

If a pastor *grievously neglects the following duties,* the Ordinary must proceed against him according to can. 2182-2185:

1. The *administration of the Sacraments,* as per can. 467, § 1 ;

2. *Sick calls,* as stated in can. 468, § 1 ;

3. *Religious instruction* for children and people, as per canons 1329-1336;

4. *Preaching* on Sundays and holydays of obligation, as per can. 1344;

5. The *custody of the parish church,* as per can. 1178;

6. The *custody of the Holy Eucharist and the holy oils,* as per canons 1265-1275 and can. 735.

CARELESSNESS IN KEEPING THE PARISH BOOKS

Can. 2383

Parochus qui paroeciales libros diligenter, ad normam iuris, non conscripserit aut servaverit, a proprio Ordinario pro gravitate culpae puniatur.

Pastors who are careless in keeping records and pre-

*serving the parish books, as prescribed by law, shall be
punished by their own Ordinary according to the gravity
of their fault.*

The books here mainly, though not exclusively, intended are:

1. The *Baptismal* Book, which must be kept according
to can. 470 and canons 776-778. It should, besides the
entry, contain four vacant columns for recording (a)
confirmation, (b) marriage, except the marriage of conscience (can. 1107), (c) subdeaconship and (d) solemn
profession, — the two latter on account of their being
matrimonial impediments,

2. The *Confirmation* Book, to be kept according to canons 798-799.

3. The *Matrimonial* Book, to be kept according to can.
1103, but omitting the marriage of conscience (can.
1107) though not omitting the record of an eventual
declaration of its nullity (as per can. 1988).

4. The *Obituary* Book, to be kept according to can.
1238. This is the *norma iuris* mentioned here, as well
as in the Roman Ritual (Tit. x, c. 2). But can. 470,
§ 1 also demands a record of the census, or *status
animarum,* which should be made as carefully as possible.

Is the *pastor* obliged to keep all these books *personally?*
There is no doubt that he is *responsible* personally and
sub gravi for these books. But this does not solve the
question asked. Our answer would be as follows:
Since a man may do through another what he can do
himself,[1] a pastor may have the records kept by another.
If the pastor were impeded, either by sickness, or
absence, or by reason of a very poor handwriting, he
certainly could entrust this work to others. Therefore

[1] *Reg. Iuris* 68 *et* 72 *in* 6°.

we cannot see why it should be wrong to entrust the assistant or curate with this task.

Another obligation is that of properly preserving the books mentioned (can. 470, § 4).

The *penalty* is arbitrary, but preceptive. The Ordinary, says a decision, may proceed with canonical penalties, which means that either censures or vindictive penalties may be employed if necessary.[2] The time of the canonical visitation offers a good opportunity for inspecting these books.[3]

NEGLIGENCE ON THE PART OF THE CANONICUS THEOLOGUS AND POENITENTIARIUS

Can. 2384

Canonicum theologum et poenitentiarium in suis muneribus obeundis negligentes, Episcopus gradatim compellat monitionibus, comminatione poenarum, subtractione portionis fructuum iis assignandae qui illorum vices suppleant; et perdurante per integrum annum negligentia post monitionem, suspensione a beneficio plectat; negligentia vero producta per aliud semestre, ipso beneficio privet.

If the *canonicus theologus* or the *canonicus poenitentiarius* should neglect their duties (see can. 308-401), the *bishop* shall proceed as follows:

1. He shall serve them with a canonical *warning* (see canons 2143 and 2307), which may contain a *threat of penalties,* and then, if this warning goes unheeded, he may *deprive* them of *part of their revenues* and give them

---

2 S. C. Sacrament., March 6, 1911, nn. II et IV (*A. Ap. S.,* III, 102 f.).   3 Bened. XIV, *"Firmandis,"* Nov. 6, 1744, § 9, 10.

to those who take the place[1] of the neglectful priests.

2. If *they continue their negligence for one year after this canonical warning* they shall be *suspended from their benefice* (see can. 2280).

3. If their *negligence is protracted* for another six months, *i. e.,* for eighteen months altogether from the date of the canonical warning, they shall be *deprived* of their respective benefices.

APOSTATES A RELIGIONE

Can. 2385

Firmo praescripto can. 646, religiosus, apostata a religione, ipso iure incurrit in excommunicationem, proprio Superiori vel, si religio sit laicalis aut non exempta, Ordinario loci in quo commoratur, reservatam, ab actibus legitimis ecclesiasticis est exclusus, privilegiis omnibus suae religionis privatus; et si redierit, perpetuo caret voce activa et passiva, ac praeterea aliis poenis pro gravitate culpae a Superioribus puniri debet ad normam constitutionum.

Apostates *a religione* are those who, having made *profession of perpetual vows,* whether solemn or simple, unlawfully leave the religious house with the intention of not returning, or who, having lawfully left the house, do not return to it, with the intention of withdrawing themselves from religious obedience. A perverse intention is presumed after a month of unlawful and unjustified absence (can. 644).

Apostates in another sense are those who publicly deny

---

[1] The place of a *canonicus theologus* may, in this case, be assigned by the bishop to either a secular or a religious priest; S. C. C., April 27, 1630 (Richter, *Trid.,* p. 19, n. 29).

the Catholic faith, clerics who elope with a person of the
opposite sex, or who attempt marriage (can. 646).
There is no doubt that those also must be considered
apostates who *transfer themselves to another religious
institute, i. e.,* another religious order or congregation,
without the necessary dispensation.[1] The superior of
the institute to which a religious of another order or congregation has repaired, is obliged to make him return
to his own institute or, at least, to notify his lawful
superior.[2]

It may be asked whether religious who leave their
own convent and without due permission transfer themselves to a monastery or convent of the same order, must
be considered apostates. The constitution of Paul IV
answers in the affirmative,[3] for the text " *extra claustra
suorum regularium locorum degunt*" (to live outside
their own regular convents) can mean nothing else but
that those religious who leave the convent of their profession without the necessary permission are considered
apostates. However, we believe that a distinction must
now be made between centralized and non-centralized
orders, of which latter the Benedictines furnish an example. For the essence of apostasy, as the term implies,
is desertion or defection from the religious state one has
chosen by perpetual vows, and subsequent withdrawal
from the obedience due to one's legitimate superior.
Centralized orders have a central or supreme superior
who represents the entire institute. Profession is made
in these centralized orders, not for a certain house, but
for the province or order, which depends on their Con-

---

[1] Paul IV, " Postquam." July 20,
1558, § 8 (*Bull. Luxemb.*, I, 834).
[2] S. C. EE. et RR., Aug. 11,
1758 (Bizzarri, *l. c.*, p. 330).
[3] *L. c.*, § 1, 2; even those who
held a benefice, *i. e.*, a parish or
office of their own order without
the necessary permission, were considered apostates; *ibid.*

stitutions.[4] The consequence is that one may transfer himself from one monastery to another, and still remain under the same higher superior, and hence he does not violate the vow of obedience. This is clearly expressed in can. 632. The same canon, however, requires an Apostolic indult for a transfer from one independent monastery to another independent monastery, even though it be of the same (so-called) order. Here we have a clear indication of the distinction between various organizations.

The consequence is that unlawful desertion of an autonomous monastery, even though the deserter repairs to another one of the same order or congregation, constitutes apostasy, if the other marks concur. With regard to Benedictine congregations much, of course, depends on whether the subjects of single monasteries pronounce their profession for the congregation as such, or for the individual house. If profession is made for an individual religious house, apostasy is verified in case of illegitimate desertion of that house, even if the deserter would straightway repair to another house of the same congregation. As stated elsewhere,[5] no apostasy or flight would be implied if a religious would seek redress with the Provincial or President or General in case of unjust vexation or manifestly unjust condemnation.

Our canon first states that can. 646 remains in force, and therefore those mentioned therein must be considered apostates. Then it lays down the *penalties* for apostates from religious institutes, as follows:

1. They *ipso facto incur excommunication*, which is *reserved*

[4] Also on papal privileges; Lezzana, *Summa Quaestionum Regularium*, Venet., 1637, p. 187, n. 11.

[5] See Vol. III of this Commentary, pp. 382 f.; Lezzana, *l. c.*, p. 188, n. 8.

a) To *their own higher superior,* according to can. 488, n. 8, *i. e.,* to the abbot of the monastery, or to the superior general or provincial, or their equals in power, if the apostate is a member of a *clerical exempt institute;*

b) Or to the *local Ordinary* in *whose diocese the apostate is stationed,* if he is a member of a lay or non-exempt organization.

From this censure only the exempt religious superior, or the Pope, or the delegate or successor of the religious superior, can validly absolve, according to can. 2245. Can. 519 cannot here be applied, for this censure is not merely one reserved by or in the religious institute, but reserved by common law to the religious superior.

Under can. 2340, the apostate, if he obstinately remains under censure for one year, becomes suspect of heresy and must be treated as such according to can. 2315. This may be a case of censure reserved to the *local Ordinary,* if the apostate belongs to a lay or non-exempt religious congregation, either papal or diocesan, male or female. The vicar general is competent to absolve from this censure even without a special commission (can. 198).

2. Such apostates are furthermore *debarred ipso facto* from all *legitimate ecclesiastical acts,* according to can. 2256, n. 2.

3. They are, moreover, *ipso facto deprived of all the privileges* granted to *their order or congregation,* but not of the privileges of the clerical state.

4. If they *return,* they remain *forever* deprived of the *active and passive vote,* and therefore cannot licitly [6] vote or be candidates for any elective office. If such a one is desired for an office, he can not be elected, but

---

6 See can. 167.

must be postulated, according to can. 179, and in the petition the reason would have to be stated. If a dispensation were granted, we think it would also restore the right to the active vote.

5. They must, in proportion to the seriousness of the case or the gravity of their offence, *be punished with other penalties by their superiors*, who are in this case bound by the constitutions. A decree of the S. Congregation of the Council[7] admonishes bishops to seek out such unfortunates and return them to their superiors, and exhorts the latter to receive them with paternal kindness.

Formerly such apostates had to do public penance, were excommunicated and forbidden to exercise any clerical office. If a monk received any sacred order during the time of his apostasy, he needed an Apostolic dispensation to exercise its functions.[8] A peculiar penalty was decreed by Paul IV: apostates from any order or congregation had to wear a black biretta with two white stripes running around its whole circumference.[9] But this was abolished by Pius IV.[10]

It may be added that a religious institute *cannot be held responsible* for *debts* contracted by apostate or fugitive religious.[11]

FUGITIVE RELIGIOUS

Can. 2386

Religiosus fugitivus ipso facto incurrit in privationem officii, si quod in religione habeat, et in sus-

---

7 Sept. 21, 1624, § 4, 5 (Richter, *Trid.*, p. 433, n. 21).

8 Cc. 1-3, C. 20, q. 3; c. 69, Dist. 50; c. 6, X, V, 9.

9 " *Postquam*," July 20, 1558, § 6.

10 " *Sedis Apostolicae*," April 3, 1560, § 3.

11 Lezzana, *l. c.*, n. 19; can. 536.

pensionem proprio Superiori maiori reservatam, si sit in sacris; cum autem redierit, puniatur secundum constitutiones, et si constitutiones nihil de hoc caveant, Superior maior pro gravitate culpae poenas infligat.

Fugitive religious, according to can. 644, § 3 are such as leave a religious house without the permission of their superior, but with the intention of returning. It does not matter whether such a one leaves with or without the religious habit.[1] The difference between apostasy and flight consists in the intention.

1. A *fugitive religious ipso facto*

a) *Loses any office he may hold in his institute,* whether that office be high or low. Hence a higher superior, a conventual prior or prioress, an assistant, procurator, or procuratrix, porter or portress, those who hold a pastoral office in the name of their organization, *i. e.,* a parish fully incorporated into the monastery (not a secular benefice or office) — all lose their office if they withdraw from obedience.

b) If the fugitive is a *cleric in higher orders,* he incurs *suspension reserved to* the *major superior* of the institute (can. 488, n. 8).

Note that these penalties are *latae sententiae* and, therefore, *per se,* require a declaratory sentence only under the circumstances mentioned in can. 2223, § 4.

---

[1] S. C. C., Sept. 21, 1624, § 4 (*l. c.*); Lezzana, *l. c.*, p. 188, n. 7. Whether the flight is accomplished by day or by night is immaterial. If *expositi, i. e.,* religious who hold an office outside the religious house, leave their post or trust, they cannot strictly be called fugitives. (Suarez, *De Relig.,* tr. VIII, l. III, c. 1. ed. Paris., 1860, t. XVI, p. 278). However, if they withdraw from the obedience due to their superiors for more than one month, they would have to be considered apostates. In this case the essential point is withdrawal from obedience.

The *suspension* here understood is the general one of can. 2278, § 2.

2. In case of the *fugitive's return, he shall be punished according to the respective constitutions,* and if these contain nothing on the matter, the major superiors shall inflict fit penalties in proportion to *the gravity of the fault.* Here, too, it must be observed that local Ordinaries and religious superiors should strive to bring fugitives back to their religious houses.[2]

Both canons 2385 and 2386 suppose a return, and distinguish two kinds of penalties: a severer one for the act itself, and a milder one after the culprit's return. Does the penalty established for the mere act of apostasy or flight cease after the culprit's return? By no means. For censures cannot be removed except by absolution, and vindictive penalties are removed only by dispensation. Both, however, should be imparted soon after the culprit's return, whilst the other penalties, which are preceptive, are to be inflicted according to the constitutions or the prudent judgment of the superior, who, however, is not at liberty to let the culprit go entirely unpunished, because penal measures are intended for the public welfare and the protection of discipline.

PROFESSION VOID BY REASON OF DECEIT

Can. 2387

Religiosus clericus cuius professio ob admissum ab ipso dolum nulla fuerit declarata, si sit in minoribus ordinibus constitutus, e statu clericali abiiciatur; si in maioribus, ipso facto suspensus manet, donec Sedi Apostolicae aliter visum fuerit.

[2] S. C. C., Sept. 21, 1624, § 4 *(l. c.)*

A *profession may be invalid* for any one of the reasons stated in can. 542, n. 1. Besides, can. 572, § 1, n. 4, expressly states that *dolus* [1] (fraud or deceit) on the part of the candidate invalidates a religious profession. Therefore, if a candidate deliberately concealed any of the reasons stated in can. 542, n. 1, his profession would be invalid. The respective constitutions may also contain an invalidating impediment, for instance, a certain disease, especially of an incurable kind, like consumption, epilepsy, etc. If the religious is afflicted with such a defect and conceals it, his profession is invalid.[2] The declaration of nullity, in the last instance, belongs to the S. Congregation of Religious.

A religious whose profession has been declared null and void on account of deceit admitted by him shall be punished as follows:

1. If he is a *cleric with minor orders, he is to be cast out from the clerical state,* but he may be readmitted as a lay brother, provided he repeats the novitiate and makes a new profession. This penalty is *ferendae sententiae,* and, therefore, requires a trial and a condemnatory or declaratory sentence, after the fact is verified.

2. If he is a *cleric in higher orders, he is ipso facto suspended until the Apostolic See shall have made provision for him.* The Pontifical Commission for the Interpretation of the Code has decided that canons 2386, 2387, and 2389 must also be applied to delinquent members of *religious associations* (can. 673), provided they lead a life in common and are of clerical rank.[3]

---

[1] "*Dolus proprie sumptus importat iniuriam in decipiendo, et effectum seu damnum illatum per talem iniuriam, seu errorem seu ignorantiam*"; Suarez *De Voto*, tr. VI, l. I, c. 11, n. 4 (t. XIV, 793). It is the injury caused by deceit which produces, if nothing else, i. e., no material damage, at least error or ignorance, which in itself is an evil.

[2] S. C. C., July 6, 1726 (Richter, *Trid.*, p. 426 ff. n. 14).

[3] June 2-3, 1918, n. VI (*A. Ap. S.*, X, 347).

MARRIAGE ATTEMPTED BY CLERICS AND RELIGIOUS

Can. 2388

. § 1. Clerici in sacris constituti vel regulares aut moniales post votum sollemne castitatis, itemque omnes cum aliqua ex praedictis personis matrimonium etiam civiliter tantum contrahere praesumentes, incurrunt in excommunicationem latae sententiae Sedi Apostolicae simpliciter reservatam; clerici praeterea, si moniti, tempore ab Ordinario pro adiunctorum diversitate praefinito, non resipuerint, degradentur, firmo praescripto can. 188, n. 5.

§ 2. Quod si sint professi votorum simplicium perpetuorum tam in Ordinibus quam in Congregationibus religiosis, omnes, ut supra, excommunicatio tenet latae sententiae Ordinario reservata.

By ecclesiastical law *clerics in higher orders, i. e.*, from subdeaconship onward, and *regulars or nuns with solemn vows,* cannot validly contract an ecclesiastical marriage,[1] and the Church consequently looks upon such marriages as mere "attempts." There must be a genuine attempt at *matrimony* to incur the penalty stated in this canon; mere concubinage is not sufficient. A valid marriage presupposes mutual consent, a certain form, and freedom from diriment impediments. There is only one form, *viz.*: marriage before a Catholic minister and at least two witnesses, which Catholics are obliged to observe under pain of nullity.[2] Therefore, if they

---

1 We say: an ecclesiastical marriage, because the civil law, in most countries, does not debar them from contracting a civil marriage.

See canons 1072 and 1073; this Commentary, Vol. V, pp. 187 ff.

2 See can. 1094, 1099.

would contract marriage before a non-Catholic minister it would be null and void by reason of lack of the prescribed form. Yet even in that case the censure would not be incurred, for it would be a species of civil marriage,[3] which is possible in our country, because non-Catholic ministers can and do perform the ceremony in the name of the law. Another possibility of complying with the form would be that mentioned in can. 1098. Besides, it might happen that the Catholic minister would be deceived. Otherwise the probability of clerics observing the required form would be exceedingly small.

The *consent* must be given internally as well as externally, and is generally presumed after puberty.[4] The question arises: May this consent coexist together with the knowledge or belief that the marriage will be void? For instance, if the contracting parties would, besides the impediment of sacred orders (celibacy) or vow, suffer from affinity or consanguinity, could they have real consent? The Code (can. 1085) expressly states the affirmative. The censure, therefore, would be incurred even under this knowledge of nullity,[5] provided it was directed to a matrimonial relation, and not merely to a concubinage.

It may also be asked whether the censure would be incurred if the marriage were null and void, not from a mere diriment impediment, but also from *lack of consent*. D'Annibale[6] and others deny that the censure would follow such a fictitiously attempted marriage. This opinion is acceptable because consent is no doubt the essential element of marriage. But trouble might

---

[3] S. O., Dec. 22, 1880 ad 1 (*Coll. P. F.*, n. 1544).

[4] See can. 1082; this Commentary, Vol. V, pp. 223 f.

[5] S. O., Jan. 13, 1892, ad 5 (*Coll. P. F.*, n. 1777).

[6] *Comment.*, 1894; p. 101, n. 157; Lehmkuhl, II, 969.

arise in the external forum, which presumes internal consent whenever external consent is given.[7] Hence in the external forum a marriage is supposed to exist if there is a semblance (*figura et species*) of matrimony, as is the case, *e. g.*, in a *civil marriage, i. e.*, one contracted before a civil magistrate without the prescribed ecclesiastical forum. This no doubt is generally the case where persons forbidden by ecclesiastical law attempt to contract marriage. But the Code lays under censure also the *party* who contracts with one forbidden to marry. This is a relative impediment, following the individual character of the matrimonial contract. Our text, then, states:

1. *Clerics in higher orders, and regulars or nuns with solemn vows of chastity,* who *presume to contract a marriage, even though it be only a civil one,* and

2. *All those who presume to contract such a marriage with one of the aforesaid persons,*

3. *Incur excommunication latae sententiae, simply reserved to the Apostolic See.*

4. *Clerics* who, after a canonical warning, do not retrace the step within the time set by the Ordinary. (a) *forfeit all the offices* they may hold, just as if they had formally resigned, for which no further declaration is required; and (b) shall be *degraded,* which requires a condemnatory, or at least a declaratory, sentence, after the term set in the canonical warning has expired.

Note that the penalty is incurred[8] only after *solemn* profession and that the profession must be valid and

---

7 See can. 2200, § 2.

8 Therefore those members of the Society of Jesus who have made only simple vows, although these produce for them the same effect, in this regard, as the solemn vows (Gregory XIII, *"Ascendente,"* May 25, 1584) do not incur the penalty; D'Annibale, *l. c.,* n. 156.

the vow absolute and pronounced after the temporary vows had been taken.[9]

The term "*praesumentes*" supposes full knowledge and deliberation. *Knowledge* is here directed to the fact that the marriage is null and void and contrary to ecclesiastical law. It also supposes knowledge of the penalty.[10] Therefore *supine or crass ignorance* would excuse one from incurring the censure. This ignorance would have to be directed to the fact that the marriage was (supposedly) contracted and that it is null and void. This is true also concerning another hypothesis. It may be that the parties concerned did not realize the nullity of their marriage at the moment they contracted it, but learned of its nullity afterwards, and continued their matrimonial or rather concubinarian relation. Even in this case the censure would not be contracted.[11] But it must be added that in clerics and religious such ignorance is almost impossible, unless their mental condition be impaired.[12] On the other hand it is not impossible that they should doubt and gradually persuade themselves that their ordination or profession was not according to law, or defective, or invalid. Consequently, they may also deem their marriage valid. Much easier is it to assume ignorance in the other contracting party, who is not bound by the ties of the clerical state or vow. However, even there affected ignorance would not excuse.[13] *Deliberation* requires freedom of the will, which is certainly impaired by grave fear. Therefore it is commonly held [14] that grave fear (*metus gravis*) excuses one

---

9 See can. 574, § 1; can. 1309.
10 Can. 2229, § 2.
11 Avanzini, n. 39; Pennacchi, *l. c.*, II, p. 24.
12 Hollweck, *l. c.*, § 230, p. 300, note 4.

13 The *affectata*, admitted by Pennacchi (II, p. 23) can no longer be defended on account of can. 2229, § 1.
14 Pennacchi, *l. c.*, II, p. 22 f.; D'Annibale, *l. c.*, p. 101, n. 157.

from censure. Grave fear may be caused by serious threats of imprisonment or death, no matter whence they come, provided it is inflicted for the purpose of contracting this particular marriage.[15] Even clerics and religious may be subjected to such threats.

§ 2 of can. 2388 sets forth the penalty for *religious with simple perpetual vows.* This penalty is *excommunication latae sententiae, reserved to the Ordinary.* " *Ut supra,*" says the text; therefore:

1. All religious who have taken simple perpetual vows incur this excommunication;

2. Also those who contract a marriage with one perpetually professed,—

3. Provided, however, they *presume* to contract such a marriage, according to what was said on presumption.

In regular *orders* the lay brothers or lay sisters generally pronounce simple perpetual vows, which can now only be taken after temporary vows lasting at least three years (can. 574. § 1).

In congregations, either papal or diocesan, all the members, even though their institute be exempt (like that of the Passionists and that of the Redemptorists), pronounce only simple vows after the temporary vows.

The other penalties, *i. e.,* loss of office and degradation, are not to be applied to these.

The *Ordinary* to whom the censure is reserved, is the *local* Ordinary with regard to non-exempt clerical institutes and nuns with solemn vows; with regard to members of exempt clerical institutes the Ordinary is the competent religious *superior major.*

15 See can. 1087, § 1.

VIOLATIONS OF COMMUNITY LIFE

Can. 2389

Religiosi legem vitae communis constitutionibus praescriptae in re notabili violantes, graviter moneantur et, emendatione non secuta, puniantur etiam privatione vocis activae et passivae et, si Superiores sint, etiam officii.

Can. 594 insisted upon community life for all religious. Here we have the penal sanction of this law, which provides that:

1, *Religious who in a serious matter transgress the law of common life prescribed by their Constitutions shall be earnestly warned.* This warning may be first paternal and then canonical, according to can. 2307, in order to serve as juridical basis for further procedure;

2. If *no amendment follows,* the *culprits shall be deprived of the active and the passive vote,* and

3. If they are *superiors, they shall also be deprived of their office.*

We need not add more than a few remarks to what we have said elsewhere on this subject.[1]

a) A *res notabilis* is a matter intrinsically or extrinsically serious. A matter is *intrinsically* important or serious if it is of great weight in preserving discipline or the special purpose of the respective institute. Thus the *peculium* seriously affects the whole religious life, especially of the Mendicant Orders. Thus also the choir service might seriously impair institutes which have solemn divine office for their main or chief object, as the Benedictines.

[1] See Vol. III of this Commentary p. 303 ff.

A matter is *extrinsically* serious if it is apt to have grave consequences, *e. g.,* by reason of the influence of the transgressor.

That superiors are not exempt, nay liable to severer punishment than inferiors, is evident from our text. This holds good also as to the common table and the vow of *poverty*. The latter binds the superiors as well as their subjects. Therefore, says a decree of Clement VIII, they are not allowed to retain anything, either movable or immovable, for their own person, neither can they give permission to anyone to possess anything of whatsoever kind for himself. As to the *common table,* the same decree says that all, including the superiors, should be satisfied with the same quantity and quality of food and wine, unless excused by infirmity.[2] This decree is merely a further declaration of the Tridentine decree,[3] and was again embodied in a decree of the S. C. Concilii.[4]

The penalty is *(ferendae sententiae)* privation of the active and the passive vote as well as of office. Superiors therefore should issue a canonical warning, and after that proves ineffective, *must* inflict the penalty, which is preceptive (can. 2223).

If the *superiors are delinquent,* the local Ordinary is the competent authority to proceed in case of non-exempt religious, according to can. 618. In case of exempt religious, the local Ordinary should paternally admonish the superior, and if he does not obtain the desired result, report to the Holy See, as per can. 617.

---

2 " *Nullus omnino,*" July 25, 1599. § 2, 4 (*Bull. Luxemburg.,* III, 891). The *law of residence* also concerns superiors (can. 508) and belongs to community life.

3 *Trid.,* Sess. 25, c. 2, *de reg.*

4 S. C. C., Sept. 24, 1624, § 1.

This canon also applies to members and superiors of societies that do not take the three vows, but lead a common life, for instance, the Fathers of the Precious Blood.[5]

5 *Commissio Pont.*, June 2-3, 1918 (*A. Ap. S.*, X, 347).

TITLE XVIII

CRIMES COMMITTED IN CONFERRING, RECEIVING, AND RELINQUISHING ECCLESIASTICAL DIGNITIES, OFFICES, AND BENEFICES

This entire Title concerns a purely ecclesiastical matter. The preliminary notions are supposed from former titles, especially from Book II, Title IV, on ecclesiastical offices, also Title IV, on benefices, as well as from the particular canons on special obligations, like the oath of Cardinals, the blessing of abbots, and the profession of faith.

VIOLATION OF THE FREEDOM OF ELECTIONS

Can. 2390

§ 1. Libertatem electionum ecclesiasticarum quovis modo per se vel per alios impedientes, vel electores aut electum, peracta canonica electione, propter eam quoquo modo gravantes, pro modo culpae puniantur.

§ 2. Quod si electioni a collegio clericorum vel religiosorum peragendae, laici vel saecularis potestas sese illegitime, contra libertatem canonicam, immiscere praesumpserint, electores qui hanc immixtionem sollicitaverint vel sponte admiserint, ipso facto privati sunt pro ea vice iure eligendi; qui vero suae electioni taliter factae scienter consenserit, fit ad officium vel beneficium, de quo agitur, ipso facto inhabilis.

This canon protects the liberty of elections in general

(§ 1) and particularly against unlawful interference by the secular power (§ 2).

§ 1 has two clauses. The first regards freedom before or at election. Those, it says, *who in any way, either themselves or through others, impede the freedom of ecclesiastical elections, shall be punished according to the gravity of their guilt.*

a) *Ecclesiastical elections* are those mentioned in canons 160 ff., especially of bishops, abbots *nullius* or prelates *nullius,* abbots or superiors of religious (also female) institutes, of the vicar capitular or administrator, of synodal examiners, judges and pastors consultors.[1]

An election, according to our Code, may take place by balloting or by compromise. It is also generally taught that postulation, presentation, and nomination were intended by the Decretal[2] from which our text is taken.[3] The scope of this canon no doubt is to safeguard the freedom of the Church.

b) *Freedom* is required, because it is essential, as for every truly human act, so especially for such transactions as depend on the choosing of a fit or worthy superior. Hence any contrary custom is styled a corruption.[3]

c) The freedom of election may be endangered in many ways, *e. g.,* by violence, serious threats, grave fear, deceit, directly or indirectly.[4]

d) The undue influence may be exerted by the *persons themselves* who endeavor to impede the electors, or through intermediary agents, including *mandantes.* Thus the voters themselves may be the executioners of the will

---

1 See can. 329, § 3; 321; 432; 506; 385; 1574. As to the *papal election* see can. 166 or "*Vacante Sede.*"

2 C. 12, 6°, I, 6, *de electione.*

2 Cfr. Schmalzgrueber, I, 6, n. 67;

Maschat-Geraldi, *Institutiones Canonicae,* 1, 6, n. 17 (*ed. Venet.,* 1760, I, 237).

3 C. 14. X. I, 6.

4 See can. 169, and this Commentary, Vol. II, p. 133.

of one who is by right excluded from asserting any influence in the election. The Decretals mention especially blood relations.[5] But other relatives, friends, pastors, chaplains — who sometimes exert more power than the law or their office permits — also Ordinaries and religious superiors may become guilty of such interference.

Those *who on account of the result, in any way vex the voters or the elected candidate after the canonical election has been completed, shall be punished according to the gravity of their guilt.* This vexation may be exercised by malicious defamation, withdrawal of support, material damage, or bodily injury. But these molestations must be inspired by the result of the election, which is here supposed to have taken place in a canonical way. If the vexations were inspired by personal spite or family reasons, the crime would not be verified. The *persons* aimed at by these vexations are the voters and the person elected by them, and no one else.[6]

The *penalty,* which according to the Decretals was excommunication *latae sententiae,* is *now arbitrary* but *preceptive* (can. 2223).

§ 2 concerns unlawful *interference by the lay or secular power with the elections of clerical or religious bodies.* The interference, to fall under this canon, must be directed *against canonical freedom.* It may consist of any act that is injurious to the freedom of the election. Thus it would be against canonical election if a layman would be freely and spontaneously admitted to cast his vote,[7] or if the magistrate, no matter what his name or title, would be asked for permission to hold the election, or to cast a vote for a certain person;[8] or if any lay or

5 C. 12, X, 6°, I, 6.
6 Eichmann, *l. c.,* p. 219.

7 C. 28, Dist. 63.
8 Cc. 14, 43, X, I, 6.

secular power were present under the pretext of safe-guarding the election.[9]

The *penalty* does not concern those who unjustly interfere,[10] but

a) *The electors who either solicit or spontaneously admit such interference.* Consequently, if the lay power threatens or creates grave fear in the minds of the electors, the penalty is not incurred.[11] The *voters are by this canon deprived ipso facto of the right of ballot,* but only for this one time *(pro ea vice),* i. e., for the election or ballot to be cast after this election, which is invalid on account of unlawful interference.

b) The person unlawfully *elected,* if *he knowingly consents* to an election held under such circumstances, *is ipso facto unfit* for the *office or benefice* to which he has been elected with the interference of the lay power. Knowledge (can. 2229, § 2) here means being aware of the lay interference, not of the penalty. The inability is restricted to the one elective office or benefice which was to be conferred — *quoad ius ad rem* — by this one invalid election. Since the text says: office or benefice, not only dignities [12] are intended, but any office or benefice, even that of a religious superioress and her assistant or secretary, where such officers are elected.

If the lay interference were sanctioned by a special and express agreement of the secular power with the Church, as, *e. g.,* a concordat, it would not be unlawful.[13] Neither is the prohibition of lay interference here to be understood as applying to elections performed by laymen,

9 Cfr. Maschat, *l. c.;* Schmalz-grueber, I, 16, n. 69.

10 The election would be null and void; see can. 166.

11 C. 43, X, I, 6; Schmalzgrueber, *l. c.,* n. 68.

12 C. 43, X, I, 6 only mentions dignities (see Hollweck, *l. c.,* p. 309, § 241, note 4); but our text is wider.

13 Maschat, *l. c.,* I, 6, n. 17; Schmalzgrueber, *l. c.,* n. 69.

as, for instance, in cases where they lawfully elect a pastor [14]; for the text explicitly says: an election held by a clerical or a religious body.

ELECTION, NOMINATION OR PRESENTATION OF UNWORTHY CANDIDATES; NON-OBSERVANCE OF ESSENTIAL FORMALITIES

Can. 2391

§ 1. Collegium quod indignum scienter elegerit, ipso acto privatur pro ea vice iure ad novam electionem procedendi.

§ 2. Singuli vero electores qui substantialem electionis formam scienter non servaverint, possunt pro gravitate culpae ab Ordinario puniri.

§ 3. Clerici vel laici qui indignum scienter praesentaverint vel nominaverint, iure praesentandi vel nominandi ipso facto pro ea vice carent.

This canon contains two specifically distinct enactments: one directed towards the person elected, presented, or nominated (§§ 1 and 3), the other concerning the essential formalities of election (§ 2).

§1. *A college that has knowingly elected an unworthy candidate, is ipso facto deprived, for that time, of the right of proceeding to a new election.*

1. A *college* is the elective body as such, *i. e.*, as a body, and therefore the penalty falls upon the members of this body, as such. Such a body would be a cathedral chapter or a group of religious endowed with the right of electing their superior. But it may also be a congregation, according to can. 455; because the text does not say: a college of clerics or religious.

14 Can. 455.

2. Who is unworthy *(indignus)?* The Code uses the term *idoneus* almost exclusively to signify a fit person.[1] Here it employs the word *indignus.* Is unfit and unworthy the same? According to a Decretal[2] it would seem that the words *indignus* and *inidoneus* have the same meaning. Worthy *(dignus)* is the one who possesses the necessary qualifications, as prescribed by law, and also the necessary competency for the office in question. Unworthy *(indignus)* is he who lacks one or the other qualification required by law.[3] These definitions, however, seem to apply to *fit* and *unfit* just as well, and therefore some other element is plainly required to render the distinction more adequate.

Dignus includes juridical as well as moral qualities, or, in other words, it combines the strictly technical qualifications prescribed for an office by law with moral fitness or equipment; or, perhaps, still better, *he* is worthy who possesses all the qualities positively prescribed by law and is without the negative qualities that render one unworthy of holding a benefice. The latter are, for instance, excommunication, interdict, suspension, deprivation of the passive vote, infamy, etc.[4] Therefore we may say that *dignus* includes *idoneus,* but adds to it moral aptitude for the respective office.

But is this the meaning of *indignus* in our text? We believe it is. For *indignus* here cannot simply mean *non-idoneus,* since a person who is not-fit on account of

---

1 See can. 153, § 2; 331; 399 (*aptiores*); 434; 435; 504 (*inhabiles*).

2 C. 29, X, III, 5.

3 Reiffenstuel, I, 6, n. 204, Schmalzgrueber, I, 6, n. 15, also assumes *dignitas* to be identical with *idoneitas,* under three headings: *aetatis maturitas, gravitas morum*

et litterarum scientia; the *gravitas morum* he distinguishes into two defects or rather absence thereof: *rimen et aliud impedimentum canonicum,* among the latter censures; but these might just as well be referred to crimes.

4 See can. 2265, § 1; 2275; 2283; 2291, n. 11; 2294.

a merely technical law, can still be postulated.[5] Thus, for instance, a religious who is too young to be elected to an office, according to can. 504, can be postulated for that office. Thus a mother general who has served two successive terms, must now be postulated for a third by the S. Congregation of Religious.[6] But no one can proclaim her "unworthy" on that account. The same appears from the quotations appended to our canon by Card. Gasparri. Thus a dean of a cathedral chapter was elected vicar-capitular, but his election was annulled not only on account of irregularities, but also because he was under suspension *ex informata conscientia*.[7]

3. If, then, the electors elect one whose unworthiness is *known* to them, they are, for *this time only, deprived of the right to proceed to a new election*. This supposes that the first election was invalid and, therefore, null and void.

The next question is: How is the invalidity of an election to be ascertained? If an invalid election needs ratification by the superior or presiding officer, it is his business to declare that it is invalid. After this is done, the electors who knowingly voted for an unworthy candidate, are deprived of the right of proceeding to a new election, and the superior who is entitled to confirm or ratify is authorized to elect another, according to can. 178. If for one reason or another the superior should decline to exercise this right, he may return it to the college, and in this case the whole college would again be entitled to vote.[8]

If the election,————for instance, of a vicar capitular

---

5 Thus also Eichmann, *l. c.*, p. 220 f.

6 S. C. Rel., March 9, 1920 (*Am. Eccl. Rev.*, Vol. 63, p. 498 ff.).

7 S. C. C., Nov. 4, 1722 (Richter, *Trid.*, p. 370, n. 2).

8 Eichmann, *l. c.*, p. 221.

(can. 438), ——— requires no ratification, the fact of the unworthiness of the candidate must be ascertained by either a declaratory or a condemnatory sentence, or must at least be notorious. Such a declaration would have to be issued by the presiding officer or in the form of a protest from the innocent members, and in this case we believe that the innocent members, though in the minority, could proceed to the election immediately (*in continenti*).[9]

§ 2. *Individual electors who knowingly fail to observe the essential formalities, may be punished by the Ordinary in proportion to their guilt.* Essential formalities, according to our Code, are:

a) The calling of all the chapter members; if more than one-third has not been called, the election is invalid (can. 162, § 3);

b) The election of two tellers and the secret collection of the votes,

c) The publication of the votes and comparing them with the number of electors,

d) The proclamation of the election and the elected (see canons 171 and 174).

If any one of these formalities was omitted, though the electors, or at least some of them, *knew* of the necessity of observing them, the guilty ones *may* be punished.[10] This punishment is facultative.

§ 3. *Clerics or laymen who knowingly present or nominate an unworthy person for office, are ipso facto de-*

---

9 Reiffenstuel, I, 6, n. 260.

10 We suppose by him who is entitled to ratify the election, generally the superior; thus the local ordinary may punish religious at whose elections he presides; the provincial or president may punish the electors regular. The Sacred C. of Religious, to which the acts in some cases must be forwarded, would also be competent.

prived of the right of presentation or nomination, for this one time.

To what was said above concerning *indigni* nothing need be added except that it is easier for laymen than for clerics to plead ignorance as an excuse. The *ea vice* must be understood as stated above. As soon as the Pope or bishop has rejected the unworthy person and selected another, the punishment ceases, and the electors may again nominate or present a candidate.

SIMONY IN ECCLESIASTICAL OFFICES, BENEFICES, AND DIGNITIES

Can. 2392

Firmo praescripto can. 729, delictum perpetrantes simoniae in quibuslibet officiis, beneficiis aut dignitatibus ecclesiasticis:

1°. Incurrunt in excommunicationem latae sententiae Sedi Apostolicae simpliciter reservatam;

2°. Ipso facto privati in perpetuum manent iure eligendi, praesentandi, nominandi, si quod habeant;

3°. Si clerici sint, praeterea suspendantur.

The crime of simony, so heartily detested by the Church, has been previously mentioned in connection with penal laws.[1] What it is and how far it extends has been clearly explained. Can. 729 renders any simoniacal provision of offices, benefices, or dignities null and void.[2] This enactment is here repeated. Consequently any simoniacal election, postulation, nomination, presentation is null and void *ipso iure*. Besides, any

---

[1] See can. 2324, 2327, 2371.
[2] Except the papal election; see can. 160 and *"Vacante Sede."*

simoniacal appointment to, or exchange of, offices, benefices or dignities, or any simoniacal alienation or advowson or payment for appointment or presentation, retention of, or agreement to pay, revenues or parts thereof, also parochial concursus — are illegal and subject to punishment.[3] Not included is real simony practiced for the purpose of entering the religious state.

Simony, as here intended, not only includes real (*realis*), but also *confidential* or conventional simony, provided it be not purely mental. The present canon decrees that *those who commit the crime of simony* in *any ecclesiastical office, benefice or dignity:*

1. *Incur the excommunication latae sententiae simply reserved to the Apostolic See,* and

2. *Are ipso facto deprived forever of the right electing, presenting, or nominating, if they possess that right.*

3. If the perpetrators *are clerics, they should also be suspended.*

The last-named penalty is *ferendae sententiae,* but preceptive (can. 2223), and the suspension is general (can. 2278, § 2).

NEGLECT OF RATIFICATION OR INSTITUTION

Can. 2393

Omnes qui iure eligendi, praesentandi vel nominandi legitime fruuntur, si, neglecta auctoritate illius cui confirmatio vel institutio competit, officium, beneficium aut dignitatem ecclesiasticam conferre prae-

---

[3] See X, V, 3; c. 2, Extrav. Comm., V, 1; Pius IV, "*Romanum Pontificem,*" Oct. 17, 1564; Pius V, "*Cum primum,*" April 1, 1566; "*Quanta Ecclesiae,*" April 1, 1568; "*Intolerabilis,*" June 1, 1569; N. Garzia, *De Beneficiis Ecclesiasticis,* P. VIII, c. 1 (*ed. Venet.,* 1630, Vol. II, p. 131 ff.).

sumpserint, suo iure pro ea vice ipso facto privati manent.

One who is elected and requires ratification *(confirmatio)*, must ask for this confirmation according to can. 177, § 1 ; one who has been postulated, must ask to be admitted according to can. 181, § 1 ; one who has been nominated or presented, needs institution according to can. 148, § 1. These acts are here understood, not the *institutio corporalis* or *installatio*.[1] The Code says: *Those legitimately endowed with the right of electing, presenting, or nominating, if they presume to confer an ecclesiastical office, benefice, or dignity by setting aside the authority of the one who is entitled to ratify the election* (respectively, to admit postulation) *or to grant institution, are ipso iure deprived of their right for this one time.*

Here *dolus*, or rather ignorance and lack of deliberation, is pre-supposed. The reason for this penalty lies in the fact that by the act of election, or nomination, or presentation, one acquires only a *ius ad rem, i. e.*, not a full right, but merely a claim to the office, benefice, or dignity, whilst the actual preferment is granted by those who enjoy the right of confirmation or institution. Neglect to seek ratification or institution is, therefore, a perversion of the real act of preferment and a slur on the proper authority.[2]

1 Eichmann, *l. c.*, p. 225 is wrong in mentioning this.

2 See c. 23, X, I, 6 (postulation); c. 2, X, I, 10 (advowson of regulars).

ILLEGALLY TAKING POSSESSION OF ECCLESIASTICAL OFFICES, ETC.

Can. 2394

Qui beneficium, officium vel dignitatem ecclesiasticam propria auctoritate occupaverit vel, ad ea electus, praesentatus, nominatus in eorundem possessionem vel regimen seu administrationem sese ingesserit, antequam necessarias litteras confirmationis vel institutionis acceperit easque illis ostenderit, quibus de iure debet:

1°. Sit ipso iure ad eadem inhabilis et praeterea ab Ordinario pro gravitate culpae puniatur;

2°. Per suspensionem, privationem beneficii, officii, dignitatis antea obtentae et, si res ferat, etiam per depositionem, cogatur a beneficii, officii, dignitatis occupatione eorumque regimine vel administratione statim, monitione praemissa, recedere;

3°. Capitula vero, conventus aliique omnes ad quos spectat, huiusmodi electos, praesentatos vel nominatos ante litterarum exhibitionem admittentes, ipso facto a iure eligendi, nominandi vel praesentandi suspensi maneant ad beneplacitum Sedis Apostolicae.

This canon distinguishes two different ways of taking possession: the *corporalis institutio* (can. 1443, § 2) for offices or benefices of free appointment, and the assumption of offices to which a claim has been obtained by election, nomination, or presentation. The offices or benefices to which one is freely appointed are taken possession of by bodily institution or installation, which is reserved to the local Ordinary. This last in the series of appointive acts presupposes actual appointment or *ius in re*. However, as can. 1443, § 1, says, no one should take possession of a benefice conferred on him on his own authority.

Those elected, presented, or nominated, need letters of confirmation or institution, which they must obtain from the proper authority and show to those who are entitled to see them. Thus a bishop elected and confirmed must show the bulls to the chapter or consultors,[1] before he can take possession of, govern, or administer his diocese.

1. *Those who act contrary to this law are ipso iure rendered incapable of holding the office, benefice, or dignity in question* and, *besides, shall be punished by the Ordinary in proportion to the gravity of their fault.* Consistorial as well as non-consistorial, secular as well as religious, residential and non-residential, curata and non-curata benefices are comprised in this law.[2] But the office, benefice, or dignity must have been actually obtained, because the appointment is supposed to have been made, the election ratified and the nomination and presentation accepted.

In our country the installation of pastors is not always performed; and, consequently, this canon does not concern pastors in dioceses where this formality is usually omitted. But the other clause concerning the papal letters for prelatical offices also holds here.[3] The penalty is vindictive, but *latae sententiae,* and therefore needs a dispensation from the superior to whom the installation

---

1 See can. 334, § 3; 293, § 2; 312, § 1; 322, § 1.

2 C. 5, 6° I, 6; c. 3, Extrav. Comm., I, 3; Innocent VIII, *"Ad reformandum,"* 1485; Paul IV, *"In-* cumbentia,"* Nov. I, 1557; Hollweck, l. c., 312, § 246.

3 Pius IX, *"Romanus Pontifex,"* Aug. 28, 1873 (*A. S. S.,* VII, 401).

or ratification by right belongs, *i. e.*, either the local Ordinary or the Pope.

2. *By suspension from, or privation* [4] *of, the benefice, office, or dignity already obtained and,* if necessary, *even by deposition, must the culprit be* compelled to give up his office, benefice, or dignity and immediately to relinquish the government and administration thereof; but this latter deposition, being *ferendae sententiae*, requires a canonical admonition (can. 2307).

3. *Chapters, convents, and other communities that admit persons elected, presented, or nominated to the administration or government of an office, benefice, or dignity before the exhibition of the letters of appointment, remain ipso facto deprived* of the right of electing, nominating, or presenting as long as it pleases the Apostolic See *(ad beneplacitum Apostolicae Sedis).* [5]

Aliique may mean any community or corporation that enjoys the right of election, *e. g.*, a chapter under a prelate or abbot *nullius*.

ACCEPTANCE OF AN OFFICE NOT VACANT DE IURE

Can. 2395

Qui scienter acceptat collationem officii, beneficii vel dignitatis de iure non vacantis et patiatur se in eius possessionem immitti, sit ipso facto inhabilis ad illa

---

[4] Privation is possible, because they really had a *ius in re*, not only *ad rem*.

[5] "*Apostolicae Sedis*," V, 1: "*Suspensionem ipso facto incurrunt a suorum Beneficiorum perceptione ad beneplacitum S. Sedis Capitula et conventus ecclesiarum et mon-* *asteriorum aliique omnes, qui ad illarum seu illorum regimen et administrationem recipiunt Episcopos aliosve Praelatos de praedictis ecclesiis seu monasteriis apud eandem S. Sedem quovis modo provisos, antequam ipsi exhibuerunt litteras apostolicas de sua promotione.*"

postea assequenda aliisque poenis pro modo culpae puniatur.

As we have explained elsewhere, an office may become vacant *de iure* or *de facto* or both ways.[1] It becomes vacant *de iure* if the title to it is lost, as per can. 183. An office must be vacant at least *de iure* to be legally conferred; any provision made otherwise is null and void (can. 150, § 1).

Our canon says:

Whoever knowingly accepts an appointment to an office, benefice, or dignity that is *not vacant de iure* and *allows himself to be put in possession thereof, is rendered ipso facto incapable of obtaining this office, etc., afterwards* and, besides, shall be punished otherwise in proportion to his guilt. Note the word *scienter* according to can. 2229, §2, and the copula *et*, which signifies that one permits himself to be illegally installed after having knowingly accepted an illegal appointment. The text, following the old law,[2] mentions actual appointment *(collationem)* and hence a mere promise of a benefice to become vacant in future is not forbidden.

RETENTION OF INCOMPATIBLE OFFICES

Can. 2396

Clericus, qui assecutus pacificam possessionem officii vel beneficii cum priore incompatibilis, prius quoque retinere praesumpserit contra praescriptum can. 156, 1439, utroque privatus ipso iure exsistat.

Concerning incompatible offices and benefices, consult

1 See Vol. II of this *Commentary*, p. 107.

2 C. 6, X, III, 8; Maschat, *l. c.*, III, tit. 8, n. 5 f.

canons 156 and 1439.[1] Note also that the second office or benefice must be peacefully possessed, *i. e.,* there must be no litigation in connection with it. It supposes, therefore, not only appointment or preferment, but actual possession by bodily installation.

Therefore, the law punishes *with the loss of both benefices a cleric who, having taken peaceful possession of another office or benefice incompatible with one already possessed by him, dares to retain both.*

How soon this penalty is effective, the Code does not expressly state, but it may be deduced from the text. The word *praesumpserit* supposes a knowledge of the incompatibility of the two offices. The term *assecutus* (perfect) supposes tranquil possession. The moment these two conditions are verified, therefore, the penalty goes into effect. Formerly it was assumed that a month must have elapsed[2]; but the Code does not favor this assumption.

REFUSAL OF THE CARDINAL'S OATH

Can. 2397

Si quis ad dignitatem cardinalitiam promotus, iusiurandum, de quo in can. 234, emittere recusaverit, ipso facto cardinalitia dignitate privatus perpetuo maneat.

The duty of a cardinal is, as Sixtus V declared,[1] to assist the Vicar of Christ on earth by advice and collaboration in governing the Church. This naturally re-

---

1 See Vol. II of this Commentary, pp. 113 f.

2 Hollweck, *l. c.,* p. 318, § 257,

note 3; Reiffenstuel, III, 5, n. 338, rejects this view.

1 "*Postquam,*" Dec. 3, 1586, § 19 (*Bull. Luxemb.,* II, 611).

quires personal presence, at least occasionally. Hence the same Pontiff ordered that no one absent from the Curia should be created a cardinal, or rather receive the red biretta, blessed by the Pope and transmitted by a special courier, unless he gives oath into the hands of an ecclesiastical dignitary that he will visit the Holy City within one year. A copy of this oath was to be immediately forwarded to the Pope. Then the penalty contained in our text is added: " If any *one promoted to the cardinalate refuses to take this oath, he is ipso facto and forever deprived of the cardinalitial dignity.*" [2] No declaratory sentence is required.

NEGLECT OF EPISCOPAL CONSECRATION

Can. 2398

Si quis ad episcopatum promotus, contra praescriptum can. 333 intra tres menses consecrationem suscipere neglexerit, fructus non facit suos, fabricae ecclesiae cathedralis applicandos; et si postea in eadem negligentia per totidem menses perstiterit, episcopatu privatus ipso iure manet.

The Council of Chalcedon (451) and other synods [1] insisted upon the necessity of episcopal consecration for those called to the plenitude of sacerdotal power. Our canon is the sanction to can. 333. It provides that anyone promoted to the episcopacy, *who neglects to receive the episcopal consecration* within *three* months after receiving the Apostolic letters of appointment, *is deprived of the*

2 Said Constitution added that if the Cardinal does not come to Rome, the same penalty follows.

But our text leaves that to the Pope to decide.

1 See c. 2, Dist. 75; c. 1, Dist. 100.

revenues of his office, which are in that case to be applied to the building fund of the cathedral, not to the *mensa episcopalis*. This obligation becomes effective ninety days after date of the reception of the papal letter, and binds *ex iustitia*.

If the appointee neglects to receive the episcopal consecration for *another term of three months, he is ipso facto deprived of the episcopal office*,[2] without any further declaration. However, it appears to us that can. 2223, § 4, concerning the public weal, would find application here.

FORSAKING ONE'S POST

Can. 2399

Clerici maiores, munus a proprio Ordinario sibi commissum, sine eiusdem Ordinarii licentia, deserere praesumentes, suspendantur a divinis ad tempus ab Ordinario secundum diversos casus praefiniendum.

Not only the law of obedience, but also the residential or diocesan obligation and ordinary courtesy demand that a cleric stick to the position or post entrusted to him by his Ordinary.[1] The present canon is a sanction of can. 128. The *munus* intended comprises all kinds of offices with which a cleric may be entrusted. Only in case the clergyman had no " place " in the diocese and was not properly incardinated, would he be allowed to go elsewhere.[2] But even then he should at least *ask* for permission to leave.[3] Not to forsake the charge assigned means to " stick to it " as long as the bishop

---

2 *Trid.*, Sess. 23, c. 2, *de ref.*
1 See can. 127, 128, 143.

2 S. C. C., Dec. 5, 1574 (Richter, *Trid.*, p. 207, n. 3).
3 S. C. C., June 12, 1604 *(ib.)*.

deems it necessary. This obligation is attached to the office or charge, and even clerics who have been ordained on the title of their own patrimony are not exempt from this law.[4]

The text says: *Clerics in higher orders, who without the Ordinary's permission, dare to relinquish a place or position assigned* to them by their Ordinary, *shall be suspended a divinis for a period* to be determined by the Ordinary, as the case may require.

This vindictive penalty (can. 2298, n. 2) presupposes malice and knowledge of the evil consequences apt to follow such conduct. Resignation, if properly tendered and accepted (can. 190), does not establish the crime.

RESIGNATION OF AN ECCLESIASTICAL OFFICE INTO THE HANDS OF LAYMEN

Can. 2400

Clericus qui in manus laicorum officium, beneficium aut dignitatem ecclesiasticam resignare praesumpserit, ipso facto in suspensionem a divinis incurrit.

A cleric who dares to resign an ecclesiastical office, benefice, or dignity into the hands of laymen, ipso facto incurs suspension a divinis. Here the act of resignation itself is punished, and justly so, because, as ecclesiastical offices, etc., cannot be received from laymen, neither can they be resigned into their hands. The Decretals [1] from which our text is taken supposed that the clergyman received his office or benefice from laymen, and therefore pronounced privation.

4 *Ibid.*
1 C. 8, X, I, 9; Hollweck, *l. c.*, p. 317, § 257. But our text does not suppose re-acceptance — only resignation.

Laymen are all persons not initiated into the clerical order, even though they be trustees or hold a so-called ecclesiastical office.[2] The offices here intended are all kinds of offices, either of election, or presentation, or nomination. Presumption, however, is supposed (can. 2229, § 2). The suspension is not reserved (see can. 2253, n. 1).

RETENTION OF OFFICE DESPITE PRIVATION OR REMOVAL

Can. 2401

Si quis in detinendo officio, beneficio, dignitate, non obstante legitima privatione aut remotione, persistat, aut ne ea dimittat, moras illegitime nectat, ea, prae-missa monitione, deserere cogatur per suspensionem a divinis aliasve poenas, depositione, si res ferat, non exclusa.

By privation and removal legitimately decreed and inflicted, an office becomes vacant *de iure* and may there-fore be conferred upon another person.[1] Thus one who holds two incompatible offices is deprived *ipso iure* (can. 2396) of both and they become vacant by law (can. 2396; see can. 156). A pastor, whether removable or irremov-able, may be removed according to law, and in that case has to leave his pastoral residence as soon as possible.[2] If *he continues to hang on to an office, benefice, or dignity, of which he has been lawfully deprived, or from which he has been removed, or if he sets up an unlawful opposition,* he shall be (canonically) warned, and if the warning proves fruitless, compelled to leave the office,

---

2 Reiffenstuel I, 9, n. 5.

1 See can. 151; 183, § 1; 2298, n. 6; 2299, § 1, 3.

2 See can. 2147-2161.

benefice or dignity, by *suspension a divinis* and, if necessary, by *deposition.*[3]

Morae illegitimae properly means unlawful delay caused in the execution of a sentence or decree. Lawful would be an appeal from the sentence of privation, which is a vindictive penalty, and also *recourse* from a decree of the Ordinary against removal (can. 2153). Pending an appeal or recourse, no canonical warning should be issued, because the text presupposes *unlawful* delay.

NEGLECT TO RECEIVE THE ABBATIAL BLESSING

Can. 2402

Abbas vel Praelatus *nullius*, qui contra praescriptum can. 322, § 2, benedictionem non receperit, est ipso facto a iurisdictione suspensus.

An abbot nullius or a prelate nullius who is required by an Apostolic mandate or by a statute of his institute to receive the *abbatial blessing* (to be imparted by a bishop) and *neglects to receive* it within three months from the date of receiving the Apostolic letters of appointment or confirmation, *is ipso facto suspended from jurisdiction*[1]*;* provided no lawful impediment prevented him from receiving the blessing.

NEGLECT OF PROFESSION OF FAITH

Can. 2403

Qui contra praescriptum can. 1406 fidei professionem

---

sine iusto impedimento emittere negligat, moneatur, praefinito quoque congruo termino; quo transacto, contumax, etiam per privationem officii, beneficii, dignitatis, muneris, puniatur; nec interim beneficii, officii, dignitatis, muneris fructus facit suos.

Those who are obliged to make profession of faith are enumerated in can. 1406. This profession is distinct from the oath to be administered by the consecrating bishop to a bishop-elect, and therefore the oath cannot take the place of the profession[1] (can. 1406, § 1, n. 3). The Orientals, too, are bound to make this profession according to the newly prescribed formula.[2]

Our canon says that whoever, contrary to can. 1406, neglects to make profession of faith, unless prevented by lawful impediment,

1. Shall be warned canonically, a suitable time being granted within which he may comply with his obligation;

2. If he permits the fixed term to go by and stubbornly persists in his refusal, he shall *be punished* even by *privation* from office, benefice, dignity or charge, and

3. Meanwhile (*i. e.*, as long as his contumacy lasts) *he shall not be entitled to the income* from his benefice, office, dignity, or charge and is, therefore, obliged to make restitution if he takes any part of it.

---

[1] S. C. P. F., Jan. 10, 1875 (*Coll.*, n. 1429). The *iuramentum* in the *Pont. Rom.*, "*De Consecratione Electi in Episcopum.*"

[2] S. C. P. F., July 16, 1878 (*ib.* n. 1429), and the formula *ib.*, Vol. II, 122 f.; the formula for the Latin Church, *ib.*, p. 97 f.

TITLE XIX

ABUSE OF ECCLESIASTICAL POWER OR OFFICE

This Title, too, *per se,* contains purely ecclesiastical matter, yet there are canons inserted here which may bring the Church into conflict with the civil power. Thus official documents may be abused and passed to persons for whom they are not intended. Ecclesiastical officials may be bribed and provoke a civil suit. All this is comprised under the general term *abuse. Power* refers to those who exercise either jurisdiction proper or domestic power, whilst *office* comprises every charge of public trust. It is precisely the abuse of public confidence and the damage accruing to public welfare that the Church wishes to prevent by these penal enactments.

ABUSE OF ECCLESIASTICAL POWER

Can. 2404

Abusus potestatis ecclesiasticae, prudenti legitimi Superioris arbitrio, pro gravitate culpae puniatur, salvo praescripto canonum qui certam poenam in aliquos abusus statuunt.

Abuse of ecclesiastical power shall be punished by the lawful superior according to his prudent judgment and in proportion to the gravity of the fault, with due regard, however, to the canons which inflict distinct penalties for certain abuses.

There may be overzealous, or imprudent, or revengeful prelates, who are too ready to inflict penalties, especially censures, before they have lawful proofs against the culprit.[1] Then there is "the root of all evil,"[2] avarice, which may prompt some to be too lenient in granting favors, absolutions, or dispensations,[3] or in meting out penalties. Another abuse of power would be to demand pecuniary contributions on the occasion of episcopal or canonical visitations.[4] Some abuses are especially singled out in the following canons, whilst others have already been mentioned, for instance, absolution without the necessary faculties (can. 2338) and conferring of orders (can. 2370, 2373).

TAMPERING WITH DIOCESAN DOCUMENTS

Can. 2405

Vicarius Capitularis aliive omnes, tam de Capitulo, quam extranei, qui documentum quodibet ad Curiam episcopalem pertinens sive per se sive per alium subtraxerint vel destruxerint vel celaverint vel substantialiter immutaverint, incurrunt ipso facto in excommunicationem Sedi Apostolicae simpliciter reservatam, et ab Ordinario etiam privatione officii, beneficii, plecti poterunt.

The reader will have noticed that the Code is very particular about official books and documents. The present canon sanctions by censure the enactments issued on this head.

---

1 C. 11, C. 2, q.: "*excommuni-care, antequam causa probetur.*"
2 I Tim. VI, 10.

3 C. 3, X, V, 37.
4 C. 2, 6° III, 20; *Trid.*, Sess. 24, c. 3, *de ref.*

1. The *vicar capitular* (our administrator during the vacancy of the episcopal see) *as well as the members of the chapter* (our diocesan consultors), *as well as outsiders* (for instance, the secretary or chancellor of the diocese, or other officials of whatever name or rank, clerics or laymen) incur the *excommunication simply reserved to the Holy See:*

2. If *personally or through intermediary persons they withdraw, or destroy, or conceal, or substantially alter* [1] *any document belonging to the episcopal court,* which certainly is identical with our diocesan court. By *documents* are understood the papers or entries mentioned in can. 1813, § 1; — but not only such as are issued by the diocesan officials and abstracts of which are kept in the diocesan archives, but also such as are sent to, or received by, the episcopal court; in other words, all documents which concern persons, property, or rights of the diocese, as, *e. g.,* petitions, accusations, criminal and civil acts, dispensations, appointments, concursus and examination papers, establishments,[2] dedications, consecrations of churches and chapels, parishes and missions, inventories, deeds, abstracts, receipts, and also civil documents addressed to the diocesan court. Private letters, unless they bear on ecclesiastical as connected with civil or criminal procedure, do not belong to the diocesan court.

3. The penalty is *ipso facto excommunication, simply reserved to the Apostolic See.* Note that no presumption or knowledge or rashness is required (see can. 2229). Transgressors may furthermore *be punished by the Ordinary by privation from office or benefice.*

[1] A substantial alteration may happen if the initials or the surname of a person are changed.

[2] Also documents fixing boundaries, the distinction between removable and irremovable parishes, etc.

PERFIDIOUS AND NEGLECTFUL HANDLING OF
OFFICIAL DOCUMENTS

Can. 2406

§ 1. Quicunque officio tenetur acta vel documenta seu libros Curiarum ecclesiasticarum vel libros paroeciales conficiendi, conscribendi aut conservandi, si ea falsare, adulterare, destruere vel occultare praesumpserit, suo officio privetur aliisve gravibus poenis ab Ordinario pro modo culpae puniatur.

§ 2. Qui vero acta, documenta vel libros hos legitime petenti exscribere, transmittere seu exhibere dolose detrectaverit aliove quovis modo officium suum prodiderit, privatione officii vel suspensione ab eodem et mulcta ad arbitrium Ordinarii pro gravitate puniri potest.

§ 1. *Whoever is obliged by his office to compile, write or keep records or documents of ecclesiastical courts or parochial books, shall be deprived of his office* and be severely punished in proportion to his guilt by the Ordinary, if *he dares to falsify, adulterate, destroy, or conceal any of these documents.* This concerns especially *chancellors* and *notaries,* who have charge of diocesan and secret archives, and keep the records of ecclesiastical, civil and criminal trials, and also of trials for beatification.[1]

Administrators or the diocesan board of *trustees* are responsible for an accurate and faithful inventory of the documents and instruments relating to church property.[2]

---

[1] See can. 375-378, also, for elections, can. 171, § 5; then, canons 1585; 1621-1625; 1645, § 2; 1811; 1874, § 5; 1946, § 2, n. 1; 2142; 2144.

[2] See can. 1522; 1523, n. 6.

Those in charge of *Mass stipends* and *Mass foundations* must take good care of their books.[3]

Pastors are responsible for their parish books.[4] These are especially mentioned, whilst the records, documents, or books are supposed to belong to the "*curia ecclesiastica,*" or ecclesiastical court. *Curia* means court and hence signifies not only the papal or Christian court *par excellence,* but also the episcopal court. Here it comprises all chapters, cathedral as well as collegiate, and also religious chapters,[5] *i. e.,* corporations which have corporate rights acknowledged as such. All the officials of such *curiae* are here intended, and all their official documents. But religious houses of female congregations are not included, because the local Ordinary and the religious superiors are responsible for them.[6]

The officials named are to be punished if they *presumptuously* commit an act here prohibited.

§ 2. *Officials who maliciously refuse to copy, transmit, or produce such records, documents or books to those who are lawfully entitled* to have a copy thereof, or to have them *forwarded or shown, or who in any way betray their office, may be punished* by privation or suspension from office and, *in addition thereto, be fined* if the Ordinary deems it proper, in proportion to the seriousness of their crime. This concerns not only the *notaries* or *chancellors* of dioceses, but also the vicars-general and the priests entrusted with the government of a diocese according to can. 381. The notaries and pastors have to give out abstracts of or extracts from ecclesiastical registers, or let those who are entitled to see them inspect the original papers.[7] Pastors are obliged to communicate

---

3 Can. 843, § 1; 1549.
4 Can. 470.
5 Du Cange, *Glossarium*, I, 1257; see can. 383.

6 Can. 535.
7 Can. 384.

marriage records to the pastor in whose parish the parties have been baptized.[8] The officials of the court from which appeal is made are bound to forward the acts to the court of appeal.[9] Title deeds must be safely kept and not allowed to come into the possession of interested, much less of maliciously inclined, persons.[10]

The *pecuniary penalty* is of ancient date and was applied to the church that had suffered from the malicious conduct of these officials.[11] *Privation and suspension* must be strictly referred to the office itself, and are vindictive penalties.

ATTEMPTED BRIBERY OF DIOCESAN OFFICIALS

Can. 2407

Qui Curiae officiales seu administros quosvis ecclesiasticos, iudices, advocatos vel procuratores donis aut pollicitationibus ad actionem vel omissionem officio suo contrariam inducere tentaverit, congrua poena plectatur et ad reparanda damna, si qua illata sint, compellatur.

Whoever attempts, by gifts or promises, to induce ecclesiastical officials or ministers of the (diocesan or ecclesiastical, also Roman) court — judges, advocates, or procurators, — to an action or omission contrary to their office, shall be punished according to his deserts and compelled to repair any damage that may have been caused by his conduct. Here the *inchoate* crime of bribery is punished, and the punishment is inflicted on those who make the attempt *(conatus delicti)*, no matter whether it is or is not successful.[1]

8 Can. 1103, § 2; 470, § 3.
9 Can. 1644, 1890; Bened. XIV, "*Ad militantis*," March 30, 1741.
10 See cc. 33, 40, C. 12, q. 2.
11 *Ibid.*
1 See 2212, § 3, § 4.

Such attempts may be made by gifts or promises. Can. 1624 forbids the acceptance of any kind of presents, even food or drink. Promises are punishable even if given conditionally. The object or aim of the attempt is to cause an official to commit or to omit an act contrary to the obligations of his office. The positive act *(actio)* may be committed by the judge who refuses his services to such as lawfully ask him, or who violates an entrusted secret, or declares himself competent when he is not, or deliberately renders an unjust sentence.[2]

Lawyers and procurators may betray their office by unjust acts or illegal means.[3]

By *omission* judges become guilty in cases which require official *(ex officio)* procedure if they omit to execute the sentence or fail to forward the acts to the court of appeal.[4] A doubt may arise as to couriers and beadles, because they may be laymen,[5] and the text only mentions ecclesiastics. However, since they are in the service of the ecclesiastical court, they no doubt incur the above-mentioned penalty if they violate the official secret or neglect to carry out summonses or orders to the detriment of the party concerned.

OVERCHARGE OF TAXES

Can. 2408

Taxas consuetas et legitime approbatas ad normam can. 1507, augentes aut ultra eas aliquid exigentes, gravi mulcta pecuniaria coerceantur, et recidivi ab officio suspendantur vel removeantur pro culpae gravi-

---

[2] Can. 1608; 1625, § 1. 1644; 1890; Eichmann, *l. c.*, p.
[3] Can. 1666. 235.
[4] Can. 1618; 1938: 1920, § 2; [5] Can. 1591-1593.

tate, praeter obligationem restituendi quod iniuste perceperint.

With the exception of taxes for matrimonial dispensations and funeral services (see can. 1056 and 1234), all other taxes and stole fees must be fixed by a provincial council or meeting of the bishops and be approved by the Apostolic See (can. 1507).

Those *who charge more than the customary and legally established taxes, or permit or demand something beyond* the taxes fixed and determined, shall be *checked by heavy fines,* and in case of *relapse,* be *suspended* or *removed,* according to the gravity of their fault. They are, besides, obliged to *make restitution* of the ill-gotten goods. *Free* gifts or donations in excess of the taxes are not forbidden and may be lawfully kept by the recipient. The penalties of *suspension* and *removal* are *ferendae sententiae,* but may become obligatory in a serious case of relapse. The gravity of the fault must be gauged by the character of the offender, his stubbornness, the persons who were overcharged, and the amount of the overcharge. The fines are to be applied according to can. 2297.

ILLEGAL ISSUANCE OF DIMISSORIAL LETTERS BY THE VICAR CAPITULAR

Can. 2409

Vicarius Capitularis concedens litteras dimissorias pro ordinatione contra praescriptum can. 958, § 1, n. 3, ipso facto subiacet suspensioni a divinis.

According to can. 958, § 1, n. 3, the vicar capitular

(our administrator), with the *consent* of the chapter (our diocesan consultors), may issue dimissorial letters after the vacancy of the episcopal see has lasted one year.

Within the first year the vicar capitular may grant such letters only to *arctati*.[1] If he would issue dimissorials without the consent of the chapter, or within the first year of vacancy, he would *ipso facto* incur *suspension a divinis*, which, however, is not reserved.

RELIGIOUS SUPERIORS GRANTING ILLEGAL DIMISSORIALS

Can. 2410

Superiores religiosi .qui, contra praescriptum can. 965-967, subditos suos ad Episcopum alienum ordinandos remittere praesumpserint, ipso facto suspensi sunt per mensem a Missae celebratione.

Can. 965 prescribes that religious superiors, who are entitled to issue dimissorials according to can. 964, should address them to the bishop in whose diocese is located the religious house of which the ordinand is a member.[1] Can. 966 enumerates the cases in which religious superiors are permitted to have their subjects ordained by another bishop, provided the diocesan chancellor testifies to the existence of one of the reasons. Can. 967 warns superiors against fraudulent dealing.[2] Can. 2410 sanctions these enactments thus: *Religious superiors who dare to send their ordinands to another bishop are ipso facto suspended from saying Mass for one month.*

Note the term *praesumpserint*. There would be no

---

1 See Vol. IV of this Commentary, pp. 427 f.

1 See Vol. IV of this Commentary pp. 434 ff.

2 See Vol. IV of this Commentary pp. 442 f.

presumption if a religious order had a privilege permitting it to have its members ordained by any Catholic bishop; nor would there be presumption if they would act thus under the impression that all regulars possessed such a privilege; or that this privilege was still valid, which may really be the case. Neither would there be presumption if the diocesan officials would refuse to issue an attestation that the bishop is absent or does not hold ordinations. For the law grants the religious this right, and if the diocesan officials unjustly or unreasonably refuse it, the religious are entitled to assert the law, which is more than a mere formality of attestation. This canon also applies to religious living a common life according to can. 673, if their community enjoys the privilege of granting dimissorials to its members.[3]

ILLEGAL ADMISSION TO NOVITIATE OR PROFESSION

Can. 2411

Superiores religiosi qui candidatum non idoneum contra praescriptum can. 542, aut sine requisitis litteris testimonialibus contra praescriptum can. 544, ad novitiatum receperint, vel ad professionem contra praescriptum can. 571, § 2 admiserint, pro gravitate culpae puniantur, non exclusa officii privatione.

Religious superiors who
1. Have received *into the novitiate candidates*
a) Who under the common law cannot be admitted *either validly or licitly,* as per can. 542, the whole of which is here intended; or who

---

3 Commissio Pontif. 2-3 June Vol. X, p. 347.
1918, in Acta Apostolical Sedis,

b) Have received *candidates into the novitiate without testimonial* letters, as prescribed by can. 544; or who

2. Have *admitted novices,* although fit, before their novitiate was completed, to *temporary profession,* as forbidden by can. 517, § 2; — *shall be punished according to the gravity of the fault; if necessary, by privation from office.*[1]

The first part of this canon (n. 1; a and b) also applies to religious societies, with due regard to their constitutions.[2]

Observe that presumption or ignorance is not admitted in the text, the reason being that every superior worthy of the name is supposed to know and to apply these essential laws.

TRANSGRESSIONS CONCERNING DOWRIES AND NOTIFICATION OF THE ORDINARY

Can. 2412

Religiosarum etiam exemptarum Antistitae pro gravitate culpae, non exclusa, si res ferat, officii privatione, ab Ordinario loci puniantur:

1°. Si contra praescriptum can. 548 dotes puellarum receptarum quoquo modo impendere praesumpserint, salva semper obligatione de qua in can. 551;

2°. Si contra praescriptum can. 552 omiserint Ordinarium loci certiorem facere de proxima alicuius admissione ad novitiatum vel ad professionem.

Religious superioresses, even of exempt institutes,

---

1 If a professed member leaves the institute, her entire dowry, except the interest, must be restored to her (Can. 551, § 1); in case of transfer can. 551, § 2 must be observed.

2 *Commissio Pont.,* June 2–3, 1918 (*A. Ap. S.,* X, 347).

shall be punished by the local Ordinary according to the gravity of their fault,— if necessary, by *privation from office,* —

1. If they *dare to expend* the dowries of their members contrary to can. 549; [1] or

2. If they *neglect to notify the local Ordinary of the admission of candidates to the novitiate, or of novices to profession,* as required by can. 552.

The canon here quoted requires a threefold notification: 1°. before admission to the novitiate, 2°. before admission to the temporary profession, 3°. before admission to the perpetual profession. But no information, either formal or informal, is required for the annual renewal of vows, which is customary in some religious institutes. Some sisterhoods renew the vows every year after the temporary profession, for the space of three or five years. For such renewal no notification is required.

Observe that the first section of this canon supposes presumption *(praesumpserint)*. Therefore, if the superioress thought it proper to expend the dowries of her nuns for building a school or a chapel, or for some other purpose, because the money was ready at hand and she forgot the ruling of can. 549, the local Ordinary may be lenient, and instead of dealing out a penalty, may read to her said canon; provided the case is not too serious.

§ 2 contains no mention of presumption, because religious superiors are supposed to know this law and to respect the authority of the Church.

RELIGIOUS SUPERIORS INTERFERING WITH THE CANONICAL VISITATION

Can. 2413

§ 1. Antistitae quae post indictam visitationem religiosas in aliam domum, Visitatore non consentiente, transtulerint, itemque religiosae omnes, sive Antistitae sive subditae, quae per se vel per alios, directe vel indirecte, religiosas induxerint ut interrogatae a Visitatore taceant vel veritatem quoquo modo dissimulent aut non sincere exponant, vel eisdem, ob responsa quae Visitatori dederint, molestiam, sub quovis praetextu, attulerint, inhabiles ad officia assequenda, quae aliarum regimen secumferunt, a Visitatore declarentur et Antistitae officio, quo funguntur, priventur.

§ 2. Quae in superiore paragrapho praescripta sunt, etiam virorum religionibus applicentur.

This canon is the penal sanction of can. 511–513, as far as the canonical visitation concerns the religious themselves, not the visiting superior, although the latter is under strict obligation to make the visitation at the time stated in law and according to the approved Constitutions of the resp. institute.[1]

Note that the Code does not adopt the severe penalties laid down in the Decret.ls against nuns who rashly attempt to impede episcopal visitation. They incurred *ipso facto* excommunication notwithstanding all their

[1] See Vol. III of this Commentary, pp. 133 ff.; also Pellizzarius, *Tractatus de Monialibus*, Rome, 1755, p. 315; cap. X, n. 65 (this edition was corrected by F. Montani; the first edition had been placed on the Index); Lezzana, *Summa Quaest. Regul.*, 1637, p. 239; this obligation is said to rest on natural and divine law.

privileges.[2] Neither does our text suppose presumptuous violence, as when religious shut their doors by force against the canonical visitor. If this should happen, the visitor would be justified in meeting force with force, and also to pronounce excommunication against such unruly religious.[3]

The persons affected by this canon may be divided into two principal classes.

1. *Religious superioresses who, after a visitation has been duly announced, transfer religious to another house against the will of the visitor.*

Antistitae are the superior general as well as the provincial, provided the latter is in any way entitled to transfer religious to another house or usurps this right against the rule of the institute. The purpose of such conduct palpably is to remove such as may testify against the superioress.

Post indictam visitationem supposes that the visitation was announced, but a formal announcement is not required if the visitation is held regularly every five years. Yet the law supposes an express announcement. This all the more since, as a rule, the canonical visitation should be made known to the religious, so that they may prepare themselves for it.[4]

The *transfer* may be only temporary and most probably it will be made under one pretext or another. But it does not matter whether it was made permanently or temporarily, if it was done against the express will of the visitor (*visitatore non consentiente*). We say *express*, because the text supposes that the visitor forbade or did not consent to the transfer. Neither does it matter

---

[2] C. 2, Clem. III, 10.

[3] Pellizzarius, l. c., p. 299; cap. X, n. 24.

[4] Lezzana, l. c., p. 373; cap. 27, n. 2.

whether the transfer was made to a *religious house of* the same or of another province, or to a local house or colony or summer resort.

2. The second clause considers two different momenta: one before or on the day of the canonical visitation, the other afterwards.

a) *All religious, whether superiors or subjects, who induce other religious to keep silence or misrepresent the truth in any way or explain things insincerely when asked by the visitator, no matter whether the religious induce other religious to do these things themselves or through intermediary persons, are to be declared incapable of holding any office involving the government of others and deposed from the office of superiors.*

The inducement may be made *directly*, especially by superiors, by way of command, threat, etc., or *indirectly* by promises or flattery or special attention, without expressing special reference to the visitation.

The intermediary persons may be outsiders, servants, students, parents, relatives, friends. It is required, however, that these inducements produce an *effect* upon the religious. For not the mere attempt is intended, as in can. 2407.

The phrase *ut interrogatae*, supposes that the religious was asked by the visitor. There is no *strict and general obligation compelling religious to present themselves of their own accord before the visitor.* This obligation only arises if the visitor imposes it on all religious without exception, or if the rule or Constitutions demand it. However, if the visitor calls one, she (or he) is obliged to obey. Nor are they allowed to keep silence *(tacere)* if he asks them questions, for that would be tantamount to contempt for authority. Occult crimes, of which there is no rumor, must not be revealed, nor faults or transgressions which have already been corrected.[5]

On the other hand the religious *are not allowed* to *dissimulate* or to make untruthful statements concerning either disciplinary or financial matters.

b) *Religious, either superiors or inferiors, who, under any pretext, vex other religious on account of answers given to the visitor* are to be punished in the same way.

The *pretext* may be a species of zeal or promotion, but in fact is removal. Reproaches, private or public remarks, signs of displeasure, may also be used to vex others. Quite different, of course, would be a paternal or maternal admonition based on the results of the canonical visitation.[6]

3. The *penalty* for these transgressions enumerated under 1 and 2 is as follows: *They shall be declared incapable of holding any office which implies government of others, and, if they are superiors, they shall be deprived of their office.*[7]

Offices implying "government of others" are those held by superiors —— general, provincial, or local; also by mistresses of novices, assistants, prefects or directrices of schools or academies, also pastors and chaplains. Those who themselves spurn authority are not fit to rule others.

§ 2 of can. 2413 says that what has been prescribed *in the preceding paragraph also applies to male institutes.*

---

5 *Ibid.* see this Commentary, Vol. III, pp. 138 f.

6 Here a remark may be permissible: The visitor is not allowed to reveal the names of those who "had something to say" to the religious superior; much less is he allowed to give their names to the confessor or chaplain. This would be an abuse of trust, apt to cause jealousy, rancor, aversion, nay even enmity.

7 There is no special penalty provided for a visitor who abuses his power or office; but can. 2404 is applicable to him.

'And since the text does not distinguish between exempt and non-exempt, all are included. But the visitor must perform this duty himself, and only in case of a lawful impediment may he substitute another, who, however, must belong to the same order or congregation, because he should know the rules and constitutions.[8] The visitor intended in § 1, on the other hand, is the local Ordinary or prelate regular with regard to nuns with solemn vows; whether the female visitor is included, seems doubtful.[9] This canon is also applicable to religious societies who lead a common life.[10]

SUPERIORESS VIOLATING FREEDOM OF CONSCIENCE

Can. 2414

Antistita quae contra praescriptum can. 521, § 3, 522, 523 se gesserit a loci Ordinario moneatur; si iterum deliquerit, ab eodem officii privatione puniatur, illico tamen certiore facta Sacra Congregatione de Religiosis.

Superiors of female religious institutes who violate the rules laid down in can. 521, § 3, can. 522, and can. 523, shall be warned by the local Ordinary (see can. 2307). If they commit the same offence again, they *shall be deprived of their office* and *the S. Congregation of Religious shall be immediately notified* of the fact. It is unnecessary to add anything to what we have said under the canons quoted,[11] except that it is the *local*

---

8 Lezzana, *l. c.*, p. 251; cap. 18, n. 92.

9 At least we hardly believe that she could inflict the penalties mentioned.

10 *A. Ap. S.*, X, 347.

11 See Vol. III of this Commentary, pp. 159-164; Vol. IV, pp. 269f.

Ordinary, not the religious superior, much less the pastor or chaplain, who may proceed thus.

LAUS DEO ET REGINAE PACIS

END

GENERAL INDEX

This general index is made on the *English* text, though not exclusively, quite a number of *Latin* terms being inserted for the convenience of those accustomed to the ecclesiastical terminology. The Roman number refers to the Volumes, the arabic to the pages.

The canons contained in the eight volumes are distributed as follows:

Volume I: Canons   1-86:   General Rules; Public Law of the Church.
Volume II: "   87-486:   The Clergy and Hierarchy.
Volume III: "   487-725: Religious.
Volume IV: "   726-1011; 1144-1153: Sacraments and Sacramentals.
Volume V: "   1012-1143; 1960-1992: Marriage Law.
Volume VI: "   1154-1551: Administrative Law.
Volume VII: "   1552-2194: Ecclesiastical Trials.
Volume VIII: "   2195-2414: The Penal Code.

INDEX